THE MONETARY-FINANCIAL SYSTEM

LESTER V. CHANDLER

Princeton University

Harper & Row, Publishers

New York   Hagerstown   San Francisco   London

Sponsoring Editor: John Greenman
Project Editor: Claudia Kohner
Designer: T. R. Funderburk
Senior Production Manager: Kewal K. Sharma
Compositor: Bi-Comp Incorporated
Printer and Binder: The Maple Press Company
Art Studio: Vantage Art Inc.

THE MONETARY-FINANCIAL SYSTEM

Library of Congress Cataloging in Publication Data

Chandler, Lester Vernon
    The monetary-financial system.

    Includes index.
    1. Finance. 2. Money. I. Title.
HG173.C48   332   78-13618
ISBN 0-06-041219-4

CONTENTS

iii

PREFACE

The goal of this book is to present an overall view of the structure and functioning of our contemporary monetary-financial system in a way that can be understood by anyone with the equivalent of a year of economics. The term "monetary-financial" in the title reflects my belief that monetary institutions and financial institutions now overlap to such a great degree that they are best viewed as parts of a larger whole. And the term "system" implies that the many parts are so interdependent and interactive that they function as an organic unit. Although it deals extensively with these separate parts, the book emphasizes their common functions, principles, and interrelationships.

This approach might be called "evolutionary." The text begins with the simplest arrangements and proceeds to more complex ones, stressing the reasons for monetary and financial innovations. For example, it starts with the potential gains from trade in real goods and services, including both spot exchanges and exchanges involving time, and notes that the potential gains are so great that some trade occurs even under an inefficient system of pure barter. Then it describes how the invention and use of even a simple type of money—and later of various types of direct financial claims—promote both operational and allocational efficiency in exchange processes.

Chapter 4 brings us to the contemporary sources and uses of saving in the United States and the principal processes through which positive saving is translated into investment and dissaving. The next three chapters deal with financial intermediaries. They emphasize principles and practices common to all types of intermediaries, but they also discuss differences among the types, major reasons for the development of monetary intermediaries, and the functions of specific nonbank intermediaries. Chapters 8 through 11 describe various branches of the financial markets, both primary and secondary; and Chapter 12 "fits all the pieces together."

The first twelve chapters examine the roles of the monetary-financial system in promoting operational and allocational efficiency in exchange processes. Chapters 13 and 14 shift the focus to macroeconomic aspects of money and finance. The simple macroeconomic model employed provides a framework for analyzing processes through which monetary policies achieve, or fail to achieve, their objectives. This model helps to demonstrate how shifts of the "real" variables affect the monetary-financial system. The final chapter speculates on some likely changes to come in the structure and functioning of the system.

This is not an exhaustive treatise on money and finance. It concentrates on interrelationships among basic principles and institutions of money and finance in order to display the monetary-financial system as a functioning unit.

This volume bridges common topics in economics and finance, and it may be used in several ways. Its coverage of nonbank financial intermediaries, financial markets, interrelationships of banks with other sectors of the financial system, and the transmission of the effects of monetary policy actions through financial markets supplies the core for various money and banking or financial institutions courses, depending on their emphasis. It offers an alternative framework to students not specializing in money or finance who seek a broad understanding of the field. It also provides students concentrating in the field a cohesive overview with which to prepare for advanced courses. Parts of the book may be used as supplementary readings in more specialized courses, such as those in macroeconomics in which the principal text deals only briefly with the roles of the financial system.

Like other academic writers of books on economics, I am convinced that my product "could be read with great profit by the intelligent layman with an interest in the field." Potential readers are warned, however, that this book offers no advice on "How to Make a Billion Without Hardly Trying," no stories on "High Jinks in High Places," and no sex. Of course, such omissions will not matter to students.

So many people have been helpful, directly or indirectly, that it is not possible to list all their names. However, I would like to acknowledge the valuable contribution of Phyllis Durepos, who somehow converted my scribblings into legible form.

1
THE
BASIC FUNCTIONS
OF MONEY
AND
FINANCE

The fundamental function of any monetary and financial system, no matter how simple or complex, is to promote efficiency in the processes of exchange or trade in real goods and services, and thus to contribute to economic welfare. This statement suggests several related questions. In what ways are exchanges of real goods and services beneficial? How do money and finance promote efficiency in trade? What is meant by "efficiency" in this context?

To answer the last question first, we distinguish two types of efficiency—*transactions,* or *operational, efficiency* and *allocational efficiency.* Transactions, or operational, efficiency refers to economizing on the use of scarce real resources in carrying out exchange processes. Exchange processes are not costless in real terms. They require the time and energy of the traders themselves, the services of brokers and others, materials and supplies, and the services of land and equipment to perform the required functions of gathering and analyzing information concerning trading opportunities, consummating trade transactions, and settling trade accounts. Obviously, scarce resources used to effect transactions are not available to satisfy other wants. Also, high costs reflecting inefficiencies in transactions usually lead to a sacrifice of some allocational efficiency. Allocational efficiency is the degree to which potential gains from trade are exploited. Complete allocational efficiency would mean that all opportunities for potential gains from trade are exploited; there would remain unexploited no opportunities for trade that would make at least one party feel "better off" without making another feel "worse off." A system is allocationally inefficient to the extent that potential gains remain unexploited.

At least two important questions remain: What are the nature and sources of benefits from trade? In what specific ways do money and finance contribute to transactions and operational efficiency? We shall find that trade is of several types, each presenting opportunities for gains, and that money and finance play varied roles in the different types of exchange. We shall deal in turn with the major types of trade, starting with the simplest: pure spot exchange. Also, we shall until further notice assume that all trade occurs under a system of pure barter, with no money, no concept of a monetary unit of account, and no type of financial instrument or claim.

PURE SPOT EXCHANGE

Spot exchange refers to the exchange of goods or services "on the spot"; the entire transaction is consummated without the passage of any significant amount of time. Within this broad category is *pure exchange.* This refers to a situation in which each potential trader has an initial endowment of specific types of goods, and neither the amount nor the composition of the stock of goods is altered in the trading process. Yet experience has shown that all parties in a pure exchange transaction can be made to feel "better off," or to enjoy greater total utility or satisfaction.

Many examples could be cited to clarify the principles involved, but the age-old example of an exchange of apples for oranges will serve as well as any. Suppose that your initial endowment is a large number of oranges while mine is a large number of apples. Assuming that we can arrive at some mutually acceptable terms of trade, we can both increase our total utility or satisfactions through an exchange of at least some of my apples for at least some of your oranges. Such gains in utility may result because of differences in our preference functions for oranges versus apples; in general, my subjective valuation of oranges relative to apples may be greater than yours. Yet even if we have the same preference functions we may gain from trade because of differences in our initial endowments. You have so many oranges that the marginal utility of any one orange is less than that of an apple, while I have so many apples that the marginal utility of any one apple is less than that of an orange. We will have exhausted the potential gains from trade only when we have exchanged apples and oranges up to the point at which our subjective marginal valuations of apples relative to oranges are exactly the same.

Thus, the potential gains from pure spot exchange are in the form of increases in the total utility or satisfactions of the traders.

PURE SPOT EXCHANGE UNDER A BARTER SYSTEM

Many of the potential gains from pure spot exchange, and from other types of trade as well, are likely to be sacrificed if pure barter is the only available method of effecting exchanges, for barter typically involves high transactions costs and is also allocationally inefficient. To illustrate these difficulties, let us visit a one-day market fair attended by at least a hundred potential traders. Each trader arrives with an initial endowment of a specific type of goods that he hopes to exchange for other goods of greater utility to him. Each therefore engages in a process of search and bargain. He searches for opportunities to exchange his goods for others that are highest on his preference list and bargains to get the largest possible amounts of those goods in exchange.

Jones is a trader whose initial endowment is a goat. He hopes to find quickly "a double coincidence of wants." That is, he hopes to find someone who both wants a goat more than anything else and offers the specific types of goods that he wants most. This is likely to be difficult and may even be impossible. Jones may easily find someone who wants a goat more than anything else, but the type of goods offered by that person may be low on Jones's preference scale, or he may easily find someone who offers exactly the goods that he wants most but who attaches little value to a goat. After a long and unsuccessful attempt to find a double coincidence of wants, Jones may engage in a series of barter transactions—trading his goat for a sheep, the sheep for some millet, and the millet for cloth—to get a collection of goods that are higher on his preference list. Even after all this effort he may end up with a collection of goods whose total utility to him is lower than that of some other collection he might have acquired if his knowledge of market opportunities had been greater and his costs of search and bargain lower.

Your reaction to all this may well be, "Even under a system of pure barter they ought to be able to devise a more efficient market. Why don't they establish auctions for the various types of goods, or stores to deal in them?" Suppose they do establish auctions for the various classes of goods, each to occur at a specified time and place in the market. Jones and other goat suppliers will appear at the goat auction, as will those who want to acquire goats. But conspicuously absent may be those in a position to offer the types of things that Jones wants most. He may therefore go to the place auctioning off the types of things that he most prefers, only to find that no one there will give much for a goat. Another problem of auctions under pure barter is that all bids would have to be in the form of offers of specific goods. For example, the bids for a goat may be, respectively, three young pigs, four bushels of rye, and three yards of cotton cloth. Which is the highest bid? You can answer this only if you know prevailing barter rates of exchange.

Alternatively, you might attempt to improve the efficiency of the market by setting up a store to deal in goats. In this role, you could well become the area's greatest expert on goats, knowing all about the qualities of goats and accumulating much information about supply and demand conditions relating to goats. But in the absence of money, you would have to accept a wide variety of other specific goods in exchange for the goats that you sell, and you would have to keep an inventory of many types of goods to pay for the goats that you buy, and you could hardly be expected to become an expert on the qualities and the demand and supply conditions pertaining to so many things. Also, in the absence of some common unit of account, you would find it impossible to establish a meaningful accounting system. Suppose, for example, that between the beginning and the end of some period the net changes in your assets are as follows: increases of three male goats, two pigs, four yards of cotton cloth; and decreases of two female goats, three leather pouches, a copper kettle, and fifty arrows. What, if any, is your net income for the period?

In summary, pure barter is a highly inefficient method of effecting exchanges, involving high search and bargain costs and allocational inefficiency. It was to remedy such inefficiencies that societies invented money.

PURE SPOT EXCHANGE IN A MONEY REGIME

Suppose now that the society has invented and uses money. It has a monetary unit of account, in terms of which it measures and states the values, or prices, of all other things. Suppose they call this unit a "dollar," and express the values of all other things in terms of the number of dollars that each will command. This greatly simplifies the measurement and statement of relative values. It also makes possible meaningful accounting systems, for all assets, liabilities, income, and costs can be measured in the common unit.

The society also has some "thing" that serves as money—something that is generally acceptable in payment for goods and services of all types. Many different "things" can serve this function—things such as precious metals, fishhooks, and baked clay. The essential requirement is that the "thing" be generally accepted in payments. We shall assume that in this simple society money is composed of gold and silver coins of various denominations in terms of dollars.

Markets and exchange processes can be much more efficient in a money regime. For example, Jones can take his goat directly to the goat auction, where the supply of and demand for goats is concentrated, and sell the goat to the bidder offering the largest number of dollars. He can then take the dollars to an auction of the things he wants most and buy at the lowest prevailing price. His search and bargin costs have been greatly reduced. He avoided the costs of searching for a double coincidence of wants, and the bargaining process was simplified by the competitive bidding by goat buyers and the competitive offers by sellers of the things he wanted to acquire.

Alternatively, Jones might elect to sell his goat to a goat dealer. Stores and other middlemen establishments can operate much more efficiently in a money regime. For example, as a goat dealer in a money regime you need only two types of inventory—goats and money. You can become a real expert on goats and goat markets and realize the achievable economics of specialization and scale. The same is true of other goat dealers and of middlemen for other goods. Thus Jones can check the prices offered by the various goat dealers, who are likely to be located close to one another, and sell to the one offering the highest price. Then he can take his dollars to the middlemen offering the goods he wants most, who are also likely to be located close to one another, and buy from those offering the best bargains.

In summary, the use of money as a medium of exchange reduces the real costs of search and bargain and enables traders to acquire the specific combinations of goods and services that they prize most. It makes possible a more efficient organization of markets, doing so by separating the act of supplying a specific good or service from the act of demanding another specific type of good or service. Sellers receive money, which is "generalized purchasing power" or "a bearer of options," that enables them to choose freely among all the available types of goods and services. It makes possible the establishment of specialized markets for each type of goods and services with various types of middlemen who can exploit the economies of specialization and scale and amass the large amounts of information that are required for efficient, competitive markets.

SPOT EXCHANGE WITH PRODUCTION

The gains from trade discussed up to this point have resulted from exchanges of a fixed stock of specific goods. We now turn to exchanges that are an integral part of a production process and that serve to increase the total volume of goods and services available to the community. We could never have approached our present high levels of real output—whether measured as total output, output per capita, or output per man-hour of work—in the absence of a high degree of specialization. Only under specialization is it possible to allocate the various types of labor and natural resources to their lines of comparative advantage, to exploit the potential economies of scale, and to amass and use the huge amounts of knowledge and skills required by modern technologies.

Exchange is a necessary concomitant of specialization in production. Specialized producers must obviously exchange their output, directly or indirectly, for the things that they want. But exchanges in a system of specialized production include far more than trade in finished outputs. They also include trade in the various types of inputs, as workers and owners of land and other property trade their services for claims on other things. And they include huge amounts of trade among producing units in intermediate goods and components, as each unit buys from others the goods or services that the others can supply more economically.

The economy could never have approached its present levels of specialization and productivity under a system of pure barter exchange, for this system is, as we have seen, very costly in real terms and allocationally inefficient. The use of even a simple type of money has increased greatly the efficiency of exchange processes, thereby encouraging specialization and increasing output. In every market involved— markets for finished output, markets for labor and other inputs, and markets for intermediate materials and components—the use of money as a medium of exchange has reduced the real costs of search and bargain, facilitated the establishment of middlemen capable of achieving the economies of specialization and scale in exchange processes, promoted the accumulation and use of information concerning supply and demand conditions for the various goods and services, and fostered competition.

MONEY AS A STORE OF VALUE

Up to this point we have concentrated on the functions of money as a medium of exchange or payments, implicitly assuming that a recipient of money quickly spent it for something else. However, a recipient of money may hold it as long as he wishes before spending it, or even refrain from spending it at all. This function of money is referred to as "a store of value," or "money as an asset." This function is not, of course, unique to money; it can be served by any asset that has a value in terms of its ability to command other things in exchange. As a store of value, money has both advantages and disadvantages in comparison with other valuable things. Among its advantages are these:

1. Low custodial and other carrying costs. Most types of money can be held at low explicit carrying costs and do not deteriorate physically with the passage of time.
2. Safety or stability of value of principal, stated in monetary units as "A dollar is always a dollar." This quality is especially useful in storing value to pay debts and other obligations that are fixed in terms of monetary units.
3. Complete "liquidity." Being itself generally acceptable in payment, it can be used directly and at any time to make payments. To exchange other assets for money with which to make payments often involves delay and transactions costs.

On the other hand, money has at least two potential disadvantages as a store of value:

1. Lack of explicit income. Most types of money yield no interest or other explicit income, or at best a low rate. In contrast, most other assets yield income in the form of interest or dividends, additions to productivity, or consumer utility.
2. Loss of real purchasing power through price inflation. In periods when there is a general increase in the prices of other things, holders of money lose real purchasing power. On the other hand, they gain real purchasing power when the general level of prices declines.

We shall later have more to say about money as an asset or store of value and its role in portfolio policies.

EXCHANGES INVOLVING TIME

Having surveyed spot exchanges, we turn now to "exchanges involving time." We shall consider such questions as these: What are the principal types of exchanges involving time, and what are the potential gains from each? What are the shortcomings of pure barter as a means of effecting such exchanges? What are the roles of money in such exchanges? Why do such exchanges give rise to the creation of financial instruments or claims other than money itself, and what are the various functions of such instruments? Why do such exchanges involve the payment and receipt of interest, or some other payment that is essentially interest?

THE NATURE OF EXCHANGES INVOLVING TIME

In a spot exchange, the entire transaction is consummated so quickly that the length of time involved is virtually insignificant. However, time is an essential ingredient in exchanges involving time, and the length of time involved is an important determinant of the terms of such exchanges. In such exchanges, one party surrenders goods, or purchasing power over goods, at one point in time in exchange for the promise of another party to repay goods, or purchasing power over goods, at some stated time or times in the future. Repayment may be in the form of a single payment or of two or more payments on stipulated future dates. For simplicity we assume at this point that there is a single repayment to be made at the end of one year. Typically, a unit of goods or of purchasing power available today is not considered to be exactly equivalent to a unit of goods or purchasing power available a year from now. Instead, the present good or purchasing power typically commands a premium in terms of future goods or purchasing power. To put the same thing another way, the future good is exchanged at a discount in terms of present goods. For example, suppose that 100 units in the present are exchanged for a promise to repay 115 units a year hence. In effect, this is an interest rate of 15 percent a year. The reasons for such premiums and discounts will be developed later.

Exchanges involving time can, of course, occur under a pure barter system. But as a means of effecting such exchanges pure barter is, if anything, even less efficient than it is for effecting spot exchanges. Suppose, for example, that under a pure barter system you wish to acquire goods and services today in exchange for your promise to repay goods a year hence. You want two things; you want a one-year loan or credit at the lowest available rate of interest, and you want now those specific goods and services that you prize most for consumption or production purposes. You may be unable to find anyone who is willing and able to make the loan to you and who can also supply the specific things that you want most. Even if you find such a person, he may demand an exorbitant rate of interest. You may therefore borrow from the lender offering the lowest rate of interest, receiving at that time specific goods that do not best fit your needs, and then barter them for the things you want most. Later, before the time of repayment, you may have to engage in further barter transactions to obtain the specific types and amounts of the goods that you promised to repay.

In a money regime the entire process is much simpler and more economical. You can borrow money from lenders offering the lowest rate of interest and use the money to buy goods from sellers offering the best bargains. Then, sometime before the repayment date, you can sell goods and services to the highest bidder and use the money proceeds to repay the loan. Thus, the use of money as a medium facilitates separation of the function of providing loans or credit from the function of supplying goods, permits exploitation of the economies of specialization and scale in both types of markets, and fosters competition in those markets, thus increasing both transactions and allocational efficiencies.

EXCHANGES INVOLVING TIME IN A MONEY REGIME

In exploring further the principles relating to exchanges involving time we shall assume that a society has abandoned barter because of its inefficiencies and has become fully monetized, but that it is still a relatively simple society. Its monetary unit of account is the dollar, and all assets and income are measured in dollars. Its money consists solely of gold and silver coins, which yield no interest or other explicit income. It has not yet invented any type of financial claim other than money itself, so that the types of assets available for holding are limited to physical goods and money. It has no government, and therefore no taxes and no government expenditures. The society is composed of several thousand households, which are its basic income and producing units. Production units have not yet become differentiated from households.

During each period the society produces a flow of output or income, which it states at an annual rate and values in terms of dollars. Until further notice we shall assume that the price level remains stable so that the dollar value of output is a true index of real output or income. Total output is composed of two major classes. "Consumption" is that value of output purchased by households for current consumption purposes. "Investment" is the value of output used to maintain and increase the stock of capital goods. All of the value of income or output produced during a period accrues to the various households as rewards for their contributions to the value of production. These accruing income shares take the forms of wages and other compensation for labor, and income received for the use of land and other property owned by the households.

During any period, a household disposes of its accruing income in two ways. One part it spends for consumption. The remainder it "saves," or uses for "saving." If we use the symbols Y for a household's income for a period, C for its consumption during the period, and S for its saving,

$$S = Y - C$$

During any period, a household's consumption may be exactly equal to, less than, or greater than its current income. A household whose consumption is exactly equal to its income during a period will be referred to as a "zero saver" or "balanced unit." One whose consumption is less than its current income, so that its S is positive, will be called a "positive saver" or "surplus unit." And one whose consumption exceeds its current income, so that its S is negative, will be called a "negative saver," a "dissaver," or a "deficit unit."

The pages immediately following will consider exchanges involving time on income and product account, or on income and output account. In such trades, command over output at one point in time is exchanged for command over output at one or more times in the future. For example, you may surrender some of your current saving, which represents a claim on output today, in exchange for a claim on output or other resources at some stated time or times in the future. We shall be interested in the potential gains from such exchanges and in the methods developed to facilitate these types of exchange. We start with exchanges involving time on consumption account.

EXCHANGES INVOLVING TIME ON CONSUMPTION ACCOUNT

With limited total resources, each household faces the problem of maximizing the total utility or satisfaction that it will derive from its lifetime consumption. The latter is limited to the household's initial net wealth, which may be positive or negative, plus its lifetime income but minus its planned bequests to heirs. To simplify exposition we shall assume that any planned bequests by a household are exactly equal to its initial net wealth, so that its lifetime consumption is limited to its expected lifetime income.

It would be a rare coincidence if each household could maximize its total lifetime utility by consuming in each and every period an amount exactly equal to its income in that period. This is because the marginal utility of consumption would be greater in some periods than in others if consumption in each period were exactly equal to the household's income in that period. For example, in some periods a household's income will be so large relative to its current wants that the marginal utility of using all of its income for current consumption would be very low. In other periods its income will be so small relative to its needs and wants that consumption in excess of its current income would yield very high marginal utility. The household can obviously increase its total lifetime utility by shifting some of its consumption from periods when it would yield only low marginal utility to periods when its marginal utility would be higher.

For such reasons, a household will not, in general, consider $1 worth of consumption now to be exactly equivalent to $1 worth of consumption a year hence, or at some other time in the future. The subjective valuation of present consumption in terms of future consumption is commonly called the *rate of time preference* or *rate of impatience*. For example, if a household considers $1 worth of consumption today to be exactly equivalent to $1.30 worth of consumption a year hence, we say that its rate of time preference or impatience is 30 percent a year. With given attitudes toward present versus future consumption and given expectations concerning present and future levels of income and wants, present consumption is subject to a diminishing marginal rate of time preference. (The marginal rate of time preference will be designated by MTP.) This is partly because higher levels of current consumption would satisfy progressively less urgent current wants, and partly because satisfaction of more current wants would require the household to forgo satisfaction of progressively more urgent wants in the future.

At any time, marginal rates of time preference at levels of consumption equal to current income are likely to differ widely from household to household. For example, your current income relative to your current wants may be quite low but you confidently expect that your future income will be much higher relative to your future wants. Your MTP may therefore be quite high. On consumption equal to your current income your MTP may be 30 percent or more; for some consumption in excess of your current income your MTP would be 29 percent; on still more it would be 28 percent, and so on. The Smith household is in a quite different position. Its current income is high relative to its current wants, but it expects that its future income will be lower relative to its future wants. Its MTP is therefore low, perhaps only 2 percent at a level of consumption equal to its current income. Smith would be happy to save and forgo some present consumption if rewarded with at least 2 percent more consumption a year hence and would forgo even more present consumption if offered higher rates of reward for waiting.

It is obvious that both you and Smith can increase your total lifetime utilities by exchanging consuming power now and consuming power in the future. You would be happy to pay $1.29 a year hence to get another dollar of consuming power now; Smith would be happy to supply a dollar of consuming power now in exchange for $1.02 a year hence. At any intermediate rate of exchange you both gain. You and Smith will have exhausted the potential gains from trade only when you have exchanged up to the point at which the MTPs of you and Smith are equal. The same principles apply to all households. Potential gains in utility arise because of differences in MTPs, and the potential gains from exchanges of present and future consuming power are fully realized only when the MTPs of all households are brought into equality.

The transactions and allocational efficiencies of exchanges of present and future consuming power would be quite limited in a society whose only assets were physical goods and money itself. Some exchanges of this type could, of course, be effected through transfers of these assets. For example, you could finance consumption in excess of your current income by making a net reduction in your holdings of money and physical assets. But even if your asset holdings are adequate for this purpose, and they may not be, a net reduction of your assets could be costly. A net reduction of your stock of money could leave you with inadequate amounts for transactions purposes, and net sales of your physical assets could involve high transactions costs and deprive you of assets that are highly useful for production or consumption purposes. Also, Smith or any other positive savers may surrender present consuming power, taking in exchange a net increase in their holdings of money or physical assets. But money yields no explicit income, and they may have little desire to increase their holdings or physical assets. For such reasons, many of the potential gains from exchanges involving time are likely to remain unrealized in a society whose only assets are physical goods and money itself.

Efficiency can be increased greatly by the invention and use of financial claims other than money. In this case, the financial claims will be in the form of a debt or credit claim. For example, Smith surrenders to you at one point in time $100 in money or $100 worth of goods or services, in exchange for which you create and deliver to Smith your promise to pay $100 a year hence, together with an agreed-upon amount of interest. You have become a debtor and Smith a creditor. To you, the financial claim is a debt liability; to Smith it is an asset. In any case, the creation of a debt or credit claim has served as an instrument for exchanging present and future purchasing powers.

The existence and terms of a debt or credit claim can be evidenced in various ways. Simplest and least satisfactory is *parole credit,* which is evidenced only by an oral agreement between debtor and creditor. This often leads to disputes, and in any case such claims are difficult to sell to third parties. *Book credit* is evidenced only by entries in a creditor's books. Though widely used, book credit also leaves room for disputes and is usually lacking in salability to third parties. The great bulk of outstanding debt is evidenced by written *debt or credit instruments,* which are clear evidence of the existence and specific terms of a debt or credit claim. Aided by favorable laws and legal precedents to protect and enforce the rights of debtors, creditors, and holders, many of these instruments enjoy wide transferability or salability. This quality is highly important, for it increases the liquidity of a financial claim and is one method of reconciling differing maturity preferences of debtors and creditors. For example, I may prefer to issue to you a debt claim with a maturity of five years, but there is some chance that you may want money for other purposes before that time. You may nevertheless buy the five-year claim, relying on its salability as a means of recovering your money when you want it.

The financial claims discussed above are members of a broader category, which we shall call variously "direct financial claims," "direct securities," and "direct financial instruments." Such "direct" claims are financial claims against all types of entities except financial institutions. Thus, they include claims against households, nonfinancial business firms, governmental units, colleges, and so on. They are of two major classes: direct debt or credit claims, such as those discussed above, and direct equity, or ownership, claims. The latter will be discussed later. We shall postpone until a later chapter discussion of "indirect financial claims" or "indirect securities," which are claims against banks and other financial intermediaries.

The creation and use of direct financial claims to effect exchanges involving time on income and product account have three different but related types of effects.

1. Allocation effects. In the case considered above, the creation and issue of direct consumer debt claims served as a vehicle or instrument for transferring or allocating command over current output for consumption purposes from positive savers to dissavers, thereby enabling the trading households to increase the total utility derived from their lifetime consumption. In this sense the allocation effect is to increase the efficiency of consumption.

2. Portfolio effects. The creation of direct financial claims, which are liabilities of their issuers but assets to their holders, enriches the array of assets available to asset holders and makes possible portfolios with more favorable combinations of income, safety, and liquidity. These claims are usually less safe and liquid than money itself but, unlike money, they yield an explicit income. Some households will consider them superior to holdings of at least some types of physical goods because their yields may be higher, they are safer and more liquid, and they do not involve the storage and maintenance costs attached to some types of physical goods. To the extent that these claims make available to savers more attractive combinations of income, safety, and liquidity, they encourage both saving and the transfer to others of this command over resources.

3. Macroeconomic effects. These refer to effects on the overall rate of spending for output, or aggregate money demands for output. Considered by itself, positive saving tends to decrease aggregate money demands for output, for it is that part of a household's income that it does not return to output markets as spending for current consumption. One way of preventing an actual decline of total spending is for other households to consume in excess of their current incomes. Thus to the extent that the creation of consumer debt claims succeeds in translating the positive saving of some households into dissaving by others, it serves to maintain the level of total money demands for output. We shall later have much more to say about such macroeconomic effects.

SAVING AND INVESTMENT

We now turn to another class of exchanges involving time—exchanges in the processes of saving and investment, or capital accumulation. Most societies discover at an early stage that they can increase their total output over time by accumulating and using a stock of capital goods. By capital goods we mean goods that are produced by man and not consumed immediately but are instead used to enhance production of goods and services in the future. In primitive societies the stock of capital goods is usually small relative to the population, and the goods are rather simple in form. They include such things as seeds, simple instruments for tilling the soil, livestock, spinning wheels, looms, tents or houses, and weapons. However, in the United States and other modern economies, production is enhanced by the use of huge stocks of capital goods of many types. Some of these have only short useful lives; among these are such things as fertilizers and inventories of raw materials and goods in process. Others have such long useful lives that they are called "fixed capital." Among these are houses, apartments, and other structures; machines and other durable equipment in mining, manufacturing, and farming; transportation equipment; irrigation systems; and communication systems. Such capital goods increase total output over time in the sense that the services that they render during their useful lives increase output by more than the original cost of the capital good.

Our primary interest here is in the processes of saving and investment. While "capital" refers to a stock of capital existing at a stated point in time, "investment" is a flow during some stated period, usually measured at an annual rate. Investment is the value of output during a stated period that is used to maintain or increase the stock of capital goods. In this period, some value of output—or, more basically, of productive resources—is "vested in" or "congealed in" the form of durable capital goods, which will yield valuable services over a considerably longer period, perhaps twenty years or more.

Saving is a necessary condition for investment. If a society used its entire output for current consumption, no resources would be available for capital accumulation. In a monetized economy, saving usually takes the form already described—failure to spend some part of current money income for consumption. In effect, saving serves to free factors of production from the task of producing goods and services for current consumption and makes them available to produce new capital goods. However, the latter can occur only to the extent that someone, savers themselves or others, spends for investment—only to the extent that they demand output for capital formation.

Since the rate of overall investment is limited to the scarce flow of output represented by saving, total social output can be maximized only if investment is confined to those types of new capital goods that will add most to the value of output. We shall use the term "marginal efficiency of investment" to denote the average annual rate of return over the cost of an investment good. For example, suppose that some new capital good that costs $1000 will, over its useful life, increase the value of output of a firm by an amount sufficient to cover the original cost of the capital good and a further average annual amount equal to 15 percent of its original cost. In this case the marginal efficiency of investment is 15 percent. In contrast, some other investment may have only a much lower marginal efficiency rate, such as 2 percent.

Saving could, of course, be translated into investment without the creation of any financial claims if every household in every period spent for investment an amount exactly equal to its own current saving. However, a system relying exclusively on self-finance of investment would be highly inefficient. Some scarce resources would be used for types of investment with very low marginal efficiency rates while investment opportunities with much higher rates of marginal efficiency remained unexploited, and serious sacrifices of potential productivity would result. For this there are several reasons:

1. Differences in managerial skills. The marginal efficiency of investment depends heavily on managerial skills in selecting the most appropriate types of capital goods, combining them appropriately with labor and other productive factors, and directing production processes. Ability to save and ability to manage are by no means perfectly correlated. Wealthy heirs and successful physicians, lawyers, athletes, and entertainment artists may be large positive savers but possess little ability, and perhaps even less inclination, to establish and manage productive establishments. On the other hand, some households with little ability to save may possess excellent managerial ability and many opportunities for investment with high rates of marginal efficiency.
2. Differences in existing stocks of capital goods relative to other productive factors. For some entities, the marginal efficiency of investment may be low because they already possess such large stocks of capital goods relative to their supply of labor and land. For others, the marginal efficiency of investment is high because their stock of capital is so small relative to their other productive factors.
3. The "lumpiness" of some individual investment projects. Some individual projects with the highest rates of marginal efficiency may require outlays beyond the capacity of a household to finance from its own current saving. For example, the most highly pro-

ductive investment opportunity available to a household may be the sinking of a tube well and the installation of a pump to provide water for irrigation and family use. Lacking resources for such a large outlay, the household may be forced to confine its investment to smaller projects with much lower marginal efficiency rates, such as purchases of buckets to carry water from a distant pond.

4. Failure to achieve maximum economies of scale. To achieve maximum total output, enterprises in every line of economic activity must be enabled to command enough resources to exhaust the available economies of scale. This size varies from industry to industry. In some lines, such as operation of repair shops, specialty stores, or truck farms, optimum scale may be reached with resources small enough to be supplied by a single household. At the other extreme, however—in such lines as steel manufacturing, generation and distribution of electricity, and electronic communications—economies of scale persist until an enterprise commands assets running into the millions or even billions of dollars.

When self-investment opportunities available to different households have differing marginal efficiency rates, exchanges of saving, representing command over resources for investment, can both increase total social output and yield net gains to the exchangers. Suppose, for example, that available to you are various investment projects with marginal efficiency rates in excess of 20 percent. In contrast, the Green household, a positive saver, has no investment opportunity with a marginal efficiency rate in excess of 8 percent. A transfer of investing power from Green to you will increase total output and can increase the net incomes of both of you. Green enjoys a net gain if you give her any rate of return in excess of 8 percent; you make net gains if you give her any rate of return below the marginal efficiency rate on your investment. The potential gains from such exchanges are fully exploited only when exchanges of command over resources for investment have been carried to the point at which marginal efficiency rates of all entities have been brought into equality.

The most efficient method of effecting exchanges of this type is through the creation and issue of direct financial claims. In the example above, you would create a direct financial claim against yourself and transfer it to Green in exchange for money representing some of her current saving. This may be a direct debt or credit claim, essentially similar to those used in effecting exchanges of present and future consuming power. In this case, you will promise to repay fixed dollar amounts of principal at some stated time or times in the future, together with agreed-upon amounts of interest to be paid at specified times. Or the direct claim may be an *equity* claim, in which you create and transfer to Green a share of ownership in the enterprise. In effect, you and Green become co-owners, sharing claims on the assets and income of the enterprise on some agreed-upon terms.

We noted earlier three different but related effects of the creation of direct consumer debt to finance dissaving. We can distinguish similar effects of the creation and sale of both equity and debt claims to finance investment:

1. Allocation effects. The creation and sale of these claims serve as a vehicle for transferring or allocating command over current output from savers to spenders for investment. To the extent that this process succeeds in allocating the scarce supply of saving to the types of investment with the highest rates of marginal efficiency and away from investment with lower marginal efficiency rates, it enhances the efficiency of investment, increases total output, and affords net gains to the exchangers.
2. Portfolio effects. The creation and sale of very large amounts of equity and debt claims to finance investment greatly enrich the array of assets available to asset holders and make possible portfolios with still more favorable combinations of income, safety, and liquidity. It thus increases the attractiveness of saving and of transferring investment power to others.
3. Macroeconomic effects. As already noted, positive saving, considered by itself, tends to decrease aggregate money demands for output. Investment spending is one way, and in our economy is usually the largest way, of "offsetting" the deflationary effect of positive saving. To the extent that the creation and sale of equity and debt claims to finance investment succeed in translating the part of current money income that is not spent for current consumption into spending for investment purposes, it serves to maintain the level of total money demands for output. This important issue will receive much attention in later pages.

BUSINESS FIRMS

As growth in the size of markets and advances in technology make advantageous the use of larger-scale enterprises, productive activities become less closely associated with individual households and new legal forms of business organizations or firms evolve. Legally, *a sole proprietorship* or *individual enterprise* is simply an individual in his role as the owner of an enterprise. This type of firm has important advantages in lines where relatively small size is not a serious handicap. It can be established or terminated with a minimum of legal formalities, management responsibility is concentrated in the owner, and the owner has a strong incentive to operate the firm efficiently. For such reasons, sole proprietorships continue to be more numerous than any other type of business firm. However, this form has serious limitations. For one thing, the owner has unlimited legal liability for the debts of the firm; creditors may claim not only his business assets but his other assets as well. Also, the firm's assets are limited to the amount contributed by the owner and such amounts as he can borrow from others.

This limitation is relaxed to some extent in a *partnership,* which is legally a firm jointly owned by two or more persons. A partnership can amass more resources from equity contributions by its multiple owners and from its larger borrowing power. However, several legal aspects of the partnership have limited its popularity:

1. Any partner can make contracts, within the scope of the firm's lines of business, that are legally binding on all the partners. One imprudent or dishonest partner can be a calamity for all.
2. Each partner has unlimited joint and several liability for all the debts of the partnership. Thus a creditor can require one partner to surrender all his assets to meet the firm's obligations, and that partner's only recourse is to sue his partners for reimbursement.
3. On the withdrawal of any partner, because of death or for any other reason, the partnership is dissolved, and a new partnership must be formed or the firm liquidated.

In view of these legal provisions, it is easy to understand why it is difficult to form a partnership of a thousand, or even a hundred, persons and why partnership claims are usually not very marketable.

Many legal types of business organizations have evolved to remedy at least some of the shortcomings of the partnership form, but by far the most successful of these has been the *business corporation.* A corporation is a legal entity, chartered under the laws of a state or the federal government, and endowed with legal powers to own and operate property, to enter into legal contracts, and to sue and be sued in the courts. Several attributes of the corporation account for its widespread use:

1. It is legally endowed with perpetual life. Its human owners may come and go, but the corporation goes on forever—if it can survive financial vicissitudes. In this respect it is much like a college, a church, or a governmental unit. This attribute is especially useful to enterprises using large amounts of durable capital that will yield its full returns only over a long period.
2. Its ownership shares are endowed with *limited liability*. After the corporation has been paid the full sales price of a share, the shareholder cannot be assessed to meet the debts of the corporation. Thus no holder of fully paid shares can lose more than he paid for the shares.
3. Its ownership shares are freely transferrable from shareholder to shareholder. Most corporations do not stand ready to buy and retire shares that they have issued, but shareholders typically expect that they can get money when they want it by selling to someone else—perhaps at a profit.

Because of such attributes, the corporation has become the dominant legal form of business organization in many lines. In terms of asset size, many corporations are quite small—some less than a million dollars. However, corporations with assets exceeding $100 million are far from rare, and some have assets running into the billions. Firms of such size can easily overcome problems related to the "lumpiness" of individual investment projects and can exploit fully all the economies of scale. Some of the largest corporations have more than a million shareholders, and debt claims against them are held directly or indirectly by millions more.

OTHER EXCHANGES INVOLVING
TIME ON INCOME AND PRODUCT ACCOUNT

Households and business firms are not the only entities in our society that engage in exchanges involving time on income and product account and that create direct financial claims against themselves. All types of governmental units—federal, state, and local—engage in similar activities. Each unit could, of course, adhere strictly to "the rule of an annually balanced budget," spending in each period an amount exactly equal to its income from taxes, fees, and other revenues. In practice, they often depart from this rule. In some periods they spend for output less than their current income. This excess of their current income over their current spending is usually called a government "surplus," but we call it government "saving" because it represents that part of the government income, and of national income, that the government does not use to demand current output. Governments ordinarily use their current saving to retire outstanding financial claims against themselves, but they can also purchase financial claims against others. In these ways money representing government positive saving is transferred to others, who may use it as they see fit.

In other periods a governmental unit spends more than its current income. It is a "dissaver," or a "deficit" unit. To finance its deficit, it typically creates and issues direct financial claims against itself, usually debt claims. Again, we can distinguish three types of effects of the creation of direct financial claims. The allocation effect is to transfer command over current output and productive resources from savers to governmental units. The portfolio effect is to enrich the array of assets available to asset holders. The macroeconomic effect is to offset the contractionary effect of positive saving by others.

We shall merely mention here similar activities by other types of entities in our society—universities and colleges, churches, fraternal organizations, and so on. In some periods such entities spend for current consumption and investment less than their current income. Such positive saving is ordinarily used to repurchase and retire financial claims against the entities or to purchase financial claims against others. In other periods they are deficit units, and they typically cover their deficits by selling some of their financial claims against others or by creating and issuing direct financial claims against themselves.

CREATION OF DIRECT FINANCIAL CLAIMS IN EXCHANGES THAT ARE NOT ON INCOME AND PRODUCT ACCOUNT

In all the cases examined up to this point, direct financial claims were created in exchanges involving time on income and product account. That is, the direct claims served as an instrument or vehicle for transferring command over current output. We merely mention here and leave for later discussion the fact that direct financial claims are sometimes created to facilitate transfers of assets that are not a part of current output. For example, an entity creates and sells debt, or sells equity claims against itself, to finance the purchase of land or an "old" house, factory, or other physical asset. Such transfers can increase total utility if the asset yields more utility to the transferee than to the transferor, and they can increase total output if the buyer can use the asset more productively than the seller. For example, total output can be increased if productive assets are transferred to a buyer with greater managerial ability or if the buyer is enabled to achieve greater economies of scale or a more economical combination of the various factors of production.

CONCLUSION

Since we have, up to this point, confined our attention to relatively simple societies and simple monetary and financial arrangements, we still have a long way to go to arrive at a faithful picture of the complex monetary-financial system of today. Yet we have already discovered some basic facts, functions, and principles that are an essential base for our later analysis of more complex systems. Among these are the following.

1. Societies discover at an early stage various types of potential gains from exchanges of real goods and services. Pure spot exchanges of a given stock of goods yield gains in the form of increased total utility for the traders. The gains from spot exchanges that are an integral part of a specialization-exchange technology of production are in the form of both increased real output and greater satisfaction from any given amount of output. Exchanges involving time on income and product account enhance total utility, or total output, or both. Such exchanges of present and future consuming power enable households to allocate their consumption more advantageously through time, thus increasing the total utility derived from their lifetime consumption. Exchanges on saving and investment account increase total output by allocating scarce investment power to its most productive uses and users. The gains from these various types of exchanges are so great that some trade occurs even under an inefficient system of pure barter.

2. The basic function of money is to increase the transactions and allocational efficiencies of exchange processes. The use of a monetary unit of account in measuring and stating the values of all things facilitates the computation and statement of relative values, makes possible meaningful accounting systems, and generally promotes precise calculations of costs and benefits. The use of some "thing" that is generally accepted as a medium of exchange or payments reduces the real costs of search and bargain and makes possible a more efficient organization of markets of all types—markets for finished output, for labor and other inputs, for intermediate materials and components, and for financial

claims of all types. It does this by making feasible the establishment of market institutions capable of achieving economies of specialization and scale in exchange processes, the accumulation and use of great amounts of information concerning the things traded, and competition in the various markets.

3. The basic function of direct financial claims is to facilitate and make more efficient exchanges involving time. Such claims serve as an instrument or vehicle for transferring command over current output from positive savers to those who wish to use it for dissaving or investment. Unlike money itself, these claims usually yield an explicit return in the form of interest or its equivalent in other forms. We have found two basic reasons for the emergence of a positive rate of interest: (a) positive rates of time preference and (b) positive rates of marginal efficiency of investment. Dissavers are willing to pay interest because they consider a dollar's worth of consumption now more valuable than a dollar's worth available only at some time in the future. Spenders for investment are willing to pay interest because a dollar invested now enables them to undertake investment that will increase the value of output by more than a dollar in the future. At a zero or negative rate of interest, the forthcoming supply of positive saving would be insufficient to meet the total demands by dissavers and spenders for investment.

4. The creation of direct financial claims enriches the array of assets available to owners of wealth. In a pure barter system, only physical goods are available to asset holders, and these differ greatly in their barterability, in their yields of explicit or imputed income, and in their costs of storage. The introduction of money provided an asset with perfect safety of principal value in terms of monetary units and perfect liquidity, but most types of money yield no explicit income and lose purchasing power in times of price inflation. The creation of direct financial claims adds a wide variety of assets that yield explicit income and possess varying degrees of liquidity and safety of principal. Some are almost as safe and liquid as money itself but yield some income; others are less liquid and safe but promise higher rates of return. The availability of such a wide variety of assets encourages both saving and the willingness of savers to part with money in exchange for other assets.

5. Ideally, a monetary and financial system would achieve not only maximum efficiency in the allocation of resources but also the macroeconomic objective of maintaining a stable price level and a continuously full-employment level of output. Saving, dissaving, and investment play crucial roles in this process. An ideal financial system

would assure that positive saving would always be translated into spending for output in the form of dissaving and investment at such a level as to maintain full employment. Unfortunately, actual monetary and financial systems have not yet reached this degree of perfection.

SELECTED READINGS

Chandler, L. V., and Goldfeld, S. M. *The Economics of Money and Banking.* 7th ed. New York: Harper & Row, 1977. Chaps. 1–3.

Smith, P. T. *Economics of Financial Institutions and Markets.* Homewood, Ill.: Richard D. Irwin, 1971. Chaps. 1, 2.

2

CERTAINTY, UNCERTAINTY, AND RISK

This chapter consists of two main parts. The first presents a model of a perfectly competitive financial market. This model assumes, among other things, complete knowledge and perfect certainty. The second part relaxes this assumption and deals with uncertainty and risk and some of their principal implications for the financial system.

MODEL OF A PERFECTLY COMPETITIVE FINANCIAL MARKET

The preceding chapter discussed the potential gains from exchanges involving time and how the creation and use of direct financial claims can increase both the operational and the allocational efficiencies of these exchanges. This section will extend that analysis, indicating how a perfectly competitive market could achieve an optimum allocation of scarce saving among its many potential uses and users. Our model makes many simplifying assumptions, as all economic models must, and some of the assumed conditions differ in various ways and degrees from those of the real world. Nevertheless, the model is highly useful for several purposes:

1. Some of its conclusions remain largely valid under actual market conditions.
2. It provides benchmarks against which the performance of actual markets can be measured.

3. It helps us to identify the major sources and types of imperfections of competition in actual markets, and to indicate the effects of such imperfections on market performance.

In order to focus attention on private consumption, saving, and investment by households and business firms, we shall assume that there is no government. Also, in order to concentrate on the allocative functions of the market we shall assume that the latter simultaneously achieves its macroeconomic objective of maintaining total real output or income at its full-employment level.

The things exchanged in our model financial market are money representing current saving, and direct financial claims or securities. Money is supplied by positive savers to demand direct securities. Direct securities are supplied to demand money for two purposes: some are supplied by dissaving households to get money to pay for the excess of their consumption over their current incomes; and some are supplied by households and business firms to finance their investment spending in excess of their own current saving. In exchanges of money and direct securities there is some rate of exchange or price; this is an interest rate, which is stated in terms of percent per annum. Exchanges in this market are facilitated by efficient brokers and dealers and others performing middleman functions. We shall not discuss these functions further at this point but shall merely assume that middlemen perform them with maximum efficiency and supply their services at marginal cost. It will be convenient at the beginning to assume that transactions costs are zero, but this assumption will obviously have to be relaxed later.

Conditions in our market conform fully to those of perfect competition:

1. There are so many suppliers and demanders of funds, each constituting such a small part of the total, that no one entity can affect the level of interest rates by varying the quantity demanded or supplied by it. Moreover, all compete and do not enter into collusion. Each is a "price taker," not a "price maker." That is, each takes the prevailing interest rate as a given fact and adjusts its own decisions to that fact.
2. The market is characterized by full information known with perfect certainty. All participants know with certainty not only prevailing interest rates and security prices but also the future behavior of these rates and prices. Each household knows with certainty its present and future levels of income and wants, and this information is made fully available to those who may provide funds to the

household. Every potential spender for investment knows with certainty the rates of marginal efficiency of all investment projects available to it, and this information is made available to potential suppliers of funds.

A world of full information known with perfect certainty is a riskless world. There are no surprises, pleasant or unpleasant. All future events, known with certainty, are "discounted" to the present; that is, they are reflected in the terms of financial contracts. There are no defaults on financial contracts, for no entity can acquire funds in excess of its ability and willingness to repay. But within this limitation, all entities have full access to the financial market at the prevailing rate of interest. In this riskless world, all financial claims are perfect substitutes for each other, so that there emerges a single market rate of interest.[1] The rate of interest is an explicit price or reward to those who supply funds in the market, and an explicit cost to those who acquire funds in the market. It is also an opportunity cost—the value of an opportunity lost—to those who do not make their funds available in the market. To use any part of your current income for consumption, or to finance your own investment, "costs" the interest that you might have earned by lending the funds in the market.

Let us now look at the objectives of the various actual and potential participants in the market.

1. Objectives of households in determining their rates of consumption, saving, and dissaving. The objective of every household is to maximize the total utility derived from its lifetime consumption. Knowing with certainty the levels of both its present and future incomes and needs, it will determine the marginal rates of time preference (MTPs) of various rates of present consumption. It will then consume up to that amount, but only up to that amount, at which its MTP is equal to the market rate of interest. It will save any part of its income on which its MTP is below the market rate of interest, and it will borrow to finance any consumption in excess of its current income on which its MTP exceeds the market rate of interest. Thus, the MTPs of all households will be equated to the interest rate.

---

[1] This statement must be modified to the extent that there are differences in the transactions costs of acquiring, holding, and disposing of the various financial claims. However, at this point we are still assuming that such transactions costs are zero. We also assume implicitly that the community does not expect the level of interest rates to change in the future. The significance of this will be discussed later.

2. Objectives of positive savers. The objective of all positive savers is to maximize the income received from the use of their saving. To this end, they will use their saving to finance their own investment only to the extent that the marginal efficiency rate on their own investment is in excess of, or equal to, the market rate of interest. They will supply the rest of their saving to the market.
3. Objectives of spenders for investment. The objective of all spenders for investment is to maximize their net income. To this end, they undertake all investments on which the marginal efficiency rate is in excess of, or equal to, the market rate of interest, but they shun any investment opportunity whose marginal efficiency rate is below the market rate of interest.

Thus for all spenders for investment, and for every type of investment, the marginal efficiency rate will be equated to the market rate of interest.

During any period, the competitive efforts of the various market participants to achieve their objectives will be reflected in the market in supply and demand functions of the type depicted in Figure 2 — 1. The supply function represents total positive saving during the period minus any amounts used by individual positive savers to finance their own investment. The demand function represents amounts of saving demanded by individual households to finance consumption in excess of their current incomes plus amounts demanded by individual spenders for investment to finance investment in excess of their own current saving.

Demand and supply are equated at the equilibrium interest rate, *OB*. Supply at that interest rate is limited to the amount *OA;* more supply would be forthcoming only at higher interest rates. This supply is only sufficient to satisfy that part of demand represented by the section of the demand curve at or above the interest rate *OB*; the part of the demand lying below that level will remain unsatisfied. The market rate of interest serves to ration or allocate the scarce supply. Which demands are satisfied, and which left unsatisfied? All of the available supply will be allocated to satisfy demands by dissavers for amounts with MTPs in excess of or equal to the interest rate and to finance investments with marginal efficiency rates in excess of or equal to the interest rate. None of the scarce supply is allocated to finance consumption on which the MTP is below the interest rate or to finance investments with marginal efficiency rates below the interest rate.

This perfectly competitive financial market has achieved com-

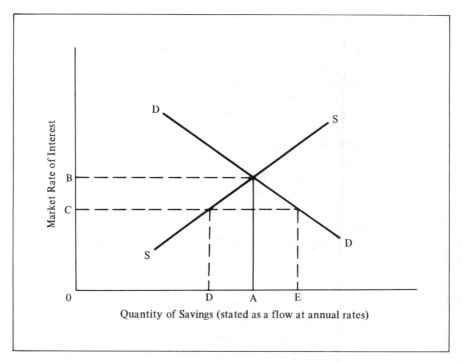

Figure 2–1   **Supply of and Demand for**
Saving in a Perfectly Competitive Market

plete allocational efficiency in the sense that it has exhausted all opportunities to make one participant feel better off without making another
feel worse off. Every household, with full access to the market, has
adjusted its consumption and saving in such a way as to equalize its MTP
to the market rate of interest. Thus the MTPs of all households are
equalized, and there remain no unexploited opportunities to increase
total utility by transfers of consuming power from households with
lower MTPs to households with higher MTPs. This market has also
achieved maximum efficiency in allocating the scarce supply of saving
available for investment. The marginal efficiency rate on every type of
actual investment has been brought into equality with the market rate of
interest, so that there remain no unexploited opportunities to increase
total output by shifting investment away from uses with lower marginal
efficiency rates to those with higher marginal efficiency rates.
    In the above processes, the market rate of interest appeared in

several roles—as a reward to positive savers, as a cost to dissavers and spenders for investment, and as an allocator of scarce resources. What would be the effects if the market rate were prevented, through official restriction or otherwise, from achieving its equilibrium level? Suppose that, because of a general dislike for higher interest rates or strong pressures from debtors, the government imposes a legal ceiling on interest rates at a level significantly below the equilibrium level. Let this level be represented by the vertical distance *OC* in Figure 2 − 1. One effect may be a departure of total output or income from its former full-employment level. But even if this does not occur, there will be adverse allocational effects. At the ceiling rate *OC*, the quantity of saving supplied will be only *OD*, while the quantity demanded is the larger amount, *OE*. Demand will exceed supply by an amount represented by the horizontal distance *DE*. This excess demand is likely to lead to the emergence of black markets with illegal interest rates in excess of the ceiling. The allocational effects of these illegal rates may be more efficient than those of the ceiling rate but not as efficient as those resulting from the equilibrium rate. The most adverse allocational effects are likely to result if the ceiling is effectively enforced. The quantity of saving supplied to the market will be reduced, as households consume more and save less. Households will consume all of their incomes with MTPs at least equal to the ceiling rate, and save only that part on which their MTP is less than *OC*. They would have felt better off if they had been allowed to earn the higher interest rate *OB* and had saved more. Also, positive savers will use more of their own saving to finance their own investment and supply less to the market. They will themselves invest in all projects with marginal efficiency rates at least equal to the ceiling rate and will offer in the market only that part of their saving on which their own marginal efficiency rates are below the ceiling rates. This has two types of adverse effects. It means that the income of positive savers is less than it would be if they were free to lend at the higher interest rate *OB*. It also means that total output will be reduced because some part of saving will be used for projects whose marginal efficiency rates are below those on some investment opportunities that remain unexploited.

How will the saving that continues to flow to the market be allocated or rationed? The ceiling rate is too low to perform this function and to eradicate excess demands. Nonprice methods of rationing or allocation will be employed, and there is no assurance that these will allocate the supply to those demanders with the highest MTPs and the highest marginal efficiency rates. Instead, the supply may go largely to members of the family, close friends, business associates, and those willing to offer bribes and other favors. The result may be large losses of utility and productivity.

This is not to say that the government should never limit interest rates by direct actions. When financial markets are highly imperfect, such action may be beneficial. However, even under these conditions the advocates of government restriction should bear the burden of proof.

In summary, a perfectly competitive financial market characterized by full information known with perfect certainty would be a relatively simple market. Except for differences in transactions costs, all direct financial claims would be perfect substitutes for each other, and there would be at any time only one market rate of interest. Rules for rational decision making would also be relatively simple. For savers, it would be: maximize the net income from your saving. For spenders for investment it would be: maximize net income. To this end, undertake all investments with marginal efficiency rates in excess of or equal to the market rate of interest.

Unfortunately, financial processes and markets become more complicated in a real world characterized by many types and degrees of uncertainty and risk.

UNCERTAINTY AND RISK

In the idealized world of full information known with perfect certainty, every participant in financial transactions could forecast precisely and with certainty the outcome of each alternative course of action. There was no risk that outcomes would differ from those forecasted. In the real world, however, outcomes are uncertain; they are only matters of probability. Some outcomes are much more probable than others, and some may have a very high probability, but there almost always remains some probability, however small, that the actual outcome will differ significantly from the most probable. Some of these deviations will be pleasant surprises; others will be disappointing and even ruinous. Risk is an inevitable concomitant of uncertainty. To develop this point we shall now consider the major sources and types of uncertainty that generate risk relating to the future prices and net rates of return on financial claims.

SOURCES AND TYPES OF UNCERTAINTY AND RISK

The market price of a financial claim depends on both the market rate of interest or discount at which future receipts are discounted and the expected amounts and timing of those future receipts. Thus, uncertainties can be divided into two broad classes: (1) uncertainties concerning the future course of market rates of interest or discount; and (2) uncertainties concerning the amounts and timing of future receipts.

MARKET RISK

Market risk arises out of uncertainties concerning future rates of interest or discount. It is the risk that a future rise of interest rates will lower the prices of outstanding securities. The principles are clearest in the case of debt claims with fixed dollar amounts of interest and a fixed principal amount repayable at some stated time in the future. For example, an outstanding debt claim may promise to pay $60 a year in interest and $1000 at maturity. If the prevailing market yield on other closely similar securities is 6 percent, the market price of this security will be approximately $1000.[2]

Suppose now that the market yields on this type of security fall from 6 to 4 percent, so that new issues selling for $1000 promise to pay only $40 a year in interest. The price of the debt claim promising to pay $60 a year in interest will rise; competing buyers will bid the price up until the average annual yield over the market price, including both annual interest receipts and the difference between market price and maturity values, is no greater than yields on other similar obligations. How much the price will rise depends on the security's remaining time to maturity. The longer the remaining time to maturity, the greater will be the price increase. For example, the price increases accompanying a fall of the interest rate from 6 to 4 percent will be 1.9 percent on a 1-year maturity, 16.4 percent on a 10-year maturity, and 31.4 percent on a 25-year maturity. (See Table 2−1.)

Suppose, on the other hand, that market yields on this type of obligation rise from 6 to 8 percent, so that new $1000 issues promise to pay $80 a year in interest. The price of outstanding debt obligations of the same maturity must fall enough to raise their average annual yields to 8 percent. How much the price of a security must fall depends on its remaining time to maturity. The longer the remaining time to maturity, the greater will be the decline of its price. For example, the price declines accompanying a rise of interest rates from 6 to 8 percent are 2 percent on a 1-year maturity, 14 percent on a 10-year maturity, and 22 percent on a 25-year maturity. These examples suggest that in a world in

---

[2] The relationships between interest rates and security prices are discussed further in the following chapter.

Table 2 — 1   **Market Values of a Bond Promising to Pay**
$1000 at Maturity and $60 a Year in Interest

		Applicable Rates of Interest or Discount		
		4 Percent	6 Percent	8 Percent
Remaining Years	1	$1019.40	$1000.00	$981.10
to Maturity	5	1089.80	1000.00	918.90
	10	1163.50	1000.00	864.10
	20	1276.60	1000.00	802.10
	25	1314.20	1000.00	785.20

Source: Bond tables.

which the future course of interest rates is uncertain, market risk is by no means negligible, especially on longer-term obligations.

Common stocks and other equity claims are also subject to market risk. Though equity claims and debt claims are not perfect substitutes for each other, they do compete for places in the portfolios of investors and their rates of return are interrelated. Suppose, for example, that a share of common stock is expected to yield some flow of dollar returns in future years and that these expectations remain unchanged. If yield rates on debt obligations are low, investors will bid up the price of the share until its expected yield over its market price is comparably low, though not necessarily the same. However, if yield rates on debt claims are high, investors will buy and hold ownership shares only at prices low enough to yield comparably high rates of return, though not necessarily the same rates.

UNCERTAINTY OF AMOUNTS
AND TIMING OF FUTURE RECEIPTS

Risk also arises out of uncertainties concerning the future dollar amounts and timing of receipts on specific financial claims. This applies to both debt and equity claims. There is no certainty that any debtor will pay fully, promptly, and without controversy or expensive litigation; the actual outcome is a matter of probabilities, though the probabilities differ greatly among debtors. This risk is called *default risk*. Actual default obviously injures the creditor. However, creditors can be hurt even in the absence of actual default if the probability of default increases, for increased probability of default will lower the market price of the security.

There are also similar risks arising out of uncertainties concerning the future flows of dollar returns on shares of common stock and other ownership claims.

Expected receipts may fail to be forthcoming because of bad faith on the part of the issuer of a security, but even greater risks arise out of uncertainties concerning the future values of the incomes and assets of the issuers themselves. Most issuers of financial claims probably act in good faith but they, as well as holders of financial claims against them, can become victims of adverse and imperfectly foreseen future events. Among these are such things as recessions and depressions; natural catastrophes, such as droughts or floods; illness and loss of income in a family; unexpectedly low revenues or high costs for a governmental unit; and a host of hazards for individual business firms, such as decreases of demand for their output, decreased supplies of important inputs, long labor disputes, and deterioration of management.

In short, many types of uncertainty and risk are inherent in the operations of business firms and other issuers of financial claims. Some risks can be reduced or eliminated through insurance, diversification, or other methods, but some cannot, or could be eliminated only at prohibitive cost. The remaining uncertainty and risk must be reflected in one or more of the classes of financial claims issued by the entity. The first impact is on residual ownership claims, but highly adverse events can endanger the ability of an entity to meet its debt obligations fully and promptly.

DECISION MAKING UNDER UNCERTAINTY

In a world of uncertainty, a decision maker contemplating the purchase of a financial claim or a new capital good obviously cannot know with certainty the future rates of return on the asset. He can at best only estimate the range of possible outcomes and the probability of each. This is illustrated schematically in Figure 2−2. Expected rates of return, including both current income and changes in principal value, are shown on the horizontal axis. The subjective probability of each expected rate of return is measured vertically. Even if we feel certain about the subjective probability distribution of possible outcomes, we cannot know which outcome will actually be realized. We can estimate the most probable outcome and the mean or average expected outcome. In this example, both are the expected rate of return $E(R)$. However, there are some probabilities that the rate of return actually realized will be above $E(R)$ and some probabilities that it will be lower. Actuarially, the chances

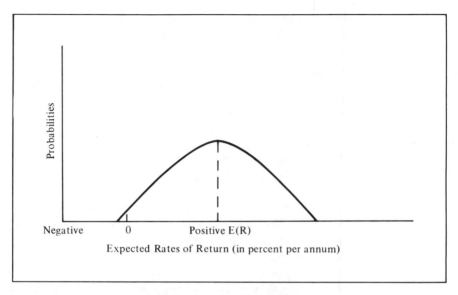

Figure 2–2   **A Subjective Probability Distribution
of Expected Rates of Return on Some Asset**

of returns above *E(R)* balance the risk that the rate of return will be lower. However, as we shall emphasize later, it is unlikely that most buyers and holders will feel that the probabilities of returns in excess of *E(R)* compensate exactly for bearing the risk that the realized rate of return will be lower, or even negative.

For measuring risk, there is no single way that is most satisfactory for all purposes. However, one measure that is commonly used is the *standard deviation*.[3] This measures the average amount by which the various possible outcomes deviate from the mean expected return, *E(R)*. It is a measure of the dispersion of the expected outcomes. Thus risk is low if the possible outcomes are bunched closely around *E(R)*, but it increases as the possible outcomes are dispersed more widely.

On what types of information and analysis can a rational decision maker base his subjective probability distribution of expected future outcomes? As John Maynard Keynes emphasized, there is no workable alternative, in forming our expectations as to the course of future events, to the usual practice of ascertaining recent trends and the present situation and projecting them into the future, modifying them only to the

---

[3] For the precise meaning and methods of computing standard deviation, see any text on elementary statistics.

extent that we have more or less definite reasons for expecting changes.[4] Thus rational forecasting involves two interrelated parts:

1. To achieve as good an understanding as is economically feasible of relevant past developments and current conditions. This involves gathering data; ordering the data and analyzing them in an attempt to find patterns of behavior, lines of causation, and trends or developments relevant to future behavior; and disseminating the data and analyses for use by decision makers.
2. To try to identify prospective forces and events that may cause conditions in the future to differ from those in the present and the recent past and to estimate the nature, timing, and magnitude of such changes. Some can be predicted with considerable confidence for at least short periods; others are less predictable.

ECONOMIC AND FINANCIAL INTELLIGENCE

Tremendous amounts of economic and financial data relating to current conditions and past events are available to aid forecasters and decision makers. These are of many types, of which only a few can be mentioned here.

1. Data relating to financial markets. These include not only quotations of current prices and yields on a wide range of financial claims but also statistical series portraying behavior in the past.
2. Data relating to gross national product and its components. These data, together with macroeconomic theory, serve as major bases for forecasters of output, income, price levels, profits, employment, and demands for many specific types of goods and services included in national output.
3. Data relating to issuers of securities and to specific security issues. Information concerning past, present, and future budgets of the federal government, state governments, and at least the larger municipalities is available nationwide, and the financial conditions and prospects of small governmental units are known at least locally. Also available on a nationwide basis is much intelligence relating to several thousand of the larger business corporations. Much of this is supplied in accordance with the federal "truth-in-securities" laws, first enacted in 1933 and 1934 and since amended many times. With some exceptions, corporations

---

[4] John Maynard Keynes, *The General Theory of Employment, Interest and Money* (New York: Harcourt, Brace and World, 1936), p. 148.

may make public offerings of securities only after issuing a prospectus containing full and fair disclosure of all facts that could affect significantly the financial performance of the company and the income and values of its securities. Periodic reports with similar disclosures are required of companies whose securities are listed for trading on the national securities exchanges and of some of the larger corporations whose securities are traded only in over-the-counter markets—that is, outside the organized exchanges.

Such data are analyzed and used as a basis for forecasts by securities-rating services, commercial and academic research organizations, investment advisory services, analysts in financial institutions, and others. The results are widely disseminated through newspapers, magazines, investment advisers, representatives of brokers and dealers, and so on. The wide availability of such intelligence helps the securities of these companies command a nationwide, and even an international, market.

Such advantages are not available to many issuers of financial claims, including most households, sole proprietorships, partnerships, and small corporations. Information about these types of issuers is often limited in both quantity and reliability and largely confined to the locality or region in which the issuer is located. In some cases this proves to be no disadvantage; the issuer can acquire funds from local or regional sources on terms no more onerous than those prevailing in the national markets. In other cases, however, lack of knowledge in other regions concerning the issuer's financial prospects produces monopoly power for local and regional suppliers of funds. In financial markets, as in others, ignorance is the enemy of competition and allocational efficiency.

Even if we had complete and accurate intelligence concerning the past and the present, we would still face the problem of identifying forces that will cause conditions in the future to differ from those of the past and the present and of estimating the nature, magnitude, and timing of such changes. Until such time as we can do this far more accurately than is now possible, uncertainty and risk will remain.

PORTFOLIO CHOICE UNDER UNCERTAINTY

We noted earlier that in a riskless world of perfect certainty the rule for optimum portfolio choice would be simple: Choose the asset with the highest rate of return, net of transactions costs. This rule is not appropriate in a world of uncertainty. Under conditions of uncertainty, rational choices among assets involve not only their mean expected rates of return but also their degrees of risk and the attitudes of buyers toward risk bearing.

A little experiment may help to elucidate some of the issues involved. You are asked to write out answers to the questions below, to request a number of your acquaintances to do the same, and then to compare the answers. Having ample funds, you face the problem of choosing between assets A and B shown in Figure 2−3. Both have the same mean expected rate of return, $E(R)$, which we assume to be 8 percent, but their risks differ greatly. Asset A is riskless, but B is risky, as evidenced by the fact that possible outcomes range from minus 10 percent to plus 26 percent. Now for the questions:

1. If the prices of A and B are the same, which asset would you prefer? If you are indifferent between them, record "indifferent."
2. If the certain rate of return on A is 8 percent, at what mean expected rate of return on B would you be indifferent between the two assets? The yield differential that would make the two assets equally preferred by you is a sort of quantitative index of your attitude toward risk bearing.

Now that you and your acquaintances have recorded and compared your answers, let us explore their significance. Those whose answer to Question 1 was "indifferent" are described as *risk neutral.* Their

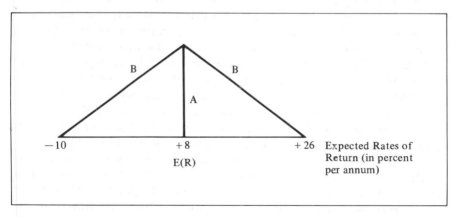

Figure 2−3   **Assets with Differing Risks**

choices among assets are based solely on mean expected rates of return and are not affected by differing degrees of risk. To them, the disutility of bearing the risk that the actual rate of return on asset B will be below $E(R)$ or even negative is exactly balanced by the utility of possible returns above $E(R)$. Those who chose A over B are said to be *risk averters*. At the same mean expected rate of return they prefer less risky assets and will hold riskier assets only if compensated by a higher $E(R)$. The extent to which the mean expected rate of return on B must be above that on A to make the two assets equally preferred is a sort of index of the degree of risk aversion. Those who chose B over A are said to be *risk lovers*. At the same mean expected rate of return they prefer riskier over less risky assets, and to get more risk they are willing to accept a lower $E(R)$. To them, the utility of the possibility of realizing rates of return in excess of $E(R)$ more than offsets the disutility of the possibility of realizing only lower rates of return.

I cannot predict with certainty the outcome of our little experiment. I do predict, however, that a majority of the respondents were revealed as risk averters. I also predict that significant differences in attitudes toward risk bearing were revealed. Some respondents may have been risk neutral and others risk lovers. Even among the risk averters, there were probably significant differences in their degrees of risk aversion.

Differences in attitudes toward risk bearing reflect to some extent personal differences among decision makers—differences in such things as personal goals, life styles, self-confidence, metabolism rates, and earlier training and experience. You may, or may not, find that your acquaintances who are most risk-averse tend to be generally conservative and cautious in their conduct, and that those who are least risk-averse or even risk lovers are generally less cautious and even inclined to be daring. However, there are more objective circumstances that affect willingness to bear risk. For example, one may be highly risk-averse because his income and net worth are such that a loss, or even a reduction of income, would bring real hardship, or because he has such large fixed-dollar commitments to others that a loss would threaten his solvency. Another may be less risk-averse or even a risk lover because he has so much other wealth and income that a loss would not bring hardship, or because he has only relatively small fixed-dollar commitments to others. But for whatever reasons, differences in attitudes toward risk bearing exist, and they help explain differences in portfolio choices.

Up to this point we have concentrated on two attributes of financial claims that are relevant to portfolio choices under conditions of uncertainty—mean expected rate of return and risk. If we use the term "safety" to mean the inverse of risk, we can say that choices depend on the mean expected rate of return and safety. Now we must introduce another attribute of an asset—its degree of *liquidity*. This is akin to safety but somewhat different.

LIQUIDITY

The term "liquidity" is widely used in economic and financial circles to denote an important attribute, characteristic, or condition. Though its general connotations are clear, it is often used imprecisely and with variable meanings. To develop more precise meanings, we shall discuss three aspects: (1) the liquidity of an entity, such as a household, a governmental unit, a business firm, or a financial intermediary; (2) sources of liquidity to an entity; and (3) the liquidity of an asset.

LIQUIDITY OF AN ENTITY

To begin with, we distinguish between the *solvency* and the *liquidity* of an entity. Solvency concerns the relationship between the values of the total assets and total liabilities of an entity. An entity is solvent if the value of its assets, given sufficient time to exchange them for money, exceeds its total liabilities, and its degree of solvency is measured roughly by the ratio of its assets to its liabilities. It is insolvent if its liabilities exceed its assets. On the other hand, liquidity refers to the ability of an entity to make payments not only fully but also promptly. An entity is illiquid to the extent that it cannot do so, or can do so only at considerable cost. An entity may, of course, be both insolvent and illiquid, but it may be illiquid even though it is highly solvent. For example, its assets may be "frozen," in the sense that they cannot be exchanged for money quickly or can be sold quickly only at prices far below their longer-run values. Insufficient liquidity to meet maturing debt obligations fully and promptly can carry heavy penalties. Even if the entity escapes bankruptcy or costly financial reorganization, it jeopardizes its creditworthiness and its future access to funds. Thus, sufficient liquidity to meet its debt obligations fully and promptly is highly important to an entity, but liquidity also carries further benefits, such as ability to buy supplies as needed from those who charge the lowest prices, ability to take advantage of bargains as opportunities appear, and flexibility in adjusting the composition of its assets.

Though liquidity is advantageous to an entity, it usually costs something in the form of explicit costs or sacrifice of potential income.

Each entity therefore faces problems of deciding how much liquidity to buy and how to acquire it at minimum cost. This brings us to the sources of liquidity for an entity.

SOURCES OF LIQUIDITY TO AN ENTITY

All types of entities have three major sources of liquidity: (1) current receipts; (2) borrowings; and (3) sales of assets.

Rational management of liquidity requires that an entity project for future periods both its flow of payments and its flow of receipts. The former includes both its maturing financial debts and other payments that it plans to make. The latter includes not only its projected income for the period but also such things as its maturing debt claims against others, proceeds from a planned net reduction of inventories, and net inflows of funds to a financial intermediary. Some of these flows can be predicted with a high degree of confidence; others are more uncertain. In some cases, an entity finds that its projected receipts are well in excess of its projected expenditures for debt payments and other purposes, so that it need not have recourse to other sources of liquidity. In other cases it finds that its projected expenditures exceed its projected receipts, or that it could be put into an illiquid position by an unexpected need to spend or by a shortfall in its expected receipts. It therefore needs recourse to some other source of liquidity, at least on a standby basis.

Capacity to borrow is a second source of liquidity for an entity. The adequacy and attractiveness of this source depend on the amount that the entity can borrow relative to its projected needs, the degree of certainty that the credit will in fact be available even under adverse circumstances, and the quickness and cheapness of borrowing. Some entities, and especially those with high credit ratings, rely on borrowing as a major source of liquidity. However, borrowing is a less adequate and attractive source of liquidity as the amount that can be borrowed is smaller relative to an entity's projected needs, as the availability of credit becomes less certain, as the time required to get a loan is longer, and as borrowing costs are higher relative to the cost of achieving liquidity in other ways. It is for such reasons that most entities rely to at least some extent on the third major source of liquidity—sales of assets.

LIQUIDITY OF AN ASSET

By the liquidity of an asset we mean its capability of being exchanged for money quickly and without loss of value. Thus two dimensions are involved—time and stability of value. Money itself is perfectly liquid; being generally acceptable at face value in payment of debts and in purchases of other things, it is immediately available for spending and its value in terms of dollars remains constant. Other assets are liquid to the degree that they share these attributes of "moneyness," and illiquid to the degree that time is required to exchange them for money and that the net price for which they can be sold, after deducting any transactions costs that may be involved, may fall below the price at which they were acquired. Among the most liquid nonmonetary assets are time and savings deposit claims against commercial banks, mutual savings banks, savings and loan associations, and some other financial intermediaries; short-term debt claims against the federal government and some other governmental units; and short-term debts of highly regarded business firms. Among the most illiquid assets are land, buildings and many other physical assets, and equity claims and long-term debt claims that are not traded regularly in organized financial markets.

To achieve a high degree of liquidity, an asset must be virtually free of default risk and also be of such short maturity that a rise in market rates of interest would not lower its price significantly. An asset meeting these conditions can be exchanged for money in two principal ways. One way is through collection at maturity. Thus the holder of a debt claim payable on demand or within a short period can collect money directly from the debtor. The other way is through the *marketability* or *shiftability* of the asset. Though the asset still has some time to go to maturity, its holder can get money immediately by selling it to others through a market mechanism. As we shall emphasize later, financial markets serve as creators of liquidity.

We conclude that in a world of uncertainty and risk, rational choices among assets depend on mean expected rates of return, expected degrees of risk and liquidity, and attitudes of holders toward bearing risk and illiquidity. Each portfolio manager presumably seeks to achieve some optimum combination of these characteristics. Portfolio compositions are likely to differ from one holder to another both because of differences in expectations concerning mean rates of return and degrees of risk and liquidity on the various available assets, and because of differences in preferences, or subjective trade-off values, among income, safety, and liquidity.

RISK AND DIVERSIFICATION

Diversification of holdings of financial assets would occur to only a very limited extent in a riskless world in which all future outcomes were known with perfect certainty. Each holder would simply concentrate his holdings on that financial claim, or the small group of financial claims, with the highest rate of return, net of transactions costs. However, in a world of uncertainty and risk, diversification of assets becomes useful and widely practiced as a means of reducing risk. The general principle is that by pooling a number of different financial claims, outcomes on the portfolio as a whole can be predicted with less uncertainty and therefore less risk. To the extent that it is successful, diversification enables a holder to achieve a given rate of return at less risk, or a higher rate of return at any given amount of risk.

We shall later have much more to say about diversification. At this point two comments will suffice. First, households themselves often diversify their portfolios by holding direct financial claims against numerous other households, governmental units, and business firms, and also by holding various differing types of financial claims, such as a mixture of equity and debt claims and debt claims of differing maturities. Second, one reason, but not the only one, for the invention and widespread use of financial intermediaries is their ability to achieve better diversification at lower cost.

DECISION MAKING BY ISSUERS OF FINANCIAL CLAIMS UNDER CONDITIONS OF UNCERTAINTY

In a world of uncertainty, holders of financial claims are not the only ones concerned with safety and liquidity as well as mean expected income; issuers of financial claims share these concerns. For example, decision makers in a business firm usually do not find it optimal to strive for the highest mean expected income without regard to risks of insolvency and illiquidity. Since survival of the firm as a successful going concern is usually a highly valued objective, management shudders at the prospect of insolvency or inability to meet its debts promptly and fully. Moreover, management is presumably concerned with the financial welfare of its shareholders, who are interested in the safety and liquidity as well as the mean expected income on their shares. Both the income-safety-liquidity position of the firm itself and the income-safety-liquidity characteristics of its shares are affected by decisions relating to the types and amounts of its investment and to the methods used to finance its investment.

INVESTMENT CRITERIA

As noted earlier, rules for rational decision making by spenders for investment would be simple in a world of perfect certainty, in which marginal rates of efficiency are perfectly predictable for all investment projects. They would be:

1. Rank all investment projects in accordance with their rates of marginal efficiency.
2. Undertake all projects whose rates of marginal efficiency exceed the market rate of interest.

In an uncertain world, neither rule is optimal unless the decision maker is risk neutral. Investment projects are likely to differ not only in their mean expected rates of marginal efficiency but also in their degrees of risk. For example, project A may have a mean expected rate of marginal efficiency of 12 percent and a high degree of risk, while project B has a mean expected rate of marginal efficiency of only 9 percent but a much smaller risk. A decision maker who is a risk lover or is risk neutral or only slightly risk-averse may rationally prefer project A while one who is quite risk-averse may rationally prefer project B.

Also, under conditions of uncertainty, it need not be rational to undertake all investment projects whose mean expected rates of marginal efficiency exceed interest costs on the funds used for investment. Suppose, for example, that the mean expected rate of marginal efficiency on a project is 8 percent and that the interest rate on borrowed funds is $7\frac{1}{2}$ percent. The gross margin of $\frac{1}{2}$ percent may be sufficient to induce investment if the attendant risks are quite small or the decision maker is no more than slightly risk-averse. However, it may be insufficient if the attendant risks are larger or the decision maker is more than slightly risk-averse.

We find, then, that under conditions of uncertainty, decisions relating to both the types and amounts of investment are based not only on relationships between mean expected rates of marginal efficiency and the cost of funds to the firm but also on the degrees of risk and illiquidity involved and on the attitudes of decision makers toward risk bearing.

METHODS OF FINANCE UNDER UNCERTAINTY

In a riskless world of perfect certainty, a firm's objective would be to maximize its net income, and to this end it would determine the composition of its security issues solely on the basis of their relative financing costs, including transactions costs. Otherwise, it would be indifferent between equity and debt issues and among the various maturities of debt. However, in a world of uncertainty it will usually not make such decisions solely on the basis of the relative costs of funds because the composition of its issues affects the risks of insolvency and illiquidity of the firm itself and also the income and risk characteristics of ownership claims against it.

Consider first the choice between equity claims and debt claims as methods of finance. Since ownership claims are only residual claims against the assets and income of the firm and do not promise to pay fixed dollar amounts at specified times, the firm cannot be forced into bankruptcy for failure to make such payments, though the management may face difficulties if it disappoints its stockholders too much. On the other hand, since debt claims are legal obligations to pay fixed dollar amounts at specified times, failure to meet these obligations fully and promptly brings at least a loss of financial reputation and often bankruptcy and financial reorganization. The practice of using debt claims to finance at least a part of a firm's requirements is called *trading on the equity.*

Three effects of issuing debt claims as a method of finance should be noted:

1. Debt issues enhance the risk of illiquidity—the risk that the issuer will be unable to meet its obligations promptly and fully.
2. Since debts are fixed in terms of dollars while the dollar values of a firm's assets may fall, the use of debt financing enhances the firm's risk of insolvency.
3. The use of debt increases the mean expected rate of return on equity claims if the mean expected rate of return on the firm's assets exceeds the interest rate on debt, but it also increases the riskiness of the equity claims.

An example may clarify these points. In order to isolate the effects of differences in the firm's financial structure—in this case the division between debt and equity claims—we make the following assumptions:

1. The firm's total assets (A) are a fixed amount and are not affected by the composition of financial claims against the firm.
2. The nature of the firm's operations is given, and neither the realized rate of return (g) on its assets, nor the amount of the firm's risk concerning its future income before interest and the value of its assets, is affected by its financial structure.
3. All of the firm's earnings in excess of its interest payments and other costs accrue to its stockholders.

The total assets (A) of the firm are equal to the sum of its debt and equity issues. Symbolically,

$$A = D + E \qquad\qquad (1)$$

where

D = value of assets acquired by the issue of debt claims

E = value of assets acquired by the issue of equity claims, either by the sale of such claims or by retention of net profits for the account of shareholders

If we use the symbol b to denote the fraction of assets acquired through debt issues and $(1 - b)$ to denote the fraction acquired through equity issues, we can rewrite equation (1) as

$$A = bA + (1 - b)A \tag{2}$$

Using g to denote the firm's annual rate of return on its assets, its annual earnings are gA. Let us use i to denote the annual interest rate on debt claims. The dollar returns accruing to stockholders each year consist of two parts. The first is the firm's earnings on the assets contributed by holders of equity claims, or $g(1 - b)A$. The second is the difference between the firm's earnings on assets contributed by holders of debt claims and the interest rate on those claims, or $(g - i)bA$. Thus,

$$\text{Annual dollar earnings accruing to equity} = g(1 - b)A + (g - i)bA \tag{3}$$

Let us divide through by the value of the equity contribution, $[(1 - b)A]$, to get the percentage rate of return (R) on equity. We find that,

$$R = g + (g - i)\frac{b}{1 - b} \tag{4}$$

Thus R, the rate of return on equity, depends on the rate of return on the firm's assets (g), the difference between the firm's rate of return on its assets and the interest rate on its debt $(g - i)$, and the ratio of debt to equity $[b/(1 - b)]$.

Table 2 − 2 shows the behavior of R at selected rates of g and at various ratios of debt to total assets, assuming the interest rate on debt to be constant at 7 percent.[5] If the firm finances entirely through equity issues, that is, if $b = 0$, the rate of return on equity is exactly equal to the firm's rate of return on its assets, and the riskiness of the equity claims on income account is exactly the same as the riskiness of the firm's earning rate on its assets. However, R will exceed g if g exceeds i, and the excess of R over g is increased by both increases of $(g - i)$ and increases of b. For example, if $g = 15$ percent and $b = 3/4$, R is 39 percent. Thus,

[5] This example oversimplifies in at least two ways. First, the rate of interest that a firm must pay is likely to rise as the ratio of debt to total assets is increased. Second, the example ignores tax considerations.

Table 2 — 2   **Rates of Return on Equity with Variable Rates of Return on a Firm's Assets and a Variable Financial Structure** (*interest rates on debt assumed constant at 7 percent*)

Rate of Return on the Firm's Assets (g)	Rate of Return on Equity			
	$b = 0$	$b = \frac{1}{3}$	$b = \frac{1}{2}$	$b = \frac{3}{4}$
15	15	19	23	39
10	10	11.5	13	19
7	7	7	7	7
3	3	1	-1	-9
0	0	-3.5	-7	-21

trading on the equity can have favorable leverage effects on the rate of return to equity if g exceeds i. Unfortunately, however, leverage also operates in the downward direction if g turns out to be lower than the rate of interest on debt, and the effects become increasingly adverse as i exceeds g by greater amounts and as the ratio of debt to total assets is increased. For example, suppose that $b = 3/4$ and g turns out to be 3 percent; R will be a negative 9 percent. Those with a taste for the gruesome may enjoy computing R if g turns out to be negative and $b = 3/4$.

A higher ratio of debt to the initial value of the firm's assets also increases its risk of insolvency. For example, if $b = 3/4$, a 25 percent decline in the value of the firm's assets will wipe out completely the value of equity claims against assets.

The effect of debt financing on the welfare of shareholders who are concerned with the riskiness as well as the mean expected rate of return on their shares is ambiguous. Since a firm presumably issues debt only when the mean expected rate of return on acquired assets exceeds the rate of interest on debt, debt financing serves to increase the mean expected rate of return on equity. But it also increases the riskiness of shares. Thus, high ratios of debt to assets may be applauded by shareholders who are risk lovers or only slightly risk-averse, but not by those who are highly risk-averse. For example, shares in a firm with a highly risky rate of return on its assets and a high debt ratio may be favorites for plungers but hardly suitable for the legendary widows and orphans.

Suppose now that a firm has decided on the total value of assets that it wishes to acquire and how much to finance through equity issues and how much to finance through debt issues. It still has to decide on what types of debt claims to issue, including the maturities of the claims. It could, of course, issue many different maturities, but at this point we shall consider only two—very long-term bonds and very short-term debts. It could issue only long-term bonds, or only short-term debts, or various combinations of the two. It will rarely be indifferent among the various possible maturity compositions of its debt. In arriving at such decisions, it will consider not only effects on the sum of expected interest and financial transactions costs over time but also effects on the firm's risk of illiquidity.

A firm could rely on a succession of one-year debts to meet all its debt financing needs, including the financing of highly durable buildings and equipment that will yield their full returns only over a long period. It may do this because it expects that the transactions costs and average short-term rates of interest over the long period will be less than the transactions costs and the interest rate on long-term bonds. However, this course of action exposes the firm to two types of risk:

1. Risks of illiquidity. The firm has obligated itself not only to pay interest but also to repay its debt at the end of each year, expecting to do the latter by issuing new short-term debts. However, it may not be able to renew its debt, or may be able to do so only at very high cost. This may result from an unexpected general credit stringency or crisis, or from an unexpected deterioration of the firm's creditworthiness.
2. Risks of an unexpected rise of short-term rates. The average interest costs on a succession of short-term debts may then be greater than the fixed contractual rate on a long-term bond.

The firm can avoid or decrease markedly both of these risks by relying on long-term mortgages or bonds to meet all its debt financing needs. It may regret this long-term commitment if future interest rates prove to be unexpectedly low, but this is the price of insuring against the risk of higher future rates. Firms usually do not find it advantageous to issue long-term debt to meet temporarily high financing needs. For example, suppose that a firm's current financial needs are very large, but that it expects its financial needs to be smaller in the future because it intends to reduce its inventories or other assets or expects large cash inflows from depreciation allowances and retained earnings. If it met all current needs by issuing long-term debt it would later have excess funds. It could, of course, use such funds to acquire financial claims against others or to purchase some of its bonds in the market and retire them.

This could be profitable if future rates of interest turned out to be substantially higher than the fixed rate on the bonds and if its bonds could be purchased and retired at a substantial discount. However, there is also the risk that future rates of interest will be so low that yields on financial claims, net of transactions costs, will be below the fixed rate on the bonds and that its bonds can be purchased and retired only at a high price. To avoid such risks, firms often prefer to issue short-term debt to finance temporarily large short-term needs.

DIFFERENTIATION OF FINANCIAL CLAIMS

We find, then, that in determining the composition of their issues, business firms and other issuers consider not only relative financing costs but also effects on their own liquidity and safety. They are willing to incur some additional cost to achieve more liquidity and less risk, but they would like to minimize the additional cost. For this purpose, they must take into account the preferences of potential buyers and holders, and the latter's preferred balances of income, safety, and liquidity differ considerably from one holder to another. Many individual issuers find it advantageous to issue several types of securities with differing income-safety-liquidity characteristics to appeal to these differing preferences and trade-off values among potential holders. Some of the options available to an issuing corporation are shown in Table 2−3.

Table 2−3   **A Simple Financial Structure of a Corporation**

DEBT CLAIMS
    Long-term debt
        Bonds and mortgages with first claim on stated amounts of income and assets
        Debentures and other long-term debt with stated amounts of claims subordinate to first claims
    Intermediate-term debt: maturity 1−5 years
    Short-term debt: maturity 1 day−1 year

EQUITY CLAIMS
    Preferred stock: claims prior to those of common stock against a stated amount of earnings and a stated amount on liquidation of the firm
    Common stock: residual claims junior to all those above.

Long-term debt claims will appeal most to holders who attach a high value to the assurance of a fixed rate of return over a long period and are least deterred by the market risk inherent in such long-term debt claims. Such holders may have differing attitudes toward default risk. Some may be willing to accept a significantly lower rate of interest in exchange for a first, or senior, claim on all the firm's income and assets. Others, for only a slightly higher interest rate, are willing to hold debentures or other long-term claims subordinate to the senior bonds. Intermediate-term debt will appeal most to those who want to reclaim their funds earlier, do not attach so much importance to a fixed rate of return over a long period, and are more averse to market risk. Short-term debt will be most appealing to those who place a high premium on liquidity and are most averse to market and default risks.

In general, equity claims will appeal most to those who are least risk-averse or are risk lovers. However, because preferences differ among equity holders, some firms issue two or more classes of shares. Preferred stock is given a claim prior to that of common stock against a stated amount of earnings and a stated amount of assets on liquidation of the firm. Common stock is the final residual claimant and appeals to those who are least risk-averse or are risk lovers.

It may well turn out, however, that on balance the preferences of issuers of securities differ significantly from the preferences of buyers and holders. For example, in order to protect their own liquidity and safety positions, issuers may strongly prefer to issue mostly equity and long-term debt claims, which would be considered by holders to be illiquid and risky. But holders, on balance, may have a strong preference for highly liquid and safe assets. Under such conditions, issuers might be able to sell their preferred combinations of issues only at very high financing costs, while holders could achieve their preferred degrees of safety and liquidity only at the cost of a large sacrifice of income. Methods of reconciling, or intermediating between, such differing preferences can benefit both issuers and holders. We have already mentioned two of these methods. One is through market facilities that enhance the salability or marketability of a security. This enables issuers to issue securities conforming more closely to their own maturity preferences and enables holders to recover money when they want it. The other is through diversification, which can create for a portfolio as a whole a degree of safety greater than that of the individual securities in the portfolio. We shall find later that a major function of a financial intermediary is to intermediate between the preferences of issuers and those of asset holders. It buys from issuers direct securities conforming more closely to their preferences, and creates and issues to asset holders financial claims with income-safety-liquidity characteristics conforming more closely to the preferences of the holders.

CONCLUSION

Financial markets in the real world are not characterized by full information known with perfect certainty concerning both present conditions and future events. Instead, uncertainties and risks of many kinds and degrees are pervasive. Many phenomena observable in actual markets can be fully understood only in light of such uncertainties and risks. To mention only a few: The great differentiation of securities issues, the structure of prices and yields on different financial claims, the widespread practice of diversification as a means of reducing risk, and the use of financial intermediaries as creators of safety and liquidity. Departures from the conditions assumed in the perfectly competitive model are indeed numerous and significant.

Our stress on market imperfections should not, however, lead us to the negative conclusion that the model of a perfectly competitive market is completely irrelevant and useless. It remains both relevant and useful for three related reasons:

1. The model provides a performance benchmark—maximum efficiency in the allocation of scarce financial resources—against which the performance of actual markets can be measured. Behavior in real markets is better and more easily understood as modifications of, or departures from, behavior in a perfectly competitive model than it could be with no such benchmark.
2. Some of its conclusions remain valid, with appropriate modifications, for actual markets. Actual markets are imperfect, but they do resemble the model.
3. The model helps us identify the various sources and types of imperfections and to analyze the effects of each on the performance and efficiency of the financial system. This is especially useful because some of the imperfections are at least partially remediable. For example, public policy can lessen monopoly power and promote competition, thus enhancing the allocative efficiency of markets. Relevant information can be increased and disseminated more widely and cheaply. Forecasting can be made more reliable. And the degrees of uncertainty and risk can be reduced in

various other ways, including diversification and many types of insurance. We shall deal further with these things in later chapters.

SELECTED READINGS

Baumol, W. J. *Portfolio Theory: The Selection of Asset Combinations.* New York: General Learning Corporation, 1970.

Smith, P. F. *Economics of Financial Institutions and Markets.* Homewood, Ill.: Richard D. Irwin, 1971.

INTEREST RATES
AND ASSET
PRICES

Though we have already mentioned, in a preliminary way, the nature and measurement of interest rates and some relationships between the latter and certain asset prices, our treatment up to this point has been much too brief and general to provide a solid foundation for discussions in later chapters. The major purpose of this chapter is to remedy this situation. We start with some rudiments of the mathematics of finance.

SOME MATHEMATICS OF FINANCE

As already noted, the existence of a positive rate of interest reflects the fact that one dollar in the present typically exchanges for more than one dollar available only at some time or times in the future. Since financial claims differ widely in their denominations and in remaining years to maturity, we need some common unit for measuring and comparing the quantitative relationships between their present and future values. For this purpose, we use interest rates, stated in percent per annum, or more technically, average annual yields to maturity, taking into account not only explicit interest payments but also any difference between present value and maturity value. Interest rates or yields are always stated as percentages of present value. They are often written as whole numbers, such as 4 or 8 percent, but computations require the use of the decimal form, such as 0.04 or 0.08. Quantitative comparisons of present and future values involve four variables: the present value, the future value or values, the number of years between the present and the times of availability of the future values, and the rate of interest. If we know the number of years to the time of availability of the future payments and the values of two of the other variables, we can easily compute the value of the remaining variable.

SIMPLE INTEREST OR DISCOUNT

We start with a simple case in which $100 in the present is exchanged for a single payment of $106 at the end of a year. It will be convenient to use the following symbols:

$$P = \text{present value} = \$100$$
$$F = \text{future value one year hence} = \$106$$
$$i = \text{the interest rate} = 0.06$$

If we know the values of P and F, we can compute the value of i.

$$i = \frac{F - P}{P} = \frac{106 - 100}{100} = \frac{6}{100} = 0.06 \text{ or } 6\%$$

If we know the values of P and i, we can compute the value of F.

$$F = P + Pi$$

or

$$F = P(1 + i) = \$100(1.06) = \$106$$

If we know the values of F and i, we can arrive at the value of P by discounting F at the rate of interest, i. Discounting is the process of arriving at a present value by deducting interest from amounts that will become available only at a later time or times. In effect, simple discounting answers this question: what present value (P) put out at simple interest rate i would be equal in value to F by the time that F becomes payable? In other words, find that value of P at which $P(1 + i) = F$. Multiplying both sides of this equation by $1/(1 + i)$, we get the formula for simple discounting:

$$P = \frac{F}{1 + i}$$

In our example,

$$P = \frac{\$106}{1.06} = \$100$$

Two points relating to discounting should be borne in mind:

1. The discount or interest rate is stated as a percentage of present value.
2. The higher the discount rate, the lower the present value relative to future values.

COMPOUND INTEREST AND DISCOUNT

In the above examples relating to simple interest, we assumed that interest was added only once a year—at the end of the year. We come now to compound interest and compound discounting. With compound interest the lender receives interest on the original principal amount and also on accumulated interest. Most debt obligations running more than a year carry compound interest, and many with maturities of no more than a year carry compound interest because interest is added more than once a year. We shall deal first with the latter case. Suppose that $1 is invested at the beginning of the year at a stated annual interest rate of 6 percent. The accumulated value (F) at the end of the year is given by the formula:

$$F = \left(1 + \frac{i}{X}\right)^X$$

where

i = the stated annual rate of interest

X = the number of times that interest is added during the year; $1/X$ is the length of each interest period, stated as a fraction of a year

$\dfrac{i}{X}$ = the rate of interest for each interest period

$F - 1$ = the effective rate of interest—the equivalent in simple interest

We have already noted that if $X = 1$, F will be $1.06 and the effective rate of interest will be 0.06, or 6 percent. Now suppose that $X = 2$; interest is added at the end of six months and again at the end of the year. In this case, 3 cents in interest will be added at the end of six months, so that $1.03 will earn interest during the second half of the year. The value of F will be $1.0609, and the effective rate of interest will be 6.09 percent. The data in Table 3−1 reveal that the shorter each interest period is, the larger F will be and the higher the effective rate of interest will be. The extreme case is called "continuous compounding." In this case each interest period is almost infinitely short; interest is added almost continuously.

Table 3−1   **Values of F at the End of One Year,**
                and the Effective Rate of Interest, for each
                $1 Invested at the Beginning of the Year with i = .06

X = the Number of Times Interest Is Added Annually	Formula for F	Value of F	Effective Interest Rate: F minus 1
1	$(1 + .06)$	$1.06	.06
2	$\left(1 + \dfrac{.06}{2}\right)^2$	1.0609	.0609
4	$\left(1 + \dfrac{.06}{4}\right)^4$	1.06136	.06136
6	$\left(1 + \dfrac{.06}{6}\right)^6$	1.06152	.06152
12	$\left(1 + \dfrac{.06}{12}\right)^{12}$	1.06168	.06168
365	$\left(1 + \dfrac{.06}{365}\right)^{365}$	1.061831	.061831
X approaches infinity		1.061837	.061837

We turn now to compound interest and compound discounting in debt contracts running more than a year. Suppose that you lend one dollar of present value at an effective annual rate of interest i. At the end of one year you will have $\$(1 + i)$. Reinvesting this, you will have at the end of the second year $\$(1 + i) (1 + i)$, or $\$(1 + i)^2$. And so on. The first columns of Table 3−2 show the accumulated values at the end of n years resulting from lending $1 now at a compound interest rate of 6 percent. The effective yield of a 6 percent compound rate is obviously greater than a simple 6 percent rate, and the difference increases with the passage of time. For example, over a 10-year period, 6 percent interest compounded is equivalent to 7.91 percent in simple interest.

Compound discount asks and answers this kind of question: What is the present value of some stated amount available only at the end of n years in the future? Using F_n to denote the amount available at the end of n years, we can describe the discounting process this way: find that present value (P), which if put out for n years at compound interest rate i, would be equal to F_n. That is, $P(1 + i)^n = F_n$. Multiplying both sides of the equation by $1/[(1 + i)^n]$, we get $P = F_n \cdot 1/[(1 + i)^n]$, which is the formula for compound discounting. The last two columns of Table 3−2 show the present values of $1 available n years hence discounted at a compound rate of 6 percent. It should be evident that the higher the

Table 3−2   **Compound Interest and Compound Discount at 6 Percent**

Number of Years (n)	Value n Years Hence		Equivalent in Simple Interest (Percent)	Present Value of $1 n Years Hence	
	Formula	Dollar Value		Formula	Dollar Value
1	$(1 + i)$	$1.06	6.0	$\dfrac{1}{1+i}$	$0.9434
2	$(1 + i)^2$	1.1236	6.18	$\dfrac{1}{(1+i)^2}$	0.8900
3	$(1 + i)^3$	1.1910	6.37	$\dfrac{1}{(1+i)^3}$	0.8396
4	$(1 + i)^4$	1.2625	6.56	$\dfrac{1}{(1+i)^4}$	0.7921
5	$(1 + i)^5$	1.3382	6.76	$\dfrac{1}{(1+i)^5}$	0.7473
6	$(1 + i)^6$	1.4185	6.98	$\dfrac{1}{(1+i)^6}$	0.7050
7	$(1 + i)^7$	1.5036	7.19	$\dfrac{1}{(1+i)^7}$	0.6651
8	$(1 + i)^8$	1.5938	7.42	$\dfrac{1}{(1+i)^8}$	0.6274
9	$(1 + i)^9$	1.6895	7.66	$\dfrac{1}{(1+i)^9}$	0.5919
10	$(1 + i)^{10}$	1.7908	7.91	$\dfrac{1}{(1+i)^{10}}$	0.5584

Source: Interest tables.

discount rate, the lower will be the present value of each dollar available at some stated time in the future. For example, the present value of a dollar payable at the end of 10 years is 55.84 cents if the discount rate is 6 percent, but only 46.32 cents if the discount rate is 8 percent.

CAPITALIZATION

In all the preceding examples, present value was exchanged against a single payment to be received at a stipulated time in the future. However, many financial contracts, including debts, provide for payments at different times. For example, a buyer of a consumer installment loan receives in return a promise to pay $65 a month for 36 months. The buyer of a long-term, amortized mortgage receives in return a promise to pay $230 a month for 25 years. And the buyer of a bond receives in return a promise to pay a stream of annual interest payments plus a repayment of principal at the maturity of the bond. In all such cases, the present value of the financial claim is simply the sum of the present values of the individual future payments. The process of arriving at a present capital value by discounting a stream of future returns is called *capitalization*.

Let us consider further a bond promising to pay $60 in interest at the end of each of the next 10 years and to repay $1000 in principal at the end of 10 years. As already noted, the present value of the bond (P) is the sum of the present values of the various future receipts. That is,

$$P = \frac{\$60}{1+i} + \frac{\$60}{(1+i)^2} + \frac{\$60}{(1+i)^3} + \frac{\$60}{(1+i)^4} + \frac{\$60}{(1+i)^5} + \frac{\$60}{(1+i)^6} + \frac{\$60}{(1+i)^7}$$
$$+ \frac{\$60}{(1+i)^8} + \frac{\$60}{(1+i)^9} + \frac{\$60}{(1+i)^{10}} + \frac{\$1000}{(1+i)^{10}}$$

Knowing the values and timing of the future stream of payments, we need only to find an appropriate value for i in order to compute the present value of the security. This raises a question common to all cases of discounting: what interest rate should be used? This is highly relevant, for at any time there is an array of interest rates in the market, the differences reflecting differences in maturity and in degrees of risk and liquidity. The answer is: use that prevailing rate of interest generally applicable to other financial claims of the same or closely comparable maturity and degrees of risk and liquidity. To discount at a lower rate of interest would yield a present price for the security so high that a buyer would realize a rate of return below that available on other comparable issues. To discount at a higher rate would yield a present price so low that a buyer would realize a rate of return above that attainable on other comparable issues. Each buyer would like this, of course, but competition among buyers is likely to force prices to such levels as to equalize rates of return on comparable issues.

To compute present values at various rates of interest by ordinary computational methods would indeed be tedious, especially for bonds running 30 years or more. Fortunately, however, bond tables providing solutions are generally available, and computers can be programmed to provide the answers almost immediately. Table 3—3 shows the present values of our hypothetical 10-year bond at three different rates of interest or discount. It is apparent that the present value tends to vary inversely with the level of interest rates, that a rise of rates will decrease

Table 3–3   **Present Values of a 10-Year Bond Paying $60 a Year in Interest and $1000 at Maturity**

| Year | Present Values of Interest Receipts at the End of Each Year, Discounted at | | |
	3 Percent	6 Percent	8 Percent
1	$ 58.25	$ 56.60	$ 55.55
2	56.56	53.40	51.45
3	54.91	50.38	47.63
4	53.31	47.53	44.10
5	51.76	44.84	40.84
6	50.25	42.30	37.81
7	48.79	39.91	35.01
8	47.36	37.64	32.42
9	45.98	35.51	30.01
10	44.65	33.50	27.79
Total present value of interest receipts	$ 511.82	$ 441.60	$402.61
Present value of principal repayment	744.09	558.40	463.19
Present value of the bond[a]	$1255.91	$1000.00	$865.80

[a] Because of rounding, items may not add to totals shown.

the price of the bond, and that a decline of rates will raise the value of the bond. By consulting a bond table you can confirm an earlier statement: the longer the remaining time to maturity, the greater will be the effect of a given change in the level of interest rates on the price of a security.

With the terms of a debt contract fixed—its maturity, and the timing and dollar amounts of its interest and principal payments—it is only through changes in its market price that its average annual yield to maturity can be brought into line with yields on other comparable securities. A change in the market price of a debt obligation alters its average annual yield to maturity in two ways: (1) by changing its *current yield,* which is simply the ratio of its fixed dollar interest payments to its market price, and (2) by changing the relationship between the market price and the fixed redemption price, thereby changing the amount of capital gain or loss accruing to the buyer during the remaining life of the bond. For example, Table 3–3 shows that a rise of the relevant market rate of interest from 6 to 8 percent would lower the price of our hypothetical bond from $1000 to $865.80. This fall of the price would raise the current yield from 6 to 6.93 percent, or $60/$865.80. Also, one who bought the bond for $865.80 and redeemed it for $1000 ten years later would realize a capital gain of $134.20. Thus, the simple average annual dollar return to the holder would be $60 + $13.42, or $73.42.[1]

On the other hand, a fall of the relevant rate of interest from 6 to 3 percent would raise the price of the bond from $1000 to $1255.91. The current yield would decline from 6 to $60/$1255.91, or 4.78 percent. Moreover, one who bought the bond at the high market price and redeemed it 10 years later at $1000 would suffer a capital loss of $255.91, or an average of $25.59 a year. Thus, the simple average annual dollar return would be $60 − $25.59, or S34.41.

CAPITALIZATION OF PERPETUAL RETURNS

The formula for determining the present capital value of an infinite series of uniform annual payments is very simple; it is

$$P = \frac{a}{i}$$

where

P = present value
a = annual dollar returns at a uniform amount in perpetuity
i = the applicable rate of interest or discount, stated in decimal form

For example, suppose that the annual return on a perpetual bond is $50. P will be $1250 if $i = 0.04$, but only $500 if $i = 0.10$. This formula is also useful for arriving at approximate present values for a series of payments that are not infinite but run for a very long time, such as 50 years. This is because the present value of payments to be received beyond 50 years is quite small if discounted at an interest rate much above zero.

CAPITALIZATION OF FUTURE
RETURNS ON OTHER DURABLE ASSETS

The process of arriving at a present capital value by discounting future receipts is by no means limited to debt obligations; it applies to all

---

[1] This is equivalent to a simple annual rate of return of 8.48 percent, but because the capital gain is not realized until the maturity of the bond, the compound rate of return is only 8 percent.

durable, income-yielding assets. In many cases, however, the process of capitalization is more difficult, for one or both of two reasons:

1. The asset carries no promise of a fixed stream of future receipts, and the stream that will be realized is more difficult to predict.
2. It is more difficult to determine the appropriate rate of interest to be used for discounting.

CAPITALIZATION AND SHARE PRICES

In general, a share of common stock has a positive present value or price only because a flow of future earnings is expected to accrue to that share. But neither the amounts nor the timing of those future earnings is fixed by contract, and neither is perfectly predictable. Some potential holders are therefore likely to have more optimistic expectations than others, though their differences are likely to be narrowed to the extent that they rely on the same sources for information and forecasts. Each potential holder reasons as follows: "I will hold that stock only at a price that will yield a rate of return at least equal to that available on other stocks of comparable risk and liquidity." We may call this "the required rate of return." Thus we can envision the existence, at any time, of a demand function for a given stock. Some would hold it only at a low price because they expect future earnings to be low, or because they consider it to be highly risky and illiquid, or because they are highly averse to bearing risk and illiquidity. Others are willing to buy and hold it at higher prices because they expect higher earnings per share, or consider it less risky and illiquid, or are less averse to bearing risk and illiquidity. Out of the competition of buyers and sellers emerges a price that will at least temporarily equate the total demand for the stock to the total supply of the stock outstanding.

The financial press reports daily P/E and E/P ratios for a large number of stocks. P is the current market price per share, and E is the dollar amount of earnings per share during the preceding year. P/E is called "the price-earnings ratio," or "the price-earnings multiple." E/P is "the earnings-price ratio." At any time, these ratios for different stocks differ widely. For example, we might observe the following in the market:

Stock	P/E	E/P
A	20	0.05
B	10	0.10
C	5	0.20

What accounts for such differences? These could reflect solely differences in "required rates of return." For example, holders might be willing to hold Stock C only at an expected 20 percent rate of return because it is considered so risky and illiquid, but be willing to hold Stock A at only a 5 percent rate of return because it is so superior in these respects. Also relevant, and in many cases more important in explaining differences in price/earnings multiples, are differences in the expected behavior of future earnings per share. For example, earnings on Stock A may be expected to rise at least 8 percent a year; earnings on Stock B to rise little, if at all; and earnings on Stock C to show a downward trend. Thus expected future rates of return on the various stocks may be roughly equal despite the large differences in their current price-earnings ratios.

As indicated earlier, the "required rate of return" used in discounting expected future earnings on stocks is related to the prevailing yield on long-term bonds. With given expectations concerning future earnings per share, an increase or decrease of bond yields tends to decrease or increase share prices.

DISCOUNTING AND THE PRESENT
VALUE OF DURABLE PHYSICAL ASSETS

The process of discounting expected future returns to arrive at a present value is by no means confined to financial assets; it applies as well to physical assets that are of value because they will yield future returns. Suppose, for example, that you, and others, are offered a piece of land that will yield an annual rent, net of real estate taxes, of $1000 in perpetuity. What is its present value? You and competing buyers will reason as follows: "I will buy it only at such a price as will yield a rate of return at least equal to that available on other assets of comparable risk and liquidity." If the competitive rate of return is 6 percent, the value of the land will be $16,667 [$1000/.06 = $16,667]. But if the competitive rate of return is 12 percent, the present value of the land will be only $8333 [$1000/0.12 = $8,333].

CAPITALIZATION AND INVESTMENT DECISIONS

In dealing with rational decision making relating to new investment or capital formation, economists use two different approaches, though they are closely related. We have already mentioned the first approach, which involves a comparison of the marginal rate of return over the cost of the investment good with the rate of interest, the latter representing the annual "rental cost" of the funds used to finance the investment. We noted that in a riskless world of perfect certainty the rational rule would be "Undertake all investment on which the marginal efficiency rate is at least equal to the interest rate."

This rule requires modification in a world of uncertainty and risk unless the decision maker is risk-neutral. The decision maker first estimates the mean expected rate of return over cost (m) and some measure of risk. He then determines what may be called his "minimum required compensation for risk bearing," this being stated as an annual percentage of the cost of the project. We shall designate this by r. The modified rule for rational decision making is "Undertake all those investments on which $(m - r)$ is at least equal to the interest rate. Or, to put the same thing another way, "Undertake all those investments on which the mean expected rate of return exceeds the interest rate by enough to compensate you adequately for risk bearing." These formulations make it clear that, with given expectations relating to m and r, a decrease of interest rates tends to increase investment spending, and a rise of interest rates has the reverse effect.

The second approach, which many economists prefer, involves a comparison of the cost of an investment project with its present capitalized value. The spender ascertains the cost of the investment good by getting quotations from suppliers and contractors. Two steps are involved in arriving at the present capitalized value of the investment good:

1. Estimate the annual amounts of additional "cash flow" that will be generated as a result of the investment. This is equal to the increase of annual depreciation allowances plus the increase of annual net earnings after deducting any increase of associated expenses except interest costs on the funds used to finance the investment. Not only the annual amounts but also the timing of the additional cash flows is important.
2. Arrive at a present capitalized value of the investment good by applying an appropriate discount rate to the expected additions to cash flows. The appropriate discount rate (d) is composed of two parts. The first is the interest rate (i) on the funds used to finance the investment. The second is "the minimum required compensation for risk bearing" (r). Thus $d = i + r$.

In principle, the process of arriving at the present capitalized value of an investment good is the same as that of arriving at the present value of a bond or other longer-term financial claim. In all such cases, compound discounting is employed.

The final step is to compare the present value of the investment good with its cost. The rational rule is "Purchase all investment goods with a present value at least equal to their cost, but shun those with present values below their cost." Again we find that an increase of interest rates tends to discourage investment; it does so by lowering the present value of investment goods, thereby decreasing the demand functions for them. And a decrease of interest rates tends to increase investment, doing so by increasing the present value of investment goods and thereby raising demand functions for these goods. We shall have many occasions to refer back to these findings.

THE TERM STRUCTURE OF INTEREST RATES

In a previous section we maintained that in a competitive financial market, yields on different financial claims with the same maturity would tend to differ by no more than enough to compensate for differences in transactions costs and in degrees of risk and illiquidity. However, we have not yet considered relative yields on financial claims with differing maturities. We shall now do this by exploring briefly the principal theories of the term structure of interest rates.

The central question considered by theories of the term structure of interest rates is this: Suppose that two or more debt obligations are exactly the same in all other respects but that they differ in their remaining time to maturity. What, at any time, will be the equilibrium relationships among the interest rates or yields on the various maturities, with interest rates or yields measured by average annual rates of return to maturity? In considering this question, we shall follow the common practice of using as an example direct debt obligations of the U.S. Treasury that differ only in their maturities, which typically range from a few days to more than 20 years, and assume that the default risk on all maturities is zero.[2] Also, we shall until further notice assume that transactions costs are zero.

---

[2] In statistical testing of theories of the term structure it is necessary to exclude Treasury obligations with special characteristics, or to make adjustments for such differences. For example, some are acceptable at face value in payment of death taxes but others are not. Some with the same maturities are callable on different dates. Other differences could be cited.

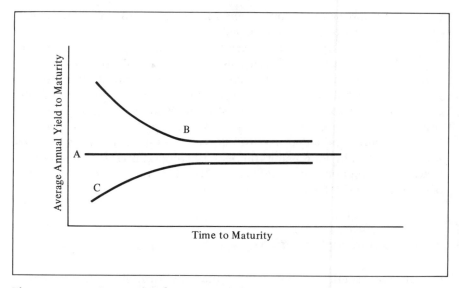

Figure 3–1   **Some Simple Patterns of Term
Structures Observed at Different Times**

Figure 3–1 shows some simple patterns of the term structure of yields that have actually prevailed at different times. These are often called "yield curves."[3] Curve A is called a "flat curve," indicating approximate equality of short-term and long-term yields. Curve B, a "descending curve," shows short-term rates significantly above long-term rates. Curve C is an "ascending curve," with short rates significantly below longer rates. These phenomena raise at least one important question: Why should the patterns of the term structure differ so much at different times?

We shall examine in turn the three leading hypotheses concerning the term structure: the liquidity premium hypothesis; the market segmentation hypothesis; and the expectations hypothesis.

THE LIQUIDITY PREMIUM HYPOTHESIS

This hypothesis asserts that because holders place a "premium" on liquidity and because short-term claims are generally more liquid

---

[3] The shapes of actual yield curves are often more complicated. For example, at the very short maturities the curve often slopes upward even if the rest of the curve slopes downward. Also, there are sometimes gentle "humps" in the curve in the intermediate maturities.

than longer-term claims, short-term yields will generally be below longer-term yields. This is not inconsistent with our earlier conclusions. However, proponents of this hypothesis face two difficulties. The first is that the market may not be dominated by holders who place a premium on liquidity. Though short-term claims may indeed be more liquid, they also subject the holder to uncertainty concerning the rate of return he will get when he reinvests funds after the maturity of his short-term claim. One can easily envisage a market dominated by holders who place a premium on an assured rate of return over a longer period and are therefore willing to accept a lower yield on longer-term claims. However, even if the market is dominated by holders who place a premium on liquidity, adherents of this hypothesis face a second difficulty; they cannot explain why short-term rates are sometimes significantly higher than longer-term rates. (See Curve *B* in Figure 3 − 1.)

THE MARKET SEGMENTATION HYPOTHESIS

In its strongest form, this hypothesis holds that the market for debt claims of differing maturities is so highly segmented that there are, in effect, separated markets for short-term and long-term claims. Neither issuers nor holders consider short and long claims to be substitutes for each other, and there is no mobility of funds among the differing maturities. The term structure therefore depends on demand-supply conditions in the separate market for short maturities relative to demand-supply conditions in the separate market for long maturities.

This extreme version of the segmentation hypothesis is not credible. There is ample evidence that short and longer maturities are substitutes for each other, though not perfect substitutes. For instance, issuers shift the maturity composition of their issues in response to changes in interest differentials, and holders shift the maturity composition of their portfolios in response to changes in such differentials. In its less extreme and more plausible form, the segmentation hypothesis is known as "the preferred habitat hypothesis." The preferred habitat of some issuers is in short maturities while the preferred habitat of other issuers is in longer maturities, and the various issuers will shift out of their preferred maturity habitats to other maturities only if rewarded by lower interest costs. Similarly, the various holders have their preferred maturity habitats and will shift to other maturities only if rewarded by higher yields. According to this hypothesis, the term structure still depends on relative supply-demand conditions in the various partially segmented markets. We shall have more to say about this later.

THE EXPECTATIONS HYPOTHESIS

In its pure form, the expectations hypothesis states that the shape of the term structure at any time depends on expectations concerning future levels of interest rates. The curve will be flat if people expect future rates to be the same as those presently prevailing, it will be ascending if they expect future rates to be higher than those presently prevailing, and it will be descending if they expect future rates to be lower than those presently prevailing.

To develop the reasoning behind the pure expectations hypothesis, we shall continue to assume that both transactions costs and default risk are zero and add three further assumptions:

1. All participants in the market know with certainty, or act as though they knew with certainty, the levels of interest rates that will prevail at all times in the future, and all participants have the same expectations. They see no risk of an unexpected capital loss because of an unexpected rise of interest rates and no "risk" of an unexpected capital gain because of an unexpected fall of interest rates.
2. The motive of every holder is to maximize his net return over each holding period. Note that the rates observable in the market are average annual rates of return to maturity, but that each potential holder bases his decisions on expected net rates of return, which take into account not only current income but also capital gains or losses, over holding periods of various lengths that may be shorter or longer than a security's remaining time to maturity.
3. Short maturities and longer maturities are substitutes for each other, and they are perfect substitutes at a term structure of rates that will equalize their yields over holding periods of various lengths. For example, you can derive a return over a long holding period by purchasing a long maturity or by purchasing a succession of short maturities. And you can derive a return over a short holding period by purchasing a short maturity or by purchasing a longer maturity and selling it at the end of the short holding period.[4] You will be indifferent between short and longer maturities only when their net rates of return are equal for each holding period.

[4] Though we shall concentrate on decision making by holders, it should be noted that issuers have similar options. For example, an issuer can finance long-term needs by issuing a long maturity or a succession of short maturities, and he can finance short-term needs by issuing a short maturity or by issuing a long maturity and repurchasing it in the market when his short-term needs terminate.

A few simple examples will clarify the principles involved. Suppose that you, amply endowed with funds, are asked to choose now between two securities, each selling for $100. One is a one-year maturity that will return $106 at the end of a year. The other is a two-year maturity paying $6 in interest at the end of one year and returning $106 at the end of two years. Will you be indifferent between the two maturities? If not, which will you prefer? You should be indifferent between them if, and only if, you expect the rate of interest on one-year maturities to be 6 percent at the beginning of next year. In this case you can earn an annual rate of 6 percent over a two-year holding period by purchasing the two-year maturity or by purchasing the one-year maturity and reinvesting the funds at 6 percent at the end of a year. And you can earn 6 percent for a one-year holding period by purchasing the one-year maturity or by purchasing the two-year maturity and selling it at the end of a year. You would experience neither a capital gain nor a capital loss on the sale, for $106 discounted for one year at 6 percent is $100. Note that in this case the market yields on one- and two-year maturities are the same; the yield curve is flat. Extending this reasoning, we can say that if you and other investors expect that rates on one-year maturities will remain unchanged indefinitely, the yield curve will be flat for all maturities.

Suppose, however, that while the present rate on one-year maturities is 6 percent, you and other buyers confidently expect that a year from now the rate on one-year maturities will be 8 percent. In this case you will not be indifferent between the maturities. If you buy the one-year maturity and reinvest the funds in another one-year maturity at the beginning of next year at 8 percent, your rate of return for a one-year holding period will be 6 percent and your average rate of return over a two-year holding period will be 7 percent—6 percent for one year and 8 percent for the second. However, if you purchase the two-year maturity, your rate of return over a two-year holding period will be only 6 percent and your net rate of return for a one-year holding period will be only 4 percent, because you will suffer a capital loss of approximately $2 when you sell the security at the end of a year at a discount rate of 8 percent. ($106/1.08 is approximately $98.)[5] With the current rate on one-year maturities at 6 percent, you will be indifferent between the maturities only if the current rate on two-year maturities is 7 percent, which is the average of the current 6 percent rate on a one-year maturity

[5] To be precise we should use compound interest and discount and geometric means. However, simple interest and arithmetic means are easier to use and will illustrate the principles involved.

and the expected rate of 8 percent on one-year maturities one year hence. Note that in this case the term structure is represented by an ascending curve. Extending this reasoning, we can say that when future rates are expected to be above present rates the yield curve will be ascending, and that at the present time the market yield on each maturity will be an average of the expected yields on one-year maturities during the period between the present and the maturity date of the security. This is illustrated by the example in Table 3−4. The yield curve is clearly ascending through at least the six-year maturities. If you and other holders expect that the 10 percent rate on one-year maturities will persist indefinitely, the yield curve·on maturities beyond six years will ap-

---

Table 3−4   **Expected Interest Rates and the
Term Structure of Interest Rates**

I. Interest rates expected at the beginning of Year 1 on one-year maturities at the beginning of Years 1 to 6

Year	Expected Rates on One-Year Maturities (In Percent)
1	6
2	8
3	9
4	10
5	10
6	10

II. The term structure of interest rates at the beginning of Year 1 consistent with the expectations shown in I above

Years to Maturity	Yields on the Maturities
1	$\dfrac{6}{1} = 6.0$
2	$\dfrac{6 + 8}{2} = \dfrac{14}{2} = 7.0$
3	$\dfrac{6 + 8 + 9}{3} = \dfrac{23}{3} = 7.66$
4	$\dfrac{6 + 8 + 9 + 10}{4} = \dfrac{33}{4} = 8.25$
5	$\dfrac{6 + 8 + 9 + 10 + 10}{5} = \dfrac{43}{5} = 8.60$
6	$\dfrac{6 + 8 + 9 + 10 + 10 + 10}{6} = \dfrac{53}{6} = 8.86$

proach 10 percent and become flat. Suppose, however, that you and other holders expect that soon after six years yields on one-year maturities will begin to fall below 10 percent and will then stabilize at about 8 percent. The result will be a "hump" in the yield curve for maturities in about the eight-to-nine-year maturity range. The yield for these maturities will be about 9 percent but will then begin to fall toward 8 percent for longer maturities.

There remains one other case to be considered. Suppose that at the beginning of Year 1, when the rate on one-year maturities is 6 percent, you and other investors expect that one year hence the rate on one-year maturities will have fallen to 4 percent. In this case you should prefer a two-year maturity with a 6 percent rate over a one-year maturity with the same rate. If you buy the two-year maturity, your rate of return for a two-year holding period will be 6 percent, and if you sell it at the end of a year at a discount rate of 4 percent, your net return for a one-year holding period will be about 8 percent because you will reap a capital gain of about $2. ($106/1.04 is approximately $102.) With the rate on one-year maturities at 6 percent, you will be indifferent between one-year and two-year maturities only if the yield on the latter is 5 percent. With this rate structure, both securities will yield 5 percent for a two-year holding period and 6 percent for a one-year holding period. You will reap a capital gain of approximately $1 if you sell the two-year maturity at the end of a year at a discount rate of 4 percent. ($105/1.04 is approximately $101.) Note that in this case the yield curve is descending. Extending this reasoning, we can say that when future rates are expected to be below present rates, rates on short maturities will be higher than those on longer maturities.

The expectations hypothesis is a useful explanatory device. It helps explain the observed market phenomena of flat, ascending, and descending yield curves and does so on the basis of credible assumptions concerning the behavior of investors and without recourse to any assumption of market segmentation. However, one must agree with critics that one set of assumptions in the pure expectations hypothesis is somewhat unrealistic—the assumption that all participants in the market know with certainty, or act as though they know with certainty, the levels of interest rates at all times in the future, and that all participants have the same expectations. In fact, participants know that they cannot predict the future with such precision and certainty, and their forecasts of future events may be diverse. Fortunately, an expectations hypothesis based on less restrictive assumptions is still useful for explanatory purposes. We shall now consider a version called the "predominant-opinion hypothesis." By this we mean a view of the future that is widely enough shared to dominate market behavior at any time. Let us consider three different examples.

Example 1. "As we view the future, we see no particular reason to expect that interest rates will be significantly higher or lower than they are now. Of course, they may rise a bit and bring capital losses, but it seems just as likely that they will fall and bring welcome capital gains." In the face of such expectations, the yield curve is likely to be fairly flat.

Example 2. "Interest rates are now abnormally low by historical standards, and this is due to temporary circumstances. Of course, they may fall a bit further, but it is far more probable that they will soon begin to rise to more normal levels. In these circumstances, we would just as soon make short-term loans at very low interest rates as to buy higher-yielding bonds and later suffer capital losses." In such cases the yield curve is usually ascending.

Example 3. "Interest rates in general, and especially short-term rates, are at or near their historic highs. They may, of course, rise a bit more, but it is far more probable that they will soon begin to decline, and when that happens there will be nice capital gains on the longer-term maturities. We will make short-term loans only if their yields are high enough to compensate us for forgoing the opportunity to buy bonds now and reap capital gains later." In the face of such expectations the yield curve will be descending.

Though such modified versions of the expectations hypothesis are less elegant and precise than the pure version, they are helpful in explaining market behavior.

SUMMARY OF THE TERM STRUCTURE

What role should each of the three main hypotheses play in a synthetic theory of the term structure of interest rates? We can answer this only in qualitative terms. A modified version of the expectations hypothesis must play an important role, for neither the liquidity premium hypothesis nor the market segmentation hypothesis nor the two of them together can explain the observed market phenomena of flat, ascending, and descending yield curves. The liquidity premium hypothesis should also have a place, for it is true that, other things equal, holders will accept a lower return in exchange for greater liquidity. When the yield curve is approximately flat through most of the maturity range, yields on the shortest maturities are often lower. And even when the yield curve is descending, short-term yields may be lower than they would be in the absence of a liquidity premium. Though the market segmentation hypothesis in its extreme form must be rejected, this is not true of its milder version, the preferred-habitat hypothesis. There is indeed a high mobility of funds among the various maturities, but it would be unrealistic to expect this mobility to be perfect, especially in the short run. For example, the appearance of a large new supply of long-term bonds may well raise the yields on long-term debts relative to short-term yields, at least in the short run.

CONCLUSION

In a sense, this chapter has been an interruption of our description and analysis of the structure and functioning of our monetary-financial system. Yet it has presented materials that are essential for a clear understanding of numerous things to be considered later. For example, we shall have many occasions to deal with simple and compound interest rates, simple and compound discounting, processes of capitalization, effects of changes in interest rates on the present value of durable assets, both financial and physical, and the term structure of interest rates.

SELECTED READINGS

I. **Mathematics of finance**

>   Simpson, T. M., Pirenian, Z. M., and Crenshaw, B. H. *Mathematics of Finance.* Englewood Cliffs, N.J.: Prentice-Hall, 1931.

II. **Term structure of interest rates**

>   Conard, J. W. *An Introduction to the Theory of Interest.* Berkeley: University of California Press, 1959.
>   Malkiel, B. G. *The Term Structure of Interest Rates: Expectations and Behavior Patterns.* Princeton: Princeton University Press, 1966.
>   _____. *The Term Structure of Interest Rates: Theory, Empirical Evidence, and Applications.* New York: General Learning Corporation, 1970.

INCOME, SAVING, AND INVESTMENT

Having explored the basic principles and functions of money and finance without much reference to specific times, institutions, or empirical facts, we now turn to the present-day American system. This chapter consists of two major parts. The first deals briefly with the outstanding stock of direct financial claims on a recent date. The second deals at greater length with flows of income or output, saving, dissaving, and investment during stated periods of time, and with some of the relations between these flows and transactions in direct financial claims.

THE OUTSTANDING STOCK
OF DIRECT FINANCIAL CLAIMS

Table 4–1 shows the stock of outstanding direct financial claims in the United States at the end of 1975. These included claims against every major type of entity in our society except financial institutions. This outstanding stock consisted of all the direct securities that had been created earlier, in many cases years earlier, and that had not been re-tired through repayment or default. The size of this stock—$3,494 bil-lion, or nearly $3.5 trillion—is indeed impressive. In fact, it is so huge that it is difficult to comprehend by those of us accustomed to thinking in terms of smaller magnitudes. It may therefore be helpful to note that this amount is equal to more than $15,000 for each of the men, women, and children in the United States at that time.

Table 4 – 1   **Outstanding Direct Financial Claims
in the United States, December 31, 1975**
(in billions of dollars)

Issuer	Type of Direct Financial Claim	Amount Outstanding
U.S. Government	Debt	$ 510.8
State and local governments	Debt	240.3
Households	Debt	782.8
Nonfinancial domestic business	Corporate equities	854.7
Nonfinancial domestic business	Debt	834.4
Rest of world	Debt	271.0
Total		$3494.0

Source: Board of Governors of the Federal Reserve System, *Flow of Funds Accounts.*
Note: The table does not include the value of equity claims against unincorporated business firms.

The data suggest the extent to which the bonds of self-finance
have been broken. We imagined earlier a simple system in which no
household or other entity could spend for consumption and investment
during any period more than its own income during that period. In this
society, there were no financial claims other than money, so that asset
holders were limited to money and direct ownership of physical assets.
Now we find that huge amounts of command over resources have been
transferred through the creation and sale of direct equity and debt
claims. Households, the ultimate claimants to wealth, continue to hold
some physical goods and net equity claims against unincorporated business firms that they control, but a major part of their wealth is now in
the form of financial claims against others that they hold directly or
indirectly.

We also noted earlier that one effect of the creation of direct
financial claims is to enrich the array of assets available for the
portfolios of asset holders. The data in Table 4 – 1 suggest not only the
huge amount but also the wide variety of direct securities available for
portfolios. About 25 percent of the total was in the form of equity claims
against nonfinancial corporations, and these differed markedly in their
yield-risk-liquidity characteristics. The debt claims, making up about 75
percent of the total, differed greatly in their maturities—ranging from
those payable on demand to those maturing only after 40 years or
more—and also in their income-safety-liquidity characteristics. Asset

holders wishing to assemble a portfolio of direct securities conforming to their preferences are certainly offered a long and varied menu from which to choose.

We shall later discuss the huge volume of trading in outstanding securities in various branches of the secondary-securities markets. The data above indicate the large stock of such securities at least potentially available for trading. Many, perhaps most, of these trades are not directly related to current flows of new saving, dissaving, and investment but instead reflect adjustments and readjustments of the portfolios of asset holders. However, some purchases and sales of issues already outstanding do serve to transfer purchasing power over current income or output. For example, positive savers transfer a part of their current saving to others by purchasing outstanding issues, and some dissavers and spenders for investment acquire funds by selling some of their holdings of financial claims against others. We shall have more to say about this later.

NATIONAL INCOME OR OUTPUT

We now turn our attention to flows on national income and product account. Our central interest will be in flows of saving, dissaving, and investment. However, these flows affect other flows in the national income and product accounts to such a great extent and are in turn affected to such a great extent by the other flows that they can be analyzed satisfactorily only within the general framework of the national income and product accounts. We shall explore such questions as these: What are the major classes of expenditures for output, which determine the money value of national output or income? How do members of the nation dispose of the income shares accruing to them? What part of national income is saved, and what are the principal types and sources of saving in the United States? How much is spent for investment, and what are the principal classes of investment? Through what processes is positive saving translated into spending in the forms of dissaving and investment? What roles do financial transactions of various types play in these processes?

GROSS NATIONAL PRODUCT (GNP)

The specific measure of national income or product that we shall use is officially called "gross national product or expenditure," and is popu-

Table 4 — 2   **GNP as the Value of Output, or**
Expenditures for Output, 1960 — 1976
(in billions of dollars)

Year	GNP	Personal Consumption Expenditures	Gross Private Domestic Investment	Government Purchases of Goods and Services	Net Exports of Goods and Services
1960	$ 506.0	$ 324.9	$ 76.4	$100.3	$ 4.4
1961	523.3	335.0	74.3	108.2	5.8
1962	563.8	355.2	85.2	118.0	5.4
1963	594.7	374.6	90.2	123.7	6.3
1964	635.7	400.4	96.6	129.8	8.9
1965	688.1	430.2	112.0	138.4	7.6
1966	753.0	464.8	124.5	158.7	5.1
1967	796.3	490.4	120.8	180.2	4.9
1968	868.5	535.9	131.5	198.7	2.3
1969	935.5	579.7	146.2	207.9	1.8
1970	982.4	618.8	140.8	218.9	3.9
1971	1063.4	668.2	160.0	233.7	1.6
1972	1171.1	733.0	188.3	253.1	−3.3
1973	1306.6	809.9	220.0	269.5	7.1
1974	1512.9	889.6	214.6	302.7	6.0
1975	1528.8	980.4	189.1	338.9	20.3
1976	1706.5	1094.0	243.3	361.4	7.8

Source: U.S. Department of Commerce, *Survey of Current Business*, January 1976 and July 1977.
Note: Because of rounding, items may not add to totals shown.

larly known as GNP. It is the market value of the output of goods and services produced by the nation's economy during a stated period of time before deduction of depreciation charges and other allowances for business and institutional consumption of durable capital goods. It is usually stated at an annual rate. It avoids double counting and includes the nation's entire output once and only once. Thus, it measures the value of all output at its point of final sale, and this value includes all the values added at earlier stages of processing and handling.[1]

[1] For excellent descriptions of GNP and other income concepts, as well as useful empirical materials, see *The National Income and Product Accounts of the United States, 1929–1965*, U.S. Government Printing Office, 1966, and *Survey of Current Business*, U.S. Government Printing Office, 1976. For later data, see the *Survey of Current Business* for July and August of each year.

GNP can be viewed and measured in at least two principal ways: (1) as the market value of output, or expenditures for output, during a stated period, and (2) as the sum of the shares of gross income accruing to the members of the nation during the period. For any period, the latter must be exactly equal to the former. We shall deal first with GNP as the market value of output. It should be remembered that since GNP is valued at current prices in each period, changes in GNP from period to period reflect changes in both the rate of real output and the average price per unit of output.

GNP for any period is the sum of four broad classes of expenditures for output: (1) personal consumption expenditures; (2) gross private domestic investment; (3) government purchases of goods and services; and (4) net exports of goods and services. Let us look briefly at each of these.

PERSONAL CONSUMPTION EXPENDITURES

These include household expenditures for three broad classes of output to be used for consumption purposes:

1. Consumer services. Among these are such things as passenger transportation services, services of barbers and beauticians, rental values of houses, and hospital and medical services.
2. Nondurable consumer goods, including such things as food, beverages, clothing, and medicines.
3. Durable consumer goods, such as passenger cars, TV sets, furniture, and electric and gas household appliances. New housing construction is not classified as a durable consumer good; it is included in investment, to be discussed below.

GROSS PRIVATE DOMESTIC INVESTMENT

This includes all private expenditures for output to be used to maintain and increase the stock of private capital. It is "gross" because it includes values of output purchased not only to make net additions to the capital stock but also to offset current depreciation of capital. It includes the following broad classes of expenditures:

1. new residential structures
2. other new private structures, such as office buildings, hotels, factory buildings, and new private dams

3. producers' durable equipment, such as machinery, power equipment, trucks, railroad cars, power lines, and store fixtures
4. net changes during the period in business inventories of raw materials and goods in process

Note that the term "investment," as used here, has nothing directly to do with financial markets; it refers, instead, to private expenditures for output to be used for capital formation purposes.

GOVERNMENT PURCHASES OF GOODS AND SERVICES

This includes all purchases of goods and services by federal, state, and local governments. These purchases are of two principal types:

1. services of government officials and employees, both civilian and military
2. purchases of goods and services produced in the private sector, including such things as new military equipment and supplies, new construction for government use, telephone service, and the millions of other goods and services used by modern governments.

NET EXPORTS OF GOODS AND SERVICES

In each period, the rest of the world purchases exports of goods and services from the United States, thus contributing to total demands for American output. Also in each period, Americans use part of their incomes to purchase goods and services from the rest of the world. The excess of our exports over our imports can be viewed as either the net contribution of the rest of the world to spending for American output, or as net income receipts by the United States on export and import account. Some part of these net receipts is usually given back to the rest of the world in the form of gifts and grants. The remainder is called "net foreign investment." This is equal to exports *minus* imports and *minus* also net gifts and grants to the rest of the world. Net foreign investment is an offset to positive saving in the United States. When it is positive, it reflects foreign spending for our output in excess of the amount of American payments to them for imports, gifts, and grants. When net foreign investment is negative, it is a form of American dissaving, for it reflects the fact that Americans have paid more to the rest of the world for imports and as gifts and grants than they received as income from exports of goods and services.

We shall use the term "gross investment" to denote the algebraic sum of gross private domestic investment and net foreign investment.

At times it will be convenient to use the following notations for GNP and its components.

y = GNP
C = personal consumption expenditures
I = gross private investment = gross private domestic investment plus net foreign investment
G = government purchases of goods and services.

Thus, the value of output during any period can be expressed as $y = C + I + G$.

DISPOSAL OF NATIONAL INCOME

As noted earlier, the total of income shares accruing to members of a nation during any period must be exactly equal to the value of output created during that period, or $C + I + G$. These shares accrue initially in the form of indirect business taxes, which are income for the government; depreciation allowances on business capital; wages, salaries, and other compensation for labor; rentals; interest; and profits. It is intuitively clear that income creation and disposal involve a circular flow. Spendings for output create values of output, which accrue to income receivers, who spend for output, and so on. However, in analyzing the disposal of income, we shall deal not with the initial accruals of income shares but with the "disposable incomes" of various groups. By the "disposable income" of any unit or group, we mean the amount of income remaining at its disposal after taxes and after transfer receipts or payments. We shall distinguish three major groups—households or persons, business firms, and government. The disposable income of households or persons will be designated by y_h, that of business firms by y_b, and that of government by y_g. For any period, the sum of these shares of disposable income is equal to GNP; that is, $y = y_h + y_b + y_g$. This relationship is illustrated in Table 4−3.

GOVERNMENT DISPOSABLE INCOME (y_g)

As is painfully evident to households and business firms, very large amounts of taxes accrue in every period to the federal, state, and local governmental units. These taxes are of many kinds—personal in-

Table 4—3   **Disposable Gross Income in the United States, 1960—1976**
(in billions of dollars)

| | | Personal | | | Business | Government | | |
| | | | | | | | | |
Year	GNP	Dispos-able Income	Con-sump-tion	Sav-ing	Dispos-able Income	Dispos-able Income	Pur-chases of Goods and Services	Sav-ing
1960	$ 506.0	$ 342.0[a]	$ 324.9	$17.1	S 58.7	$103.4	$100.3	$ 3.1
1961	523.3	355.2	335.0	20.2	59.8	103.9	108.2	−4.3
1962	563.8	375.6	355.2	20.4	67.0	114.2	118.0	−3.8
1963	594.7	393.4	374.6	18.8	70.1	124.7	123.7	0.7
1964	635.7	426.5	400.4	26.1	76.3	127.5	129.8	−2.3
1965	688.1	460.5	430.2	20.3	84.6	138.9	138.4	0.5
1966	753.0	497.8	464.8	33.0	91.2	157.4	158.7	−1.3
1967	796.3	531.3	490.4	40.9	93.7	166.0	180.2	−14.2
1968	868.5	574.0	535.9	38.1	98.2	193.2	198.7	−5.5
1969	935.5	614.8	579.7	35.1	101.7	218.6	207.9	10.7
1970	982.4	669.4	618.8	50.6	101.3	209.5	218.9	−9.4
1971	1063.4	725.5	668.2	57.3	115.7	215.4	233.7	−18.3
1972	1171.1	782.4	733.0	49.4	131.0	249.6	253.1	−3.5
1973	1306.6	880.2	809.9	70.3	140.2	275.8	269.5	6.3
1974	1412.9	961.3	889.6	71.7	137.8	299.5	302.7	−3.2
1975	1528.8	1060.6	980.4	80.2	179.2	274.6	338.9	−64.3
1976	1706.5	1159.9	1094.0	65.9	206.6	325.8	361.4	−35.6

Source: *Survey of Current Business,* January 1976 and July 1977.
[a] The data in this column appear in the national income accounts as "disposable personal income less interest paid and transfer payments to foreigners."
Note: The careful reader will note small differences between the value of GNP for a period and the sum of disposable income shares. These statistical discrepancies arise from basing some estimates on data relating to the value of output and basing other estimates on data relating to income shares.

come taxes, corporate taxes, property taxes, taxes on production and sales, contributions for social insurance, and so on. These obviously tend to decrease the disposable incomes of taxpayers. Also in each period, the government makes large transfer payments to the private sectors. Government transfer payments in any period are those payments for which the government receives no goods or services in return. They consist of such things as old-age security benefits, aid to the indigent, unemployment benefits, subsidies, veteran's benefits, and interest on the federal debt. These tend to increase the disposable incomes of the private sectors. Government disposable income in any period is equal to its total tax collections minus its transfer payments to others.

The government disposes of its disposable income in two ways. Some it uses to purchase goods and services. This is the G discussed above. The rest it saves. We shall call this "government saving" and denote it by S_g. Thus, $y_g = G + S_g$, and $S_g = y_g - G$. S_g may be either positive or negative. We shall sometimes refer to negative S_g as "government dissaving," or "government deficits."[2]

Government saving is essentially similar to private saving. Positive government saving, like positive private saving, represents a part of current disposable income that can be made available to finance dissaving and investment spending by others. A governmental unit ordinarily uses its positive saving to retire financial claims against itself, and the former holders of these claims can use the funds to finance their own consumption or investment, to retire financial claims against themselves, to purchase financial claims against others, to increase their holdings of money, and so on. Government dissaving, like private dissaving, requires that the dissaver somehow acquire funds from others to cover the excess of its expenditures over its current disposable income. Governments ordinarily do this by creating and selling direct financial claims against themselves.

The last column of Table 4–3 shows that, as a group, American governmental units—federal, state, and local—were positive savers in some years and large dissavers in others. These data greatly understate the gross activities of governmental units in supplying and demanding funds in financial markets, for they reflect the algebraic sum of the positive saving of some units and the negative saving of others. In most periods, some governmental units are positive savers and supply funds in financial markets while others incur deficits and demand funds in financial markets.

Though dissaving by a governmental unit may sometimes reflect ineptitude and poor financial management, such a unit often has good reasons to incur deficits during some periods. Wars, and especially full-scale wars, usually occasion dissaving by national governments as those governments seek to command a major part of national output but are unable or unwilling to raise taxes enough to cover their full costs. Economists usually consider wartime tax efforts to be inadequate and

[2] In the national income accounts, what we call positive government saving is officially called "government surplus on income and product account," and what we call negative government saving is officially called "government deficit on income and product account."

not sufficiently anti-inflationary, but it is probably true that, at least in full-scale wars, tax increases sufficient to cover total government expenditures would require tax rates so high as to threaten civilian incentives to work and to produce efficiently. A major part of the outstanding debt of the federal government arose out of deficit spending during World War I, World War II, the Korean War, and the Vietnam War.

Government dissaving in peacetime is often induced by an unusual decline of the government's tax income, an unusual increase of its need to spend, or both. This often happens to state and local governments because their incomes are reduced by a general or localized business recession or depression or because unfavorable local or regional events, such as a flood or a drought, require extraordinary expenditures. The position of the federal government in the face of a recession or depression is worthy of special note. In such periods, federal revenues fall automatically and sharply, for each decline of GNP decreases the principal federal tax bases—personal income, corporate profits, production and sales, and payrolls. The government could, of course, avoid dissaving by raising effective tax rates, but this would lower private disposable incomes and thereby tend to lower private demands for output. Or the government could seek to avoid dissaving by decreasing its expenditures, but this would both decrease the government's own demand for output and lower its contribution to private disposable incomes. It is now generally accepted that in such depressed periods the government should not raise taxes or decrease its expenditures but should become a dissaver, even though this involves the creation and sale of government debt, and that if the recession threatens to become deep or prolonged the government should seek to increase its dissaving by decreasing effective tax rates, by increasing its expenditures, or both. Thus, the creation of new government debt claims during recession or depression periods serves a dual purpose: it enables the government to acquire resources in excess of its current disposable income; and it is an integral part of an economic stabilization policy to combat recession and unemployment. On the other hand, positive government saving, representing an excess of government tax collections from the private sectors over government expenditures to those sectors, can be a useful method of combating actual or threatened price inflation.

Much government dissaving, and especially dissaving by state and local governments, is associated with the acquisition of highly durable goods for government use. Among these are new highways, streets, bridges, water and sewer systems, schools, other public buildings, and sports stadiums. Two aspects of these things are conducive to government dissaving during the period of their acquisition. First, many of them are very expensive relative to the current disposable income of the governmental unit. Second, they are highly durable, yielding useful services over many years. Taxpayers living in the jurisdiction at the time such goods are purchased would consider it unfair to impose on them the entire cost of the durable improvements in view of the fact that future residents will receive much of the benefit. For such reasons, it is common for governmental units to borrow to pay for expensive durable goods and then to repay principal and interest over the useful life of the goods. Thus, much of the outstanding debt of state and local governments, and especially the latter, was created in the process of accumulating what may properly be called "public capital goods."

BUSINESS DISPOSABLE INCOME (Y_b)

Great amounts of gross income flow to business firms during each period, representing the contributions of the latter to the value of output. A large part of this gross income is paid to others for their contributions to production. These are in the form of wages, salaries, and other compensation for labor; interest; rentals; and dividends to shareholders. Taxes must also be paid. However, some part of business gross income remains at the disposal of business firms; this we call business disposable income and denote by Y_b. This consists of two principal parts: (1) depreciation and other capital consumption allowances during the period, and (2) retained, or undistributed, corporate profits. The latter is simply the amount of net profits after taxes that firms do not distribute as dividends to their owners. Since corporations as such do not purchase goods and services for personal consumption, all of Y_b is saved. This is officially called "gross business saving." We shall designate it by S_b and ask the reader to remember that $S_b = Y_b$.

Since depreciation and other allowances for capital consumption during a period have come to constitute such a large part of gross business saving, and even of gross national saving, further comments on them may be useful. They are not a part of a firm's net income; in fact, they are a part of its costs of production. However, they are a part of the firm's gross income, and of gross national income, that remains at its disposal. In popular parlance, they are a part of the firm's "cash flow." An example will illustrate the principles involved. Suppose that in some year a firm acquires, for $1 million, a durable capital good that is expected to have a useful life of 10 years. It would be inappropriate to charge the entire cost of the capital good to production costs of output during the year of acquisition, for the capital good will yield productive services over a much longer period. The initial cost should be "written off," or amortized, over the predicted useful life of the capital good. Suppose that the firm uses a simple "straight-line" formula over a 10-year period, with a depreciation allowance of $100,000 a year. This amount will be included in the firm's costs of production during each of those years, but it will represent a part of the firm's gross income that remains at its disposal.

The high rate of S_b in the form of depreciation allowances reflects both the huge stock of depreciable capital goods used by American business and the desire of many managements to "write off" the cost of a capital good in a period significantly shorter than the latter's probable useful life. This is encouraged by taxes on business net profits, for larger depreciation allowances tend to decrease taxable current profits.

The other component of S_b, retained or undistributed profits, is almost always positive for business firms as a group, though it became negative during some of the worst years of the great depression of the 1930s as profits turned into losses and some corporations continued to make dividend payments. Even in the rare cases in which retained profits are negative for business firms as a group, they are not negative enough to offset the large positive component of S_b in the form of depreciation allowances.

Several pitfalls should be avoided. Depreciation allowances should not be confused with replacement of capital goods. The former, as we have seen, represent annual accruals over the useful life of an asset. Replacement, if it occurs at all, is likely to occur at specific points in time. Replacement of a particular capital good may not occur at all; the firm may find more profitable uses for its depreciation allowances. Nor should it be assumed that because a firm has positive gross saving during a period it will use these funds to acquire new capital goods of any sort. It may indeed use at least some of its S_b for this purpose, but it may also find it more profitable to use some or all of these funds for other purposes—to retire debt, to acquire existing capital goods or financial claims, to acquire newly created financial claims against others, or even to increase its money balances. A management devoted to promoting the economic welfare of the owners of the firm would never invest in projects within the firm whose rates of marginal efficiency were below the rates of return available in other uses.

HOUSEHOLD (OR PERSONAL) DISPOSABLE INCOME (Y_h)

During each period, households receive income of two broad types. The first and largest is their reward for the use of their labor and property. This is in the form of wages and other compensation for labor, interest, rentals, incomes of proprietors of unincorporated business, and dividends from corporations. The other part consists of transfer payments received from government and business in such forms as social security, unemployment, and veterans benefits; aid to the indigent; and business pensions. Total household or personal income is the sum of these two parts. However, households are liable for various types of personal taxes—personal income taxes, property taxes, contributions for social insurance, and so on. Total household or personal disposable income (Y_h) is equal to total household or personal income minus personal taxes.

Y_h is disposed of in two ways. One part, by far the larger, is spent for current output to be used for consumption purposes. This is the C discussed earlier. The rest is saved. We call this personal saving and denote it by S_p. That is, $Y_h = C + S_p$, and $S_p = Y_h - C$. Thus, personal saving in any period is simply that part of personal disposable income that is not used to purchase current output for consumption purposes. For households as a group, S_p is almost always positive, though it became negative in the worst years of the great depression, when personal disposable incomes fell to abnormally low levels. An important proposition for income analysis is that S_p varies positively with Y_h. When households enjoy an increase of Y_h, they increase C, but by a smaller amount, and also increase S_p. When households experience a decrease of Y_h, they decrease C, but by a smaller amount, and also decrease S_p.

Total personal saving during any year, as shown in Table 4–3, is the algebraic sum of the positive saving of some households and the negative saving of others. In effect, dissaving is netted out of positive saving, and only the positive remainder is shown. Even during the years when S_p is highly positive, millions of households are dissavers. Moreover, an individual household may be a positive saver during some parts of a year and a dissaver in others. For these reasons, the data do not reflect the full magnitude of the gross amounts of funds supplied in financial markets by households, and they do not record all the funds demanded in financial markets by dissaving households. They do, however, show the net flow of personal saving available to finance investment and government dissaving.

Dissaving is widely practiced among American households despite lingering feelings in some quarters that to consume beyond one's current income is unwise, dangerous, and perhaps even sinful. Some dissaving may indeed reflect poor foresight and unwise household management of scarce resources. Yet there are good reasons why a rational household attempting to maximize its total satisfactions from its lifetime income should dissave during some periods. One reason is a temporary loss or reduction of income because of such things as unemployment, illness of the family breadwinner, a bad year for the family enterprise, or a bad crop for a farmer. Another is an unusually large need, such as a need for expensive hospital and medical services. Still another is to acquire an education. Personal expenditures for educational services are officially classified as purchases of consumer services. There is good reason for this, since the one being educated may enjoy the educational process and be enabled to derive greater satisfaction from his enhanced knowledge and understanding. However, at least some part of expenditures for education may be viewed as "investment in human capital," for the acquired knowledge and skills enable the person to increase his lifetime earnings.

Most families find it advantageous to go through rather long cycles of dissaving, saving, and dissaving. To illustrate the point, let us look at the lifetime history of a hypothetical "typical family" and divide its history into three stages. The first stage extends from the time of marriage until the children have terminated their formal education, the second from that time until the breadwinner reaches retirement, and the third from retirement to death. The family has good reason to expect that its income will start at a relatively low level, gradually rise to a peak when the parents are close to middle-age—perhaps when they are in their forties or early fifties—stay at approximately this peak level until the breadwinner reaches retirement, and then drop sharply.

In the first stage, when its income is still below the expected peak, the family faces many needs—to accumulate a stock of durable consumer goods; to pay for the birth of children; to meet rising costs as the children grow older and more demanding; and, usually most expensive of all, to "see the kids through college." A family would find it difficult to be a positive saver during all of the years in this stage, and it is likely to be a dissaver during at least some of them. Conditions change in the second stage. The family's income is at or near its peak, and the children are now "on their own" and, in most instances, of no expense to the parents. Moreover, with retirement only about two decades away, the parents become acutely aware of the need to accumulate wealth for use in their old age. Families are likely to be positive savers during this stage and to achieve their largest stock of wealth by the end of the stage. This wealth may be in various forms, such as houses and other physical goods and equity and debt claims against others. A common form is an annuity policy, with a value that includes both earlier contributions to an annuity company and the accumulated income thereon. In the third stage, when its current income has been reduced by retirement of the breadwinner, the family is likely to be a dissaver. It will probably finance at least part of its dissaving by selling its physical assets and financial claims against others. If it receives annuity payments, which represent largely a return of values accumulated earlier, the annuity company in effect sells to others some of the financial assets accumulated earlier for the retired family's account.

The nation's population at any time consists of millions of families in each of the three stages of family history. Much of the dissaving during any year involves intergenerational transfers of consuming power, which are effected primarily through intergenerational transfers of financial claims. As a group, families in the third stage finance their dissaving by selling financial claims, directly or indirectly, to families that are younger. As a group, families in the first stage are likely to be at best only small positive savers and small net purchasers of financial claims. Families in the second stage, as a group, are the largest suppliers of consuming power to the others and the largest net purchasers of financial claims from them. The consumption preferences of both those of us who are old and those of you who are still young would be thwarted in the absence of the thrifty second-stagers. But we need not feel that we are exploiting the second stagers. They will later become third-stagers and you youngsters second-stagers.

Much household dissaving and creation of consumer credit in any period are associated with the very large amounts of durable consumer goods purchased by American families. These include such things as automobiles, motorcycles, campers, pleasure boats, power lawnmowers, color TV sets, washing machines and dryers, refrigerators, and furniture. Two characteristics of these durable goods are conducive to the use of consumer credit. First, units of many of these things are so expensive that most families would find it difficult to pay for them out of current income without raising their total consumption expenditure above their disposable incomes during the period in which these things are purchased. Second, these goods are highly durable, yielding consumer services over a number of years. Households could, of course, acquire the use of such goods without buying and owning them. For example, they could patronize commercial laundries instead of buying washers and dryers. Or they could lease the durable goods from others, paying periodic rentals for their use. This is sometimes economical, especially when the durable goods are used only infrequently. In most cases, however, it is cheaper in the long run to buy the goods. Families can, and sometimes do, postpone purchases of durable goods until they have saved enough to pay for them. In this case, dissaving during the period of purchase is financed by drawing down other accumulated assets of the household. However, postponing purchases requires that in the interim the family forgo the use of such goods. Families often decide, therefore, that it is "only good business" to "borrow and buy now, pay later."

In purchasing and paying for durable goods, families often go through a dissaving–positive-saving cycle. They are dissavers during the period of purchase, thereby incurring consumer debt, and are positive savers in later periods in order to reduce their debt. To the extent that debt repayments exceed depreciation of the goods, a family increases its net worth in the form of its equity in the goods. It is unlikely that American households could have accumulated such a huge stock of consumer durable goods in the absence of consumer credit facilities.

GROSS SAVING

We have now identified the three broad components of gross saving in the United States. Personal saving (S_p) is that part of household disposable income not spent for consumption. Gross business saving (S_b) is the sum of business capital consumption allowances and retained net earnings. Government saving (S_g) is that part of the government's disposable income not used to purchase output. If we use the symbol S to denote total gross saving, we can write: $S = S_p + S_b + S_g$. The same thing can be expressed in another way: S is that part of gross national output (y) in any period that is not demanded for consumption (C) or as government purchases of goods and services (G). Thus $S = y - C - G$. In some cases it will be convenient to use the first formulation and in other cases the second.

Let us now look at some major facts concerning gross saving in the United States. One fact that stands out in Table 4−4 is the very small fraction of S contributed by government saving. In many of the years, governmental units as a group were dissavers, or deficit units. Thus they appeared in financial markets as net demanders of funds and net suppliers of securities. Even when they were positive savers, their total contribution was very small relative to the total. It should be noted, however, that these units can have important impacts on financial markets as they alternate between being, on balance, positive savers and net suppliers of funds, and being dissavers and net demanders of funds.

Table 4−4   **Sources and Uses of Gross Saving in the United States, 1960−1976**
(in billions of dollars)

	Saving					Investment		
Year	Total Gross Saving	Total Private Saving	Per- sonal Saving	Gross Busi- ness Saving	Govern- ment Saving	Total Gross Invest- ment	Gross Private Domestic Invest- ment	Net Foreign Invest- ment
1960	$ 78.9	$ 75.8	$17.1	$ 58.7	$ 3.1	$ 78.2	$ 76.4	$ 1.7
1961	75.8	80.0	20.2	59.8	−4.3	77.3	74.3	3.0
1962	83.6	87.4	20.4	67.0	−3.8	87.6	85.2	2.4
1963	89.6	88.9	18.8	70.1	0.7	93.4	90.2	3.2
1964	100.1	102.4	26.1	76.3	−2.3	102.3	96.6	5.7
1965	115.4	114.9	30.3	84.6	0.5	116.3	112.0	4.3
1966	122.9	124.2	33.0	91.2	−1.3	126.1	129.5	1.6
1967	120.3	134.6	40.9	93.7	−14.2	122.1	120.8	1.2
1968	130.8	136.3	38.1	98.2	−5.5	130.2	131.5	−1.4
1969	147.5	136.8	35.1	101.7	10.7	144.2	146.2	−2.0
1970	143.4	151.9	50.6	101.3	−9.4	141.4	140.8	0.5
1971	155.4	173.0	57.3	115.7	−18.3	156.8	160.0	−3.2
1972	177.5	180.4	49.4	131.0	−3.5	179.2	188.3	−9.0
1973	216.8	210.5	70.3	140.2	6.3	219.4	220.0	−0.6
1974	204.4	209.5	71.7	137.8	−3.2	210.1	214.6	−4.5
1975	195.1	259.4	80.2	179.2	−64.3	201.0	189.1	11.8
1976	237.0	272.5	65.9	206.6	−35.6	242.5	243.3	−0.9

Source: U.S. Department of Commerce, *Survey of Current Business,* January 1976, and July 1977,
various tables. Statistical discrepancies between estimates for gross saving and those for
gross investment are not shown in the table.

One striking fact about gross private saving is its large magnitude,
whether measured in terms of annual dollar flows or as a percentage of
GNP. (See Tables 4−4 and 4−5). In the years covered by these tables, it
ranged between 14.6 and 16.9 percent of GNP. Perhaps such a high ratio
should be expected in view of the nation's high per capita income and
output. More surprising may be the small fraction of gross private saving accounted for by personal saving. This ranged from 21.3 to 34.3
percent in the years covered by the tables. As a group, households saved
between 5 and 8.9 percent of their disposable incomes. It will be remembered, however, that personal saving is a net figure, reflecting the
excess of positive saving by some households over the dissaving of
others.

Gross business saving accounted for between 65.7 and 78.9 percent of total gross private saving in the years covered by the tables. Capital consumption allowances were by far the largest component; in every year except two they were equal to more than 50 percent of gross private saving. Retained corporate net earnings were smaller, and more variable, ranging between 3.5 and 23.7 percent of gross private saving. Corporate managements have various motives for retaining some of a firm's net profits after taxes: to enable stockholders to avoid personal income taxes on dividends; to finance additions to the firm's assets without recourse to financial markets; to avoid reducing dividends when net profits fall; and to preserve and increase the independence, security, prestige, and emoluments of the management.

Thus, so-called "nonfinancial" business firms play major roles in

Table 4 – 5   **Some Data Relating to Gross Private Saving, 1960 – 1976**

| Year | Gross Private Saving as a Percentage of GNP | Components as Percentages of Gross Private Saving | | | |
		Personal Saving	Total Gross Business Saving	Capital Consumption Allowances	Undistributed Corporate Profits
1960	15.0	22.6	77.4	62.9	14.5
1961	15.3	25.3	74.7	61.2	13.5
1962	15.5	23.3	76.7	57.8	18.9
1963	14.9	21.1	78.9	58.8	20.1
1964	16.1	25.5	74.5	53.3	21.2
1965	16.7	26.4	73.6	50.0	23.6
1966	16.5	26.6	73.4	49.7	23.7
1967	16.9	26.6	73.4	53.6	19.8
1968	15.7	28.0	72.0	54.1	17.9
1969	14.6	25.7	74.3	60.3	14.0
1970	15.5	33.3	66.7	59.8	6.9
1971	16.3	33.1	66.9	57.4	9.5
1972	15.4	27.4	72.6	58.2	14.4
1973	16.1	33.4	66.6	55.9	10.7
1974	14.8	34.2	65.8	64.8	1.0
1975	17.0	30.9	69.1	62.7	6.4
1976	16.0	24.2	75.8	65.7	10.1

Source: Computed from data in Tables 4 – 3 and 4 – 4 above.

financial processes—as the largest spenders for investment, as issuers of both equity and debt claims, and as major sources of gross saving.

We turn now to gross private investment, noting its magnitudes and its components. For any period, this is equal to total private saving plus positive government saving or minus government dissaving.

GROSS PRIVATE INVESTMENT

This is the algebraic sum of net foreign investment and gross private domestic investment. (See Table 4–4 above.) Net foreign investment is by far the smaller part of the total. Even in years when it is positive, it is equal to only a small fraction of the total, and in some years it is negative. Thus gross private investment is largely gross private domestic investment. The latter usually ranges between 14 and 17 percent of GNP. Its major classes of components in recent years are shown in Table 4–6.

Net changes in business inventories or stocks of raw materials, goods in process, and finished goods account for only a very small fraction of the total. However, changes in the rate of expenditures for this type of investment have important short-run cyclical effects on GNP and employment. Fixed investment is by far the larger part of the total. Expenditures for new residential structures—both single-family and multifamily—fluctuate widely but are almost always a significant part of total fixed investment. In the years covered by the table, they ranged between 25 and 31 percent of total fixed investment. New nonresidential structures are of many types—industrial, commercial, religious, private educational, hospital and other institutional, public utility, and so on.

New producers' durable equipment is also of many types—tractors and other types of farm equipment, power converters and machinery in factories and mines, communications equipment, transportation equipment, store fixtures, and so on. Expenditures for these things are usually considerably larger than those for either residential structures or for nonresidential construction.

SUMMARY OF SAVING AND INVESTMENT

The data above relate to what may be called "net gross saving," for they measure the excess of total gross positive saving over the amount of total negative saving, or dissaving, during a period. For example, personal saving (S_p) is equal to total household positive saving minus

Table 4—6 Gross Private Domestic Investment, 1969 – 1976
(in billions of dollars)

Components	1969	1970	1971	1972	1973	1974	1975	1976
NET CHANGE IN BUSINESS INVENTORIES	$ 9.4	$ 3.8	$ 6.4	$ 9.4	$ 17.9	$ 8.9	$ -11.4	$ 13.3
FIXED INVESTMENT— TOTAL	136.8	137.0	153.6	178.8	202.1	205.7	200.6	230.8
Residential structures	37.9	36.6	49.6	62.0	66.1	55.1	51.5	68.0
Nonresidential structures	35.7	37.7	39.3	42.5	49.0	54.5	52.9	55.8
Producers' durable equipment	63.3	62.8	64.7	74.3	87.0	96.2	96.3	106.1
Total	$146.2	$140.8	$160.0	$188.3	$220.0	$214.6	$ 189.1	$243.3

Source: U.S. Department of Commerce, *Survey of Current Business*, January 1976, and July 1977, various tables.

household dissaving, and government saving (S_g) is equal to total positive saving by governmental units minus dissaving by governmental units. Unfortunately, we do not have data revealing the total amount of positive saving during each period. However, we do know that it is much larger than "net gross saving," because during each period millions of households are positive savers while others are dissavers and some governmental units are positive savers while others are dissavers.

We noted earlier that positive saving, considered by itself, tends to reduce total expenditures for output, for it represents that part of national income that is not used to purchase output for consumption and government purposes. Positive·saving can be "offset," or reinjected into expenditures for output, in three principal ways:

1. through expenditures for gross private investment
2. through expenditures in the form of household dissaving
3. through expenditures in the form of government dissaving.

As we shall see in the next section, all positive savers—whether they are households, business firms, or governmental units—face this question: "What shall we do with the money representing our positive saving?" And household dissavers, government dissavers, and spenders for private investment face a common question: "Where and how do we get the money to finance our expenditures in excess of our current disposable incomes?"

TRANSLATION OF POSITIVE SAVING INTO DISSAVING AND INVESTMENT

Though the national income and product accounts provide invaluable information concerning the types and sources of positive saving on the one hand and the types and amounts of dissaving and private investment on the other, they provide almost no information relating to questions that will be our central concern in this section: How, and through what channels and instruments, is the positive saving of some entities translated into expenditures in the form of dissaving and investment? How and to what extent does the translation occur without transactions in financial markets? What are the roles of financial markets in the process? We shall now begin to remedy these deficiencies. For this purpose, the flow-of-funds accounts, developed and published by the Board of Governors of the Federal Reserve System, are highly valuable.

As a first step, we identify in Table 4 – 7 the various ways of disposing of positive saving and the various sources of funds to dissavers and spenders for investment. The left-hand column lists the various ways that a positive saver—be it a household, a business firm, or a governmental unit—can dispose of, or use, the flow of money receipts representing its positive saving. The right-hand column shows the various ways that a dissaver or spender for investment can acquire money to finance its dissaving or investment. In the center appears an empty box, labeled "financial markets." At this stage we are not yet prepared to describe its many components. We shall say only that it includes many types of brokers and dealers to facilitate exchanges between money and financial claims, and also many banks and other types of financial intermediaries that buy and hold direct financial claims for their own account and that create and sell financial claims against themselves. The latter are the "indirect financial claims" that were mentioned earlier.

It will be convenient to start with the right-hand column, showing the various sources of funds to dissavers and spenders for investment. Since dissavers, by definition, have no current positive saving, they cannot rely on this source of finance. However, many spenders for investment, and especially business firms, rely at least partially on their own current saving. A second method of financing current dissaving or investment is to sell "old" physical assets, such as land, buildings, or equipment. A third method is to reduce the entity's money balance. None of the above methods involves directly any transaction in financial claims.

Table 4 – 7   **Some Flows Related to Saving and Investment**

Disposal of Funds by Positive Savers		Sources of Funds to Dissavers and Spenders for Investment
I. Purchase new investment goods		I. Own current saving
II. Purchase "old" physical assets		II. Sell "old" physical assets
III. Increase money balance		III. Decrease money balance
IV. Purchase "old" financial claims against others	Financial markets	IV. Sell holdings of financial claims against others
V. Purchase newly created financial claims against others		V. Create and sell new financial claims against self
VI. Retire financial claims against self		

A fourth method of financing dissaving or investment is to sell some of the entity's holdings of financial claims against others. This obviously involves transactions in financial markets, but it does not alter the total stock of securities outstanding. Though we do not know what part of total dissaving and investment is financed in this way, it must be significant because both households and business firms often accumulate claims in some periods in order to make large expenditures later. For example, a household saves and accumulates claims that it will later sell to make a down payment on a house, to buy a car, or to make some other large expenditure, and a business firm acts similarly to be in a position to build a new plant or to buy expensive equipment. A final, and highly important, method of financing dissaving and investment is for the entity to create and sell financial claims, either equity or debt claims, against itself. This clearly involves transactions in financial markets and it serves to increase the stock of outstanding direct financial claims.

Let us turn now to the left-hand column of Table 4–7, which shows the various ways that positive savers can dispose of, or use, the money representing their positive saving. A positive saver may, as we have seen, use at least some of its saving to purchase new investment goods. It may also purchase "old" physical goods, such as land, buildings, or equipment, thus transferring some of its saving to the sellers of the "old" physical assets. It may also use some of its current saving to increase its own money balance. None of the above methods involves directly any transaction in financial claims.

A saver may use its saving to purchase outstanding equity or debt claims against others, thus transferring funds to the sellers of the claims. This clearly involves financial transactions, but it does not serve to change the size of the stock of outstanding claims; it merely shifts ownership of those claims. Though we do not know how much saving is transferred in this way, we do know that the amount is large. For example, many households prefer to buy "seasoned securities" rather than new, unfamiliar issues, and business firms that are positive savers often buy outstanding claims solely for their income and liquidity or to achieve some degree of control over the issuer. A positive saver may also purchase newly created financial claims against others, including both direct financial claims against other nonfinancial units and indirect financial claims against financial intermediaries.

Finally, a positive saver may use at least some of its current saving to retire outstanding financial claims against itself. For example, a household may reduce its mortgage or pay off other debt; a governmental unit may retire debt claims against itself; and a business firm may reduce its short-term or long-term debt or, less frequently, buy up and retire equity claims against itself. In these ways current saving can be transferred to those who formerly held claims against the positive savers. Note that this is the one use of positive saving that tends to reduce the outstanding stock of direct financial claims.

We can now consider further a question mentioned earlier: What is the relative importance of the various possible methods of translating positive saving into spending in the forms of dissaving and private investment? Though available data do not permit precise answers, they do support important general conclusions.

1. The creation and sale of new direct financial claims has become a major method of financing dissaving and investment. Table 4 − 8 presents some relevant data. Column 3 shows, for the various years, the amounts of gross private investment plus government dissaving or minus positive government saving. This measures the net amounts of funds needed to cover these expenditures. Column 4 shows, for each of these years, the amounts of funds raised in financial markets by the nonfinancial sectors. This is the net increase of outstanding direct securities during each year—the amounts of new issues less the amounts of direct securities retired. Column 5 shows the amounts of funds raised in financial markets as percentages of the amounts of funds required for the purposes shown in Column 3. It will be noted that in no year since 1960 has this percentage been below 53.9 percent, and in recent years it has been considerably higher. Because of certain characteristics of the data, we cannot conclude that these percentages portray precisely the fractions of total dissaving and private investment on income and product account that were financed through the creation and sale of new direct financial claims. For one thing, Column 3 does not include funds required to finance household dissaving. Also, the nonfinancial sectors sometimes issue new securities to acquire assets that are not included in the income and product accounts—such things as liquid financial assets and "old" physical goods. On the other hand, Column 4—showing the net increases in direct securities outstanding, or total new issues less retirements—clearly understates the gross amounts of new direct securities created and sold by the nonfinancial sectors, for we know that in any year positive savers retire very large amounts of outstanding financial claims against themselves. Despite all these necessary qualifications, we can validly conclude that in a typical year considerably more than half of all dissaving and private investment on income and product account are financed through the creation and sale of new direct financial claims.

Table 4 — 8   **Gross Private Investment, Government Saving, and Funds Raised in Financial Markets by Nonfinancial Sectors**
(amounts in billions of dollars)

Year	Col. 1 Gross Private Investment	Col. 2 Government Saving	Col. 3 Col. 1 plus Government Deficit or Minus Government Surplus	Col. 4 Funds Raised in Financial Markets by Non-financial Sectors	Col. 5 Col. 4 as a Percentage of Col. 3
1960	$ 78.2	$ 3.1	$ 75.1	$ 33.1	44.1
1961	77.3	−4.3	81.6	44.3	54.3
1962	87.6	−3.8	91.4	54.3	59.4
1963	93.4	0.7	92.7	58.2	62.8
1964	102.3	−2.3	104.6	67.1	64.1
1965	116.3	0.5	115.8	70.4	60.8
1966	126.1	−1.3	127.4	68.7	53.9
1967	122.1	−14.2	136.3	83.4	61.2
1968	130.2	−5.5	135.7	97.8	72.1
1969	144.2	10.7	133.5	91.7	68.7
1970	141.4	−9.4	150.8	101.6	67.4
1971	156.8	−18.3	175.1	156.3	89.3
1972	179.2	−3.5	182.7	169.4	92.7
1973	219.4	6.3	213.1	202.0	94.8
1974	210.1	−3.2	213.3	189.6	88.9
1975	201.0	−64.3	274.4	205.6	74.9
1976	242.5	−35.6	278.1	268.3	96.5

Sources: Data on investment and saving are from Table 4 — 4 above. Data on funds raised in financial markets are from *Federal Reserve Bulletin,* November 1976, p. A.56, and from various tables in Board of Governors of the Federal Reserve System, *Flow of Funds Accounts.*

2. Another unknown, but undoubtedly significant, fraction of positive saving is translated into dissaving and investment through transactions in outstanding financial claims. Positive savers make funds available by purchasing outstanding claims against others and by purchasing and retiring outstanding claims against themselves, and dissavers and spenders for investment acquire funds by selling some of their holdings of outstanding claims against others.

3. Though positive savers can and do dispose of some of their saving by increasing their holdings of money and "old" physical assets, and dissavers and spenders for investment can and do acquire funds by reducing their holdings of such assets, this method accounts for no more than a small fraction of all transfers of positive saving.

4. A significant amount of positive saving continues to be used by savers themselves to finance their own investment spending. This is especially true of business saving. But this is no longer the major method of transforming saving into investment.

In summary, we have come a long way from that simple system, imagined earlier, in which every individual household, business firm, and governmental unit could spend for consumption plus investment in any period no more than its own current disposable income. The restraining bonds of self-finance have indeed been broken. A major part of saving is now transferred from positive savers to others for their use, and most of these transfers are effected through various types of financial transactions.

CONCLUSION

This chapter has carried us several more steps toward an understanding of the roles of financial instruments in the processes of saving, dissaving, and investment in the United States. It has identified the major types and sources of positive saving and the major types of dissaving and private investment. It has also identified the various ways that a positive saver can dispose of the money representing its saving and the various ways that a dissaver or spender for investment can acquire the funds needed to finance its expenditures.

Despite our progress, one essential part of the financial picture is still missing. We have yet to fill in the empty box in Table 4−7, labeled "financial markets." Through what channels and institutions are the funds supplied by positive savers made available to dissavers and spenders for investment?

Positive savers could, of course, buy the specific securities sold by dissavers and spenders for investment, doing so directly without the use of middlemen or any other sort of intermediation. Though such transactions do occur, sole reliance on such a system would be highly inefficient in both operational and allocational terms. A complex system of financial intermediaries and financial middlemen has evolved to remedy these deficiencies. The chapters immediately following will describe the roles played by various types of financial intermediaries, which acquire and hold direct financial claims and create and sell financial claims against themselves. These institutions now hold a major part of all outstanding direct financial claims, and a major part of total saving is channeled through them. Later chapters will deal with brokers, dealers, and other financial middlemen whose major function is to facilitate purchases and sales of financial claims of virtually all types.

SELECTED READINGS

I. The national income and product accounts

   A. Description and analysis of these accounts

   Branson, W. H. *Macroeconomic Theory and Policy.* New York: Harper & Row, 1972. Chap. 2.
   Wonnacott, P. *Macroeconomics.* Homewood, Ill.: Richard D. Irwin, 1974. Chap. 17.

   B. Sources of data

   U.S. Department of Commerce. *Survey of Current Business* (monthly). Data for earlier years are conveniently accessible in the annual *President's Economic Report.*

II. The flow-of-funds accounts

   A. The nature of the accounts

   Board of Governors of the Federal Reserve System. *Introduction to Flow of Funds.* Washington, D.C., 1975.
   Cohen, J. "Copeland's Money Flows After Twenty-Five Years: A Survey." *Journal of Economic Literature,* March 1972, pp. 1−25.

   B. Sources of data

   Annual and quarterly data are available from the flow-of-funds section of the Board of Governors of the Federal Reserve System. Most of the data are also published in the monthly *Federal Reserve Bulletin.*

PRINCIPLES OF FINANCIAL INTERMEDIATION

Financial intermediaries and their functions will be our central interest in this and the two chapters that follow. The distinguishing characteristic of these institutions is that they create and sell financial claims against themselves and use the proceeds to acquire and hold financial claims against others. Their assets consist largely, though not entirely, of direct financial claims against the nonfinancial sectors — households, governmental units, nonfinancial business firms, and so on. The financial claims against themselves that they create and issue are variously called indirect financial claims, indirect securities, and indirect financial instruments. Deposit claims against banks are an example. The characteristics of the indirect financial claims that they issue typically differ markedly from those of the financial assets that they acquire and hold. They differ in denominations, in maturity, and in their combinations of income, safety, and liquidity. Through such transformations, financial intermediaries intermediate between the preferences of asset holders and those of the issuers of direct securities.

The most familiar types of financial intermediaries in the United States are commercial banks, mutual savings banks, savings and loan associations, credit unions, and investment companies, but there are also several others, and new types appear almost every year.

How can financial intermediaries survive, and even thrive, in a financial system in which issuers of direct securities and ultimate suppliers of funds could completely bypass financial intermediaries and deal with each other through the widespread primary and secondary markets for direct securities? As we have seen, we all have access to financial markets in which we can choose among a wide variety of direct equity and debt claims and can make up a portfolio of money and direct securities conforming to our preferences. Moreover, the operation of a financial intermediary is far from costless in real terms. It requires the use of many types of labor, office space, computers and other equipment, communications services, and so on. The fact that financial intermediaries not only survive under these circumstances but have also achieved a dominant position in the financial system suggests that they must provide some product or service that others value and cannot produce for themselves, or can produce only at higher cost. The central purpose of this chapter is to explore the economic bases for the success, and sometimes the failure, of financial intermediaries.

CHARACTERISTICS OF
DIRECT AND INDIRECT SECURITIES

We noted earlier that the characteristics of the indirect financial claims issued by a financial intermediary typically differ significantly from those of the direct securities that it acquires and holds, and that this enables intermediaries to intermediate between the preferences of issuers and the preferences of asset holders. Issuers are enabled to issue direct securities conforming more closely to their preferences, and ultimate suppliers of funds are enabled to acquire indirect financial claims that conform more closely to their preferred combinations of income, safety, and liquidity.

The differences between the characteristics of the claims issued by an intermediary and those of the direct securities that it acquires and holds are of several kinds.

1. Differences in denominations. An intermediary can buy direct securities in denominations preferred by the issuers, which are often large, and issue claims on itself in denominations tailored to the differing preferences of ultimate savers. For example, a depository intermediary will create deposit claims in any denomination of a dollar or more. In other cases, intermediaries acquire a large number of small claims, such as consumer debts, and issue claims in larger denominations.
2. Differences in maturity. An intermediary can acquire direct claims conforming to the maturity preferences of the issuers and create claims conforming to the differing maturity preferences of asset

holders. In most cases the maturities of the claims issued by intermediaries are shorter than those of their financial assets. In some cases, however, the reverse is true. For example, a consumer finance company may issue long-term bonds, which will appeal to holders who prefer an assured fixed rate of return over a long period, and use the proceeds to buy a succession of short-term or intermediate-term consumer loans.

3. Differences in combinations of income, safety, and liquidity. A major function of financial intermediaries is to create safety and liquidity, and to do so at lower costs in terms of forgone net income than could be achieved by individual asset holders. The gain to asset holders is obvious; the gain to issuers of direct securities is that they are enabled to issue riskier and less liquid claims at a lower penalty in terms of financing costs.

ECONOMIES OF SPECIALIZATION AND SCALE

The success of financial intermediaries is based on various economies of specialization and scale. To illustrate the principles involved, we shall assume that an intermediary has acquired financial assets worth at least a few million dollars by issuing its indirect financial claims to at least a few thousand holders, and then we shall compare the results with those that would ensue if each individual holder had acquired and held directly his own portfolio of money and direct securities. Note that an intermediary with only a few million in assets and a few thousand holders of claims against it is indeed small as compared with many existing intermediaries with hundreds of millions, and even billions, in assets and hundreds of thousands of holders of financial claims against them.

The economies of specialization and scale in a financial intermediary are of many kinds. For example, they apply to safekeeping of securities; enforcement of claims against issuers of direct securities, such as collecting monthly payments on consumer installment loans and home mortgages and seeing that mortgagors pay their taxes and maintain adequate insurance; and performing large amounts of accounting and other paperwork. However, the following sections will concentrate on economies of specialization and scale as they relate to four aspects of financial operations:

1. economic and financial intelligence
2. transactions costs

3. diversification of assets
4. offsetting inflows and outflows of funds.

ECONOMIC AND FINANCIAL INTELLIGENCE

The production, analysis, dissemination, and use of the economic and financial intelligence required for rational decision making are not costless, and they involve large elements of fixed costs. Once the cost is incurred and the intelligence acquired, the latter can serve as well for a large volume of transactions as for only a small volume. Individual holders of direct securities, especially those who have only a modest amount of funds and wish to hold a diversified portfolio, find these processes expensive. Most individuals are not experts in financial analysis, and even those who are find the costs of a thorough analysis, stated as a percentage of the values of their portfolios, to be high. To avoid or reduce these costs, they often make decisions on the basis of only limited knowledge.

A financial intermediary is in a better position to exploit economies of specialization and scale in acquiring and using information. It can employ experts in the various branches of financial analysis, purchase financial intelligence from others, analyze and compare many different direct securities, and spread the costs over its large volume of assets. Managements of financial intermediaries are prone to exaggerate, sometimes grossly, the quality of their financial intelligence and their superiority in forecasting. However, they should be able to do a better job than many individual holders, and to do so at a lower cost per dollar of assets. To the extent that this is done, a financial intermediary can achieve a better yield-risk combination on its portfolio than individual holders could achieve for themselves.

TRANSACTIONS COSTS

Transactions costs are incurred in acquiring, holding, and selling direct securities. For example, a buyer must make a decision to buy, communicate with a broker or dealer, and pay a brokerage fee. When he wishes to sell, he must again communicate with a broker or dealer and pay another brokerage fee. Some of these costs are fixed in total amount, or at best do not vary proportionally with the value involved in a transaction. For example, the structure of brokerage fees typically includes a minimum dollar charge plus a percentage of value that declines as the value of the transaction rises. Thus, the fee might be $20 plus 2 percent of the first $1000 of value plus 1 percent of the next $5000 of value plus 1/2 percent of the next $10,000 of value plus 1/4 pecent of the value in excess of $16,000. The results of this fee structure are shown in Table 5—1. In this case, the fee is 4 percent on a $1000 transaction but only 0.3 percent on a $1 million transaction. The results on this fee structure are shown in Table 15—1.

Stated as a percentage of the value per year that the security is held, transactions costs decline as the holding period is lengthened and increase as the holding period is shortened. For example, in the illustration above the brokerage fee on a $1000 purchase was $40, or 4 percent. Stated as a percentage of value for each year the security is held, the fee will be only 1 percent if the security is held four years, 4 percent if it is held only one year, and 8 percent if it is held only half a year. This suggests how expensive it can be for an individual to buy a small amount of direct securities and hold them for only a short period.

A financial intermediary can reduce transactions costs far below the total that would be incurred if each individual supplier of funds acquired and held his own portfolio of direct securities. This is partly because the intermediary, able to buy and sell in large lots, can buy transactions services at lower prices. To a far greater extent, it is because the intermediary can reduce greatly the necessary volume of transactions in direct securities. This is because an intermediary need purchase securities only to the extent that its total assets increase and it need sell securities only to the extent that its total assets decline. And the phenomenon of at-least-partially-offsetting inflows and outflows virtually assures that the net increase or net decrease of an intermediary's total assets during any period will be small in relation to its total assets and also in relation to its gross outflows and gross inflows of funds. During any period, some claimants against an intermediary, perhaps

Table 5—1   **Hypothetical Brokerage Fees on
Transactions of Differing Values**

Value of Transaction	Broker's Fee in Dollars	Broker's Fee as a Percentage of the Value of the Transaction
$ 1,000	$ 40	4.0
6,000	90	1.5
16,000	140	0.9
100,000	360	0.4
1,000,000	2600	0.3

many of them, will withdraw funds, but such outflows will be at least partially, or perhaps fully or more than fully, offset by inflows from others. If outflows and inflows balance exactly, leaving the intermediary's total assets unchanged, the intermediary need not make any purchases or sales, no matter how great its gross inflows and gross outflows may be. In any case, its purchases or sales need not exceed its net inflows or net outflows.

DIVERSIFICATION OF ASSETS

We found earlier that in a world of uncertainty, diversification of assets is a useful method of reducing risk and of achieving a better combination of income, safety, and liquidity. Many households and entities other than financial intermediaries form their own diversified portfolios of money and direct securities. However, those with only modest amounts of funds at their disposal find it inconvenient and costly to achieve a high degree of diversification without recourse to a financial intermediary. Since direct securities are not infinitely divisible but are available only in discrete units, many individuals could buy only a few different issues even if they bought only one unit of each. They would also encounter high costs of gathering and analyzing information about many different issues and high transactions costs. A financial intermediary, with large amounts of assets, can diversify more effectively and much more economically.

Since diversification plays an important role in portfolio management, and in the usefulness of financial intermediaries, a few further comments are in order. The efficacy of diversification in reducing risk does not depend solely on the number of different issues in a portfolio. It depends also on the diversity of behavior of the incomes and values of the different issues. Increasing the number of issues held would not reduce risk at all if changes in all of them were *perfectly positively correlated*—if all invariably changed in the same direction and in the same proportion. In this case, the risk on the entire portfolio, measured in percentage terms, would be the same as the risk on each issue alone. The dream of every diversifier is to find different issues whose incomes and values are *perfectly negatively correlated*. That is, increases or decreases on one issue are invariably accompanied by opposite and equal changes on the other. In such cases, the combination of two issues, each highly risky, would result in a riskless portfolio. Unfortunately, it is virtually impossible to find issues with perfect negative correlation, for all are subject to some common forces to which they respond in some-what similar ways. However, diversification can reduce risk even in the absence of perfect negative correlation; all that is required is that the behavior of the issues be less than perfectly positively correlated—that their behavior be somewhat diverse. This condition is commonly met.

The incomes and values of different issues respond in somewhat diverse ways to forces that affect the entire economy. A few examples will illustrate the point.

1. A general rise of interest rates. We have already seen that prices of long-term debt claims fall more than the prices of short maturities under such circumstances. A rise of interest rates also tends to lower the prices of common stocks and other equity claims, but the very forces that induced the rise of interest rates, such as general prosperity, often raise the dollar earnings accru-ing to equity claims at least enough to prevent their prices from falling.
2. A general business recession or depression. Since business declines are usually accompanied by declining interest rates, the prices of outstanding debt claims tend to rise unless the decline of business is serious enough to bring a significant rise of default risks. On the other hand, both the incomes and prices of equity claims tend to decline. The declines are usually largest on issues by firms in cyclically sensitive industries, such as metals and heavy capital goods, and least on issues by firms in more stable industries, such as food manufacturing and public utilities.
3. General price inflation. The prices of outstanding debt obligations, with their fixed dollar amounts of interest and principal, are likely to fall because inflation is usually accompanied by rising interest rates. On the other hand, both the earnings and prices of equity claims are likely, but not certain, to rise.

Another reason for diverse behavior is that some issues and is-suers are affected by forces that do not affect others, or affect others to only a lesser extent. For example, an increase of demands for air condi-tioning may raise earnings of electric utilities and manufacturers of air conditioning equipment with only minor effects on other industries. A regional catastrophe, such as a drought or a flood, may have serious effects on households, business firms, and governmental units in the region but only small effects elsewhere. Also, of course, individual is-suers of securities are subject to diverse forces. For example, some families suffer serious losses of income while others prosper, some governmental units get into financial difficulties while others have surpluses, and some business managements deteriorate while others improve.

In short, the success of diversification as a means of reducing risk and of achieving a better combination of income, safety, and liquidity in a portfolio depends not only on the number of issues held but also on the extent to which the risks on the different issues tend to offset each other.

OFFSETTING INFLOWS AND OUTFLOWS

We found earlier that the phenomenon of at-least-partially-offsetting inflows and outflows enables an intermediary to achieve large economies in its transactions costs. It also accounts in large part for the ability of an intermediary to issue financial claims against itself that are more liquid than the direct securities that it holds. An intermediary can do this because it expects that any net outflow that it may experience will be equal to no more than a small fraction of its total assets.

Outflows from a financial intermediary are of two major types: payments of interest or other income on outstanding claims against it; and withdrawals by those who had previously entrusted funds to it. Inflows of funds are of three principal types.

1. Proceeds from issues of new claims against the intermediary.
2. Income on the intermediary's assets. (Both of the above tend to increase the total assets of the intermediary.)
3. Proceeds from maturing direct securities held by the intermediary, such as maturing debt claims and monthly receipts of payments on consumer installment debt and amortized mortgages.

All three types of inflows help an intermediary meet outflows without selling direct securities before they mature.

It is, of course, possible that an intermediary would experience large net withdrawals in some periods and large net inflows in others. This risk may be considerable if there are only a few suppliers of funds to the intermediary and if the suppliers of funds have quite similar income, expenditure, and saving patterns. However, such an outcome becomes increasingly less probable as the number of suppliers of funds to the intermediary rises into the thousands or even tens of thousands and as the suppliers have diverse income-expenditure patterns.

An intermediary bases its forecasts of outflows and inflows on many different types of information: its own past experience, the past experience of other intermediaries of the same or similar types, knowledge of the maturity schedules of its issues of indirect securities that have maturity dates, knowledge of the maturity schedule of its assets, forecasts of the income and saving of actual and potential holders of its indirect securities, and so on. However, such information does not enable an intermediary to forecast with certainty its future outflows and inflows; at best, the intermediary can only form a subjective probability distribution of possible outcomes and calculate both a mean expected net outflow or net inflow and some measure of risk, such as the standard deviation.

In some cases an intermediary can forecast with only a small degree of uncertainty that its inflows will exceed its outflows for a considerable period. For example, a life insurance company may have experienced an annual growth rate in its total assets of at least 5 percent during recent years and may calculate that premium receipts on its outstanding annuity and insurance policies plus income on its assets and proceeds from maturing assets will greatly exceed its payments to policy holders for at least 10 more years. Or a depository type of intermediary, such as a savings and loan association or a mutual savings bank, may have experienced an annual growth rate in its total deposits of at least 7 percent during recent years and see no reason to expect a lesser growth rate in the future. Such an intermediary may well decide to rely solely on future inflows to meet withdrawals and hold all, or almost all, of its assets in long-term, illiquid assets, such as long-term corporate bonds or mortgages on homes and other real estate.

In many cases, however, the management of an intermediary faces some probability that withdrawals will exceed inflows, which would decrease its total assets. For example, its expected probabilities may be as follows: The mean expected outcome is that inflows will exceed outflows enough to increase its total assets by 4 percent; there is an 85 percent probability that its total assets will rise or remain unchanged; a 10 percent probability that outflows will exceed inflows enough to reduce its total assets by as much as 5 percent; a 1 percent probability that total assets will decline by as much as 10 percent; and virtually a zero probability that its total assets will be reduced more than 10 percent. With such expectations, even a highly conservative management would probably choose to hold at least 90 percent, and perhaps more, of its assets in high-yielding, illiquid claims.

Since there is some probability, though only a small one, that outflows will exceed inflows, and since failure to meet obligations promptly and fully would spell disaster, a prudent management will arrange sources of liquidity equal to some fraction of its total assets, such as 5 to 10 percent. As noted earlier, an intermediary has two major sources of liquidity to cover any net outflows that may occur— borrowing facilities and its holdings of money and other liquid assets.[1] It is strongly impelled to buy the desired amount of liquidity at the lowest possible cost in terms of interest outlays, transactions costs, and forgone income. Though money itself is perfectly liquid and involves no transactions costs, it yields no explicit income. Highly liquid claims against others do yield an income, but acquiring and selling them may involve transactions costs. A major advantage of borrowing facilities as a source of liquidity is that interest costs are incurred only if borrowing proves to be necessary. Their potential disadvantages are that they may not prove to be reliable under adverse conditions and that borrowing costs may be high.

An intermediary's choices among these various sources of liquidity depend on its estimate of the probability and timing of net outflows, the height of transactions costs and yields on liquid earning assets, and the reliability and costs of borrowing. In practice, most intermediaries hold little money beyond their needs for current transactions purposes unless they are required by law to do so, and they rely much more heavily on holdings of liquid earning assets and on borrowing facilities.

Up to this point we have dealt with principles common to all types of financial intermediaries. We turn now to some differences in the policies and practices of the various types of intermediaries and some of the reasons for these differences.

POLICIES RELATING TO LIABILITIES AND ASSETS OF AN INTERMEDIARY

As we have already seen, a financial intermediary participates in financial markets in two principal roles:

1. As a demander of funds through its issues of indirect securities. Claims against an intermediary must compete with many other types of assets for a place in the portfolios of ultimate suppliers of funds—with money itself, with claims against other financial intermediaries, and with a wide variety of direct equity and debt

[1] See pp. 44–45 above.

securities. The amount of financial claims that an intermediary can issue and keep outstanding, and therefore the amount of assets that it can accumulate, depends on the preferences of the public and on the income-safety-liquidity characteristics of its issues as compared with these characteristics of competing financial assets. An intermediary therefore faces many important policy problems in determining the characteristics of its issues. For example, it must determine whether to issue debt claims, or equity claims, or various combinations of both; the maturities of its debt issues; and the amount of income to offer holders of its various issues.

2. As a supplier of funds through its purchases of financial claims against others. In acquiring such securities, an intermediary competes with many other purchasers and holders—with other intermediaries and with households and other bidders for direct securities. Policy makers in the intermediary must therefore decide what types of securities to acquire and in what proportions and, where they have some leeway, what prices they will bid for the various types of securities.

INTERRELATIONS OF ASSET MANAGEMENT AND LIABILITY MANAGEMENT

An intermediary's decisions relating to the characteristics of its assets and of its own issues of indirect securities are interrelated in many ways. We shall discuss only a few of these at this point:

1. Income on its assets and income paid on its issues. The average rate of return realized by an intermediary on its assets sets a limit on the rates of return that it can offer to holders of claims against it, and the latter is one determinant, but only one, of its ability to attract funds.
2. Composition of its assets and liabilities. An intermediary's risks of insolvency and illiquidity depend on the composition of its assets, the composition of its issues, and the relationship between the two. Both the market and default risks on its assets may be minimal if its assets are composed wholly of short-term debt claims, but at least the market risk will be higher as the proportion of long-term debt claims is increased. The risk of fluctuations in value will be greatest if the portfolio is composed almost wholly of common stocks. An intermediary's risks of insolvency and il-

liquidity also depend on the characteristics of the claims that it issues. For example, it can avoid risks of insolvency and illiquidity entirely, no matter how risky its assets, by issuing only equity claims that it does not promise to redeem at any time. By issuing long-term debt claims, it protects its liquidity but increases its risk of insolvency. By issuing only debt claims payable on demand or on very short notice, it maximizes its risks of both insolvency and illiquidity. A gross mismatching of assets and liabilities can be disastrous.

These few examples suggest that arriving at optimal compositions of assets and liabilities is no easy task for an intermediary concerned with its solvency-liquidity position as well as its net income.

DIFFERENTIATION OF INDIRECT SECURITIES

As noted earlier, portfolio preferences differ markedly among ultimate suppliers of funds, and a given asset holder usually wants to include in his portfolio claims with differing income-safety-liquidity characteristics. It is therefore hardly surprising that financial intermediaries differentiate their issues to appeal to such differing demands. Many individual intermediaries issue two or more types of claims with significantly differing income-safety-liquidity characteristics, and different types of intermediaries issue different types and mixes of claims. Some cater to demands for a perfectly liquid asset even if it yields no income; commercial bank issues of demand deposits are the outstanding example. Some cater to demands for high, but not perfect, liquidity plus income. Examples are the depository intermediaries and the so-called liquid asset funds that issue short-term claims against portfolios composed entirely of the safest types of short-term debt claims. Some cater to demands for a fixed rate of return over a long period. These include bond funds that issue claims against a diversified portfolio of long-term bonds. Some cater to desires to minimize income taxes. The major example is municipal bond funds, which hold diversified portfolios of tax-exempt state and local government bonds and issue claims whose income is also exempt from federal income taxes. And some cater to demands for high mean expected income even if this entails a high degree of risk. An outstanding example is the "go-go" investment companies that issue equity claims against a diversified portfolio of speculative common stocks believed to have unusually high growth potentials—which often remain potential. It is almost literally true, but not quite, that financial intermediaries as a group offer something to suit every taste.

PROBLEMS OF MAINTAINING SOLVENCY AND LIQUIDITY

Because of the very nature of their operations, financial intermediaries are subject to risks of insolvency and illiquidity. This is especially true of depository types of intermediaries and others that issue primarily debt claims that are fixed in terms of dollars. As already noted, an intermediary cannot forecast with certainty either the future values of its income and assets or its future outflows and inflows; it must operate on the basis of probabilities. It could, of course, play it safe, or almost safe, being always prepared to withstand the most adverse possible outcome. Thus, it could hold only money and the safest and most liquid types of direct securities, and it could issue only equity claims which it does not promise to redeem at any time. Such a policy would virtually assure lack of success. The intermediary could not attract funds, and it could not perform its valuable economic function of intermediation. To be effective, an intermediary must assume risks, and with risk comes the possibility that highly improbable adverse outcomes will actually happen.

Because the failure or malfunctioning of intermediaries can have serious social consequences, the government has intervened in many ways. At this point we shall mention only briefly a few of these:

1. Various laws and regulations requiring intermediaries to make full and fair disclosure of all facts materially relevant to their condition and operations.
2. Laws against fraud and malfeasance by managements of intermediaries.
3. Laws and regulations designed to prevent gross mismatching of an intermediary's assets and liabilities.
4. Insurance of some of the assets held by financial intermediaries. Outstanding examples are the insurance of home mortgages by the Federal Housing Administration (FHA) and the Veterans Administration (VA); insurance of some loans on agricultural commodities by the Commodity Credit Corporation (CCC); and insurance of loans to foreigners by the Export-Import Bank (Eximbank).

5. Insurance of claims against financial intermediaries. Government-sponsored institutions insure the first $40,000 in each account at most of the depository intermediaries.
6. Provision of "super financial intermediaries" to aid other financial intermediaries by lending to them or purchasing assets from them. Among these are the Federal Reserve, which lends to commercial banks and occasionally to others, and buys assets from banks, other intermediaries, and the public. Though the Federal Reserve creates the money that it provides, the other super intermediaries acquire funds by issuing interest-bearing financial claims against themselves. Among these are the Federal Home Loan Banks, which lend to savings and loan associations and some other holders of home mortgages, and the Federal Intermediate Credit Banks, which lend to institutions that make intermediate-term loans to farmers.

Though private intermediaries often complain about government restrictions, in some cases with good reason, there can be no doubt that the net effect of government intervention has been to promote their growth.

GOVERNMENT-SPONSORED FINANCIAL INTERMEDIARIES

Up to this point we have concentrated largely on private financial intermediaries, but we shall now note briefly that the principles of financial intermediation are also employed by institutions sponsored by federal, state, and local governments. Only the most important of these will be mentioned.

FEDERALLY SPONSORED INTERMEDIARIES

In addition to the three types of super financial intermediaries already mentioned, the federal government has sponsored in varying degrees several other types of intermediaries. Among these are the following:

1. the Federal Land Banks, which issue long-term bonds and acquire farm mortgages
2. the Banks for Cooperatives, which issue intermediate- and short-term debts and lend to various types of agricultural cooperatives

3. the Government National Mortgage Association (GNMA), which acquires funds from the Treasury and by issuing its own securities and buys residential mortgages
4. the Federal National Mortgage Association (FNMA), which issues intermediate- and long-term bonds and acquires residential mortgages
5. the Federal Home Loan Mortgage Corporation (FHLMC), which acquires funds from the Federal Home Loan Banks—which borrow funds in the market—and buys home mortgages.

Though most of the securities issued by these federally sponsored intermediaries are not guaranteed by the government, their acceptability is greatly increased by their government sponsorship, and they are generally considered to be almost as safe and liquid as direct Treasury issues of comparable maturities.

INTERMEDIARIES SPONSORED BY STATE AND LOCAL GOVERNMENTS

The various state and local governments sponsor numerous types of intermediaries, among which are the following:

1. Pension funds for teachers and other public employees. These receive contributions from employers and employees and acquire diversified portfolios of mortgages, bonds, and common stocks. Some of these funds are very large.
2. Housing finance agencies, established by some states and municipalities. These issue tax-exempt debt obligations and use the proceeds to finance housing for low- and medium-income families.
3. Dormitory authorities, which issue tax-exempt bonds and lend to colleges and universities for dormitory construction.
4. Various types of industrial development authorities, some established by states and others by local governments. These issue tax-exempt bonds and use the proceeds to attract private industry, either by lending to firms or by acquiring land and plants for their use.

IMPORTANCE OF PRIVATE FINANCIAL INTERMEDIARIES IN THE FINANCIAL SYSTEM

Private financial intermediaries as a group have become a major, and even dominant, element in the financial system. They hold a huge stock

Table 5 – 2	**Assets of Major Types of Private Financial Intermediaries, End of 1975** *(assets in billions of dollars)*		
Type of Financial Intermediary	Total Finan- cial Assets	Principal Type of Claims Issued	Principal Type of Claims Held
Commercial banks	$ 873.6	Deposits	Debts
Mutual savings banks	121.1	Deposits	Debts
Savings and loan associations	338.4	Deposits	Debts
Credit unions	37.0	Deposits	Debts
Life insurance companies	279.9	Insurance and annuity policies	Debts
Other insurance companies	77.4	Insurance policies	Equities and debts
Private pension funds	148.9	Pension claims	Equities and debts
Finance companies	98.4	Debts	Home mortgages and consumer loans
Open-end investment companies	42.2	Equities	Equities
Total	$1818.5		
Addendum: Assets of four types of depository intermediaries	$1370.1		

Source: Board of Governors of the Federal Reserve System, *Flow of Funds Accounts, 1946–1975,* December 1976.

of financial claims, they provide a large fraction of the stock of financial claims held by households, and they purchase and hold a large fraction of the annual flows of new issues of direct securities.

Table 5 – 2 indicates that by the end of 1975 the principal types of private financial intermediaries had accumulated a huge stock of financial assets aggregating more than $1.8 trillion. Of this $1.8 trillion, about $1370 billion, or 75 percent, was held by the four major types of depository intermediaries; the other intermediaries held $448 billion, or 25 percent of the total.

Table 5 – 3 shows the percentages of outstanding direct debt and equity claims held by private financial intermediaries at the end of 1975. "Direct debt claims outstanding" refers to all debt claims except those against financial intermediaries. The total of these was $3243 billion, of

Table 5—3   **Outstanding Direct Debt and Equity Claims Against Nonfinancial Entities in the United States and Holdings by Private Financial Intermediaries, December 31, 1975**
(amounts in billions of dollars)

Type of Direct Security	Col. 1 Amount Out-standing	Col. 2 Holdings by Private Financial Inter-mediaries	Col. 2 as Percentage of Col. 1
DIRECT DEBT CLAIMS			
U.S. government (net)	$ 503.8	$ 120.7	24.0
State and local government	229.6	147.4	64.4
Corporate and foreign bonds	254.3	248.8	97.8
Mortgages	795.0	616.8	77.6
Consumer credit	197.3	166.4	84.3
Other direct debt	409.0	365.2	89.3
Total direct debt	$2389.0	$1665.3	69.7
CORPORATE SHARES	$ 854.7	$ 194.7	22.8
Grand total of direct debt and corporate shares	$3243.7	$1860.0	57.3

Source: Board of Governors of the Federal Reserve System, *Flow of Funds Accounts*.

which financial intermediaries held 57.3 percent. However, the percentages held by financial intermediaries differed markedly from one type of direct financial claim to another. Financial intermediaries held only 22.8 percent of the value of corporate shares but 69.7 percent of total direct debt claims. They held nearly 84 percent of total private direct debt, but only smaller percentages of the direct debts of governmental units. Many individuals and nonfinancial business firms prefer to hold obligations of the federal government directly because of their high degrees of safety and liquidity, and many like direct debt claims against state and local governments because income on them is exempt from the federal income tax, and in some circumstances from state income taxes.

Table 5—4 shows the magnitude of household financial assets at the end of 1975, the composition of these assets, and the role of financial intermediaries as providers of financial claims for household portfolios. The total financial assets of households on that date amounted to about

$2497 billion. Households as a group elected to hold about $1475 billion, or 59.1 percent of their total financial assets, in the form of claims against financial intermediaries. About 64 percent of these consisted of currency, checking deposits, and savings accounts at depository types of intermediaries. The bulk of the remainder consisted of claims against life insurance companies and pension funds.

Household holdings of direct securities amounted to nearly $1022 billion, or 40.9 percent of their total financial assets. Of these, about 62 percent were in the form of shares in nonfinancial corporations, and only 38 percent were in the form of direct debt claims. Of the total financial assets of households, less than 16 percent were in the form of direct debt claims, and only 8 percent were in the form of direct debt claims against nongovernmental entities.

Table 5 — 4   **Household Financial Assets, December 31, 1975**
(amounts in billions of dollars)

Type of Financial Asset	Amount	Percent of Total
Total	$2496.9	100.0
CLAIMS AGAINST FINANCIAL INTERMEDIARIES		
Demand deposits and currency	165.6	6.6
Time and savings deposits;		
at commercial banks	350.7	14.0
at savings institutions	425.6	17.0
Life insurance reserves	164.6	6.6
Pension fund reserves	368.6	14.8
Total claims against financial intermediaries	$1475.1	59.1
DIRECT SECURITIES		
Corporate shares	630.5	25.3
Direct debts		
U.S. government	123.4	4.9
State and local governments	74.2	3.0
Corporate and foreign bonds	65.9	2.6
Mortgages	72.7	2.9
Other direct debt	55.1	2.2
Total direct debt	391.3	15.7
Total direct securities	$1021.8	40.9

Source: Board of Governors of the Federal Reserve System, *Flow of Funds Accounts.*

Some of the most surprising facts in Tables 5 — 3 and 5 — 4 relate to the shares of nonfinancial business corporations. Of the $854.7 billion of these outstanding, only 22.8 percent were held by financial intermediaries, while about 74 percent were held by households. The latter elected to hold 25.3 percent of their total financial assets in the form of these direct equities and only 2 percent in the form of equity claims against financial intermediaries. In view of the riskiness of many direct corporate shares, one might have expected to find the reverse—that households would shun direct equities and would hold instead equity claims against financial intermediaries. There are some trends in this direction, and larger changes may occur in the future.

The present situation is explainable in part by the fact that trust departments of banks are not considered to be financial intermediaries and that their holdings of common stock for the accounts of individuals are included in household holdings of direct equity claims. At the end of 1975 these amounted to at least $140 billion. However, the large household holdings of direct equities are also partly explainable in terms of the distribution of total wealth among households and the asset preferences of high-wealth families. As is well known, there are great inequalities in the distribution of income among households and even greater inequalities in the distribution of wealth. Households in the high-income and high-wealth brackets hold a very large fraction of all financial assets and an even larger fraction of equity claims. Several conditions combine to make such families willing to bear the risks involved in holding direct equities.

1. Ability to bear risk. With large wealth and also, in many cases, much income from other sources, they can incur losses without serious hardship.
2. Preferential tax treatment of capital gains. With their ordinary income subject to high marginal tax rates, many of these holders prefer to take their rewards in the form of capital gains, on which tax rates are much lower.
3. Their relatively low valuation of the diversification and other services offered by financial intermediaries. With a large volume of funds at its disposal, a wealthy household can, if it wishes, form and manage economically its own diversified portfolio of direct equities. Moreover, such a family may not view with favor some of the effects of a high degree of diversification. It will, of course, welcome the decreased risk of loss resulting from diversification

but not the decreased chance of extraordinarily high income or capital gains. Diversification tends to make actual outcomes cluster closer to the mean expected outcome.

4. Other reasons for holding direct equities rather than equity claims against financial intermediaries. Some households elect to hold shares in specific nonfinancial corporations in order to exercise some control over the corporations, and officers and employees of a corporation are often expected, and sometimes required, to hold some of its shares.

The data in Tables 5−2 to 5−4 related to outstanding stocks of securities on stated dates. Table 5−5 shows some relevant flows during the years 1970−1976 inclusive. Line 1 shows the total amounts of funds raised in financial markets by the nonfinancial sectors during each year, and Line 2 indicates the amounts of these funds advanced by private financial intermediaries. As shown in Line 3, the percentages of the total advanced by private intermediaries ranged between 58.3 and 86.5. The remainder was advanced by government agencies and foreign sources and by private domestic nonfinancial investors.

In summary, the above data support our earlier statement that private financial intermediaries have come to play a crucial role in the

Table 5−5   **Total Funds Raised in Financial Markets by the Nonfinancial Sectors, and Funds Advanced by Private Financial Intermediaries, 1970−1976**
(in billions of dollars)

	1970	1971	1972	1973	1974	1975	1976
1. Total funds raised in financial markets by the nonfinancial sectors	$94.9	$139.6	$166.4	$202.0	$189.6	$205.6	$268.3
2. Funds advanced by private financial intermediaries	77.0	109.7	149.4	164.9	126.3	119.9	187.3
3. Line 2 as percentage of Line 1	81.1	78.6	86.5	81.6	66.6	58.3	69.8

Source: *Federal Reserve Bulletin,* November 1976, pp. A56 −57, and Board of Governors of the Federal Reserve System, *Flow of Funds Accounts.*
Note: The above data do not include equity issues.

financial system. They hold more than half of all outstanding direct securities. They supply more than half of all the financial assets held by households. And each year they supply much more than half of all funds raised in financial markets by the nonfinancial sectors. Thus flows of funds from ultimate suppliers to ultimate users are largely flows through financial intermediaries. For these reasons, intermediaries play critical roles in the allocation of scarce funds and real resources among their alternative uses, in the macroeconomic behavior of the economy, and in the rate of economic growth.

CONCLUSION

This chapter has described in general terms the principal reasons why financial intermediaries were invented and have grown to become a major, and even dominant, element in the financial system. They have achieved this status because, through various economies of specialization and scale, they provide more economically services that are valued by both issuers of direct securities and ultimate suppliers of funds. Though their economies of specialization and scale are of many kinds, we stressed their greater ability to accumulate and use economic and financial intelligence in decision making, their ability to reduce transactions costs, their greater and more economical reduction of risk through more effective diversification of assets, and their ability to create liquidity because of the phenomenon of at-least-partially-offsetting inflows and outflows.

Though we have stressed the principles, functions, and problems common to all types of intermediaries, we have also noted briefly some of the differences among the various types of intermediaries and some reasons for such differences. The next two chapters will deal more specifically and in more detail with the principal types of intermediaries.

SELECTED READINGS

I. **Pioneering work on the theory of financial intermediaries**

Gurley, J. G., and Shaw, E. S. *Money in a Theory of Finance.* Washington, D.C.: Brookings, 1960.

II. **Other extensive treatments of financial intermediaries**

Brill, D. H., and Ulrey, A. "The Role of Financial Intermediaries in U.S. Capital Markets." *Federal Reserve Bulletin*, January 1967, pp. 18–31.

Goldsmith, R. W. *Financial Institutions.* New York: Random House, 1968.
———. *The Flow of Capital Funds in the Postwar Economy.* New York: National Bureau of Economic Research, 1965.

III. Data on the financial assets and liabilities of financial intermediaries

Flow-of-funds accounts published periodically by the Board of Governors of the Federal Reserve System. Some data are also published in the monthly issues of the *Federal Reserve Bulletin.*

MONETARY
INTERMEDIARIES

This chapter will concentrate on one class of financial intermediaries—the monetary intermediaries. The principal monetary intermediaries in the United States are the commercial banks and the Federal Reserve System, though we shall later mention others that play lesser monetary roles. These are financial intermediaries because they buy and hold financial claims—mostly direct financial claims—against others, and they are monetary institutions because they create and issue indirect financial claims against themselves that are so safe and liquid that they make up most of our money supply. The commercial banks issue demand, or checking, deposit claims that make up about three-fourths of our money supply, and most of our paper money is in the form of Federal Reserve notes, which are created and issued by the Federal Reserve banks.

We shall adopt an evolutionary approach and attempt to identify the major forces that have changed the forms of money that we use. For example, we assumed in an earlier chapter that the only type of money invented and used in our simple society was full-bodied commodity money in the form of gold and silver coins. This was a reasonable assumption, for most societies prefer such types of money during their early stages of development. The task of the monetary authority in such a system is simple; the authority accepts all the precious metal offered to it and mints it into coins, thereby certifying the weight and purity of the commodity included in the coins. However, our present system includes no full-bodied money; almost all of our money today is in the form of debt money created and issued by the monetary intermediaries. Our purpose in the following pages is to explain why such changes have come about.

EVOLUTION OF MONETARY FORMS

We found earlier that the invention and use of even a simple type of commodity money, such as gold and silver coins, was a great advance, enabling a society to obviate the diseconomies of pure barter and to achieve greater transactions and allocational efficiencies in exchange processes. However, such a simple monetary system was still flawed by disadvantages and diseconomies that would inevitably, sooner or later, provide strong incentives to develop other monetary forms to supplement, and later supplant, full-bodied commodity moneys as a medium of payments.

DISECONOMIES OF FULL-BODIED COMMODITY MONEYS

The main disadvantages of full-bodied moneys are the following:

1. The high real cost of the commodity included in the coins. The necessary gold and silver could be acquired only through domestic production or by net exports of other things, both of which require the use of labor and other scarce resources.
2. The cost of maintaining the quality of coins. Both silver and gold coins, and especially the latter, were subject to abrasion in ordinary use. In addition, many found it profitable to abuse the coins. They "sweated" the coins by shaking them in a leather bag, filed their surfaces, pared their edges, and cut notches in them. Anyone accepting such lightweight coins at face value ran the risk that others would accept them only at a discount based on their deficiency in weight. Frequent recoinages were necessary to maintain the quality of coins.
3. Risks of loss, theft, and robbery. Every society has its thieves and robbers who, whatever their deficiencies in social ethics, are acutely aware of the advantages of acquiring an asset that is difficult to identify as stolen property and that is generally acceptable in payments. These risks are serious for households, merchants, and others without security guards and adequate strongboxes.

4. The high costs and hazards of making payments over long distances. To transport gold and silver long distances over land or sea was expensive in terms of manpower and transportation facilities. Moreover, the transporters and their money were subject to the hazards of piracy at sea and theft and robbery on land.
5. The inconvenience and cost of counting coins in transactions of large value. This disadvantage is compounded if the weight and purity of each coin must be checked.
6. The absence of interest or any other explicit return on such money.
7. Dissatisfaction with the behavior of the total supply or stock of money when the latter was limited to the supply of gold and silver available for monetary purposes.

Such disadvantages and diseconomies of full-bodied commodity moneys provided strong incentives for holders to accept other forms of money and for issuers, both governmental and private, to invent and issue other types of money.

MONETARY INNOVATIONS NOT INVOLVING BANKS

Governments introduced several new types of money that did not involve the invention and use of banks. For example, some issued *representative full-bodied money.* This was paper money fully backed by an equal value of gold or silver coins or of bullion held in government vaults. It did not, of course, reduce the real cost of acquiring gold and silver, but it did reduce wear and tear on coins and the need for frequent recoinages, and it provided a type of money that was less expensive, but not less hazardous, to transport. An important long-run effect of this innovation was to accustom people to using paper money as an actual medium of payments.

Governments also issued *token coins,* especially in the smaller denominations. These were made of such base metals as lead, zinc, copper, and nickel, and their face values were usually far above the market value of their contents. Thus, their real cost and their wear and tear in use were less than those of an equivalent face amount of gold and silver coins. In issuing such coins, governments reaped a profit equal to the difference between the face values of the coins and the cost of making them.

Among the other types of money issued by governments was *fiat money*—paper money with no specific commodity content or backing. The motives for issuing such money varied from case to case. In some cases the motive was to relieve a "money shortage," which at least allegedly hampered economic activity. In other cases the motive was to increase the government's revenue. By spending small amounts for paper and printing, a government can issue fiat money with face values far above its cost of production, taking the difference as profit. Monetary history is replete with cases in which governments, hard-pressed by inadequate taxes and large expenditures for war or other purposes, seriously overissued fiat money, leading to price inflation and in some cases to worthlessness of the money. However, these lurid examples should not be allowed to obscure the fact that in many cases fiat money was issued with restraint and served efficiently as a medium of payments.

Though monetary innovations of the above types have been important, even greater innovations came with the invention and widening use of institutions that came to be called "banks."

MONETARY INNOVATIONS INVOLVING BANKS

Largely because of the hazards of loss, theft, and robbery, many merchants, wealthier households, and others came to entrust at least a part of their gold and silver to a local goldsmith, a wealthy merchant, or a money changer, who had a vault or strongbox, security guards, and a reputation for trustworthiness. At this stage, the function of the incipient banker was solely that of safekeeping the specie "deposited" with him. Let us call the banker A. Goldsmith and the typical depositor John Roe. Suppose that Roe, having deposited gold or silver with Goldsmith, later wants to make a $25 payment to Jane Wells. In the initial stage, Roe probably went to Goldsmith, withdrew the required amount of coins, and paid them to Wells. However, this required that Roe make a trip to the bank and bear the risks of loss, theft, and robbery while the coins were in his possession. Goldsmith and his depositors soon evolved more economical and less hazardous methods of payment. One was the use of a written order to pay. These are now called sight or demand drafts, or bills of exchange; the most familiar form is the bank check. The essentials of a draft, or bill of exchange, are shown in Figure 6 – 1. In this case, Roe, the *drawer*, orders Goldsmith, the *drawee*, to pay Wells, the *payee*. Since no date of payment is stated, it is understood that Goldsmith is to pay on demand or at sight. The words "or order" are important, for they indicate that Goldsmith is to pay Wells or anyone else to whom Wells may order payment. Wells can do this by *endorsing* the draft.

```
                                              Date:  July 1, 1649

     TO:  A. Goldsmith


        Pay to Jane Wells or order the sum of $25.

                                           Signed:  John Roe
```

Figure 6 – 1   **A Sight or Demand Draft or Bill of Exchange**

When Wells receives the draft in payment, she can choose among three courses of action.

1. She may withdraw coins from Goldsmith and use them as she sees fit.
2. She may surrender the draft to Goldsmith in exchange for a depositor claim against the specie held by Goldsmith. In this case the banker simply makes an entry in his books transferring the depositor claim from Roe to Wells.
3. She may endorse the draft to someone else to whom she wishes to make a payment.

The recipient then has available the three courses of action that were open to Wells. Drafts were often endorsed and transferred several times before being presented to the bank for payment or deposit.

Goldsmith and his depositors soon evolved another method of payment—the bank note. Goldsmith issued to those who left specie with him pieces of paper promising to pay stated amounts of specie. For example, a note might read: "I, Goldsmith, promise to pay to bearer on demand the sum of $X." Bank notes achieved wide circulation and usually changed hands many times before being presented to their issuers for payment.

Goldsmith-bankers and moneychanger-bankers developed in all the populous centers, and the bankers came to know each other personally and by reputation through attendance at the numerous market fairs and otherwise. They soon evolved methods of making payments over long distances that were far more economical and less hazardous than shipping gold or silver. For example, Goldsmith in London and Ambrosio in Genoa might have entered into the following types of arrangements:

1. Goldsmith agreed to honor drafts drawn on him by Ambrosio ordering payment to payees in London and vicinity, and Ambrosio agreed to honor drafts drawn on him by Goldsmith ordering payments to payees in Genoa and vicinity.
2. Though it was expected that payments made by Goldsmith for Ambrosio's account would be largely balanced by payments made by Ambrosio for Goldsmith's account, they recognized that net balances might occur at times, sometimes in favor of Goldsmith and sometimes in favor of Ambrosio. To minimize shipments of gold and silver, they agreed to settle their accounts monthly, or perhaps only once a year on the opening day of the Antwerp Fair.

Similar arrangements were made among goldsmiths and moneychangers in most of the populous centers, and bills of exchange became a principal means of transmitting payments over distances.

At this stage, the functions of the fledgling banks were solely those of safekeeping gold and silver and of providing means of payment that were cheaper and less hazardous. For these services they usually charged a fee. Holding specie equal to 100 percent of outstanding deposit and bank note claims against it, such a bank neither increased nor decreased the public's total money supply; it merely substituted one type of money for another. Suppose, for example, that the public deposits $1000 of gold and silver with Goldsmith, taking in return $1000 of claims in the form of bank notes and deposits. Goldsmith's balance sheet will appear as follows:

Assets	Liabilities
Gold and silver $1000	Bank notes and deposits $1000

The public holds $1000 less in gold and silver money, and $1000 more in the form of bank notes and deposits. The banks have not yet become financial intermediaries, for they do not hold financial claims against others.

However, the substitution of bank deposits and bank notes for gold and silver coins as actual means of payments brought several economies. It reduced wear and tear on coins, it provided cheaper and more reliable protection against theft and robbery, it reduced greatly the real costs and hazards of making distant payments, and it obviated the inconvenience of counting coins in large transactions because drafts could be drawn in the appropriate amounts. For such reasons, owners of money deposited large amounts of specie with the banks and willingly paid fees for bank services.

FRACTIONAL RESERVE BANKING

For two reasons it was virtually inevitable that banks holding specie equal to 100 percent of their deposit and note liabilities would be transformed into fractional-reserve banks. First, gold and silver held by a bank yielded no interest or other explicit income. Second, bankers gradually discovered the principle of at-least-partially-offsetting inflows and outflows. Each bank experienced specie withdrawals by its own depositors, by others to whom claims against it had been transferred, and by other banks that had received claims on it. But a bank also received inflows from its depositors as they deposited with it gold and silver and claims against other banks. Each bank discovered that net withdrawals, and therefore net decreases in its holdings of specie, were never equal to more than a small fraction, perhaps no more than 8 to 10 percent, of its outstanding note and deposit liabilities. Thus bankers came to reason as follows: "If I held gold and silver equal to only 10 percent of my note and deposit liabilities, I could still meet my promises to redeem notes and deposits on demand, and I could lend out the rest and earn an attractive interest income." The temptation was irresistible. The first loans by such bankers were probably surreptitious breaches of trust, for depositors probably expected banks to hold 100 percent specie reserves. However, the secret was soon out, and as banks earned increasing amounts of interest on their expanding loans, a banker could advertise, "We can both benefit if you leave your gold and silver with me. I will earn interest on my loans and will share the benefits with you by providing free safekeeping, by supplying you with safe and cheap methods of making payments, by enabling you to write checks for the exact amount of each payment, and by doing much of your bookkeeping for you." Many banks also offered interest on deposits. It was because of such attractions that the public came to hold a major part of its money in the form of claims against banks, and much of the available supply of gold and silver money came to be held by banks.

The development of fractional-reserve banking was a landmark in monetary and financial history. With this innovation, banks became financial intermediaries, buying and holding financial claims against others, thereby supplying funds for the use of others. They also acquired the power to increase or decrease the total money supply in the hands of the public. They could increase the total money supply by increasing their holdings of financial claims against others, and they could decrease the total money supply by reducing their holdings of financial claims against others.

To illustrate the principles involved, we shall deal with a banking system as a whole, not with individual banks, and start from a situation in which banks hold specie equal to 100 percent of their note and deposit liabilities. Their initial composite balance sheet appears as follows:

Assets	Liabilities
Gold and silver $1000	Note and deposit liabilities $1000

We shall deal with two cases of loan expansion. In Case 1, the banks buy from the public $900 worth of financial claims, either newly created financial claims or a part of the outstanding stock of such claims, and the public withdraws an equal amount of gold and silver. The balance sheet of the banks will now appear as follows:

Assets		Liabilities	
Gold and silver $ 100		Note and deposit liabilities $1000	
Loans	900		
	$1000		$1000

The public's money supply is thus increased by $900; the public still holds the $1000 of note and deposit claims against the banks and also $900 of gold and silver money formerly held by the banks as "backing" for their note and deposit liabilities. The banks feel sufficiently liquid, for they still hold specie equal to 10 percent of their liabilities. This example illustrates the principle that the banks can increase the public's money supply by expanding their loans even if borrowers withdraw all the loan proceeds in the form of gold and silver. However, in this case the ability of banks to acquire financial claims against others would be quite limited, for the banks' reserves in the form of gold and silver would soon fall below the desired ratio to note and deposit liabilities.

As the public comes to prefer to hold larger and larger fractions of its total money supply in the form of claims against banks, the probability of such large withdrawals of specie becomes smaller and smaller. At the extreme we have Case 2: As the banks purchase financial claims against others, the sellers take all the proceeds in the form of bank note and deposit claims against banks, and neither they nor others to whom they transfer the claims withdraw specie. If the banks acquire $9000 of financial claims, paying for them by issuing an equal amount of note and deposit liabilities, their balance sheet will appear as follows:

Assets		Liabilities	
Gold and silver	$ 1,000	Bank notes and deposits	$10,000
Loans	9,000		
	$10,000		$10,000

Thus, in expanding their loans by $9000, the banks have created an equal amount of new money in the form of bank notes and deposits. In effect, the banks acquired financial claims that were not money, issuing in exchange claims so safe and liquid that they serve as money. The banks still feel adequately liquid, for their gold and silver reserves are equal to 10 percent of their note and deposit liabilities.

We shall make repeated use of the following findings:

1. The commercial banking system can and does increase the total money supply by increasing its holdings of earning assets. The latter can be either newly created financial claims, such as loans to bank customers, or a part of the outstanding stock of financial claims.
2. Such net bank purchases of securities from the public provide funds for use and appear in the market as an increase in demands for securities.

If banks can increase the total money supply by increasing their holdings of financial claims, it should be credible that they can decrease the total money supply by reducing their holdings of financial claims. Suppose that, starting from the situation depicted in the last balance sheet above, the banks reduce their holdings of financial claims by $5000, and that the buyers of these claims pay for them by relinquishing an equal amount of their bank note and deposit claims against the banks. The banks' balance sheet will now appear as follows:

Assets		Liabilities	
Gold and silver	$1000	Bank note and deposit liabilities	$5000
Loans	4000		
	$5000		$5000

In this process, the public's money supply is reduced by $5000. In effect, the banks make net sales of financial claims to the public and retire an equal amount of money in the form of notes and deposits.

Thus we find that:

1. The banks can, and sometimes do, decrease the total money supply by reducing their holdings of financial claims against others.
2. Such net sales of securities by banks decrease the supply of funds for use and appear in financial markets as a decreased demand for securities.

THE ROLE OF CHECKING
DEPOSITS IN THE MONETARY SYSTEM

For many decades, demand deposit claims against fractional-reserve commercial banks have constituted approximately three-quarters of the nation's money supply, and most of these deposits were created by bank purchases of financial claims against others. Primarily because of the interest earned on their acquisitions of financial claims against others, banks have found it profitable to create and supply this type of money and to provide many services, and sometimes interest, to depositors. And the public, perfectly free to choose among all the available types of money, has elected to hold the major part of its money in this form because of its greater economy and convenience.

THE MONETARY ROLES OF SILVER AND GOLD

The first American monetary legislation, the Coinage Act of 1791, provided for the creation of full-bodied gold and silver coins, and these constituted a large part of the money supply in the early period. Our present circulating medium contains neither gold nor silver. Silver has disappeared completely from the monetary system.

The monetary history of gold is somewhat more complicated. Prior to March 1933, the United States was on an "unlimited gold coin standard." This means that the government was obligated to redeem all types of money in gold coins on demand. Thus the public could, if it wished, refuse to hold any other type of money and hold and use only gold coins. In fact, however, the public elected to hold most of its money in other forms. For example, at the end of 1932, when the total money supply exceeded $20 billion, the public elected to hold less than $200 million in gold coins. Government actions in 1933 and 1934 prohibited private holdings of monetary gold and gold certificates and concentrated all monetary gold in the Treasury. Since that time, the major function of gold has been as an international reserve, but even that function of gold has diminished greatly. No gold has been purchased for monetary purposes since August 1971. The future monetary roles of gold are uncertain. However, two things are highly probable: First, gold will never again constitute a significant part of our money supply; and, second, the nation will not allow its domestic money supply to be regulated by the size of its monetary gold stock. What the Treasury will do with the gold that it still holds remains to be seen.

SOME PROBLEMS OF COMMERCIAL BANKING

Up to this point we have not mentioned government regulation or restriction of banks and have tacitly assumed that banks were free to issue both bank notes and deposits, to determine their ratios of reserves to their note and deposit liabilities, and to determine how much money they would create by acquiring earning assets. It turned out, however, that unregulated fractional-reserve banking was subject to serious shortcomings and abuses. One was the proneness of such banks to insolvency and illiquidity. Many individual banks became insolvent or at least unable to meet fully and promptly their obligations to redeem their note and deposit liabilities. In some crisis periods virtually all banks became unable to meet their obligations or to make loans. A second shortcoming was an undesirable behavior of the money supply. In some periods, banks expanded the money supply so fast and so much as to create serious inflationary pressures; in others they either failed to expand the money supply fast enough or actually decreased it, with depressing effects on economic activity.

Such experiences with unregulated banking led to many types of government intervention, of which only a few will be mentioned at this point:

1. Termination of the privilege of note issue by private banks. In the United States, state-chartered banks lost their right of note issue during the Civil War period, and the federally chartered national banks lost theirs during the 1930s. Since then only the Treasury and the Federal Reserve may issue paper money of any kind. Now that the public prefers to hold such a large fraction of its money in the form of demand deposits, a bank can prosper without the privilege of note issue.

2. Imposition of legal minimum reserve requirements. In effect, such requirements say to a bank, "You must hold legal reserves equal to at least X percent of your deposit liabilities." As originally con-

ceived, the purpose was to force banks to maintain adequate liquidity. However, as we shall discuss later, the major purpose of these requirements today is not to provide liquidity but to help limit and regulate the volume of bank deposits, and indirectly the volume of earning assets that banks can acquire.

3. Creation of the Federal Reserve System to act as "lender of last resort." When the Federal Reserve was created in 1914, its major function was expected to be that of providing liquidity to banks in temporary difficulties and to prevent and ameliorate general banking crises and panics that had occurred much too frequently in earlier decades. However, with the passage of time the responsibilities of the Federal Reserve have become far more comprehensive and continuing, as we shall see in the following sections.

THE FEDERAL RESERVE SYSTEM

The other major type of monetary intermediary in the United States is the Federal Reserve System. This system includes a board of governors, whose members are appointed by the President with the approval of the Senate; 12 Federal Reserve banks, located in as many cities throughout the country; and a total of 25 branches of the Federal Reserve banks. However, the system has become so unified and control over its policies and actions so centralized that we shall view it as a single unit.

The Federal Reserve has many functions, including such things as check clearing and collection, regulation of commercial bank practices, and fiscal agent for the federal government. However, its major function is general monetary management—continuous management of the behavior of the money supply and, indirectly, of the volume of credit extended by commercial banks. It does this by imposing legal reserve requirements on commercial banks and by controlling the dollar volume of High-Powered Money and bank reserves. At this point we shall concentrate on its function of controlling the supply (stock) of High-Powered Money, to be designated by H.

At any time, H is the sum of outstanding coins, paper money, and deposit liabilities of the Federal Reserve banks. These are "High-Powered" in the sense that they are countable as legal bank reserves to the extent that they are acquired and held by commercial banks and that each dollar of these legal reserves can "support" several dollars of deposits.

As shown in Table 6 − 1, the stock of *H* at the end of January 1977 amounted to more than $115 billion. It will be noted that a small fraction of this total, only 9.4 percent, consisted of Treasury currency—various types of coins and paper money issued by the United States Treasury. This includes only a small amount of paper money, which consists mostly of United States notes, or Greenbacks, issued during the Civil War. There is presently no reason to expect further Treasury issues of paper money. The rest consists of coins, which are issued in the amounts required to meet the economy's need for small change. Thus the Treasury plays only a minor and relatively passive role in issuing *H*. By far the largest part of *H*—more than 90 percent—consists of Federal Reserve notes and Federal Reserve deposit liabilities, whose total is subject to close control by the Federal Reserve.

Both Federal Reserve notes and Federal Reserve deposits are merely debt claims against the Federal Reserve banks. Federal Reserve notes, which make up most of our paper money, are finely engraved but they are merely debt liabilities of the Reserve banks, and Federal Reserve deposits are only debt liabilities evidenced by entries on the books of the Federal Reserve. The Federal Reserve always stands ready to exchange its notes and deposits for each other at face value and in unlimited amounts, though it does not hold deposits of the public. Thus a bank that wants more Federal Reserve notes to hold in its vault or to meet the demands of the public can get them by surrendering an equal value of its deposits at the Federal Reserve, and a bank with excess cash can exchange it for more deposit claims on the Federal Reserve. Thus what is subject to close control by the Federal Reserve is the sum of its note and deposit liabilities. For convenience, we shall assume that changes in the total are initially in the form of changes in Federal Reserve deposits.

Table 6−1   **High-Powered Money in the United States, January 31, 1977**
(amounts in millions of dollars)

	Amounts	Percent of Total
Treasury currency (coins and paper money)	$ 10,865	9.4
Federal Reserve notes	81,198	70.3
Federal Reserve deposits[a]	23,411	20.3
	$115,474	100.0

Source: *Federal Reserve Bulletin,* March 1977, pp. A4, A12.
[a] Includes only those owned by member banks.

Table 6 — 2   **A Simplified Balance Sheet of the**
                Federal Reserve Banks, January 31, 1977
                (in millions of dollars)

Assets		Liabilities	
International reserve assets	$ 12,970	Federal Reserve notes	$ 81,198
Loans and securities		Federal Reserve deposits[c]	35,833
Loans	47		
Acceptances	191		
U.S. government securities[a]	100,924		
All other (net)[b]	2,899		
Total	$117,031		$117,031

Source: *Federal Reserve Bulletin,* March 1977, p. A12.
[a] Includes both direct obligations of the Treasury and obligations of federal agencies.
[b] This is equal to miscellaneous assets minus miscellaneous liabilities.
[c] This includes some deposits owed to the government.

How does the Federal Reserve increase and decrease the stock of its outstanding monetary liabilities? It does so by purchasing and selling assets. It creates new deposit claims against itself to pay for assets that it acquires. And when it sells assets the buyer pays for them by relinquishing an equal value of deposit claims against the Federal Reserve. Though the Federal Reserve can create and destroy H by purchasing and selling assets of any kind, in fact it buys and sells only a few major types of assets.

The first category of Federal Reserve assets shown in Table 6–2 is "international reserve assets." These consist of claims against gold, Special Drawing Rights issued by the International Monetary Fund, and foreign currencies. Purchases or sales of these assets serve to increase or decrease Federal Reserve deposit liabilities, but the Federal Reserve does not make such purchases and sales for purposes of domestic monetary management. Rather, it does so in response to the behavior of the nation's balance of international payments and to influence the behavior of exchange rates between the dollar and foreign currencies. If its purchases or sales of these assets tend to bring about undesired increases or decreases in the total supply of H, the Federal Reserve can easily compensate through offsetting sales or purchases of other types of assets.

The other, and far larger, category of Federal Reserve assets consists of its holdings of loans and securities—financial claims against others. In January 1977 these amounted to $101 billion, or 86 percent of total Federal Reserve assets. This fact justifies our calling the Federal Reserve a "monetary intermediary." The financial claims acquired and held by the Federal Reserve are of three principal types: loans, acceptances, and debts of the federal government and some of its agencies.

FEDERAL RESERVE LOANS

Federal Reserve loans are mostly to commercial banks, primarily to those that are members of the Federal Reserve System. In expanding its loans, the Federal Reserve creates High-Powered Money. For example, if it expands its loans by $100, the effects on its balance sheet will be as follows:

Assets	Liabilities
Loans +$100	Deposits +$100

The Federal Reserve has created $100 of additional deposit claims against itself to pay for its purchase of assets in the form of debt claims against others. On the other hand, the Federal Reserve retires High-Powered Money when it reduces its outstanding loans. In effect, those who repay loans do so by relinquishing deposit claims against the Federal Reserve. For example, if the Federal Reserve reduces its loans by $200, the effects on its balance sheet will be as follows:

Assets	Liabilities
Loans −$200	Deposits −$200

The Federal Reserve regulates the volume of its outstanding loans in two principal ways:

1. By changing its discount rate, which is simply the interest rate that it charges on its loans. It can discourage borrowing by charging a discount rate that is high relative to the rates that banks can earn on their assets, and it can encourage borrowing by setting a lower discount rate relative to market rates.

2. By various types of nonprice rationing. Instead of lending freely at its established discount rate, the Federal Reserve discourages "excessive" borrowing from it and may even go so far as to refuse to

make additional loans to a bank or to demand repayment of outstanding loans.

OPEN-MARKET OPERATIONS IN
ACCEPTANCES AND GOVERNMENT SECURITIES

In its early years, the Federal Reserve regulated the supply of High-Powered Money primarily through regulating its loans to banks. This method is still of considerable importance. However, for many years the Federal Reserve has relied primarily on its "open-market operations" for this purpose. These are called "open-market operations" because purchases and sales are made in the "open" or competitive market and do not imply the type of "customer" relationship involved when the Federal Reserve lends directly to a specific bank. Since the Federal Reserve buys and sells through specialized dealers, it usually does not know the ultimate sources of the securities that it buys or the ultimate buyers of the securities that it sells. These can be either banks or nonbanks.

In its open-market operations, the Federal Reserve purchases and sells two types of debt claims—acceptances and debts of the U.S. government.[1] The latter consist mostly of direct debt obligations of the Treasury but also include some obligations of federal agencies. Federal Reserve operations in acceptances have been small in recent decades, but its operations in government securities have been huge.

In purchasing acceptances or government securities, the Federal Reserve creates new High-Powered Money. For example, suppose that it purchases $4 billion of government securities, paying for them by adding to deposit accounts at the Federal Reserve. The effects on the Federal Reserve's balance sheet will be as follows:

Assets	Liabilities
U.S. government securities +$4 billion	Deposit liabilities +$4 billion

In this operation, the Federal Reserve has created $4 billion of new High-Powered Money.

On the other hand, the Federal Reserve reduces the stock of High-Powered Money when it makes net sales of securities. Suppose,

[1] The acceptances are bankers' acceptances. That is, they are time drafts drawn on a commercial bank and "accepted" by that bank. By writing "accepted" on such a time draft, the bank makes it a binding obligation to pay.

for example, that it sells $3 billion of securities, and that buyers pay for them by relinquishing an equal amount of deposit claims against the Federal Reserve. The following direct effects will appear on the balance sheet of the Federal Reserve:

Assets	Liabilities
U.S. government securities −$3 billion	Deposit liabilities −$3 billion

In this operation, $3 billion of High-Powered Money has been destroyed.

Open-market operations are a highly flexible instrument for regulating the supply of High-Powered Money, for the Federal Reserve can at its own discretion determine whether to buy or sell and when and how much to buy or sell. Also, as we shall see later, the market for government securities is so efficient that the Federal Reserve can consummate quickly even very large transactions.

AN OVERVIEW OF THE AMERICAN MONETARY SYSTEM

It will be useful to summarize at this point some major characteristics of the present American monetary system.

1. Our circulating medium contains no full-bodied money. Instead, it consists of token coins, a small amount of fiat paper money issued by the Treasury, larger amounts of paper money issued by the Federal Reserve, and checking deposits issued by commercial banks. Demand deposits typically make up about three-fourths of the money supply.

2. Most of our money is created by the Federal Reserve and commercial banks acting as special types of financial intermediaries. It is true that the Treasury issues some money and that the Federal Reserve has created some money in its purchases of international reserve assets, but most of our money—well over 90 percent—is created through Federal Reserve and commercial bank purchases of financial claims against others. In the process of purchasing and holding financial claims of various types and maturities, the Federal Reserve in effect transforms them into High-Powered Money. The commercial banks buy and hold financial claims of various maturities and degrees of risk and liquidity and transform them into money in the form of demand deposits.

CONTROL OF THE MONEY SUPPLY

Though we shall postpone to a later chapter a more detailed discussion of monetary management by the Federal Reserve, it will be useful to discuss briefly at this point the factors that determine the maximum stock of money that can be outstanding, and in the process to identify the major methods that the Federal Reserve can use to control the money supply.

These propositions are of central importance:

1. The maximum amount of deposits that the commercial banking system can create by purchasing and holding financial claims against others depends on both its dollar volume of legal reserves and the height of the legal minimum reserve ratio.
2. The Federal Reserve has two principal methods of controlling (1) above: (a) By determining the height of the legal minimum reserve ratio against bank deposits; and (b) by regulating the size of the stock of H and bank reserves.

We define the money supply (M) as the sum of currency in circulation outside the banks (C) and the volume of demand deposits (D), so that $M = C + D$. In our first simplified model we assume that the commercial banks issue only one type of liability (D), and that they hold only two types of assets, which are legal reserves (B) and financial claims against others (L). Thus $B + L = D$, for total assets must equal total liabilities.

We shall first address this question: What is the maximum stock of M that can be outstanding with a given stock of H? We shall assume for this purpose that the Federal Reserve fixes H at $100 billion. H is used for two purposes—to meet the public's demand for currency (C) and to provide legal reserves for the commercial banks (B). Thus $H = C + B$, and $B = H - C$. The latter expression highlights the fact that the dollar volume of reserves available to banks is equal to H minus the amounts demanded by the public as C. With a given stock of H, the maximum stock of M depends on two things:

1. The height of the legally required ratio of reserves to D, as determined by the Federal Reserve. This will be designated by r. This determines the maximum number of dollars of D that can be supported by each dollar of legal reserves (B). For example, if $r = 0.10$, $D/B = \$10$, but if $r = 0.20$, $D/B = \$5$. In our first numerical example, we assume that $r = 0.125$, or $1/8$, so that $D/B = \$8$.

2. The public's choices between C and D as forms of holding money. Note that the fractions of M held in these forms are determined by public choices, not directly by the Federal Reserve or the commercial banks. This is an important determinant of maximum M because each dollar of H can support only one dollar of C, but each dollar of H in bank reserves can support several dollars of D. Let us use a to denote the fraction of M that the public elects to hold in the form of C and $(1 - a)$ to denote the fraction it elects to hold in the form of D. (In the mid-1970s, a was approximately 0.23 and $(1 - a)$ approximately 0.77). Thus, $C = aM$ and $D = (1 - a)M$. Substituting these into our earlier definitional identity, $M = C + D$, we get

$$M = aM + (1 - a)M \qquad (1)$$

M will have expanded to its maximum only when all the available stock of H is absorbed in meeting the demand for currency in circulation (aM) and as required reserves against D, or $r(1 - a)M$. Thus M has expanded to the maximum when

$$H = aM + r(1 - a)M$$

or

$$H = M[a + r(1 - a)] \qquad (2)$$

Multiplying both sides of Equation 2 by $1/[a + (1 - a)r]$, we get the equation that we need to determine the maximum money supply, M.

$$M = H \cdot \frac{1}{a + r(1 - a)} \qquad (3)$$

In words, this states that the maximum money supply varies directly with the size of H and inversely with the public's demanded ratio of C to M and the height of the legal reserve ratio. Banks are usually impelled to expand to the maximum because to stop short of this would mean that they had failed to acquire the maximum amount of earning assets (L).

To get a numerical example, let us assume some values for the variables that are not far different from those prevailing in the mid-1970s.

$$H = \$100 \text{ billion}$$
$$a = 0.23$$
$$(1 - a) = 0.77$$
$$r = 0.125$$

Inserting these into Equation 3, we get M = $100 billion × 1/[0.23 + (0.125 × 0.77)], or M = $100 billion × 1/0.3265 = $306.28 billion. From this we can derive other desired values, which will be rounded to the nearest billion.

$$C = 0.23M = \$70$$
$$D = 0.77M = 236$$
$$L = D - B = 206$$
$$B = H - C = 30$$
$$rD = .125D = 30$$
$$C + rD = 100$$

These data indicate that M has indeed expanded to the maximum, for all of H is absorbed by $C + rD$, and the banks' legally required reserves are equal to their actual reserves. The balance sheet of the commercial banking system will be as follows (in billions).

Assets		Liabilities	
B	$ 30	D	$236
L	206		
Total	$236	Total	$236

If the banking system had created less money by acquiring earning assets (L), its actual reserves would have been in excess of its legally required reserves, but if the system had created more money by acquiring more earning assets, its actual reserves would have been below the legally required ratio.

The data in Table 6–3 support the earlier statement that with any given stock of H, the maximum amount of M that can be outstanding tends to vary inversely with the fraction of the money supply that the public elects to hold in the form of currency and also inversely with the height of legal reserve requirements against deposits. For example, reading down any column of the table reveals that at any given value or r, an increase in the fraction of its money that the public elects to hold in the form of C reduces maximum M sharply. And reading across any row reveals that with a given value of a, an increase of legal reserve requirements serves to reduce maximum M. Though not shown in the table, increases and decreases in the stock of H, with the values of a and r given, tend to produce proportional increases and decreases of maximum M. Thus, by purchasing earning assets the Federal Reserve can increase H and induce an increase of the money supply. And by

Table 6—3	The Maximum Money Supply with $H =$ $100 Billion and Various Values for a and r *(in billions of dollars rounded to the nearest billion)*			
		Values of r		
Values of a	0.08	0.10	0.125	0.25
0.10	$582	$526	$449	$308
0.23	343	326	306	237
0.40	223	217	211	182

selling earning assets it can, if it wishes, decrease H and force a decrease of the money supply.

SAVINGS AND TIME DEPOSITS AT COMMERCIAL BANKS

Up to this point we have assumed that commercial banks issue only one type of liability—demand deposits that serve as money. We did this to emphasize the monetary functions of commercial banks that enable them to increase and decrease the money supply. Now we must recognize that banks also issue other types of liabilities, principally savings and time deposit claims of various types. These are quite similar to, and competitive with, claims issued by other depository types of financial intermediaries—mutual savings banks, saving and loan associations, and credit unions. Savings deposits are usually evidenced by entries in the books of the issuing bank and in the depositor's passbook. Banks have a legal right to require 30 days' notice before withdrawal, but they ordinarily waive this and permit withdrawals at any time, the only penalty being a loss of interest. Time deposits, usually evidenced by some sort of certificate, have stated maturities, ranging from 30 days to several years. They are issued in various denominations, relatively small ones to appeal to households of modest means and larger ones to appeal to business firms and other large investors. To facilitate exposition, it will be convenient to lump together savings and time deposits at commercial banks and to denote their total by T.

Unlike demand deposits, savings and time deposits are generally not transferable in payments to third parties by checks or other orders and are therefore not a part of the circulating medium.[2] However, they are as safe as demand deposits, and at least the shorter maturities are highly liquid. They share equally with demand deposits as claims on a bank's assets, and, as is also true of demand deposits, the first $40,000 of each account is insured by an agency of the federal government, the Federal Deposit Insurance Corporation, popularly called the FDIC.

Since about the early 1950s, T has grown much faster than D. Though there were probably also other reasons why T grew faster than D, two factors have clearly been important—the legal prohibition of interest payments on demand deposits and the generally rising level of market rates of interest during this period. Federal legislation in the 1930s forbade banks to pay explicit interest on D and authorized the Federal Reserve to impose maximum , or ceiling, rates that banks may pay on T. The Federal Reserve raised the latter ceilings many times as market yields on other assets rose. Thus both households and business firms had strong incentives to economize on their holdings of D and to hold more of their assets in other forms, including T. And banks, facing rising demands for credit and experiencing only a slow growth in the volume of funds that depositors would supply by holding D, competed vigorously, by raising interest rates and otherwise, to attract holders of T.

By issuing T as well as D liabilities, banks are able to acquire and hold a larger volume of loans and securities. Depositors become willing to hold a larger total volume of deposits, $D + T$, when they are offered not only non-interest-bearing demand deposits but also a variety of interest-bearing savings and time deposit claims. And banks can create and issue a larger total volume of deposits on the basis of a given volume of legal reserves because the legally required reserve ratio against T is not nearly as high—usually only about 1/4 or 1/3 as high—as that against D. Banks can therefore acquire and hold a larger volume of financial claims against others. For example, Table 6—4 shows that at the end of January 1977 the commercial banking system held about $811.5 billion of loans and securities, an amount far greater than would have been possible on the basis of its $260.8 billion of outstanding demand deposits.

Though issuance of time as well as demand deposits enables the banking system to keep outstanding a greater amount of total deposits and to acquire a greater volume of earning assets, it reduces the amounts of D and M that can be supported by any given stock of H. This is because some part of H is absorbed in meeting reserve requirements

[2] Some exceptions will be noted later.

Table 6—4   **A Partial Balance Sheet for All Commercial Banks in the United States, January 26, 1977**
(in billions of dollars)

Assets		Liabilities	
Total loans and securities	$811.5	Demand deposits	$260.8
		Time and saving deposits	486.8
	———	Total deposits	$747.6

Source: *Federal Reserve Bulletin*, March 1977, p. A16.

against savings and time deposits. However, the Federal Reserve can, if it wishes, increase the stock of H to prevent any net depressive effects on D and M.

CONTROL OF THE VOLUME OF TOTAL DEPOSITS, $D + T$

The Federal Reserve can control the total volume of deposits, or $D + T$, that the banking system can create and keep outstanding, and indirectly the volume of earning assets (L) that the banking system can acquire, in two principal ways:

1. by regulating the dollar volume of legal reserves (B) available to the banking system
2. by setting and altering the height of legal reserve requirements against D and T.

As before, we use r to indicate the minimum fractional reserve requirement against D, and we use b to denote the height of the reserve requirement against T. We noted earlier that b is typically equal to no more than 1/4 or 1/3 or r. In our numerical example, we assume that $r = 0.12$ and $b = 0.04$.

The banking system will have expanded its total deposits and its earning assets to the maximum only when the volume of its required reserves against D and T is equal to the available volume of reserves, B. That is,

$$B = rD + bT \qquad (1)$$

Inserting our assumed values for r and b, we get

$$B = 0.12D + 0.04T$$

However, with given values for B, r, and b, the maximum $D + T$ that can be outstanding also depends on the fraction of total deposits that the public elects to hold in the form of D and the fraction that it elects to hold in the form of T. This is because r is so much larger than b, so that a shift from T to D serves to raise the average reserve requirement against $D + T$, and a shift from D to T lowers the average reserve requirement.

The numerical examples in Table 6 − 5 illustrate dramatically the effects of the public's choices between D and T on the total volume of deposits that the banking system can create on the basis of each dollar of reserves with a given level of legal reserve requirements. For example, if the public elects to hold only D, the average reserve requirement against total deposits will be 12 percent, so that each dollar of bank reserves will support only $8.33 of total deposits. At the other extreme, if the public elects to hold all of its deposits in the form of T, the average reserve requirement against total deposits will be only 4 percent, so that each dollar of reserves can support $25 of total deposits.

The freedom of the public to determine the fractions of its total deposits that it will hold in the forms of D and of T, and to change these fractions, does not mean that the Federal Reserve is thereby deprived of control over the total volume of bank deposits or of the total volume of earning assets acquired by the banking system. The Federal Reserve can prevent or offset unwanted changes in these aggregates through appropriate changes in the dollar volume of bank reserves, in the level of legal

Table 6 − 5   **Maximum Values of $D + T$ with $B = \$1, r = 0.12$, and $b = 0.04$**

Ratio of D to $D + T$	Ratio of T to $D + T$	Average Reserve Requirement Against $D + T$	Maximum $D + T$
1.0	0.0	0.12	$ 8.33
0.9	0.1	0.112	8.93
0.8	0.2	0.104	9.62
0.7	0.3	0.096	10.42
0.6	0.4	0.088	11.36
0.5	0.5	0.080	12.50
0.4	0.6	0.072	13.89
0.3	0.7	0.064	15.63
0.2	0.8	0.056	17.86
0.1	0.9	0.048	20.83
0.0	1.0	0.040	25.00

reserve requirements, or both. However, this freedom of the public does mean that the Federal Reserve, relying only on its conventional instruments, can regulate precisely the volume of D alone only by permitting changes in T, and it can regulate precisely the volume of T alone only by permitting changes in D. The Federal Reserve sometimes finds it difficult to assess the economic and financial significance of shifts in the fractions of D and T in total deposits, and therefore difficult to determine its appropriate policy responses. We shall later have more to say about this problem.

Though members of the public are free to choose the fractions of their total deposits that they will hold in the forms of D and T respectively, their decisions can be, and are, influenced by a number of policies of the monetary authorities and the commercial banks. For example, repeal of the prohibition of explicit interest on demand deposits would encourage people to hold more D relative to T and also relative to currency and other assets. Federal Reserve ceilings on rates that banks may pay on savings and time deposits are also relevant. By raising these ceilings, the Federal Reserve can encourage the public to hold more T relative to D and also relative to other financial claims, and by lowering these ceilings or refusing to raise them when yields on other assets rise, it can induce the reverse effects. Within the limits imposed by laws and official regulations, policies of commercial banks also affect public choices. For example, by providing large amounts of "free services" proportional to holdings of demand deposits, banks can encourage the public to hold more D relative to other assets. And banks can induce the public to hold more T relative to other assets not only by offering higher interest rates but also by improving the other characteristics of these claims, such as their degrees of safety and liquidity.

We shall have many occasions to emphasize that the amount of $D + T$ that the commercial banking system can issue and keep outstanding depends heavily on the explicit and implicit yields on these claims relative to yields on claims against other types of financial intermediaries and on safe and liquid direct debt claims.

WHAT IS MONEY?

How should money be defined and the supply or stock of money be measured? For more than a decade these questions have been widely debated, with no end of the controversy yet in sight. Five different measures of the money stock are published regularly, and more may evolve. These measures yield widely differing figures for the size of the money

Table 6—6   **Various Measures of the Money Stock**

Symbol for the Measures	Composition of the Money Stock	Amount Outstanding in April 1976 (in billions of $)
M_1	Currency outside the Treasury, the Federal Reserve, and the commercial banks *plus* commercial bank demand deposit liabilities to the public	$ 301.7
M_2	M_1 plus savings and time deposits at commercial banks, except large-denomination negotiable certificates of deposit[a] (abbreviation: NCDs)	691.9
M_3	M_2 plus deposits at mutual saving banks, shares of savings and loan associations, and shares of credit unions	1,141.3
M_4	M_2 plus NCDs	763.4
M_5	M_3 plus NCDs	1,212.7

Source: *Federal Reserve Bulletin,* June 1976, p. A12.
[a] Large-denomination negotiable certificates of deposit are certificates of time deposits in denominations of at least $100,000. They have stated maturity dates, but in the interim can be transferred from depositor to depositor by endorsement.

stock. For example, in April 1976 the money stock was $301.7 billion as measured by the most restrictive definition but $1212.7 billion as measured by the broadest definition. (See Table 6—6.) A difference of $911 billion can hardly be considered trivial.

From the outset we have defined money in functional terms, stating that money consists of those things, and only those things, that are generally used as a medium of exchange or payments. Of course, money also serves as a store of value, but this function is not unique to money; it is shared by all valuable assets. Applying this definition in the current American context, only two types of financial claims clearly qualify as money: currency and demand deposits. This measure is known as M_1. However, many contend that this definition is too restricted and that still other assets should be admitted to the exalted category of money. Some favor a measure called M_2, which would also include time and savings deposit claims at commercial banks, except large-denomination negotiable certificates of deposit (NCDs).[3] Others

[3] Why these NCDs should be considered to possess less "moneyness" than other forms of savings and time deposits remains a mystery to this writer.

prefer a broader measure known as M_3, which includes also what are in effect various types of time and savings deposit claims against mutual savings banks, savings and loan associations, and credit unions. M_4 is defined as M_2 plus NCDs of commercial banks, and M_5 is M_3 plus the NCDs.

Those who advocate the broader measures of M do not claim that the things they would add would qualify as money if the latter is defined as the stock of things generally used as a medium of exchange or payments. Instead, they maintain that "money" should be defined according to another criterion. It should include those "monetary magnitudes" that exhibit a highly stable relationship to the rate of expenditures for output, or GNP at current prices, and that are therefore presumably major determinants of the rate of money expenditures. They believe that the things that they would include in M in addition to M_1 are indeed important determinants of the rate of expenditures and should therefore be included in the stock of money.

We cannot even list all the issues involved in this controversy or pretend to resolve them. However, a few comments may be useful. Those who define the money supply narrowly as M_1 do not deny that the size of the stock of other things included in broader definitions of M affect the rate of expenditures. In fact, they generally agree that, other things equal, the greater the stock of these other highly safe and liquid assets, the greater will be the rate of expenditures. But the effects of these other assets on expenditure rates can be taken into account without including them in the stock of money. For example, we shall later contend that the equilibrium rate of expenditures for output is determined by both the supply function of money and the public's demand function for money balances. We shall define the money supply as M_1, thereby relegating the other candidates to the status of "near moneys." The effects of the stock of "near moneys" on the rate of expenditures is taken into account in the demand function for money balances. In general, the greater the stock of these close substitutes for money, the lower will be the public's demand for M_1 at each level of GNP, and therefore the higher will be the level of expenditures that can be supported by a given stock of M_1.

On one thing there is general agreement: any valid analysis of the determinants of the rate of expenditures must take into account the stock of "near-moneys." But whether this is done more appropriately by including them in the supply of M or by including them as a determinant of the public's demand function for money balances remains a debated question.

CONCLUSION

Through a process of evolution, the monetary system has become a system of monetary intermediaries. Our medium of exchange has not for decades contained any type of money with a commodity value equal to its face value. Only our fractional coins have any significant value as a commodity, and that is considerably below their face values. All our other types of money, constituting more than 96 percent of the total stock, consist of specific types of debt claims that have achieved general acceptability as a medium of exchange or payments. Federal Reserve notes, for all their fine paper and engraving, are but debt claims against the Federal Reserve, and demand deposits are but specific types of debt claims against commercial banks. The monetary intermediaries increase and decrease the stock of money primarily by purchasing and selling financial claims against others, mostly debt claims. Thus the Federal Reserve creates and issues High-Powered Money to pay for its purchases of interest-bearing financial claims with various maturities and degrees of risk and illiquidity, and the commercial banks create and issue demand deposits to pay for their purchases of a wide variety of earning assets, mostly direct debt claims. On the other hand, the monetary intermediaries decrease the stock of money primarily by making net sales of other types of financial claims.

Since increases and decreases in the supply of money are achieved predominantly through net purchases and sales of a wide variety of other types of financial claims by the monetary intermediaries, one would expect increases or decreases in the money supply to affect the prices and yields of other types of financial claims, at least temporarily. In purchasing additional securities to increase the money supply, the monetary intermediaries tend to bid up the prices and to lower the yields on financial claims. But this is not the end of the process, for the monetary intermediaries have altered the composition of the portfolios of the public. They have removed from the public's portfolios earning assets with varying degrees of risk and illiquidity and have substituted for them money itself, which is completely safe and liquid but yields no explicit income. Thus the public's portfolios are generally made safer and more liquid but yield less income. If its portfolio preferences have not shifted, the public can be expected to try to restore balance in its portfolios by increasing its demands for earning assets. On the other hand, when the monetary intermediaries decrease the money supply by making net sales of securities, this is reflected in financial markets as a decreased demand for securities, which tends directly to lower the prices and increase the yields on earning assets. The public's portfolios yield more income but are less liquid and safe. If their portfolio preferences have not changed, members of the public can be expected to reduce their demands for securities. We shall have more to say about this when we discuss monetary policies.

In the final chapter we shall stress that the evolution of money is by no means at end. For example, some financial intermediaries other than commercial banks are likely to be permitted to issue liabilities transferable to third parties in payment, and these liabilities may differ in some respects from demand deposits. Also, an electronic funds transfer system, already in the process of replacing the written check as a means of transferring payments, not only will perform this function faster and with greater transactions efficiency but also is likely to have other important consequences.

SELECTED READINGS

Chandler, L. V., and Goldfeld, S. M. *The Economics of Money and Banking.* 7th ed. New York: Harper & Row, 1977. Chaps. 5–10.

Tobin, J. "Commercial Banks as Creators of 'Money.' " In Dean Carson (ed.), *Banking and Monetary Studies.* Homewood, Ill: Richard D. Irwin, 1963. Chap. 22. Also reprinted in Hester, D. D., and Tobin, J. (eds.). *Financial Markets and Economic Activity.* New York: John Wiley & Sons, 1967. Chap. 1.

PRIVATE
FINANCIAL
INTERMEDIARIES

We shall now examine more closely, though not exhaustively, the principal types of private financial intermediaries in the United States. We shall be especially interested in the number of institutions of each type, the principal types of financial claims that they buy and hold, the principal types of indirect financial claims that they issue, and the roles that they play in the various sectors of the financial system.

The conditions described will be those prevailing in the mid-1970s. However, the policies and practices of some institutions are already changing and further changes appear likely. We shall note some of these as we go along, but our discussion of others will be postponed to a later chapter.

COMMERCIAL BANKS

Commercial banks are much more numerous and hold far more financial assets than any other type of financial intermediary. More than 14,500 separately incorporated banks located throughout the country operate a total of nearly 43,800 banking offices. (See Table 7 − 1.) Virtually every community has access to at least one local banking office. Some of the larger banks also have branches in foreign countries. The total assets of commercial banks, at more than $1011 billion, are more than twice those of the runner-up, the savings and loan associations.

Table 7—1   **Commercial Banks in the United States**

I. Number of banks and banking offices, June 30, 1975

Number of banks	14,570
Branches and additional offices	29,223
Total banking offices	43,793

II. Combined balance sheet of all insured commercial banks, March 31, 1977 (in billions of dollars)

Assets		Liabilities	
Cash, bank balances, and items in process of collection	$ 125.2	Demand deposits	$ 316.3
Securities	249.8	Time deposits	506.8
Loans	564.1	Other liabilities	114.7
All other	72.4	Net worth	73.7
Total	$1011.5	Total	$1011.5

Sources: Number of banks and banking offices—*Federal Reserve Bulletin,* August 1975, p. A76. Balance sheet data—*Federal Reserve Bulletin,* September 1977, pp. A18—19.

COMMERCIAL BANK LIABILITIES

As noted in the preceding chapter, the principal claims issued by commercial banks are demand deposits, which serve as money, and a wide variety of savings and time deposits. Demand deposits are equal to about 31 percent, and time and savings deposits to about 50 percent, of total bank assets. Equity claims against banks are quite small relative to bank assets, typically below 8 percent. In recent years some banks, especially the larger ones, have tended to broaden the types of liabilities that they issue, though the total of these is still much smaller than their deposit liabilities. Among these are the following:

1. Long-term debts, usually called debentures, intermediate-term notes, and short-term notes. These interest-bearing debts are not sold exclusively to customers of the issuing banks, they are evidenced by paper instruments, and they are not insured by the FDIC.
2. Sales of securities and other earning assets under repurchase agreements. In such transactions, a bank sells an earning asset at one time but agrees to repurchase it at some later time at a higher price. The difference between the repurchase price and the sales price represents interest for the intervening period.

3. Various other types of short-term borrowing. We shall discuss these later in connection with liquidity management by banks.

COMMERCIAL BANK ASSETS

Banks hold only small amounts of equity claims against others, basically because such a large part of their liabilities is stated in fixed amounts of dollars. However, as holders of debt claims against others, banks are the most versatile of all intermediaries. They hold more types of debt claims against more types of issuers than any other class of intermediary. Commercial and industrial loans are the largest single component of their earning assets. (See Table 7–2.) A majority of these have maturities within a year, but at least a quarter of them are "term" loans, with maturities ranging up to seven years or more. Banks are by far the largest single source of short-term and intermediate-term credit to business firms. They hold only small amounts of long-term corporate bonds, but they supply larger amounts of long-term funds by purchas-

Table 7 – 2   **Loans and Securities of All Commercial Banks, June 30, 1975**
(amounts in billions of dollars)

	Subtotal Amount	Total Amount	Percentage of Total
LOANS AND SECURITIES—Total		$747.9	100.0
SECURITIES—Total	$212.1		28.4
U.S. government and agencies	102.1		13.7
State and local government	101.5		13.6
Other	8.5		0.1
LOANS—Total	535.8		71.6
Commercial and industrial	179.0		23.9
Loans to individuals	101.8		13.6
Agricultural loans			
Farm mortgages	6.1		0.1
Other	19.1		2.6
Other mortgages			
On residential properties	81.4		10.9
On other properties	44.0		5.9
To domestic and foreign banks	11.2		1.5
To other financial institutions	32.4		4.3
To brokers and dealers	5.5		0.7
All other	55.3		7.4

Source: *Federal Reserve Bulletin,* May 1976, p. A16.

Table 7–3   **Commercial Bank Holdings of Selected Types**
             of Outstanding Debt Claims, December 31, 1975
             (amounts in billions of dollars)

Type of Debt	Total Outstanding	Amount Held by Commercial Banks	Percent of Total Outstanding Held by Commercial Banks
Consumer credit	$197.3	$ 90.4	45.6
U.S. government debt outside the Treasury and the Federal Reserve	343.2	85.4	24.9
State and local government	223.8	102.8	45.9
Mortgages	795.0	136.5	17.2

Source: Board of Governors of the Federal Reserve System, *Flow of Funds Accounts.*

ing mortgages on agricultural, residential, commercial, and industrial properties.

Some other types of claims that constitute only smaller fractions of total commercial bank loans and securities nevertheless represent a large fraction of the total outstanding claims of these classes. For example, banks hold about 46 percent of the total debts of state and local governments. (See Table 7–3.) These are attractive despite their lower gross yields because commercial banks are subject to the federal corporate income tax. Banks hold directly about 46 percent of all outstanding consumer credit claims, and they advance further amounts indirectly by lending to retailers and others who, in turn, extend consumer credit. Other holdings by commercial banks were nearly 25 percent of the total direct federal debt held outside the Treasury and the Federal Reserve, and 17.2 percent of all mortgages.

Commercial banks extend credit to each other and to other types of financial intermediaries in many ways, of which only a few will be noted here. Some banks hold deposit claims against other banks, usually with smaller banks holding deposits with larger banks in financial centers. These interbank deposits transfer lending power from depositing banks to banks receiving the deposits. Banks also lend to each other in many ways. Some banks borrow from others only to meet temporary liquidity needs; others borrow almost continuously. Interrelations between commercial banks and other types of financial institutions are numerous. For example, virtually all types of financial institutions hold demand deposit claims against commercial banks, and some also hold small amounts of time deposits. They also borrow from commercial banks. Table 7–2 shows $5.5 billion of outstanding bank loans to brokers and dealers and $32.4 billion of loans to other types of financial institutions, but the importance of the availability of bank credit to these institutions is even greater than these figures might indicate. This is because banks extend to these institutions *lines of credit,* under which a bank agrees to extend credit on demand up to some stated limit. This increases the liquidity of the recipient of the line of credit even if the recipient does not actually borrow. Brokers and dealers rely heavily on bank credit to finance their inventories of securities and also for the accounts of their customers who purchase securities on margin. Nonbank financial intermediaries also borrow from banks, sometimes to meet temporary liquidity needs and in other cases for longer periods or more continuously. For example, a consumer finance company may borrow from banks and retail the funds to consumer-borrowers. Or a life insurance company may borrow from banks and buy bonds or mortgages in anticipation of future inflows of funds.

Because of their versatility as lenders, commercial banks have direct contact with almost all branches of the credit markets. This enables them to readjust their portfolios and to reallocate credit in response to shifting demands and also to transmit to almost all branches of the credit markets the effects of Federal Reserve policy actions.

SIZE DISTRIBUTION OF COMMERCIAL BANKS

Commercial banks differ greatly in size. (See Table 7–4.) Each of the 5661 smallest banks, or 38.6 percent of all banks, holds no more than $10 million of deposits, and these banks collectively account for only 3.7 percent of total bank assets. At the other extreme, the largest 6.2 percent of all banks, each with at least $100 million of deposits, hold nearly 70 percent of all bank assets, and the largest 87 banks, each with at least $1 billion of deposits, hold nearly 42 percent of total bank assets. A few of the largest—notably the Bank of America in California and Citibank and the Chase Manhattan Bank in New York City—hold assets well in excess of $25 billion.

Though commercial banks of all sizes operate on the same general principles, their great differences in size are accompanied by wide differences in the variety and scope of the financial functions that they perform. The smallest banks are predominantly local institutions. Their deposits come mostly from local sources, and their loans are primarily

Table 7 — 4   **All Commercial Banks in the United States,**
Classified by Size of Deposits, December 31, 1975
(amounts in millions of dollars)

Size of Bank (in millions of dollars of deposits)	Number of Banks	Percent of Total Banks	Total Assets	Percent of Total Assets
Less than 1	194	1.3	$ 644	0.1
1 to 2	289	2.0	620	0.1
2 to 5	2,023	13.8	8,651	0.8
5 to 10	3,155	21.5	26,283	2.7
10 to 25	4,840	33.1	89,333	9.2
25 to 50	2,190	15.0	86,745	8.9
50 to 100	1,046	7.1	82,347	8.5
100 to 500	728	5.0	175,475	18.1
500 to 1000	105	0.7	93,606	9.7
1000 +	87	0.5	406,152	41.9
Total	14,657	100.0	$969,857	100.0

Source: Federal Deposit Insurance Corporation, *Assets and Liabilities —Commercial and Mutual Savings Banks*, December 31, 1975.

to local households, business firms, and governmental units. However, they do acquire claims against distant issuers through purchases in the open market. On the other hand, the largest banks do business nationwide and even internationally. Such a bank may be domiciled in New York, Chicago, or San Francisco and have no domestic branches outside its own state, but it draws deposits from foreign banks, foreign business firms, and foreign official institutions; from American business firms engaged in nationwide and even international activities; and from large firms located in the various regions. And it provides funds, either through direct loans or purchases of claims in the open market, to many foreign borrowers; to big American firms that operate nationwide and even internationally; and to the larger governmental units and business firms located in the various regions. We shall find later that the larger banks play a major role in promoting interregional mobility of funds, both by acquiring funds from all regions and by supplying funds to all regions.

Up to this point we have confined our attention to the activities that banks undertake for their own accounts; the results of these activities are reflected in the banks' own assets and liabilities. Now we turn to activities that are not reflected in a bank's own balance sheet but are closely related to the bank. Specifically, we consider bank trust departments and separate corporations closely affiliated with banks.

BANK TRUST DEPARTMENTS

Though a trust department is a part of a bank, its assets are not considered a part of the bank's assets; as trustee or agent, the department holds the assets for the accounts and benefit of others. In some cases the department has complete control of the composition of these assets; in others the trustor retains at least some degree of control.

As a group, trust departments hold a huge volume of assets — more than $325 billion at the end of 1974. Acting as trustees and agents, they held almost $200 billion for the accounts of individuals and more than $126 billion for the accounts of employee benefit plans. Table 7—5 shows the composition of these assets. More than 51 percent were in common stocks, 14.2 percent in debt claims against governmental units, and 19.4 percent in "other obligations," mostly corporate bonds. Trust departments are by far the largest institutional holders of common stock.

Some trust departments are quite small, holding only a few million in assets, but some are huge. The largest holds assets in excess of

Table 7—5   **Trust Assets of Insured Commercial Banks, End of 1974**
(amounts in billions of dollars)

	Amounts of Assets	Percent of Total Assets
Total	$ 325.3	100.0
U.S. government and agency obligations	24.6	7.6
State, county, municipality obligations	21.5	6.6
Other obligations	63.1	19.4
Common stocks	167.6	51.5
Preferred stocks	3.7	1.1
Real estate mortgages	7.2	2.2
Real estate	12.2	3.8
Savings and loan association accounts	0.7	0.2
Time deposits	13.8	4.2
Demand deposits	3.1	0.9
Miscellaneous assets	7.8	2.4

Source: Board of Governors of the Federal Reserve System, Federal Deposit Insurance Corporation, the Comptroller of the Currency, *Trust Assets of Insured Commercial Banks —1971,* Washington, D.C., 1975.

$17 billion, and at least 16 others hold assets of more than $4 billion. Though trust departments are not considered to be financial intermediaries, they are far more important than many types of financial intermediaries as purchasers, holders, and sellers of financial claims.

BANK AFFILIATES

We turn now to activities that are performed not by a bank itself but by one or more separate corporations that are closely affiliated with the bank. This typically involves a *bank holding company,* which is a corporation that controls one or more separate bank corporations and in some cases other corporations as well. *A multibank holding company* controls two or more banks through stock ownership. A *single bank holding company,* as the name implies, controls only one bank, but it usually has one or more nonbank subsidiaries. Both multibank and single-bank holding companies, and especially the latter, grew very rapidly after the mid-1960s, and more than 1600 were in existence by 1974. These have established a wide variety of nonbank subsidiaries to engage in what have been determined to be "bank-related activities." Some of these subsidiaries were established *de novo* by bank holding companies; others were already in existence as independent entities and were acquired by bank holding companies through purchase or exchange of stock. In many cases the acquired companies were among the largest in their respective lines of activity.

Among the most important types of nonbank subsidiaries of bank holding companies are the following:

1. Consumer and sales finance companies, which make loans to consumers and buy, or lend on the basis of, claims of business firms against consumers.
2. Factoring companies, which lend on accounts receivable and provide credit collection and credit analysis services.
3. Mortgage banks, which originate, sell, and service real estate mortgages.
4. Small business investment companies, which acquire debt and equity claims against small business firms.
5. Real estate investment trusts (REITs), which acquire debt and equity claims against real estate.
6. Companies providing economic and financial analysis and advice.
7. Companies providing research, appraisals, and advice concerning real estate and its development.

8. Companies financing exports and imports.
9. Equipment leasing companies, which acquire and lease equipment, such as trucks, buses, planes, and processing equipment.
10. Companies underwriting and selling credit life, accident, and health insurance.
11. Companies providing messenger services, computer services, and so on.

Though many of these companies are not engaged in financial intermediation, others are and for this purpose require large amounts of funds. Bank holding companies and their nonbank affiliates acquire funds in various ways:

1. Through loans from their bank affiliates. These are limited by the regulatory authorities to protect the soundness of banks.
2. Through issues of equity claims.
3. Through issues of debt claims, ranging from long-term to very short-term.

For example, bank holding companies issue long-term debentures and are important issuers of commercial paper—short-term, unsecured promissory notes sold on the open market. Funds raised by bank holding companies are sometimes made available to subsidiary banks through deposits, loans, and purchases of earning assets from them.

In summary, commercial banks as a group are by far the largest type of financial intermediary even if we consider only those activities that are reflected in the banks' own balance sheets. However, their roles in financial markets are further enhanced by the huge amounts of financial assets held by their trust departments and by their nonbank affiliates.

MUTUAL SAVINGS BANKS

Legally, these institutions are "mutual" or "cooperative" in form. That is, they issue no equity claims against themselves and are, in effect, owned by their depositors.[1] However, they have accumulated "general reserve" or "surplus" accounts, which serve as a buffer against declines in the values of their assets and make it feasible for them to issue deposit claims that are stated in fixed numbers of dollars.

[1] Legislative proposals, not yet enacted, would permit them to issue equity claims, if they wished, thus converting to stock savings banks.

Mutual savings banks are much less numerous and much less geographically extensive and hold a much smaller total volume of financial assets than the commercial banks. They number only 476, and most of them are located in New England and the Middle Atlantic states. (See Table 7−6.) Despite their small number and limited geographic area,

Table 7−6   Mutual Savings Banks in the United States

I. Number of mutual savings banks, December 31, 1975
   Number of mutual savings banks   476

II. Locations of mutual savings banks, December 31, 1972

Location	Number
Massachusetts	167
New York	121
Connecticut	68
Maine	32
New Hampshire	30
New Jersey	20
Washington	9
Pennsylvania	8
Rhode Island	7
Vermont	6
Total of above	468
In 8 other states—total	18
Total states = 18	486

III. Balance sheet of mutual savings banks, June 30, 1977 (in billions of dollars)

Assets		Liabilities	
Cash items	$ 2.1	Deposits	$129.2
U.S. government securities	6.1	Other liabilities	3.0
State and local government securities	2.5	General reserve	
Mortgages	83.9	accounts	9.5
Corporate and other bonds	36.4		
Other assets	10.7		
Total	$141.7	Total	$141.7

Sources: For number of banks on December, 1975, FDIC, *Assets and Liabilities of Commercial and Mutual Savings Banks,* December, 1975, Washington, D.C., 1976. For location of mutual savings banks, December 31, 1972, National Association of Mutual Savings Banks, *Fact Book,* 1973. For balance sheet, *Federal Reserve Bulletin,* September 1977, p. A29.

they have accumulated an impressive amount of financial assets — more than $141 billion. They are major financial intermediaries in the areas in which they are located, and their role in the national financial system is by no means negligible. Like most other types of financial inter-mediaries, mutual savings banks differ greatly in size. (See Table 7 — 7.) About 32 percent of them hold deposits not in excess of $50 million and collectively account for only 3.4 percent of the total financial assets of the industry. At the other extreme, the 59 largest hold nearly 61 percent of the industry's assets. Several of these, mostly located in the New York and Philadelphia metropolitan areas, hold deposits in excess of $4 bil-lion. The financial operations of the larger institutions are by no means limited to their own regions.

Mutual savings banks acquire funds almost exclusively by issuing savings and time deposit claims, which are quite similar to those issued by commercial banks. Like the latter, they have in recent years increased the variety of their issues, including issues of longer-term time deposits. They hold almost no equity claims, and most of their holdings of debt claims are of long-term maturities. For liquidity purposes, they minimize their holdings of cash and hold small amounts of government securities, mostly short-term. Real estate mortgages are by far the largest component of their earning assets. In mid-1977 these amounted to $83.9 billion, or 59 percent of the total assets of these banks. About 83 percent of the mortgages were on residential real estate, and most of the remaining 16 percent were on commercial and industrial properties.

Table 7 — 7   Mutual Savings Banks in the United States, December 31, 1975, Classified by Size of Deposits

Size of Bank (in millions of deposits)	Number of Banks	Percent of Total Banks	Total Assets (in millions)	Percent of Total Assets
Less than $10	13	2.7	$ 104	0.1
10– 25	42	8.8	828	0.1
25– 50	97	20.4	3,958	3.3
50– 100	120	25.2	9,181	7.7
100– 500	145	30.5	33,729	28.1
500– 1000	33	6.9	24,658	20.5
1000 or more	26	5.5	48,613	40.3
Total	476	100.0	$121,070	100.0

Source: FDIC, *Assets and Liabilities of Commercial and Mutual Savings Banks,* December 31, 1975, Washington, D.C., pp. 116 – 119.

Though they held less than 10 percent of all outstanding mortgages, their share of the mortgages outstanding in their own regions was, of course, higher. Long-term corporate and other bonds, primarily the former, are the other major component of their earning assets. In mid-1977 these amounted to $36.4 billion, or 26 percent of the total assets of these banks.

Both the liability and asset policies of mutual savings banks may change in the future. A few of them are already offering accounts on which negotiable orders of withdrawal can be drawn. These are popularly called NOW accounts. They are similar to demand deposits in that they can be transferred to third parties in payment, but they are dissimilar in two respects: they bear interest, and the issuer retains the legal right—almost never exercised—to require notice before withdrawal. There are also proposals that the lending powers of these banks be expanded to include consumer loans and perhaps other types as well.

SAVINGS AND LOAN ASSOCIATIONS

As a group, savings and loan associations are second only to commercial banks in number, in geographic dispersion, and in total financial assets.[2] More than 4,900 associations, some chartered by the federal government and some by the states, are spread throughout the nation and operate a total of more than 15,400 offices. (See Part I of Table 7–8.) Most of them are mutual in form, but a minority have issued equity claims and are stock institutions. The mutuals have accumulated general reserve or surplus accounts, which make it feasible for them to issue claims stated in fixed amounts of dollars. The average size of savings and loan associations is less than that of commercial banks or mutual savings banks, but the associations differ greatly in size. (See Table 7–9.) For example, the smallest 2582 associations, or 52 percent of the total number, held only 7.9 percent of the industry's total assets. At the other extreme, the 301 largest, each with at least $200 million in assets, held more than 48 percent of the industry's total assets. A few associations have assets in excess of $4 billion. As might be expected under these circumstances, some associations acquire and lend funds only locally while others acquire funds and lend over much wider areas.

[2] Though most institutions of this type are called savings and loan associations, some carry other names. For example, some are called cooperative banks in New England and homestead associations in Louisiana, and some are known as building associations or savings associations.

Table 7−8   **Savings and Loan Associations in the United States**

I. Number of savings and loan associations, end of 1975

	Number	Assets (in millions)
State chartered	2,916	$142,985
Federally chartered	2,048	195,410
Total	4,964	$338,395
Branches	10,441	
Total offices	15,405	

II. Legal form of organization   Number

	Number
Mutual	4,255
Capital stock	709
	4,964

III. Balance sheet of all savings and loan associations, June 30, 1977 (in billions of dollars)

Assets		Liabilities	
Cash and investment securities	$ 39.6	Share capital	$364.3
Mortgages	350.8	Borrowed money	20.6
Other	36.7	Other liabilities	18.7
Total	$427.1	Total	$427.1

IV. Fractions of outstanding mortgages held by savings and loan associations, June 30, 1977 (amounts in millions of dollars)

Type of Mortgage	Amounts Outstanding	Amounts Held by Savings and Loan	Percent of Total Held by Savings and Loan
1−4 family	$498.1	$283.9	47.5
Multi-family	106.1	30.5	28.7
Commercial	181.2	36.3	20.0
Farm	61.4	a	—
Total	$946.8	$350.8	37.1

Sources: For number and types of associations, U.S. Savings and Loan League, *Savings and Loan Fact Book,* Chicago, 1976. For balance sheet data, *Federal Reserve Bulletin,* September 1977, pp. A29 and 41.
a Holdings of farm mortgages negligible.

Table 7 — 9   **Distribution of Savings and Loan**
                Associations, By Asset Size, December 31, 1975

Asset Size (in millions of dollars)	Number of Associations	Percentage of Total	Assets (in millions)	Percentage of Total
Under 1	426	8.6	$ 234	0.1
1 — 5	489	9.9	1,430	0.4
5 — 10	503	10.1	4,021	1.2
10 — 25	1,164	23.4	20,836	6.2
25 — 50	1,019	20.5	38,416	11.4
50 — 100	661	13.3	50,361	14.9
100 — 150	262	5.3	34,050	10.1
150 — 200	139	2.8	25,532	7.5
200 — 300	116	2.3	28,304	8.4
300 and over	185	3.7	135,211	40.0
Total	4,964	100.0	$338,395	100.0

Source: U.S. Savings and Loan League, *Savings and Loan Fact Book,* Chicago, 1976, p. 53.

ASSETS OF SAVINGS AND LOAN ASSOCIATIONS

While commercial banks are the most versatile of all institutional lenders, savings and loan associations are among the most restricted in the types of financial claims that they acquire. They are predominantly holders of real estate mortgages, and especially of mortgages on residential real estate. (See Part III of Table 7 — 8.) Of their total assets, 74 percent are in mortgages on residential real estate and 82 percent are in mortgages of all types. Their other assets are of various types: cash, government securities, and deposits at the Federal Home Loan Banks, which are held largely for liquidity purposes; financial claims against pools of mortgages; and equity claims against the Federal Home Loan Banks which, as members, they are required to hold.

As a group, these associations are by far the largest holders of mortgages, and especially of residential mortgages. (See Part IV of Table 7 — 8.) They hold nearly 48 percent of all mortgages on one-family to four-family dwellings, more than a quarter of all mortgages on multi-family dwellings, and 44.6 percent of the value of all residential mortgages. Though they play a less dominant role in markets for commercial and industrial mortgages, they hold 20 percent of the total outstanding.

LIABILITIES OF SAVINGS AND LOAN ASSOCIATIONS

These associations acquire funds predominantly by issuing financial claims that are officially called "savings capital." They are so called because in the mutual or cooperative form of organization, "depositors' " claims are legally equity or share claims. In fact, however, associations generally advertise them as "deposits," and the public generally considers them to be essentially the same as deposit claims against commercial and mutual savings banks. They are stated in fixed amounts of dollars, and in most of the associations the first $40,000 of each account is insured by the Federal Savings and Loan Insurance Corporation. In mid-1977 these liabilities were equal to 85 percent of the total assets of the associations. Their other principal liability consisted of advances from the Federal Home Loan Banks. Such loans are sometimes very large when the associations are experiencing net withdrawals of funds or abnormally small net inflows. We shall later have more to say about this.

CREDIT UNIONS

A credit union is a cooperative organization whose major function is to provide for its own members a convenient and safe repository for their savings and a reliable source of loans at moderate rates. Members of a credit union typically have some other bond in common. For example, they belong to the same church, fraternal organization, cooperative, or labor union; they work for the same business firm or for two or more local firms in the same industry; they are employed by the same governmental unit or educational institution; or they are members of the same neighborhood association. Most credit unions still operate on principles consistent with the original concept that they should serve as institutions for mutual self-help.

Though the total assets of credit unions are still far below those of the other major types of depository intermediaries, these institutions have expanded very rapidly since World War II in number, membership, and total assets. By the end of 1975, there were some 23,000 credit unions with 31.5 million members, and they had accumulated $37 billion of assets. The typical credit union is rather small; about 75 percent have assets below $500,000, and only 15 percent hold assets in excess of $1 million.

Credit unions acquire funds by issuing to their members what are, in effect, various types of savings and time deposit claims that are quite similar to those issued by the other types of depository intermediaries. In most credit unions, the first $40,000 in each account is insured by the National Credit Union Share Insurance Fund. Most of the earning assets of credit unions are in the forms of loans to members. These are typically short-term and intermediate-term consumer loans, but credit union officials take great pride in their ability to analyze the credit needs of members, to provide financial advice, and to tailor the amounts and terms of loans to the borrowers' needs. Their other assets are principally in the form of money and short-term government securities held primarily for liquidity purposes.

THE DEPOSITORY INTERMEDIARIES—SUMMARY

The four types of depository intermediaries have one major characteristic in common: in the process of intermediation they all create and issue financial claims that are stated in fixed amounts of dollars, that are predominantly payable on demand or on relatively short notice, and that are highly liquid and safe. The similarity of these claims is enhanced by the fact that the first $40,000 in each account at most of these institutions is insured by government-sponsored agencies.

There are also significant differences in the policies and practices of these institutions with respect to both their liabilities and their assets. Commercial banks are now the only type that creates large amounts of demand deposits that serve as money, but this difference may diminish if, as seems probable, the other depositories are permitted to issue claims transferable to third parties in payment. All these intermediaries issue savings and time deposit claims designed to appeal to households, but commercial banks also issue claims fashioned to appeal to business firms and, in fact, they do attract large amounts of funds from such firms. In contrast, credit unions acquire funds almost exclusively from their member households, and mutual savings banks and savings and loan associations draw funds primarily, but not exclusively, from households.

The depository institutions differ most in the composition of their assets. Commercial banks are the most versatile of all lenders, acquiring debt claims against virtually all types of debtors and throughout the range of maturities, though their portfolios are heavily weighted with maturities in the short-term and intermediate-term ranges. In contrast, most of the holdings of mutual savings banks are in the form of long-term mortgages and bonds, and the portfolios of savings and loan associations consist largely of long-term mortgages, most of which are on residential properties.

Events in recent years have created serious doubts concerning the practice of acquiring predominantly long-term debts with funds obtained by issuing predominantly short-term claims. The ability of such an intermediary to acquire and retain funds depends heavily on its ability and willingness to offer yields comparable to those on competing short-term liquid assets. On the other hand, the average rate of return on the assets of an intermediary holding predominantly long-term debts depends on the levels of rates prevailing at the times the assets were acquired. Thus conditions are most favorable for the growth of such an intermediary when prevailing short-term rates are low relative to the average of long-term rates in the preceding years, and also low relative to prevailing long-term rates. In general, such conditions were met during the period from the end of World War II to the mid-1960s, so that the depository intermediaries, and especially savings and loan associations, enjoyed very large net inflows of funds.

However, the situation was reversed in 1966, in 1969, and on several occasions during the early 1970s, in response to inflationary pressures, excessively expansionary government fiscal policies, and restrictive Federal Reserve policies. The entire structure of interest rates rose to historically high levels, and short-term rates rose significantly above long-term rates. The latter occurred primarily because so many participants in the market believed that the current high rates were only temporary and would soon give way to lower rates. Borrowers were willing to pay the higher short-term rates to escape the necessity of entering into long-term commitments to pay the prevailing high long-term rates. And many lenders were willing to lend on short-term only if rewarded by a yield high enough to compensate them for forgoing the opportunity to receive for a protracted period the prevailing high yields on long-term debts.

The result was "disintermediation" at depository institutions, and especially at savings and loan associations. Some continued to receive net inflows, though only at a much reduced level, but many suffered large net withdrawals. There arose deep concern about the liquidity, and even the solvency, of the associations. Moreover, the residential construction industry, so heavily dependent on funds from the savings and loan associations, became deeply depressed. Several ameliorative actions were taken. The Federal Reserve kept down ceiling rates on savings and time deposits at commercial banks to lessen the flow of funds from the savings and loan associations to commercial banks. This was of only limited assistance because savers purchased high-yielding open-market assets, such as Treasury bills. Also, the Federal Home Loan Banks lent very large amounts to savings and loan associations to enable them to meet withdrawals and to maintain some flow of funds to the housing industry. Despite these actions, the residential construction industry remained depressed.

Because of these experiences, it is now clear that longer-term reforms of the financing system for housing are desirable, but what these reforms will be remains unclear. Among those proposed are the introduction of variable rate mortgages, whose rates would vary with market rates; the establishment of new intermediaries that would acquire funds by issuing longer-term claims; expanding the scope of commercial bank holdings of mortgages; permitting the nonbank depositories to issue demand deposits so they can attract more funds; and permitting them to make short-term consumer loans, and perhaps other short-term loans as well, so that their earning power, and therefore their ability to bid for funds, will not be so dependent on past levels of mortgage yields.

LIFE INSURANCE COMPANIES

With total financial assets of $334.4 billion in mid-1977, life insurance companies rank in size closely behind the savings and loan associations, and are far larger than any other nondepository type of financial intermediary. There are nearly 1800 of these institutions, with their head offices located all over the country. They differ greatly in size; the smallest have only a few million in assets and their operations are largely confined to their own regions, while the largest have assets in excess of $35 billion and are truly nationwide, and even international, concerns. Most of the largest firms are domiciled in New York, New Jersey, and Connecticut. In legal form, 91.9 percent are stock companies and only 8.1 percent are mutuals, but the latter are on the average so much larger that they hold two-thirds of the industry's total assets.

Pooling large numbers of individual risks and thereby reducing total risk, these companies provide two major types of insurance:

1. Life insurance, which insures against some of the financial hazards of "dying too soon." Most of the policies representing this insurance are issued to individuals, but very large numbers of people are

       insured under group plans covering some or all of the employees of a business firm, governmental unit, or educational institution.

2. Annuities and pensions, which insure against some of the financial hazards of "living too long." The annuitant is assured of an income even if he survives far beyond his average life expectancy. Very large numbers of annuity policies are issued to individuals, but many people have pension rights under employee benefit plans that are insured and administered by life insurance companies.

       These companies could provide both life insurance and annuity rights without accumulating a large stock of financial assets if they collected each year from their policy holders an amount just sufficient to cover their outpayments, administrative costs, and profits in that year. In fact, however, the terms of many types of insurance and annuity policies are such that payments by the policy holder during the earlier years exceed the actuarial costs of providing insurance during those years, and the excess is a form of saving. For example, in a straight-life insurance policy with fixed annual premiums, the premium exceeds the actuarial cost of insurance during the earlier years but falls below the current cost of insurance as the policy holder grows older. The insurance company therefore accumulates a "reserve of assets" to meet its later liabilities. Similarly, holders of annuity and pension policies contribute over a period of time before they begin to draw benefits, and insurance companies accumulate a "reserve of assets" to meet such future liabilities.

       In summary, the principal types of indirect financial claims issued by life insurance companies are life insurance and annuity and pension claims, and the value of these claims at any time is shown on the liability side of the companies' balance sheets as "life insurance and pension reserves." These are typically equal to at least 81 percent of the total financial assets of the companies. The remaining liabilities are miscellaneous.

Table 7—10   **American Life Insurance Companies, End of 1974**

I. Number: 1781

II. Legal form	Number	Percent of Total
Stock	1636	91.9
Mutual	145	8.1

The following facts about life insurance companies help explain their portfolio policies:

1. Because of the nature of the financial claims that they issue, they are less subject than are the depository types of intermediaries to unexpected outflows of funds. Their actuarial tables and knowledge of the age composition of their policy holders enable them to predict with a fair degree of accuracy their future payments of death benefits and annuities. Policy holders do sometimes surrender their policies for their cash values, but such actions are not taken lightly.

2. For many years the companies have experienced very large net inflows of funds, and it appears that these will continue for some years to come. These annual net inflows have averaged above $15 billion during recent years. A major reason for this is that as a result of the large recent growth in the total population, the number of people still paying premiums is very large relative to the number of those who have retired and are drawing annuity and pension benefits and also very large relative to the number of insured people who die each year.

3. Many of the policies guarantee to policy holders at least some minimum fixed rate of return. Companies therefore tend to match these fixed commitments with assets that will yield a fixed rate of return over a long period.

Because of this combination of conditions, life insurance companies rely largely on inflows of funds to meet their needs for liquidity, they hold only a small fraction of their portfolios in money and other liquid assets, and they have a strong preference for long-term securities. (See Table 7—11.) Nearly 40 percent of their assets were in long-term corporate bonds and 27.8 percent in real estate mortgages. Stocks, equal to 10 percent of their assets, were held largely for the accounts of the employee benefit plans insured and administered by them. Loans to policy holders, at $26.7 billion, were this high primarily because the rates charged by insurance companies on such loans were significantly lower than prevailing market rates.

Insurance companies are the major holders of some types of debt claims. Of the total outstanding, they held nearly 50 percent of corporate bonds, 28 percent of commercial and industrial mortgages, 17.7 percent of mortgages on multifamily dwellings, and 12.9 percent of farm mortgages, but only 2.6 percent of mortgages on one- to four-family dwellings.

Table 7—11   Assets of Life Insurance Companies, June 30, 1977
(amounts in billions of dollars)

	Amounts	Percent of Total
Total Assets	$334.4	100.0
Government securities		
Federal	5.4	1.6
State and local	5.8	1.7
Foreign	7.4	2.2
Business securities		
Bonds	133.5	39.9
Stocks	33.4	10.0
Mortgages	92.9	27.8
Real estate	10.9	3.3
Policy loans	26.7	8.0
Other assets	18.4	5.5

Source: *Federal Reserve Bulletin*, September 1977, p. A29.

OTHER INSURANCE COMPANIES

Though much less important than life insurance companies as financial intermediaries, other insurance companies have, in the course of their principal lines of business, accumulated sizable amounts of financial assets. Their main business is to insure against many types of hazards.

Table 7—12   Financial Assets of "Other
Insurance Companies," December 31, 1975
(amounts in billions of dollars)

	Amounts	Percent of Total
Total financial assets	$77.4	100.0
Demand deposits and currency	1.7	2.2
U.S. government securities	7.0	9.0
State and local obligations	34.3	44.3
Corporate bonds	12.2	15.8
Corporate shares	14.3	18.5
Commercial mortgages	0.2	0.3
Other	7.7	9.9

Source: Board of Governors of the Federal Reserve System, *Flow of Funds Accounts*.

Among these are defective titles to property; damage to property by fire, flood, hurricanes, and other natural catastrophes; marine damages and losses; damage to motor vehicles and planes; robbery, burglary, theft, and embezzlement; and corporate and personal liability for injury to others. Some companies assume only a few types of risk; others offer broader coverage.

These companies acquire funds principally by issuing insurance policies and collecting premiums from the insured, and they use some of these inflows to accumulate "reserves of assets" against their future liabilities. By the end of 1975 they had accumulated total financial assets of $77.4 billion. (See Table 7 − 12.) That 44.3 percent of these assets were in the form of state and local government obligations is largely explainable by the fact that so many of these companies are stock corporations subject to the federal corporate income tax. Their other assets consist largely of corporate shares and long-term corporate bonds.

PRIVATE PENSION FUNDS

The primary purpose of these funds, established by employers or by employers and employees jointly, is to provide pensions to employees after retirement. Contributions by employers are their principal sources of funds, though employees also contribute in some cases. Since World War II their total assets have grown very rapidly, so that by the 1970s they were second only to the life insurance companies among the non-depository types of intermediaries. Their large net inflows of funds reflected several developments: the large increase in the number of such funds; the increasing generosity of the pension plans; the increasing labor force and rising pay scales; and the very large number of active employees for whom contributions are made relative to the number who have retired and are drawing pensions.

Because of their large net inflows, pension funds rely largely on these inflows to meet their needs for liquidity, hold only a small part of their assets in liquid form, and concentrate their holdings largely in long-term securities. (See Table 7 − 13.) Corporate shares constitute by far the largest part—nearly 60 percent—of their total assets, with most of the remainder in long-term corporate bonds and mortgages. Whether or not they will continue to concentrate so heavily on equities rather than long-term debt obligations remains to be seen.

Table 7 – 13   **Financial Assets of Private Pension Funds, End of 1975**
              (amounts in billions of dollars)

	Amounts	Percent of Total
Total financial assets	$148.9	100.0
Demand deposits and currency	1.5	1.0
Corporate shares	88.6	59.5
U.S. government securities	10.8	7.3
Corporate bonds	37.8	25.4
Mortgages	2.4	1.6
Other	7.8	5.2

Source: Board of Governors of the Federal Reserve System, *Flow of Funds Accounts.*

STATE AND LOCAL GOVERNMENT RETIREMENT FUNDS

In principle, these funds are quite similar to private pension funds. Their major purpose is to provide pensions for retired employees of state and local government units, and they acquire funds primarily from contributions by employers but also in some cases from employees. Since they, too, have large net inflows of funds, their holdings are largely concentrated in long-term securities. (See Table 7 – 14.) But unlike private pension funds, they hold far more corporate bonds than corporate shares.

Table 7 – 14   **Financial Assets of State and Local Government Retirement Funds, End of 1975**
              (amounts in billions of dollars)

	Amounts	Percent of Total
Total financial assets	$106.1	100.0
Demand deposits and currency	1.7	1.6
U.S. government securities	6.8	6.4
State and local obligations	2.5	2.4
Corporate bonds	61.0	57.5
Mortgages	8.3	7.8
Corporate shares	25.8	24.3

Source: Board of Governors of the Federal Reserve System, *Flow of Funds Accounts.*

FINANCE COMPANIES

Some time ago it was customary to divide these companies into two classes: consumer finance companies, which extend consumer credit to households; and sales finance companies, which lend to retailers and other business firms, largely on the basis of their accounts receivable from customers, but also on inventories. However, during recent years the functions of these companies have become overlapped and merged to such an extent that they are now lumped together as "finance companies."

In mid-1972, there were nearly 3,000 finance companies operating about 12,000 offices located throughout the country. Many are quite small, with no more than 5 offices and less than $1 million in total assets.[3] At the other extreme, some are very large. Some of the largest are affiliates of big manufacturing and merchandising firms, which lend largely on the basis of accounts receivable from purchasers of their products. Some examples are the General Motors Acceptance Corporation, the General Electric Credit Corporation, May Department Stores Credit-Company, and the Associated Dry Goods Credit Corporation. However, some independent finance companies are also very large. For example, the Household Finance Corporation operates about 1,950 offices and has more than $4 billion of financial assets, and the Beneficial Corporation has nearly 1,500 offices and more than $2 billion of financial assets.

ASSETS OF FINANCE COMPANIES

Consumer credit is the largest component of the assets of finance companies. At the end of 1975, this amounted to $46.1 billion, or 46.8 percent of the total assets of these institutions. (See Table 7 — 15.) Most of this was in the form of installment loans, some of which were cash loans unrelated to purchases of any specific product, but more were related to purchases of automobiles and other durable consumer goods. On that date, finance companies held about 20 percent of all outstanding consumer credit and 23 percent of total installment consumer credit. They also held $9.5 billion of home mortgages.

[3] *Federal Reserve Bulletin,* November 1972, pp. 962, 966.

Table 7 — 15 **Financial Assets and Liabilities of Finance Companies, December 31, 1975** *(amounts in billions of dollars)*

Assets	Amount	Percent of Total	Liabilities	Amount
Demand deposits and currency	$ 3.9	4.1	Corporate bonds	$30.7
			Open-market paper	28.0
Consumer credit	46.1	46.8	Bank loans	16.2
Home mortgages	9.3	9.5	Other liabilities	19.2
Loans to business	39.0	39.6	Net worth	4.3
Total assets	$98.4	100.0	Total	$98.4

Source: Board of Governors of the Federal Reserve System, *Flow of Funds Accounts.*

Their loans to business, at $39.6 billion, constituted 40 percent of their total assets. These were mostly loans to retailers and wholesalers on the basis of their inventories and accounts receivable.

LIABILITIES OF FINANCE COMPANIES

Finance companies acquire most of their funds from other financial institutions rather than directly from the public. Though they do issue some equity claims, they acquire less than 10 percent of their assets in this way and rely largely on three types of debt financing (see Table 7 — 15):

1. Long-term corporate bonds, most of which are bought by other types of financial intermediaries.
2. Open-market paper, usually called "commercial paper." These are unsecured notes with maturities that rarely exceed nine months and are often much shorter. These are bought mostly by other financial intermediaries and nonfinancial business firms and to only a small extent by households. Finance companies are major issuers of commercial paper.
3. Loans from banks. As noted earlier, the availability of bank credit is more important to these institutions than their outstanding borrowings from banks might imply because they commonly have backup lines of credit at banks. In the absence of such assurances from banks, they would find it difficult, and in some cases impos-

sible, to issue on acceptable terms such large amounts of commercial paper.

INVESTMENT COMPANIES

These companies acquire funds largely by issuing equity claims against themselves and use most of the proceeds to acquire a diversified portfolio of equity claims against others. They are of two broad types: *open-end investment companies* and *closed-end investment companies*. In terms of total assets, the former are by far the larger.

OPEN-END INVESTMENT COMPANIES

These companies, of which there were more than 400 in the mid-1970s, stand ready at all times to issue new shares and to redeem outstanding shares at prices related to their current net asset value per share. The latter is simply the total net value of the company's assets divided by the number of shares outstanding. *No-load funds* sell their shares at net asset value. *Load funds* sell shares at net asset value plus a premium that in many cases exceeds 9 percent. Open-end funds typically stand ready to redeem their outstanding shares at net asset value.

The stated objectives of investment companies differ widely. Some seek high and stable income and try to avoid high risks. Others place less emphasis on current income and assume higher risk in hope of realizing large capital gains.

At the end of 1975, open-end investment companies held total financial assets of $42.2 billion, of which 79.8 percent consisted of corporate shares. (See Table 7–16.) Another 11.3 percent consisted of corporate bonds, many of which were held primarily because they were convertible at the option of the holder into common stock of their issuers. The rate of growth of these institutions has varied widely from period to period. They have received large net inflows of funds when stock prices were rising and the public optimistically expected further increases, but they have been subjected to large net outflows during periods of falling stock prices.

CLOSED-END INVESTMENT COMPANIES

These are quite similar to open-end companies but differ in one important respect: They do not stand ready to issue new shares, and

Table 7– 16   **Financial Assets of Open-End
Investment Companies, December 31, 1975**
(amounts in billions of dollars)

	Amounts	Percent of Total
Total financial assets	$42.2	100.0
Demand deposits and currency	1.2	2.7
U.S. government securities	1.1	2.6
Open-market paper	1.5	3.6
Corporate bonds	4.8	11.3
Corporate shares	33.7	79.8

Source: Board of Governors of the Federal Reserve System, *Flow of Funds Accounts.*

they do not promise to redeem their outstanding shares. Instead, they issue a fixed number of shares, and holders of these must rely on their salability in the market to recover their money. To enhance their marketability, many of these issues are listed for trading on the organized securities exchanges. Because a closed-end company does not stand ready to issue new shares, the price of its shares can rise to a premium above their net asset value, but because the company does not stand ready to redeem its stock, the price of its shares can fall below their net asset value.

OTHER FINANCIAL INTERMEDIARIES

We shall mention only briefly some other types of intermediaries that have accumulated smaller amounts of assets, though they may become larger in the future.

BOND FUNDS

These typically acquire funds by issuing equity claims and use the proceeds to acquire a diversified portfolio of long-term bonds. Though their total assets are still relatively small, they gained favor during the early 1970s, when stock prices were falling and bond yields reached historically high levels. Most of these funds hold primarily corporate bonds. However, some are *tax-exempt bond funds,* which hold diversified portfolios of state and local government bonds whose income is exempt from federal income taxes. This tax exemption is passed on to holders of claims against the funds.

LIQUID ASSET FUNDS

These first appeared in 1974. They hold only the safest and most liquid types of short-term assets, such as large-denomination certificates of deposit issued by big commercial banks, Treasury bills, prime-quality commercial paper, and bankers' acceptances. The claims issued by these funds are stated in fixed amounts of dollars, are highly liquid, and are in denominations smaller than those of the assets held by the funds. The latter charge a small management fee but make no charge for issuing or redeeming their claims. Liquid asset funds are economically feasible partly because they can economize on transactions costs and partly because some government regulations and policies discriminated against small savers. For example, the lowest-denomination Treasury bill was $10,000, and official ceilings on rates that banks might pay on passbook savings accounts and small-denomination time deposits were far below prevailing rates on certificates of deposit in denominations of $100,000 or more. Whether liquid asset funds can survive in the absence of such discriminatory official policies remains to be seen. However, there are strong indications that they will.

REAL ESTATE INVESTMENT TRUSTS (REITs)

These intermediaries began to be numerous in the late 1960s and early 1970s. Their asset policies differ widely. Some acquire only mortgages, with emphasis on mortgages on multifamily dwellings and commercial properties. Some also acquire equity claims against real estate, and some own real estate outright. Their liability policies also differ widely. In general, however, they acquire significantly less than half their funds by issuing equity claims and borrow the remainder. Though more than half of their debt is in the form of long-term mortgages and corporate bonds, they also depend heavily on short-term credit in the form of bank loans and issues of commercial paper. This financial structure proved to be most unfortunate during the 1973 – 1975 period of inflation, restrictive monetary policies, acute shortages of mortgage funds, and extraordinarily high short-term interest rates. Many REITs became illiquid and some faced insolvency. Because of these experiences, the future of REITs is uncertain, though their basic concept is economically sound if they avoid such serious mismatches of their assets and liabilities.

SECURITY BROKERS AND DEALERS

As we shall see later, the principal function of brokers and dealers in securities is not to serve as financial intermediaries; it is to serve as middlemen facilitating purchases and sales by others. However, in the course of performing their primary function they do acquire financial claims against others and do issue financial claims against themselves. Dealers hold inventories of financial claims to facilitate their operations, and brokers acquire financial claims against their customers who buy securities on margin. To finance their holdings of such assets, brokers and dealers issue some equity claims against themselves, but they se-

Table 7—17 **Direct Financial Claims Outstanding Against the Nonfinancial Sectors, December 31, 1975**
(in billions of dollars)

	Direct Corporate Equity Claims	Direct Debt Claims	Total Direct Equity and Debt Claims
Total Outstanding	$812.5	$2358.0	$3170.5
Percentage of Total Held by			
Commercial banks	—	31.6	23.5
Mutual savings banks	—	4.7	3.0
Savings and loan associations	—	14.0	10.4
Credit unions	—	1.4	1.0
Life insurance companies	3.5	10.0	8.3
Other insurance	1.8	2.3	2.1
Private pension funds	10.9	2.2	4.4
State and local government retirement funds	3.2	3.3	3.3
Finance companies	—	4.0	3.0
Open-end investment companies	4.1	0.3	1.3
REITs	—	0.5	0.3
Securities brokers and dealers	a	a	a
Total of above (in percent)	23.5	74.3	60.6

Source: Board of Governors of the Federal Reserve System, *Flow of Funds Accounts.*
[a] Less than 1/10 of 1 percent.

cure most of their funds by issuing debt claims. Most of the latter are quite short-term, are considered to be highly liquid, and are held largely by banks and business corporations.

CONCLUSION

Table 7 — 17 presents one measure of the importance of private financial intermediaries in the financial system—the percentages of all outstanding direct debt and equity claims held by these institutions at the end of 1972. As a group, these institutions held 74.3 percent of all direct debt claims, 23.5 percent of all direct equity claims, and 52.5 percent of total direct debt and equity claims. All these percentages would be significantly higher if trust departments of banks were classified as financial intermediaries, as they probably should be. The table also indicates the relative importance of the various classes of financial intermediaries as holders of direct claims. Commercial banks were by far the largest, followed in order by savings and loan associations, life insurance companies, private pension funds, and mutual savings banks. Though the other types of intermediaries held only smaller shares of the total, their aggregate holdings were by no means small.

SELECTED READINGS

I. Commercial banks

American Bankers Association. *The Commercial Banking Industry*. Englewood Cliffs, N.J.: Prentice-Hall, 1962.

Crosse, H. D., and Hempel, G. *Management Policies for Commercial Banks*. 2d ed. Englewood Cliffs, N.J.: Prentice-Hall, 1973.

II. Mutual savings banks

Grebler, L. *The Future of Thrift Institutions,* Danville, Ill.: Joint Savings and Mutual Savings Exchange Groups, 1969.

Teck, A. *Mutual Savings Banks and Savings and Loan Associations: Aspects of Growth*. New York: Columbia, 1968.

Welfling, W. *Mutual Savings Banks, The Evolution of a Financial Intermediary*. Cleveland: Press of Western Reserve University, 1968.

III. Savings and loan associations

Federal Home Loan Bank Board. *Study of the Savings and Loan Industry*. 4 vols. Washington, D.C., 1970.

Kendall, L. T. *The Savings and Loan Business: Its Purposes, Functions and Economic Justification*. Englewood Cliffs, N.J.: Prentice-Hall, 1962.

Maisel, S. J. *Financing Real Estate*. New York: McGraw-Hill, 1965.

IV. Credit unions

Croteau, J. T. *The Economies of the Credit Union.* Detroit: Wayne State Press, 1966.

Dublin, J. *Credit Unions.* Detroit: Wayne State Press, 1966.

Flannery, M. J. *An Economic Evaluation of Credit Unions in the United States.* Boston: Federal Reserve Bank of Boston, 1974.

Moody, J. C. and Fite, J. C. *The Credit Union Movement: Origins and Development, 1850–1870.* Lincoln: University of Nebraska Press, 1970.

V. Life insurance companies

Brimmer, A. F. *Life Insurance Companies in the Capital Market.* E. Lansing, Mich.: Bureau of Business Research, 1962.

Jones, L. D. *Investment Policies of Life Insurance Companies.* Boston: Harvard Business School, 1968.

Life Insurance Association of America. *Life Insurance Companies as Financial Institutions.* Englewood Cliffs, N.J.: Prentice-Hall, 1962.

VI. Pension funds

Dietz, P. D. *Pension Funds: Measuring Investment Performance.* New York: Free Press, 1966.

Gardner, E. B. (ed.). *Pension Fund Investment Management.* Homewood, Ill.: Richard D. Irwin, 1969.

Holland, D. M. *Private Pension Funds: Projected Growth.* New York: National Bureau of Economic Research, 1966.

Polakoff, M. E., et al. *Financial Institutions and Markets.* Boston: Houghton Mifflin Co., 1970. Chap. 8.

VII. Investment companies

Friend, J., and Crockett, J. *Mutual Funds and Other Institutional Investors: A New Perspective.* New York: McGraw-Hill, 1970.

Investment Company Institute. *Management Investment Companies.* Englewood Cliffs, N.J.: Prentice-Hall, 1962.

VIII. Government-sponsored intermediaries

Polakoff, M. E., et al. *Financial Institutions and Markets.* Boston: Houghton Mifflin Co., 1970. Chap. 11.

FINANCIAL MARKETS: STRUCTURE AND BASIC FUNCTIONS

At several points we have simply assumed the existence of a well-developed market for financial claims and have noted that the market performs valuable functions in enhancing the liquidity of such claims by increasing their marketability, and also in improving efficiency in the allocation of scarce financial and real resources. However, we have not yet dealt sufficiently with either the structure or the functioning of these markets. The central purpose of this chapter and of the two that follow is to remedy this situation.

ELEMENTS OF FINANCIAL MARKETS

Any market—whether it be a market for commodities, services, or financial claims—has at least four elements:

1. the "things" traded
2. suppliers of the things
3. demanders of the things
4. individuals or institutions that perform middleman functions in organizing the market and facilitating purchases and sales

We have already identified the first three elements in financial markets. The things traded are, of course, many types of financial claims. A large part of these are direct financial claims issued by almost every type of entity except financial intermediaries. Some are equity claims—

principally common and preferred stock in corporations. Others are debt claims of differing maturities and varying degrees of risk and liquidity. In addition, many types of indirect securities issued by financial intermediaries are also traded in financial markets. Examples are stocks issued by banks and other nonmutual types of financial firms and debt obligations with maturities ranging from long-term debentures to short-term commercial paper.

Suppliers of financial claims include not only every type of entity that issues new financial claims but also holders of outstanding claims who at least occasionally offer some of their holdings for sale. Demanders of financial claims include almost every type of entity in our society. Although we have stressed the roles of households and of the various types of financial intermediaries that command a huge volume of financial assets, we should not forget that some other types of institutions also play important roles as demanders of claims. Among these are the so-called nonfinancial business firms and many types of endowed institutions, such as churches, hospitals, nonprofit foundations, schools, and colleges.

Middlemen are the fourth element in financial markets. These consist of a national, and even international, network of several thousand brokers and dealers who serve all branches of the financial market. We shall discuss these further after surveying the various branches of the financial markets.

PRINCIPAL BRANCHES OF FINANCIAL MARKETS

Financial markets, in the broad sense of the term, include a number of submarkets, which are classified and cross-classified on several bases. One classification is on the basis of whether the claims traded are new issues or are already outstanding. *Primary markets* are those through which new issues are distributed from their issuers to buyers. *Secondary markets* are those in which already outstanding claims are traded. Classified on the basis of the nature of the claims traded in them, markets are of several types.

1. Corporate equity markets, in which both common and preferred stocks of corporations are traded.
2. Bond markets, for long-term debt claims against corporations and governmental units.
3. Mortgage markets, for long-term mortgage claims against various types of real estate.

4. Markets for short-term, liquid debt claims. These are popularly called *money markets.*

Though such classifications are useful for some descriptive and analytical purposes, it would be a mistake to assume that each branch is almost completely compartmentalized and that the behavior of prices and yields within each branch is independent of behavior in others. In fact, the various branches are interrelated in many ways. For one thing, the same middlemen usually operate in many branches. More important, the various types of claims are interrelated, sometimes as complements and sometimes as substitutes. For example, even though an issuer is not indifferent to the composition of its liabilities, shifts in relative financing costs can induce it to change the distribution of its issues among equities and debt claims and among the various maturities of debt claims. Similarly, buyers can be induced by changes in relative yields to change the composition of their portfolios. We shall later have more to say about arbitrage among the various branches of the market.

Primary markets and secondary markets are closely interrelated. For one thing, the terms on which a firm can sell a new issue in the primary market depend in part on the efficiency of secondary markets in providing continuous marketability, and thus liquidity, for the security after its issue. In the absence of a good secondary market for it, a new issue may have to carry a higher yield to attract buyers. Moreover, the prices and yields on new issues and those on comparable outstanding issues are closely interrelated. This is because new issues and outstanding issues are substitutes, in some cases almost perfect substitutes, in the eyes of potential buyers. A new issue cannot be sold at a yield significantly below that prevailing in secondary markets on the most comparable outstanding issues, and in a well-functioning market a new issue need not carry a yield much above that on the most comparable outstanding issues.

This is not to say that security prices and yields are determined solely in secondary markets and then imposed on new issues in primary markets. Prices and yields in both markets are determined simultaneously by total demand and total supply conditions in both markets. However, the stock of outstanding securities is so large relative to the volume of new issues during any short period, and the volume of transactions in outstanding securities is so much greater than that in new issues, that it is only a slight exaggeration to say that during short periods the prevailing prices and yields in secondary markets can dominate the terms on which new issues can be sold. It is partly, but not solely, because of this that the behavior of security prices and yields in secondary markets is so important for the economy. These economic effects include both effects of the general level of security prices and yields on overall rates of spending and economic activity, and the effects of relative yields of the various issues on the allocation of scarce financial resources among their potential uses and users.

FEDERAL REGULATION OF SECURITIES MARKETS

Before becoming enmeshed in the institutional and mechanical details of financial markets, it will be useful to consider the principal types of federal regulation that affect practices in this industry.

In 1933 and 1934, following the stock market crash of 1929, the disastrous fall of stock prices during the early years of the depression, and revelations of unwise practices and even wrongdoings in securities markets, the federal government established the Securities and Exchange Commission (SEC) and enacted a number of laws relating to public issues of new securities, trading on the organized exchanges, trading in the over-the-counter (OTC) market, investment advisers, and investment companies. These laws have been amended many times but their basic principles remain largely unchanged. Some practices are outlawed; among these are publication of false reports, circulation of false rumors, and manipulative practices of various kinds, such as bull or bear raids to raise or lower prices, and fictitious purchases and sales to create a spurious impression of public interest in a stock.

With a few exceptions, mostly for small issues and issues by governmental units, new securities may not be offered to the public before they have been registered with the SEC. Contrary to the practice in some states with "blue-sky" laws, the SEC has no authority to pass on the merits of the securities to be offered or on the fairness of the terms of distribution. It can only refuse to accept a registration until it receives full and fair disclosure of all facts materially relevant to the future of the issuer and its securities. These include information concerning the past and present financial position of the issuer, other known facts that may be relevant in the future, compensation of the underwriter, and other relations between the issuer and the underwriter. This information is supplied to the public in a prospectus.

The principle of full and fair disclosure also applies to securities listed on national securities exchanges and to over-the-counter (OTC) securities in which there is a substantial public interest. Issuers of these securities are required to file annual and other periodic reports designed to give the public current material information.

Administration of these laws relies heavily on the principle of "self-regulation under supervision by the SEC." Each national securities exchange has primary jurisdication over its members and transactions on the exchange. The National Association of Securities Dealers, Inc.—usually referred to as the NASD—has primary jurisdiction over the OTC market. These bodies are empowered to make rules not in conflict with the laws and the regulations of the SEC and are primarily responsible for enforcement of the relevant laws and regulations. However, the SEC may modify or reject rules and decisions of these bodies.

As might be expected, the principle of self-regulation is controversial. Though the various exchanges and the NASD have rendered valuable regulatory services, it is only natural that at times they have been more cognizant of the interests of their members, or of some of their members, than of the interests of others. And the SEC itself has at times been less than aggressive in promoting the public interest and in resolving sharp conflicts within the securities industry. We shall later deal with some of the controversial issues.

One provision of the securities laws is administered by the Federal Reserve; this is regulation of minimum margin requirements on loans collateraled by stocks and bonds listed on national exchanges and some traded in the OTC market when the loan proceeds are used to purchase or carry such securities. These margin requirements fix the minimum percentage of the purchase price that a buyer must pay at the time of purchase. This is an indirect way of setting maximum loan values on such securities, for the latter are equal to 100 percent minus the margin requirement. The Federal Reserve raises margin requirements to restrict the use of credit to purchase and carry such securities, and it lowers them to lessen the degree of restriction. In recent years these have ranged between 50 and 80 percent on stocks and between 50 and 60 percent on bonds convertible into stocks.

The Federal Reserve also imposes minimum margin requirements on short sales of such securities. These are sales in which the securities delivered were not owned by the seller but were borrowed from someone else. The margin requirement is stated as a percentage of the value of the borrowed securities. An increase of this margin requirement requires the seller to put up more money and thus tends to discourage short sales.

MIDDLEMEN IN FINANCIAL MARKETS

The function of middleman is performed primarily by a nationwide, and even international, network of dealers and brokers in financial claims. A dealer buys and sells for his own account and risk, hoping to cover his expenses and reap a profit from the gross margin between his selling and buying prices. The function of a broker, on the other hand, is to facilitate purchases and sales by others. For this, the broker receives a fee or commission. In some cases, a broker merely puts buyers and sellers into communication with each other so that they can enter into a transaction. In most cases, however, the broker acts as agent for a buyer or seller. At least two brokers are involved in most transactions, one serving as agent for the seller and another as agent for the buyer. Though some middlemen act only as brokers and others only as dealers, most of them—and especially the larger firms—act as both brokers and dealers.

In mid-1976, about 5300 firms were registered with the Securities and Exchange Commission as brokers and dealers in securities. However, there were also others that performed to at least some extent the function of brokers and dealers in securities without registering with the SEC. For example, some commercial banks regularly serve as brokers and dealers in securities issued by the federal, state, and local governments. Banks are also permitted, on specific requests from their customers, to forward to brokers and dealers their customers' orders to buy and sell other types of securities.

Of the registered brokers and dealers, about a quarter have their head offices in New York City, and the others are domiciled in a large number of other cities, including Chicago, San Francisco, Los Angeles, Boston, Philadelphia, Cleveland, Miami, and Dallas. Broker-dealer firms differ greatly in size. A majority are relatively small, with only a single office, a small number of officers and employees, and less than $1 million of capital. At the other extreme, some are very large. For example, in 1977 the largest firm, Merrill Lynch & Co., had 230 domestic offices, 54 offices abroad, and a total capital position in excess of $630 million. Several others had more than 25 domestic offices, and some of these also had branches and affiliates in other countries. As in many other industries, a small percentage of the firms account for a major part of the total business.

As might be expected in view of the structure of the industry, correspondent or customary relationships have developed among the smaller, more localized firms and the larger firms doing business on a national or international scale. For example, a small firm receiving a customer's order to buy or sell a security listed on a distant exchange often passes the order along to a larger firm for execution. And a larger firm, acting as an underwriter for a new issue, often invites smaller firms to retail some of the securities.

The range and mix of financial services provided by broker-dealers differ widely. Some firms act only as brokers and dealers in securities. Others, and especially the medium-sized and large firms, also offer other services. Among these are underwriting of new issues of securities, serving as financial adviser to nonfinancial business firms and financial intermediaries, arranging business reorganizations and mergers, managing investment companies and pension funds, and acting as brokers and dealers in commodities.

As a group, the 5300 firms registered as broker-dealers operate about 6300 branches located throughout the United States and other branches and affiliates abroad, and they employ about 200,000 representatives who are licensed to do business with the public. Thus, virtually all ultimate buyers and sellers of financial claims have easy access to at least one broker-dealer office. However, they sometimes communicate with broker-dealers by telephone or by placing orders through a local bank or other financial intermediary.

The various broker-dealers do business with each other, for their own accounts and for the accounts of their customers, through two principal channels. One is by meeting on the trading floor of an organized securities exchange. For example, suppose that Mr. A, who lives in Seattle, orders his local broker to sell 100 shares of XYZ common, which is listed for trading on the New York Stock Exchange, and that the order is sent to New York for execution by the head office of A's broker. In the meantime, Ms. B, who lives in Cleveland, has ordered her broker to buy 100 shares of XYZ common, and this order is sent to New York for execution by the head office of B's broker. A's broker and B's broker meet on the floor of the exchange and consummate the transaction.

All trades that do not take place on the organized exchanges are said to occur in the "over-the-counter market," popularly called the OTC market. This has been called "a market without a marketplace," for trades do not occur at a specific place. The thousands of broker-dealers effect transactions among themselves not by meeting at a specific geographic place but through a complex but rapid communications network. Information concerning offers to buy or sell specific securities is disseminated through newspapers, daily quotation sheets, a computer-

Table 8 – 1   **Registered Securities Exchanges in the United States**

In New York City:
    New York Stock Exchange
    American Stock Exchange

Regional Exchanges Outside New York City:
    Boston Stock Exchange
    Chicago Board Options Exchange, Inc.
    Cincinnati Stock Exchange
    Midwest Stock Exchange
    Pacific Stock Exchange
    Philadelphia– Baltimore– Washington (PBW) Stock Exchange Inc.
    Intermountain Stock Exchange
    Spokane Stock Exchange

Source: SEC, *Annual Report,* 1975/76, p. 77.

based system with TV outlets in the offices of broker-dealers, and telephone and telex. Transactions are usually consummated by telephone. We shall later have much more to say about the OTC market. In the meantime, it is unsafe to assume that trading on the OTC market is necessarily slower or less efficient than trading on the organized exchanges.

SECURITIES EXCHANGES

There are 10 organized securities exchanges that are registered with the SEC.[1] (See Table 8 – 1.) The New York Stock Exchange is by far the largest, with the American Stock Exchange a distant second. The others are usually referred to as "the regional exchanges."

A securities exchange does not itself engage in buying or selling securities, either for its own account or for the accounts of others. This function is performed by the brokers and dealers who are members of the exchange. The primary purposes of the exchange itself are to regulate trading practices and to provide various types of trading facilities. The latter include a building to house trading facilities, a trading floor, communications from the floor to offices of member broker-dealers, a

[1] The Honolulu Exchange does such a small amount of business and confines its activities to such small areas that it is not required to register with the SEC.

ticker and other facilities for reporting trades and prices, and facilities for clearing and settling transactions among members.

As shown in Table 8−2, securities of 3404 issuers are admitted to trading on one or more of the exchanges. Two of these issuers are the federal government and the International Bank for Reconstruction and Development, whose bonds are listed on the New York Stock Exchange. Virtually all the other issuers are corporations, most of them domestic but some foreign. Some 3889 different issues of common and preferred stocks and 2626 different bond issues are admitted to trading on one or more of the exchanges. In general, an issue that is listed for trading on the New York Stock Exchange or the American Stock Exchange is not listed for trading on the other. Only a few issues are listed on both exchanges. However, many of the issues listed for trading on one of these major exchanges are also listed on one or more of the regional exchanges. In fact, a large fraction of the dollar volume of transactions on the regional exchanges is in securities also listed on the American

Table 8−2 **Stocks and Bonds Listed for Trading on Securities Exchanges in the United States**

	New York Stock Exchange	American Stock Exchange	Exclusively on Other Exchanges	Unduplicated Total
I. Number of issues and issuers (June 30, 1975)				
Stock issues	2080	1305	504	3889
Bond issues	2380	202	44	2626
Issuers involved	1892	1280	232	3404
II. Values of stock listed on exchanges, Dec. 31, 1974 (in billions)	$511.1	$23.3	$2.9	$537.3
III. Percentages of total dollar volume of stock transactions on exchanges, 1974	83.8	4.4	11.8	100.0
IV. Dollar volume of trading on the New York Stock Exchange, 1974 (in billions)				
Stocks	$105.6			
Bonds	6.2			

Source: SEC, *Annual Report,* 1975, pp. 192 − 199.

Table 8 – 3   **Active Corporations in the United States, by Size of Assets, 1968**

Asset Size	Number of Corpora- tions	Percent of All Corpora- tions	Assets (in millions)	Percent of Total Assets
Under $100,000	890,176	57.7	$ 30,032	1.4
$100 – 999.9 thousand	552,935	35.9	164,343	7.4
$1 – 9.9 million	81,802	5.3	215,603	9.7
$10 – 24.9 million	9,125	0.6	141,238	6.4
$25 – 49.9 million	3,472	0.2	120,613	5.4
$50 – 99.9 million	1,839	0.1	127,956	5.8
$100 – 249.9 million	1,280	0.1	197,467	8.9
$250 million and over	1,041	0.1	1,218,373	55.0
Total	1,541,670	100.0	$2,215,625	100.0

Source: U.S. Department of Commerce, Bureau of the Census, *Statistical Abstract of the United States,* 1971, p. 469.

Stock Exchange or the New York Stock Exchange, primarily the latter. We shall also have occasion to emphasize that many securities listed on one of the two big New York exchanges are also traded in the OTC market. Such OTC transactions are said to occur in the *Third Market,* to distinguish them from transactions in the same securities on the floors of the two big New York exchanges.

Though bonds are traded on the securities exchanges, the latter are primarily marketplaces for stocks, both common stocks and preferred stocks. Of the 2626 bond issues listed for trading on one or more of the exchanges, 2380 were listed on the New York Stock Exchange and only 246 were listed exclusively on the other exchanges. (See Table 8 – 2.) Even on the New York Stock Exchange, the dollar volume of trading in bonds is far less than that in stocks. For example, during 1975 trading in bonds was only $9.1 billion, while trading in stocks was $133.8 billion. Even for bonds listed for trading on securities exchanges, the volume of transactions on the exchanges is far smaller than that in the OTC market. The bond market is predominantly an OTC market.

Only a very small fraction of all business corporations have their securities listed on any securities exchange. There are more than 1.5 million active corporations, but only about 3400 of these, or less than 1 percent, have any securities listed on an exchange. (See Table 8 – 3.) However, the corporations whose securities are listed are so large that they account for at least 65 percent of the value of all corporate assets. Securities of the other corporations are traded, if at all, only in the OTC market. It seems likely that the securities of at least a million of the smallest corporations are closely held by families or other small groups and rarely appear in the market. Of the remaining corporations, more than 3,300 have issues that are traded more or less actively in the OTC market, and about 30,000 others are traded at least occasionally.

No matter how measured, the New York Stock Exchange is by far the most important of the organized exchanges. For example, at the end of 1974, when the total value of stocks listed on one or more of the exchanges was about $537 billion, those listed on the New York Stock Exchange accounted for 95.1 percent, those listed on the American Stock Exchange for 4.3 percent, and those listed exclusively on the other exchanges for less than 1 percent of the total. (See Table 8−2.) Of the total dollar volume of stock transactions on exchanges during 1974, the New York Stock Exchange accounted for 83.8 percent, the American Stock Exchange for 4.4 percent, and all the other exchanges for only 11.8 percent. The fraction for the regional exchanges would be considerably smaller if transactions in securities also listed on the New York Stock Exchange were excluded.

THE OTC MARKET

As already noted, this market includes all purchases and sales of financial claims that are not effected on an organized securities exchange. The things traded in this market are therefore of many types:

1. Corporate stocks that are not listed on any exchange.
2. Corporate stocks that are listed on the New York Stock Exchange or the American Stock Exchange. This, as noted earlier, is called the Third Market.
3. Stocks listed exclusively on a regional exchange.
4. Long-term corporate and government bonds. As noted earlier, the volume of bond transactions in the OTC market far exceeds the total on all the securities exchanges.
5. Many types of short-term debt claims, such as Treasury securities, state and local government securities, bankers' acceptances, and commercial paper. Transactions in such claims are almost exclusively in the OTC market, and the trading volume is huge.

Primary markets for stocks and bonds are predominantly OTC markets. New issues are sometimes distributed through securities exchanges when they are additions to issues already listed for trading. However, stocks and bonds are in most cases distributed initially through the OTC market even if they are subsequently listed for trading on an exchange.

The middlemen in this market are, of course, the thousands of broker-dealers noted earlier. Many of these are not members of any exchange and do business solely in the OTC markets, but many, including the larger ones that account for a major part of the business in this market, are also members of one or more of the organized exchanges.

In providing continuity of trading and promoting orderly behavior of security prices in the OTC market, dealers acting as "registered market makers" play a key role. The immediate supervisory agency for the OTC markets, the National Association of Securities Dealers (NASD), designates specific dealers as "registered market makers" for specified stocks. In the OTC market, there are often numerous registered market makers for a single stock, in some cases as many as twenty-five. Also, a market maker may serve this function for several different stocks. Some of the most active market makers have large financial resources at their disposal, and it is common for the combined resources of all market makers for a specific stock in the OTC market to be very large indeed.

In becoming a registered market maker for specified securities, a dealer assumes certain responsibilities. He must quote prices for them and stand ready to buy and sell at least a minimum number of shares at the quoted prices. He is also subject to NASD rules and regulations designed to prevent unfair trading practices and unfairly wide margins between buying and selling prices.

In some cases ultimate buyers and sellers deal directly with a market maker. This is most likely to happen when the buyer or seller is a financial intermediary, a trust department, or some other institution that buys and sells in large lots. In fact, some institutions have direct wires to market makers in securities that they buy or sell most frequently and in the largest amounts. In more cases, however, an ultimate buyer or seller communicates with a broker or dealer, who in turn deals with a market maker. There is also a large volume of transactions among market makers for a specific security. These arise because one has an excessive inventory while the inventory of another is deficient, or one has an excess of buy orders while another has an excess of sell orders.

In recent years the OTC market has grown remarkably in volume of transactions, in efficiency, and in prestige. We shall see later that there are several reasons for this rapid growth, among which are the rising importance of financial intermediaries and trust departments with purchase and sell orders too large to be effected satisfactorily through the conventional auction system on the floor of an exchange, and certain restrictive practices by the exchanges, and especially by the New York Stock Exchange. At this point, however, we shall concentrate on what can only be called a communications revolution in the OTC market for stocks. Before the 1970s, information concerning prices in recent transactions and current price quotations by dealers was communicated through newspapers, daily quotation sheets issued by dealers, and telephone and telex. This communications system was adequate but expensive, information concerning prices in current transactions often became generally available only after a delay, and it was difficult to get and compare on a current basis price quotations by the various market makers.

The information system in the OTC market made a quantum leap in early 1971 when NASDAQ began operation. This is the acronym for National Association of Security Dealers Automated Quotation System. It is a computer-based system with TV outlets in thousands of offices of broker-dealers. By the end of 1976, there were 365 registered market makers quoting prices in the system. Stocks quoted in NASDAQ included nearly 2400 issues that were not listed on any exchange but had an aggregate market value of about $78 billion, and about 90 issues listed on one or more of the exchanges.

NASDAQ supplies three levels of services that a viewer can obtain by punching the appropriate buttons on a TV terminal. Level I provides current representative interdealer bid and ask quotations for each security included in the system for the information of registered representatives of broker-dealers and for customers of retail firms. Level II supplies to trading rooms of broker-dealers actual quotations by all market makers for each security included in the system. The selling prices quoted by market makers are ranked from low to high, and quoted buying prices are ranked from high to low. Thus it is easy for a buyer to purchase at the lowest quoted prices and for a seller to sell at the highest quoted prices. Transactions are consummated by telephone. Level III is similar to Level II but it also provides input facilities that enable authorized market makers to enter, change, and update their quoted buying and selling prices. Viewing at Level II, it is interesting to see how frequently market makers alter their quotations to become more competitive with others or to adjust to changes in demand-supply relations. For example, a market maker whose quoted selling price is above others and who wants to reduce his inventory of a security will lower his quoted price, which often leads to adjustments of quotations by others. Or a market maker whose quoted buying price is below those of others will adjust his quotation upward in order to cover his current sales of a stock or to rebuild his inventory. Though transactions are not consummated through NASDAQ, this system both induces and reflects competition in price quotations.

In 1974 NASDAQ expanded the system to enable subscribing brokerage firms to report the details of each transaction in stocks to the NASDAQ central computer. This trade-reporting system makes it possible for traders to verify each trade within seconds of its execution and to detect immediately any errors. It also provides more current information to investors and speeds up the clearing and settling of OTC transactions. NASDAQ innovations have already improved greatly the speed and efficiency of the OTC market and made it more competitive with the securities exchanges. A further innovation may be imminent: the system may be used to consummate transactions. Addition of appropriate equipment to NASDAQ would enable broker-dealers to communicate their orders directly to market makers and to receive through the system immediate confirmation.

OTHER TECHNOLOGICAL CHANGES

Important as it is, NASDAQ is by no means the only computer-based technology that has been introduced, is in process of being introduced, or is in the offing in the securities industry. There are also others, and their combined effects may be to alter markedly the structure and practices of the industry—the number and size of broker-dealer firms, the number of securities exchanges, and the distribution of transactions among the securities exchanges and the OTC market. One thing is certain: the introduction of computer technology can reduce markedly real transactions costs. A major reason for this is that traditional methods have involved huge amounts of paperwork and much labor—especially clerical labor, which has become increasingly expensive.

An example of a simple transaction will illustrate the processes and steps involved in traditional methods. Suppose that Ms. Seller orders her broker to sell 500 shares of XYZ Common, and that Ms. Buyer orders her broker to buy a like number of these shares. Their brokers will execute the orders on the floor of an exchange or in the OTC market. This is by no means the end of the process.

1. Stock certificates. Ms. Seller will surrender stock certificates to her broker, who will send them to a stock clearing corporation. The

latter will compare the total amounts of each stock owed by each broker and owed to each broker as a result of transactions and will inform each broker of the net amount of each stock to be delivered to or received from each other broker. Ms. Buyer's broker, after receiving the stock certificates, will send them to the transfer agent for that stock, who will cancel the old certificates, issue new ones in the name of Ms. Buyer, and deliver them to Ms. Buyer's broker, who will forward them to Ms. Buyer. These processes obviously involve much paperwork and expenses for stationery, postage, and insurance.

2. Payments. Ms. Buyer must pay her broker, who must in turn pay Ms. Seller's broker, who will pay Ms. Seller. In between there is further paperwork at a clearinghouse, which compares the gross amounts due to and from each broker-dealer and notifies each of the net amounts she is to pay to or receive from each other broker-dealer.

These inefficient and expensive methods, abetted by an unusually high volume of transactions, a shortage of "back-room" personnel in brokers' offices, and inadequate automation, led to a "paperwork crisis" in the late 1960s. Accounts became muddled, certificates were lost, a number of brokerage houses failed, and public confidence was shaken. Reform became inevitable. Though reforms are still in process and the final outcome is not fully predictable, the direction of change is becoming clear:

1. Eventual elimination of the stock certificate.[2] How soon and to what extent this can be accomplished remain problematical; some owners are apparently more impressed by engraved stock certificates than by computer printouts. However, long steps have already been taken to eliminate the stock certificate in processes of delivery, clearance, and settlement. In early 1973, there were established the Depository Trust Co. in New York City and eight regional depositories located in six states. These receive stock certificates on deposit, hold them, and issue in return claims against their computers. In our example, the seller would surrender stock certificates to her broker, who would immediately send them to either the Depository Trust Company in New York or to one of the regional depositories. From that point no further movements of the paper certificates are involved; all transfers are of claims against

---

[2] Though certificates representing debts of the U.S. Treasury have not yet been fully eliminated, a major part of that debt is now represented by entries in computers at the Federal Reserve banks. Transfers of ownership are made by appropriate entries in the computer.

a computer of the Depository Trust Company. However, buyers can, if they wish, get certificates by surrendering their claims against the computer.

By mid-1973, participants in the Depository Trust Company included not only the two big New York exchanges but also six regional exchanges and the National Clearing Corporation, which is operated by the NASD. The company held on deposit 1.5 billion shares, worth over $60 billion. It held over 4000 different issues, among which were a majority of the issues listed on the NYSE and the American Stock Exchange and over 1500 issues traded only in the OTC market. This system, or one quite similar to it, is expected to expand much further in the future.

2. Development of a more efficient clearing and settlement system. Before 1977, there were separate clearing and settlement systems for the OTC and the various securities exchanges. Now the separate systems of the OTC, the New York Stock Exchange, and the American Stock Exchange are being merged into a new entity called the National Securities Clearing Corporation (NSCC). The regional exchanges are expected to join in the near future. When fully established, the NSCC will enable all transactions to be cleared and settled regardless of the branch of the market in which the transactions occur. This system is called *continuous net settlement*, or CNS. Under this system, broker-dealers do not deliver to or receive from each other directly either securities or money; instead, each settles with the clearinghouse itself. Each delivers to the clearinghouse any net shares or net money that it owes, and each receives from the clearinghouse any net amount of shares and money that is due to it. This method is considerably faster and more economical than the older ones, and it serves to protect each broker against "fails to deliver" by other brokers.

3. Establishment, in 1970, of the Securities Industry Protection Corporation (SIPC). The purpose of the SIPC is to protect customers against loss of cash or securities in case of failure of a brokerage firm. The limit per customer is $50,000, except that claims for cash are limited to $20,000.

We shall have more to say about innovations in this industry when we discuss the proposed new National Market System.

EFFICIENCY OF FINANCIAL MARKETS

When dealing with financial markets there is a strong temptation to become so fascinated with the mechanics and with the profits or losses accruing to the immediate participants that one may fail to give adequate attention to the more basic functions and broader significance of financial markets. It may therefore be useful to emphasize again that the efficiency of financial markets has profound implications for the behavior of the real sectors of the economy, including both effects on the macroeconomic behavior of overall real output, employment, and price levels, and effects on the allocation of scarce real resources among their various potential uses.

In the following pages we shall explore briefly some issues relating to the efficiency of financial markets. As usual, we distinguish two related types of efficiency—transactions efficiency and allocational efficiency.

TRANSACTIONS EFFICIENCY

This refers to economy in the use of resources to produce and distribute the various services used to facilitate financial transactions. To achieve maximum transactions efficiency, two broad conditions must be met:

1. Each service must be produced at minimum cost. This means that firms must exploit the available economies of specialization and scale, the most favorable technology, and optimum combinations of the various factors of production. Unnecessarily high costs of producing financial services are objectionable on two grounds. First, they respresent a waste, for resources used for this purpose are not available for other uses. Second, to the extent that they are reflected in higher prices for these services, they discourage trading and result in a loss of potential utility to traders.
2. The price charged for each service must be equal to its marginal cost. A higher price would discourage use of such services, with loss of potential utility to traders. And a lower price would lead traders to demand some services whose value to them is below the marginal cost of producing them.

We shall later encounter cases in which maximum transactions efficiency was not achieved, either because financial services were not produced at minimum cost, or because they were priced too high or too low relative to their cost, or both.

ALLOCATIONAL EFFICIENCY

The most obvious function of financial markets is, of course, to facilitate exchanges of financial claims of various kinds. In some cases, financial claims are swapped directly for each other. In the bulk of transactions, however, money is used as the medium of exchange; securities are sold for money, and securities are bought with money. It is useful to view such transactions as methods of allocating and reallocating financial claims and money. Securities are obviously transferred or reallocated from sellers to buyers. This effect is important, for it enables traders in securities to readjust their portfolios in order to achieve what they consider to be the most favorable combination of income, safety, and liquidity. Several benefits can flow from this process:

1. Each holder can maximize the utility derived from his portfolio.
2. The function of the bearing risk and illiquidity can be transferred to those who will perform it at the lowest price in terms of a higher yield.
3. It can minimize the higher cost of funds to issuers of risky and illiquid securities.

Transactions in securities are also a major method of transferring or reallocating money from buyers to sellers of securities. Suppose, for example, that Mr. Seller sells $1 million of securities, either "old" or newly created, receiving in return an equal amount of money. Since money is "generalized purchasing power" or "a bearer of options," he can use it for any purpose or purposes that will yield the highest utility to him. He may, of course, use it to buy other securities, including his own outstanding issues. But he also has various other options: to add it to his money balances for transactions purposes or to improve the safety and liquidity of his portfolio; to acquire "old" physical goods; to finance consumption; or to finance new investment or capital formation. We shall emphasize here the use of such funds for investment. The price and yield at which Mr. Seller can sell his securities, whether these are his own issue or an issue by others, represent the terms on which he can acquire funds for investment. Thus the price and yield on a security, and relative prices and yields on different securities, play vital roles in investment decisions and in the allocation of scarce resources for investment.

For the structure of prices and yields on securities to promote maximum efficiency in the allocation of resources for investment, the following conditions must be met.

1. The price of each and every security must be based on, and reflect, the best information available concerning the future amounts and timing of the returns that will accrue to that security. Though these cannot be predicted precisely in a world of uncertainty and

risk, there are, as noted earlier, various means of improving the state of information and the quality of forecasting.

2. Prices of the various securities must be such that yields differ by no more than enough to compensate for differences in risk and liquidity.

Each potential spender for investment will arrive at his investment decisions by comparing the cost of funds, as represented by the yield on securities that he is in a position to sell, with the expected rate of return on investment. We assume, as we did earlier, that each spender for investment will estimate the mean expected rate of marginal efficiency (m) for each available investment project and the required rate of compensation for bearing the risk and illiquidity associated with the investment (r), and then undertake all the investment on which ($m - r$) exceeds the cost of funds.[3] He will not undertake any investment on which ($m - r$) is less than the cost of funds. The result is the most efficient allocation that can be achieved in a world of uncertainty and risk.

Any structure of security prices that resulted in yield differentials greater than those justified by differences in risk and liquidity would tend to produce misallocations of investment resources. Suppose, for example, that the prices of the securities that Firm A is in a position to sell are so high that their yields are considerably below the levels justified by their risk-liquidity characteristics. In contrast, the prices of the securities that Firm B is in a position to sell are so low that their yields are considerably above the levels justified by their risk-liquidity characteristics. Firm A, enjoying a low cost of funds, will undertake some investment on which ($m - r$) is comparably low. But Firm B, faced with a much higher cost of funds, will not undertake any investment on which ($m - r$) is not at least as high as its high cost of funds. Allocational efficiency would be improved if less investment resources were allocated to Firm A and more to Firm B.

In financial markets of maximum efficiency, competition would eradicate yield differentials greater than those justified by differences in risk and liquidity.

---

[3] See pp. 67–69 above.

CONCLUSION

We have now completed our survey of financial markets as a whole. Several submarkets can be distinguished. On the basis of the legal nature of the things traded, we have:

1. Bond markets, in which are traded long-term debt obligations, principally those of corporations and governmental units.
2. Mortgage markets.
3. "Money markets," in which are traded many types of liquid, short-term debt claims.
4. Corporate equity markets for trading in common and preferred stocks.

For most of these types of claims there are primary markets through which new issues are distributed, and secondary markets for trading in issues that are already outstanding.

In the following chapters we shall examine each of these markets more closely.

SELECTED READINGS

I. Purposes and performance of financial markets

Baumol, W. J. *The Stock Market and Economic Efficiency.* New York: Fordham, 1965.

Fama, E. F. "Efficient Capital Markets: A Review of Theory and Empirical Work." *Journal of Finance,* May 1970, pp. 383–417.

Robbins, S. M. *The Securities Markets.* New York: Free Press, 1966.

II. Over-the-counter markets

Loll, L. M., and Buckley, J. G. *The Over-the-Counter Market.* 3d ed. Englewood Cliffs, N.J.: Prentice-Hall, 1973. (This book also deals with the organized securities exchanges.)

III. Organized securities exchanges

A. Historical development of exchanges

Sobel, R. *The Big Board.* New York: Free Press, 1965. (The New York Stock Exchange and its predecessors.)

——— . *The Curbstone Brokers.* New York: Macmillan, 1970. (The American Stock Exchange and its predecessors.)

B. Structure and functioning of organized exchanges

Eiteman, W. J., Dice, C. A., and Eiteman, D. K. *The Stock Market.* 4th ed. New York: McGraw-Hill, 1966.

Shultz, B. E., and Squier, A. P. *The Securities Market —And How It Works.* Rev. ed. New York: Harper & Row, 1963.

IV. Current sources of information

National Association of Securities Dealers. Annual reports and other publications.

New York Stock Exchange. *Fact Book* (annually) and other publications.

Securities Exchange Commission. Annual reports and other publications.

9

STOCK MARKETS

This chapter consists of two main parts. The first, and longer, part deals with trading of corporate shares through the organized securities exchanges and the OTC market. The second deals with stock options.

In discussing trading through the exchanges, we shall concentrate largely on the New York Stock Exchange (NYSE) because it is by far the largest and because it operates on the same general principles as the others, but we shall at times comment on differences in practices and on interrelations among the exchanges. It will not be possible to discuss in static terms the arrangements for trading in stocks listed on the New York Stock Exchange, for these have undergone marked changes since the early 1960s, changes still continue, and the final outcome is not yet clear. We shall therefore describe the principal developments up to the mid-1970s, the situation at that time, and the general nature of probable future developments.

THE NEW YORK STOCK EXCHANGE

It will be useful to recall some of our earlier findings about this institution:

1. The NYSE does not itself trade in securities. It provides facilities for trading and trade reporting and acts as the governing body, under

supervision by the SEC, prescribing and enforcing rules regulating trading practices and the conduct of its members.

2. Only stocks listed on the exchange may be traded on the exchange floor. Less than 2000 corporations have their stocks listed on the NYSE, but these are so large that the aggregate value of their stocks constitutes significantly more than half of the value of all outstanding corporate stocks.

3. Only broker-dealers who are members of the exchange may transact business on the exchange; nonmember broker-dealers can gain access to the trading facilities of the exchange only through members—and at a price. Membership on the exchange is limited to 1366. There are some 500 member firms; these are firms that include one or more members of the exchange. These firms operate a nationwide network of several thousand offices and also have branches and affiliates in foreign countries.

TRADING ON THE EXCHANGE FLOOR

Most trading on the exchange is in "round lots" and multiples thereof; for most stocks, a round lot is 100 shares. There is also trading in "odd lots," or less than 100 shares. Some buyers pay the full price of the purchased shares; others "buy on margin." In the latter case, buyers contribute the required margin in cash and their brokers pledge the securities for a loan so that the sellers can be paid immediately and in full. In most sales sellers offer securities that they own and deliver them immediately to their brokers. However, there are also "short sales," in which sellers sell securities that they do not own. In this case, brokers borrow the securities from others and deliver them to buyers. Thus, the short-seller incurs a debt stated in terms of the number of shares borrowed. If the price of these shares should rise, the short-seller might be unable to purchase shares to return to the lender. To protect against this hazard, the short-seller is required to contribute a money margin. Minimum margin requirements against short sales are regulated by the Federal Reserve and are usually the same, or approximately the same, as those applying to purchases on margin.

Customers' orders to buy or sell can be classified in various ways, but for our purposes it is sufficient to distinguish two principal classes: *market orders* and *limit orders*. In effect, an order to buy "at market" instructs the broker, "Buy as cheaply as you can, but buy immediately." An order to sell at market means, "Sell as high as you can, but sell immediately." On the other hand, a limit order places a limit on the price to be accepted or paid. The price mentioned may be "away from" the current price, so that the order cannot be executed at once. Suppose, for example, that at some time the current price per share for a stock is $40. A limit order to buy at $38 means, "Do not pay more than $38 per share, but buy immediately when the price is at that level." A limit order to sell at $42 means, "Do not sell for less than $42, but at that price sell immediately." Under the conditions assumed above, neither of the limit orders could be executed immediately. The brokers receiving them would relay them to the specialist in the security, who would enter them in his "book," to be executed if and when the price reached the stipulated limits. Some limit orders are "good 'til canceled" (GTC); others are valid for only stipulated periods.

Members transacting business on the floor of the NYSE are of several types:

1. Floor traders, who buy and sell only for their own accounts. They are members in order to be "close to the action" and to save on commissions.
2. Brokers' brokers, who act as brokers for other brokers, primarily for commission brokers. They are often called "$2-brokers" because their commission was once $2 per hundred shares. Commission brokers employ them when they are absent from the floor or have too many orders to handle themselves.
3. Commission brokers, who act on the floor as agents for customers.
4. Odd-lot dealers, who buy and sell odd lots. They buy odd lots at a price fractionally below the current round-lot price and sell at a price fractionally above it.
5. Specialists, who serve as both brokers and dealers in the stocks for which they act as specialists.

Specialists play a crucial role in maintaining continuity of trading. Every stock listed on the NYSE is assigned to one, and usually only one, specialist.[1] Many specialists have more than one stock assigned to them. In return for this exclusive privilege, the specialist is expected to assure that all orders to buy and sell at market are executed immediately. At all times during trading hours, the specialist or his representative remains at the post where the stock is traded.

A specialist "maintains the book" for each stock in which he specializes. In this book, limit orders to buy are ranged from high to low,

---

[1] Some of the other exchanges have more than one specialist in each stock, or at least for those stocks that are traded very actively. In 1976 the NYSE began to experiment with more than one specialist for some stocks.

and limit orders to sell are ranged from low to high. When the market price reaches the limit specified in an order, the specialist buys or sells as a broker. However, the specialist is also expected to act as a dealer, buying and selling for his own account. In this role he is a "market maker"; he is expected to buy when there is an insufficiency of other buy orders at "reasonable" prices, and to sell when there is an insufficiency of other sell orders at "reasonable" prices. In short, his function is to serve as a stabilizing agent, though not to maintain completely stable prices. The extent to which a specialist should be expected to stabilize prices, and the efficacy of the various specialists in performing this function, are controversial questions.

There are elaborate rules to prevent a specialist from profiting as dealer at the expense of those who have orders in his book. The general principle is that orders in his book should always take precedence. A specialist may not buy for his own account if he has in his book any customer order to buy at that or a higher price. And he may not sell for his own account if he has in his book any order to sell at that or a lower price.

THE CONTINUOUS AUCTION MARKET

To illustrate the principles of the continuous auction market, we shall deal first with the case in which individual orders to buy or sell are of no more than moderate size—not much more than 1000 shares. Commission brokers who are members of the exchange receive such orders from all over the country and from abroad. The brokers receiving orders for a particular stock go to the trading post where the stock is traded and where the specialist and others interested in the stock congregate. Brokers with buy orders try to buy as cheaply as possible; those with sell orders try to sell as dearly as possible. Out of this competition emerge a transaction and a price that temporarily equate supply and demand. In many transactions the specialist does not participate at all; in others he buys or sells, either for orders in his book or for his own account. Such auctions continue during all trading hours, and prices respond as supply-demand conditions change.

Under the conditions described above, the floor of the exchange can indeed be a centralized marketplace in which are reflected total demand and total supply conditions for a stock. Ticker tape reports on transactions and prices are available on a current basis to potential buyers and sellers all over the nation and in many other countries. All have access to brokers, who will communicate their orders to the exchange floor, where the available supply is sold to the highest bidders. When single orders are of no more than moderate size, the specialist has enough financial and risk-bearing capacity to offset temporary imbalances of supply and demand and to maintain orderly market conditions. One observer has concluded that "before institutions rose to prominence on the equity market, the NYSE may easily have been the best securities market that ever existed."[2]

BLOCK TRADING

Block trading became increasingly important during the 1960s and early 1970s as large institutional investors—such as private pension funds, pension funds of state and local governments, investment companies, trust departments, and insurance companies—increased greatly their holdings, purchases, and sales of common stocks. Single orders to buy or sell thousands of shares worth millions of dollars became common. Specialists in the NYSE auction market cannot cope satisfactorily with such large blocks. For one thing, stock exchange rules require that specialists deal only with members of the exchange and forbid them to deal directly with institutional buyers and sellers. Moreover, few specialists have either the financial capacity or the willingness to bear the risk that would be required to prevent such large block orders from creating disorders in the auction market.

Special methods have evolved for trading blocks of stock considered too large for auctioning on the exchange floor. Some of these involve member broker-dealers, acting as "block assemblers." Instead of taking the transaction to the floor, they "go upstairs," where they negotiate the placement of the block order with other institutions or with other broker-dealers through an extensive communications system. The price is arrived at by negotiation rather than in a competitive auction. In many cases, however, block transactions do go to the floor to be "crossed"; that is, the offers to buy and sell at the agreed-upon price are presented on the floor, and the transaction is formally consummated if, as usually happens, no one offers a better price for the block.

In other cases large block orders do not go to the NYSE at all. Many of them, as we shall see later, go to the regional exchanges or the OTC market. In some cases institutions deal directly with each other in large blocks, though they often use brokers as finders and advisers. Such direct trades are said to occur on the Fourth Market.

[2] Morris Mendelson, *From Automated Quotes to Automated Trading: Restructuring the Stock Market In the United States* (Institute of Finance, New York University, 1972), p. 25.

The marked growth of institutional trading has been a major reason for the recent fragmentation of markets for listed stocks and for other changes in financial markets. However, two other factors are also relevant to these developments: the introduction of NASDAQ and other improvements in the OTC market; and certain restrictive and monopolistic practices of the NYSE. Though many of these practices are now in process of change, we shall refer to them in the present tense.

THE NYSE AS A CARTEL

From its beginnings in 1792 until the early 1970s the NYSE was a cartel, regulating the conduct of its members and access to its facilities. Officials of the exchange have contended that its rules and practices are in the public interest, for they serve to preserve the integrity of the continuous auction market and enable the exchange to police its members and enforce rules of fair trading. Whether or not one shares this assessment, some of the rules were clearly anticompetitive and have created serious market distortions. We shall now explore some of these in order to see why changes began to be introduced in the 1970s.

LIMITATION OF ACCESS TO EXCHANGE
FACILITIES BY NONMEMBER BROKER-DEALERS

We have already mentioned that the exchange places a limit on the number of its members and that only members are permitted to trade on the exchange floor. Nonmember broker-dealers have access to the trading facilities of the exchange only through its members and at a price or commission rate fixed by the governing body of the exchange. Before 1972 the commission rate imposed on a nonmember broker-dealer was exactly the same as that imposed on any other buyer or seller, but in March of that year the exchange authorized a 40 percent discount to qualified nonmember broker-dealers, imposing the condition that nonmembers should not pass along to their customers any part of the discount. Though a nonmember could thereafter retain 40 percent of the commission, this was in many cases significantly less than he could earn by executing the order on a regional exchange or in the Third Market.

This restrictive rule of the exchange tended to fragment the market for securities listed for trading on the NYSE, because nonmember broker-dealers were given a strong incentive to execute orders outside the exchange. At any time, the price of a given stock on the regional exchanges and the Third Market could be either higher or lower than that prevailing on the NYSE. As a result, customers sometimes failed to get "best execution" of their orders placed with nonmember broker-dealers. That is, a seller might receive a lower net price than that available through the exchange, and a buyer might pay a higher gross price than would result from purchases through the exchange.

LIMITATIONS OF MEMBER
TRANSACTIONS OUTSIDE THE EXCHANGE

Under the rules of the exchange, a member receiving a buy or sell order for a stock listed on the exchange was permitted to execute it on a regional exchange or in the Third Market only after receiving permission from the governing authorities of the exchange, and a separate permission was required for each outside transaction. This was only rarely sought or given.

This rule clearly promoted fragmentation of the market in the sense that it permitted persistent price differences for a stock in the various branches of the market. A member broker could not quickly eliminate such price differences by selling outside when the price there was higher, and by purchasing outside when the price there was lower. In some cases, customers of member brokers failed to get the best possible execution of their orders.

FIXED MINIMUM COMMISSION RATES

From the beginning, the governing body of the exchange decreed a fixed schedule of minimum commission rates and penalized member brokers who charged less. These rates were so high that they became actual rates, they enabled even inefficient firms to survive, and they failed to bring pressure on firms to lower their costs. The rate schedule was only remotely related to costs on transactions of various sizes. Before 1968 there were no discounts for large-volume transactions. For example, the commission charged on 10,000 shares was exactly 100 times that on 100 shares. Though a new schedule introduced at the end of 1968 provided discounts on orders of 1000 or more shares, the resulting rate structure did not reflect adequately the lower costs per unit on large transactions.

Any student of cartels could have predicted some of the results of fixing commission rates above competitive levels. With overt price competition prohibited, broker-dealers turned to various types of nonprice competition, which tended to raise their costs. They advertised extensively and expensively, operated more and plusher offices, hired more salesmen, and proliferated the number of services offered. They offered not only execution of orders, but also investment advice, free subscriptions to financial publications, and special research reports. These services were "bundled"; that is, they were all covered by one commission charge that was based on the number and value of shares traded.

This pricing method is suspect on several grounds:

1. It may lead to overtrading. Since a broker's income depends on his volume of transactions, he is tempted to advise customers to buy and sell frequently even though this may be unprofitable for the customer.

2. It tempts customers to demand services to which they attach little value but which are costly in real terms. For example, an institution that attaches little value to a broker's advice and research may nevertheless demand them because they cost it nothing extra.

3. Bundling inhibits quality and price competition in providing the various services. Even if a broker is the most efficient executor of orders, he may not be the most efficient source of investment advice or of economic and financial research. If services were unbundled and priced separately, customers could shop around and buy each from the supplier offering the best terms. As might be expected, professional investment advisers strongly favor unbundling.

Faced with high fixed rates on the NYSE, customers sought in many ways to buy brokerage services at lower net prices, and in the process stimulated the growth of trading facilities outside the exchange. Small individual investors buying and selling no more than a few hundred shares a year lacked both the incentive and the financial expertise to do this to any large extent. But institutional investors were in a far different position. With brokerage fees running into the millions every year, they had strong incentives to economize, and they had the expertise to find and create alternatives. Moreover, a series of court decisions established the fact that they were legally obliged to economize for the benefit of their beneficiaries. Institutions therefore diverted large amounts of their business to the Third Market, where there were no fixed fees, and to the regional exchanges. Some of the regional exchanges also had fixed commission rates, but these were avoided in many and complex ways, ranging from outright or secret rebates to complicated reciprocal trading arrangements. Some of the regional exchanges also admitted to membership brokerage affiliates established by some of the financial institutions. In some cases these brokerage affiliates actually executed orders for the parent institution; in other cases they were only shells established to receive discounts or rebates for the account of the parent.

MARKET INEFFICIENCIES AND DISTORTIONS

In summary, the various restrictive practices of the NYSE led to a number of inefficiencies and market distortions, some of which have already been mentioned. One of the most serious results was fragmentation of the market for stocks listed on the NYSE. We have already noted that this permitted the existence of price differentials among the various branches of the market and that customers sometimes failed to get best execution of their orders. Fragmentation also tended to reduce the quality of the market as a whole. A market can achieve maximum continuity, liquidity, and resilience only if total demand and total supply conditions are reflected in what is, in effect, a single market, and if the resources of all market makers and specialists are made available in that market to maintain orderly conditions. To the extent that the market becomes separated or fragmented, the volume of trading in a given branch is reduced, imbalances between demand and supply occur more frequently and increase price fluctuations, and the market as a whole becomes less liquid and orderly. This is especially true if market makers and specialists are not permitted to operate freely in all branches of the market.

THE BREAKDOWN OF THE NYSE CARTEL

By the early 1970s, the restrictive practices of the NYSE were under strong, and ultimately successful, attacks from many quarters — not only from financial institutions but also from the Antitrust Division of the Department of Justice, the SEC, and the Congress.

By 1977 the cartel powers of the NYSE had been largely dissipated in these ways:

1. In a series of steps, fixed commission rates were eliminated. Since May 1, 1975, commission rates on transactions of all sizes have been determined through competitive negotiation. Rates on large

transactions have been reduced sharply. In general, rates on small orders have declined less, but some brokers quote rates considerably below those prevailing earlier. Moreover, many brokers now unbundle their services and price them separately.

2. Registered brokers who are not members of the exchange now have access to the services of member brokers at negotiated commission rates, so that they can transmit orders to the exchange floor more cheaply.

3. Members of the exchange are now permitted to execute customers' orders for listed securities outside the NYSE if they can get better execution of an order in the Third Market or on a regional exchange.

These reforms have already lowered commission rates for most buyers and sellers of securities; facilitated the flow of transactions among the NYSE, the regional exchanges, and the Third Market; and reduced market segmentation. However, further changes will come with the introduction of the National Market System.

THE NATIONAL MARKET SYSTEM (NMS)

In 1975 Congress ordered the SEC and the securities industry to develop and introduce as soon as possible a National Market System (NMS). The NMS will be a computer based, electronic communications system that will facilitate flows of information and orders among the NYSE, the Third Market, and the regional exchanges to such an extent that it will indeed be a "central" or "national" market system. It will include not only exchange specialists and Third Market market makers for the listed securities but also all registered broker-dealers, whether or not they are members of an exchange. At first, eligibility for trading through the NMS may be limited to stock issues listed on the NYSE. However, the eligible list will probably be expanded, and it seems likely that in the end eligibility for trading in this system will depend not on whether a security has been listed on any exchange but on whether its quality, outstanding volume, and frequency and volume of trading make it suitable for a continuous auction market.

Though many technical details of the NMS remain to be determined, some parts of it are already in place or in process of introduction, and it is possible to describe in general terms both the structure and functioning of the system. The principal components are:

1. A consolidated reporting system. As noted earlier, this component is already in operation. It reports as they occur all transactions in the listed securities, indicating both price and volume.
2. A Composite Quotations System (CQS). For each listed security, CQS supplies quoted offers to buy and sell by specialists and market makers in all branches of the market. Bid quotations are ranked from high to low, with identification of the location of the bidders. Asked quotations are ranked from low to high, with similar identification of the location of those who quote for sale. This information is continuously available through TV outlets in thousands of brokers' offices located throughout this country and in some others.
3. An electronic Composite Limit-Order Book (CLOB). Though the CLOB is not yet in place, it is contemplated. We noted earlier that when a broker receives a limit order to buy or sell at a price that is away from the current market price, he typically gives the order to a specialist, who enters it in his book to be executed if and when the market price reaches the limit price. Now it is proposed that there be established a central computer based, electronic book in which would be entered all limit orders for each listed stock. Brokers will be permitted to communicate limit orders directly to the electronic book without the intervention of a specialist, and the latter will communicate to this book any limit orders that it receives. The computer will accumulate all such orders with identifying symbols and numbers, rank purchase orders from high to low and sell orders from low to high, and make this information available through an electronic communications network.

These three computer based communications components will make available to brokers and dealers instantaneously a large amount of information about each listed security: the volume and prices in recent transactions in all branches of the market; current buy and sell quotations by all competing market makers and specialists in the security; and a price-ranked list of all outstanding limit orders. All that remains is to use this information to compare buy and sell orders, to arrive at a price that equates demand and supply, and to execute a transaction. This could be done on the floor of an exchange or even through the books of a market maker in the Third Market. With information and orders flowing freely among all branches of the market, prices would tend to be uniform at any time.

However, it is expected by many that the NMS will have a fourth component—a facility for automated trading. This will be a large computer, which can be located anywhere, with a very extensive electronic communications network through which it can receive and send orders and other information. In effect, the computer will be instructed to conduct a continuous auction market in accordance with programmed rules. For each listed security, the computer will have stored in its memory all buy and sell quotations in the CQS and all buy and sell orders in the composite limit order book. It will also receive directly flows of orders from brokers and dealers to buy and sell at market. From these data, it will construct what are, in effect, momentary supply and demand functions for each security, find the price that will equate demand and supply at the moment, and consummate a transaction. At the same time, it will communicate the terms of the transaction to the consolidated reporting system, the brokers or dealers who bought and sold, the CQS, and the national clearing and settlement system. As new orders arrive it will repeat the process.

CONCLUSIONS

The NMS will be more efficient than the system it will replace (though the efficiency of the present system should not be understated). It will reduce the real costs of disseminating information, executing orders, and transferring titles and payments. By requiring competitive prices for financial services, it will promote economies in both the production and use of those services. And it will promote more orderly and continuous markets by ending fragmentation and by bringing all specialists and market makers for a stock into competition with one another.

Other changes are likely to come as the NMS is developed and becomes fully operational. However, we cannot forecast exactly what these changes will be because some technical details remain undetermined, technology is certain to change further, and some of the relevant laws and regulations have not yet been adopted. For such reasons, we shall merely list some possible effects and changes without predicting their probabilities:

1. Effects on the roles and functions of the organized securities exchanges. These effects are very difficult to predict, partly because many of the details of the NMS have not yet been developed. For example, it will make a difference whether transactions through the NMS are consummated automatically within the electronic system itself, or whether at least some of them are consummated through one or more of the organized exchanges. However, it seems inevitable that the

development of a truly centralized market will diminish the individual roles of the NASD and the various exchanges, both as regulators of trading practices and as providers of trading facilities. Some, or perhaps all, of the powers to function as "self-regulator under supervision of the SEC" are likely to be transferred to some central authority, which might be called a "National Market Board." And one or more central bodies may be formed to provide the principal trading facilities—the consolidated reporting system, the Composite Quotation System, the Composite Limit-Order Book, and the electronic system for automatic trade execution. Securities exchanges as we have known them may disappear. On the other hand, the organized exchanges may be interlinked electronically to become the center of the NMS.

2. Effects on the number of firms in the securities industry. With the advent of competitive commission rates, the spreading use of electronic equipment, and the accompanying sharpening of competition, the number of broker-dealer firms has already been reduced significantly through mergers and discontinuances. This trend is likely to continue for some time.

3. Effects on the geographic location of financial firms, facilities, personnel, and transactions. New York City has been indisputably the center of both the primary and the secondary branches of the securities market. There appear to have been important economies in having in close geographic proximity to one another many broker-dealers, banks, trust departments serving as registrars and transfer agents for stocks and bonds, accounting firms, law firms specializing in financial matters, foreign-exchange markets, and so on. Some of these economies of geographic concentration are likely to persist for the foreseeable future, and New York City is likely to remain a great financial center. However, the new electronic communications systems make geographic location far less important for success in this industry. It seems likely, therefore, that the securities industry will come to be less concentrated in New York City. Some firms will move all their functions to other areas, and some others will perform some functions in the City but move other functions elsewhere. One thing is almost certain: no local jurisdiction, such as New York City, can levy significant taxes on transfers of stocks and bonds without losing a large part of this industry.

THE OTC MARKET FOR STOCKS

We have already described some of the principal characteristics of this market: its general structure; the central role played by dealers acting as market makers; the complex communications system, including NASDAQ; and Third Market trading in stocks listed on one or more of the organized exchanges. The following brief comments relate to trading in stocks that are not listed on any exchange.

Facilities for trading stocks in the OTC market are indeed extensive. At the end of 1976, the immediate supervisory authority for the OTC market, the NASD, had nearly 2,900 broker-dealer member firms, which operated 6,000 offices and employed 191,000 representatives licensed to do business with the public. More than 2,600 stock issues were listed for trading in NASDAQ, and the volume of trading through that system was very large. (See Table 9 − 1.) For example, the number of shares traded through NASDAQ during 1976 was equal to nearly a third of the number traded on the NYSE and was greater than the combined totals on all other exchanges. The data above refer only to stocks listed for trading through NASDAQ. It is estimated that about 30,000 other issues are traded in the OTC market at least occasionally.

It is impossible to predict how the development of the NMS and other future events will affect trading in stocks that have formerly been traded only in the OTC market. Some of these stocks, especially those that are traded most actively, may be listed for trading through the NMS. On the other hand, the continuing development of computer based electronic communications systems—with their great capacity to accumulate, process, retrieve, and disseminate information rapidly and at low cost—may make it feasible to include in NASDAQ many stocks that formerly were not known widely enough to warrant their inclusion.

STOCK OPTIONS

The preceding sections considered transactions in which the things bought and sold are shares of corporate stocks. Now we shall consider briefly stock options. A stock option is a contract in which the seller of the contract, called the writer, agrees to buy or to sell certain shares of corporate stock at a fixed price within a named period, if and when he is called upon to do so by the buyer of the contract. An option contract almost always covers 100 shares of stock (one round lot), but a single transaction may involve several such contracts. Stock options are of two principal types—*call options* and *put options*.

CALL OPTIONS

A call option requires the writer of the option to sell the stock, at any time within the *contract period,* to the holder of the option at the

Table 9–1   **Share Trading During 1976**
            (in millions)

Market	Number of Shares Traded	Percent of Total Shares Traded
New York Stock Exchange	5360.1	63.4
NASDAQ	1683.9	19.9
American Stock Exchange	648.3	7.7
All other exchanges	764.7	9.0
		100.0

Source: NASD, *Fact Book,* 1976, p. 3.

agreed *striking price,* irrespective of the market price at the time the option is exercised. When the option is exercised, the buyer is said to "call" the stock. For the option contract, the buyer pays a *premium,* or price, which is stated in dollars. The contract period is rarely less than three months or more than a year; the most common length is six months. The striking price is the price at which the writer is obliged to sell; this is usually set equal to, or close to, the market price of the stock at the time the contract is written. The size of the premium varies from case to case, but it is often in the range of 10 to 15 percent of the value of the underlying stock.

To clarify the nature and functions of call options, we shall use an example in which we assume that you are the writer of the option and Mary Smith is the buyer, the contract relates to 100 shares of XYZ common, the contract period is six months, both the current market price and the striking price are $40 a share, and the premium is $600, or $6 a share. We further assume that your sale of the call option is fully covered by your holdings of XYZ common, which you already owned or which you purchased at the time you wrote the call contract. You could write an uncovered, or "naked," call contract, but you would really "be out in the cold" if, within six months, the market price of the stock should rise far above the striking price.

At this stage, Smith has paid you $600 for the call option, and this is yours to keep regardless of what happens to the market price of the stock during the next six months. You will keep your stock too if the market price remains below the striking price of $40 during the option period. In this case, Smith will have lost her $600, but that will be the limit of her loss no matter how much the price of the stock declines. She will make a net gain if the market price rises above $46 a share, which is the sum of the $40 striking price and the $6 premium per share. Her gain, stated as a percentage of her initial investment, can be quite large if the market price rises much above $46. Suppose, for example, that she exercises her option and sells 100 shares at a market price of $52 a share. Her gain will be $5200 minus the total cost of $4600.[3] Thus, her gain will be equal to nearly 100 percent of her initial investment in the option. In this case you, the writer, lose, in the sense that you are worse off than you would have been if you had not sold the option. If you had not sold the call, you could have sold the stock for $52 a share, but under the call contract you realize only $46 a share—the $40 striking price plus the $6 premium. If, during the option period, the market price rises above the striking price but by less than the amount of the premium per share, the holder of the call option can exercise it, sell the stock, and reduce the amount of net loss on the premium paid.

In summary, the buyer of a call option must lose if, during the option period, the market price of the stock fails to rise above the striking price by an amount at least equal to the premium per share, and the writer will lose, in the sense of an opportunity loss, if the market price rises above the striking price by more than the premium per share.[4] Most writers and buyers are fully aware of the risk of loss on individual call contracts, but they typically write and buy many contracts, hoping that the gains on some will more than offset losses on others.

In the example above we simply assumed that the premium or price of the call contract was $600, or $6 a share. Now we must face this question: What determines the price of a call contract? As a first step, we note that this price is determined in a competitive, but not necessarily perfectly competitive, market with many actual and potential writers and suppliers of options on a stock and many actual and potential buyers. Second, we ask why a buyer would be willing to pay a positive price for a call option, and why a writer would be willing to supply such an option only at a positive price. Options become useful because the future behavior of the price of a stock is uncertain. Ownership of a stock carries both an opportunity for gain if the price of the stock rises and risks of loss if the price of the stock declines. Options are instruments that transfer some of these opportunities for gain or risks of loss from the writer of the option to the buyer. A call option transfers from the

[3] We ignore here the commission costs of the transaction.

[4] We assumed in this case that the striking price was equal to the cost of the stock to the option writer. The latter may, of course, have been either higher or lower than the striking price.

writer to the buyer all the opportunities for gain if the market price of the stock rises above the striking price during the contract period, but the writer retains all the risks of a price decline.

Thus the demand function for call options depends on buyers' expectations concerning the probability that the price of the stock will rise above the striking price during the contract period and the expected extent of the price increase. The demand function will be high if buyers' expectations are very sanguine, but lower if their expectations are less so. The supply function also depends in part on the writer's expectations as to the future course of the price of the stock. If writers expect that a price rise during the contract period is improbable and will be small at best, they will tend to write call contracts at a small premium, but they will demand a higher premium if they believe that price increases will be likely and large. The supply function of call options also depends in part on the writers' expectations concerning the risk of loss because of a price decline of the stock against which they sell call options. They may be willing to supply call options only at a high price if they believe there is a serious risk of loss on the underlying securities, but at a lower price if they believe this risk is smaller.

PUT OPTIONS

Because put options are just the opposite of call options, we can deal with them more briefly. In a put option, the writer is required to buy stock from the option holder at the agreed striking price irrespective of the market price at the time of exercise. When the put option is exercised, the buyer is said to "put" the stock to the writer.

In an example symmetrical with that above, you, the writer, agree to buy from Smith, or from anyone to whom she transfers the put option, 100 shares of XYZ common at any time within the next six months at a striking price of $40 a share. For this you will receive a premium, which we shall assume to be $400. Thus the put option has transferred from Mary to you the risk that the price per share may fall below the $40 striking price. Smith retains all the opportunities for gain if the price of the stock rises, but is assured that her net realization on the stock if she sells it cannot fall below $36, or the $40 striking price minus the $4 premium per share. As writer of the put option, you assume the risk that you may have to buy the stock at $40 a share when the market price is lower.

In general, the premium or price of a put option depends on expectations concerning the probability and extent of a decline of the market price of the underlying stock below the striking price. The premium is likely to be low if such price declines are expected to be quite unlikely and small, but higher under the reverse conditions.

MARKETS FOR STOCK OPTIONS

Two components of the market for stock options can be distinguished, though they are closely related: primary markets, through which newly written options are sold; and secondary markets, in which options already outstanding are traded. Brokers and dealers are the middlemen in these markets. In some cases, brokers seek out writers and buyers of new options and act as agents in effecting transactions. In others, option writers sell options to dealers, who resell them to others.

Secondary markets for options serve to increase the marketability and liquidity of options already outstanding. This can be useful to both buyers and sellers of options. To explain why this is so, let us recall the earlier example in which you sold to Smith a six-month call option on XYZ common at a striking price of $40 a share. She may elect not to resell the option. She may let it lapse without exercising it, which she will do if the market price remains below the striking price. Or she may herself exercise the option if the market price rises above the striking price. However, if she does not wish to hold the stock, she may not exercise the option even if it would be profitable to do so, because she would have to pay a brokerage fee to sell the stock. She may find it more profitable to sell the option to someone else. The market price of a call option on one share at any time is roughly equal to the difference between the current market price of the share and the striking price per share. The price of the call option cannot fall much below this difference, because if it did competing arbitragers would rush to buy the option, exercise it, and sell the stock at the current price. However, the price of the option may rise a bit above this difference if buyers expect that the market price of the stock may rise still higher during the remaining life of the option.

Smith may have other reasons for selling the option. As time passes, she may become less optimistic about the probability and extent of a rise in the price of the underlying stock, and elect to resell the call option to someone who values it more highly than she does. If she receives any positive price she will at least regain some of the premium that she initially paid for the option.

You, the initial writer of the call option, may find it advantageous to purchase the option before it is exercised. For example, you may come to believe that a rise of the market price above the striking price is more probable and may be more extensive than you originally thought. By purchasing the option before it is exercised, you can eliminate your obligation to sell the stock.

For similar reasons, there are purchases and sales of put options in secondary markets. For example, the holder of a put option may come to believe that there is now less risk that the market price of a stock will fall below its striking price, and he may therefore sell his put option to someone who will value it more highly. Or the writer of a put option may come to believe that there is now more risk of a price decline on a stock below its striking price, and therefore may buy the put option, or one just like it, thus eliminating his obligation to buy the stock.

Before 1975, stock options were traded only in the OTC market. This market was relatively inefficient. It did not provide full information concerning prices in the most recent transactions, buyers and sellers sometimes lacked information about the most favorable trading opportunities, and methods used to effect transactions were rather expensive. However, in 1974 the Chicago Board of Trade established the Chicago Board Options Exchange (CBOE) for trading call options on more than 60 listed stocks. By 1977 four other organized exchanges had established departments to trade in call options on listed stocks—the American Stock Exchange, the Philadelphia Exchange, the Pacific Exchange, and the Midwest Exchange. These exchanges now provide the facilities necessary for efficient, continuous, and competitive trading in call options on several hundred listed stocks. These facilities include regulatory authorities to assure fair trading practices, current reporting of trades and prices, specialists and market makers, and an efficient system for clearing and settlement.

Though it is not possible to forecast future developments in the options market, it seems very likely that still other exchanges will establish options departments, that call options on more stocks will be listed for trading on the exchanges, and that at least some put options will be listed for trading. It is also possible that options will come to be traded through an electronic communications system, similar to NASDAQ.

THE ECONOMIC ROLES OF STOCK OPTIONS

At first glance it might appear that stock options serve only as instruments for transferring income or wealth from those who lose to those who gain in options transactions, and that they have no other economic effects. Such a view would ignore the facts, noted earlier, that options serve as instruments for transferring opportunities for gain or risks of loss from sellers to buyers, thereby enabling each participant to move toward his preferred portfolio balance in terms of income, safety, and liquidity. Options perform functions similar to those of financial intermediaries that intermediate between the preferences of issuers and holders, reduce risk, create liquidity, and shift risk bearing to those who will perform this function for the lowest price. Options produce such results through many types of transactions, some of which are highly complex and sophisticated. We shall use as examples a few of the simpler types of transactions.

The ability to write options can increase the demand for a stock. For example, you may be unwilling to buy and hold XYZ common if the only prospective rewards are future dividends and possible capital gains, but willing to do so if you expect a profit from writing call options against it. You feel better off because you value the premium you received for the call more highly than the opportunity for gain that you transferred to the buyer of the option. The buyer also feels better off because he values the premium he paid less highly than his acquisition of the opportunity for gain with only a lower initial investment and without the risk of loss that would be involved if he purchased the stock outright. You retain the risk of a decline in the price of the stock. However, you may, if you wish, eliminate, or at least reduce, this risk by purchasing a put option. You may feel better off because the elimination or reduction of your risk is worth more to you than the premium that you paid for the put, and the seller of the put may feel better off because he feels that the premium he received more than compensates for the risk he assumed.

Stock options are used in many ways to insure or hedge against other risks. For example, Jones has bought a stock on margin, hopefully expecting its price to rise. However, there remains some risk that the price will fall. Jones can reduce this risk, or even eliminate it, by purchasing put options. To cite a different type of example, Hardy has sold a stock short, hopefully expecting its price to fall, but there remains some risk that the price will rise. Hardy can reduce or eliminate this risk by purchasing call options against the stock.

These are only a few of the many ways that stock options are used.

CONCLUSION

Both markets for stocks and markets for stock options have undergone sharp changes during the most recent decade. These have been brought about by many forces, including various technological innovations, the growth of institutional trading in stocks, and government policies directed toward enhancing competition. Still further changes are almost certain to come, though their nature and extent are difficult to predict. Among the most likely are a continuing trend toward fewer and larger brokerage firms, changes in the relative functions of the organized securities exchanges and the OTC market, a decrease in the number of the organized exchanges resulting from mergers and perhaps also some discontinuances, and a greater use of electronic communications systems to facilitate trading.

SELECTED READINGS

I. Stock markets

Mendelson, M. *From Automated Quotes to Automated Trading: Restructuring the Stock Market in the United States.* New York: Institute of Finance of New York University, 1972.

Sobel, R. *NYSE: A History of the New York Stock Exchange 1935–1975.* New York: Weybright and Tally, 1975.

Stone, J. M. *One Way for Wall Street: A View of the Future of the Securities Industry.* Boston: Little, Brown and Co., 1975.

Subcommittee on Commerce and Finance of the Committee on Interstate and Foreign Commerce, House of Representatives, 92d Congress, 2d Session. *Securities Industry Study.* Washington, D.C.: U.S. Government Printing Office, 1972.

See also the lists of selected readings at the end of the preceding chapter.

II. Stock options

Auster, R. *Option Writing and Hedging Strategies.* Hicksville, N.Y.: Exposition Press, 1975.

Malkiel, B. G., and Quandt, R. E. *Strategies and Rational Decisions in the Securities Options Market.* Princeton: Princeton University Press, 1968.

Miller, J. T. *Options Trading.* Chicago: H. Regnery & Co., 1975.

PRIMARY MARKETS
AND
MONEY MARKETS

This chapter deals with three principal subjects: primary markets for both equity and debt claims; secondary markets for longer-term debt claims; and money markets. In some cases we shall deal with each subject separately; in others we shall deal with two or more of them together because they are so interrelated.

PRIMARY MARKETS

New securities can flow from their creators to their ultimate buyers and holders in many different ways. Some of these do not involve middlemen at all. For example, a borrower borrows directly from the bank, a household issues a mortgage directly to a savings and loan association, or a corporation offers new shares directly to its stockholders. Also, corporations sometimes place new issues directly with large financial intermediaries, such as insurance companies. However, very large amounts of new issues are distributed through middlemen serving as "investment banks." These distribute new issues of equity and debt claims for nonfinancial business corporations; for some financial institutions, such as investment companies, banks, and finance companies; for state and local governments and their agencies and authorities; for agencies of the federal government; and for foreign institutions, both governmental and private. Only rarely does the federal government sell its direct issues through investment banks; it usually distributes them through the Federal Reserve and the commercial banks.

INVESTMENT BANKING

The term "investment bank" is a misnomer, suggesting that in purchasing a new issue the purpose of the investment bank is to hold it as a portfolio investment. A more apt name would be "merchandiser of new securities," for an investment bank hopes to sell the securities as quickly as possible in order to avoid risks of a price decline. In actuality, those performing this service are usually broker-dealers, acting singly or more often as a group or "syndicate." As noted earlier, some commercial banks also performed this function before 1933, but since that time their distribution of new securities has been limited to issues of governmental units and their agencies.

A specific example will illustrate the functions of investment banking. Suppose that a business corporation wishes to sell $100 million of new stocks, bonds, or intermediate-term notes and seeks the assistance of one or more broker-dealers. In some cases the issuer consults only one group of broker-dealers and arrives at a *negotiated price* for the securities. In others, the issuer solicits *competitive bidding* by two or more groups. In any case, the functions performed by the broker-dealers can be classified under *origination, underwriting,* and *selling.* The first step is to determine precisely the economic and legal characteristics of the new security and to arrive at the price to be paid to the issuer. This involves analysis of the financial condition and prospects of the issuer, estimates of market demands for the security, registration with the SEC, and so on. At this stage only a few broker-dealers—often only two—are involved as comanagers.

The next stage is *underwriting:* broker-dealers guarantee that the issuer will receive the full agreed-upon price on a stipulated date, even if the issue is not fully sold by that time. For this purpose, an *underwriting syndicate or group* is usually formed. This is a temporary joint venture of a number of broker-dealers, in which each agrees to underwrite a specified fraction of the total issue. The number of broker-dealers involved varies greatly, depending on such things as the size of the issue, the estimated risk, and the nature and number of the expected ultimate buyers. For example, a syndicate may include only a few underwriters if the issue is small and considered relatively safe and if the entire issue is expected to be sold to a few institutional buyers. Under the reverse conditions, syndicates often include many members. For example, an underwriting syndicate for a $200 million issue would usually include at least 25 and sometimes 100 or more members.

Selling is the final stage. Here, too, there are many variations in practice. In some cases the underwriters themselves sell the entire issue through their own offices and affiliates at home and abroad, though even in this case they often "wholesale" some to other broker-dealers, who "retail" them to customers. In other cases, a *selling syndicate* is formed, including not only the underwriters but also additional brokers and dealers.

Through such processes, new issues can be distributed nationally and internationally. In many cases even very large issues are sold within a few hours.

In the case discussed above, the underwriters took the entire new issue and guaranteed a fixed price to the issuer. However, an issuer may wish to give its stockholders the right of first refusal, in which case underwriters may agree to buy at a fixed price all of the new issue that is not purchased by stockholders. In some situations broker-dealers do not agree to buy the entire issue at a fixed price, but agree only to exert their "best efforts" to sell it. This is most likely to occur when buyers' responses to an issue are highly doubtful.

In addition to distributing new issues, investment banking syndicates sometimes facilitate "secondary distributions" of securities already outstanding. For example, a major holder of a corporate stock, either an individual or an institution, that wishes to sell a very large block of shares may employ an underwriting and selling syndicate to effect the distribution.

PRIVATE PLACEMENTS

Many new issues of securities, even large issues, are neither underwritten nor offered to the public. Instead, they are *privately placed;* that is, they are sold directly by the issuer to one or more institutional buyers, such as trust departments of banks, life insurance companies, pension funds, or other financial intermediaries. In some instances, an entire new issue is purchased by a single buyer. For example, one big life insurance company may take all of a public utility issue of $30 million of bonds or preferred stock. In other instances two or more institutions share in the purchase of a new issue.

Broker-dealers often facilitate private placements. They help issuers find buyers who may be interested in such securities, and they help institutional buyers find attractive issues. They assist issuers in designing securities that will appeal to institutions and advise on various legal procedures. They also provide financial advice to purchasers.

Private placements with large institutional investors are quite common for corporate bonds, preferred stocks, and intermediate-term debt, and for state and municipal obligations.

U.S. TREASURY OBLIGATIONS

The Treasury, as noted above, rarely employs private under-writers to distribute its new issues; it relies mostly on the Federal Reserve, acting as its fiscal agent, and on the commercial banks. With the advice of the Federal Reserve, the Treasury determines the amounts and terms of its issues and communicates these to the Federal Reserve banks. The latter prepare sheets describing an issue and distribute these to their own branches, to commercial banks in their respective regions, to dealers in government securities, and to any others who may be interested. The commercial banks subscribe for their own accounts and solicit subscriptions by their customers. The Treasury sometimes encourages this by maintaining tax and loan deposit accounts at more than 11,000 commercial banks. Under these arrangements, a bank is not required to pay immediately for new securities purchased by itself and its customers; instead, the Treasury leaves the funds on deposit at the bank until they are needed for expenditure, which is often several days, and sometimes more than a week, later. For this reason, banks often subscribe to more securities than they wish to retain for a longer period, hold these until the Treasury calls for its money, and then sell them to others, sometimes directly but often through dealers in government securities. Through this network, the Treasury issues billions of dollars' worth of new securities every year. With the average maturity of its outstanding debt at only about 2.5 years, it must sell very large amounts every year to pay off its maturing debts, and its issues are, of course, greater when it has current deficits.

REAL ESTATE MORTGAGES

Real estate mortgages are a very important component of the financial system. The volume of these outstanding at the end of 1975 was $802 billion, and the annual flow of new mortgages is typically equal to a significant percentage of all funds raised in financial markets by the nonfinancial sectors. For example, during the years 1970 through 1975, this percentage for all mortgages ranged between 28.3 and 45.3 percent, and for residential mortgages alone it ranged between 20.3 and 33.2 percent (see Table 10−1). Many of these are purchased with savings in the areas in which the mortgages originate, a few directly by local savers

Table 10 – 1   **Funds Raised in Financial Markets by the Nonfinancial
Sectors Through Issues of Debt Obligations, 1970 – 1975**
(in billions of dollars)

	1970	1971	1972	1973	1974	1975
Total funds raised	$94.9	$139.6	$166.4	$190.0	$185.0	$200.3
Residential mortgages	21.3	38.3	55.3	56.8	41.6	40.7
Commercial mortgages	7.1	9.8	16.4	18.9	15.1	10.9
Farm mortgages	0.8	2.4	3.6	5.5	5.1	5.2
Total mortgages	$29.2	$ 50.5	$ 75.3	$ 81.2	$ 61.8	$ 56.8
As percentage of total funds raised						
Residential mortgages	22.4	27.4	33.2	29.9	22.5	20.3
Commercial mortgages	7.5	7.0	9.9	9.9	8.2	5.4
Farm mortgages	0.1	1.7	2.2	2.9	2.8	2.6
Total mortgages	30.0	36.1	45.3	42.7	33.5	28.3

Source: *Federal Reserve Bulletin,* November 1976, p. A56.

but many more through local financial intermediaries, such as savings
and loan associations, mutual savings banks, and commercial banks.
However, in many cases there are imbalances between local creations of
new mortgages and local demands for them. Such imbalances can be
remedied and regional yield differentials reduced to minimum levels in
two principal ways: (1) through flows of funds from other areas to financial intermediaries in the areas with excess supplies of mortgages and (2)
through sales of mortgages originating in these areas to outside buyers.

Some commercial mortgages issued by large firms with good
credit ratings have long enjoyed broad and efficient primary and secondary markets, similar to those for good corporate bonds. However, three
characteristics of commercial mortgages issued by lesser business firms
and of mortgages on residential and farm properties have made it difficult to develop geographically broad and efficient primary and secondary markets for these instruments:

1. The quality of these mortgages, which depends on the value of the
   underlying properties and the financial position of the issuers,
   varies widely.
2. Each mortgage is so small that distant potential buyers find it expensive to investigate the quality of each mortgage.
3. Servicing costs are relatively high. Someone must ensure that the

mortgagor maintains the property in good repair, keeps the property insured, pays property taxes, and makes the promised periodic payments.

Despite these difficulties, some farm and residential mortgages were sold outside the areas in which they originated even before the federal government entered this field. For example, life insurance companies purchased mortgages directly in various parts of the country, or purchased them from local banks or savings and loan associations that had originated them and would continue to service them for a fee. Mortgage brokers sometimes aided in bringing buyers and sellers together. Mortgage bankers perform more extensive functions in this field. They originate individual mortgages, put together a pool of such mortgages large enough to be attractive to institutional buyers, sell them to buyers, and continue to service them. However, these market facilities were considerably less effective than those for good corporate and government securities, so that significant regional differentials in mortgage yields persisted.

The federal government has taken many actions to improve markets for farm and residential mortgages and to increase the geographic mobility of mortgage funds—so many types of actions that we can mention here only the most important. Its principal action in the field of farm mortgages was to sponsor the establishment of twelve Federal Land Banks located in as many regions of the country. These banks sell their highly regarded bonds in the national securities markets and use the proceeds to buy farm mortgages. They now hold about 31 percent of all outstanding farm mortgages.

Federal actions in the field of residential mortgages have been more numerous and varied:

1. Insurance of residential mortgages by federal agencies—the Federal Housing Administration (FHA) and the Veterans Administration (VA). Though such insurance has been useful in expanding the primary and secondary markets for these mortgages, these agencies have been widely criticized for some of their practices, such as faulty appraisals, excessive delays and red tape, and maintenance of unrealistic ceilings on interest rates on these mortgages. For such reasons, a majority of new mortgages have continued to be uninsured by a federal agency. Uninsured mortgages are usually called "conventional mortgages." In the late 1960s, a number of private firms began to insure residential mortgages and to make secondary markets for the mortgages that they insure.

Though they insured many mortgages during their early years, it is still too early to predict how successful they will be.

2. Provision of federal charters for savings and loan associations, and insurance of the first $40,000 of each account at most savings and loan associations by a federal agency—the Federal Savings and Loan Insurance Corporation (FSLIC). These actions served to increase the total number of institutions specializing in mortgage loans, to enhance the safety of claims against these institutions, and to enable such institutions to draw funds from wider areas.

3. Establishment of the Federal Home Loan Banks, which provide funds to savings and loan associations and some other major holders of mortgages. These sell their highly rated debt obligations in the central securities markets and use the proceeds to lend to members to meet temporary needs for liquidity and to lend for longer periods in areas with large excess demands for mortgage funds. They have also established a subsidiary, the Federal Home Loan Mortgage Corporation, which provides a secondary market for home mortgages.

4. Establishment of the Federal National Mortgage Association (FNMA), which was at first a government institution but later became privately owned with continuing government sponsorship. It raises funds primarily by selling its highly regarded debt obligations in the central securities markets. Its major function was expected to be that of providing a secondary market for home mortgages, buying mortgages in some areas and reselling them in others. In practice, however, its purchases have far exceeded its sales, so that it has accumulated a large inventory of mortgages.

5. Establishment of the Government National Mortgage Association (GNMA). This agency is government-owned and acquires most of its funds from the U.S. Treasury. It buys and holds home mortgages, mostly those that receive some sort of government subsidy. It also guarantees the prompt payment of interest and principal on some mortgages and issues guaranteed bonds secured by a pool of mortgages.

As a group, these federal actions have undoubtedly increased the geographic mobility of mortgage funds, widened the primary distribution of new mortgages, and brought some improvement in the secondary market for mortgages. However, the secondary market for mortgages is still less developed than secondary markets for good long-term corporate and government debt claims.

SECONDARY MARKETS FOR BONDS

We have already noted some of the characteristics of these markets:

1. The market for debt claims, including both the primary market and the secondary market, is predominantly in the OTC market. It is true that some bonds—mostly those of the federal government and corporations—are listed on securities exchanges, and especially on the NYSE, and that the volume of bond trading on the exchanges is far from negligible. However, the volume of bond trading in the OTC market exceeds by many times the total on all the exchanges combined.
2. Most, though not all, of the middlemen in this market are broker-dealers who also serve this function for stocks.
3. The bond market is organized around dealers. This is not an auction market except in the bond-trading room of the NYSE. Ultimate buyers and sellers of bonds use brokers to gain access to dealers, but in many cases they deal directly with dealers.

CORPORATE AND FOREIGN BONDS

At the end of 1975 the outstanding volume of corporate and foreign bonds in this country was more than $317 billion (see Table 10 −2). Of this total, domestic nonfinancial corporations accounted for 80.2 percent, domestic financial corporations for 11.7 percent, and foreign issuers for 8.1 percent. Though corporations of almost all sizes issue bonds, the great bulk of those outstanding were issued by medium-sized and large corporations, most of which are widely known. Of the total volume of these bonds outstanding, financial intermediaries held more than 78 percent; households held less than 21 percent of the total. The percentage for financial intermediaries would be higher and that for households lower if trust departments holding bonds for household accounts were considered to be financial intermediaries. Thus the market for corporate bonds is primarily an institutional market, and single transactions are typically in fairly large amounts.

As already indicated, this market is organized around dealers acting as specialists. For some bond issues, and especially for large issues, there are numerous specialists. When a dealer advertises that he "specializes" in a certain bond or category of bonds, he usually does not mean that he confines his trading to those securities; he means only that he stands ready at all times to buy or sell the securities in large amounts in trades with ultimate buyers and sellers and with brokers and other

Table 10 — 2 **Outstanding Corporate and Foreign Bonds and Their Holders, December 31, 1975**
(amounts in billions of dollars)

I. TYPES AND AMOUNTS OUTSTANDING

Type of Issuer	Amount	Percent of Total
Nonfinancial corporate business	$254.3	80.2
Financial corporations		
Finance companies	30.7	9.7
Commercial banks	4.5	1.4
REITs	2.1	0.6
Foreign	26.5	8.1
Total	$317.2	100.0

II. HOLDERS OF THE TOTAL ABOVE

Type of Holder	Amount	Percent of Total
Commercial banks	$ 8.6	2.7
Mutual savings banks	17.5	5.5
Life insurance companies	105.5	33.3
Private pension funds	37.8	11.9
State and local government retirement funds	60.9	19.2
Open-end investment companies	4.8	1.5
Brokers and dealers	1.4	0.4
Total of above	$348.7	78.4
Households	65.9	20.8
Rest of world	2.6	0.8
Total	$317.2	100.0

Source: Board of Governors of the Federal Reserve System, *Flow-of-funds accounts.*

dealers. These specialist dealers function much like market makers for a stock. Institutional investors, and especially the larger ones, often deal directly with a specialist. However, many buyers and sellers of bonds gain access to the specialist through the nationwide network of brokers and other dealers.

DEBTS OF STATE AND LOCAL GOVERNMENTS

The special attraction of these securities, popularly called "municipals," is that income on them is exempt from federal income taxes and also, in most cases, from any income taxes levied by the state in which the security originates. As might be expected, therefore, they are held largely by households in the higher-income brackets and by nonfinancial corporations and financial institutions subject to the federal corporate income tax. At the end of 1975, households held 32.2 percent, and financial intermediaries 63.9 percent, of the total. The principal institutional holders were commercial banks, with about 45 percent of the total.

Municipal securities are of many types and carry widely differing degrees of risk. Some are direct obligations of the issuing governmental unit, backed by "the full faith and credit" of that unit. Their quality therefore depends on the financial responsibility of the governmental unit that issues them. At the other extreme are tax exempt bonds that are issued not by a governmental unit itself but by some sort of "authority" established by one or more governmental units, that are not guaranteed by any governmental unit, and that depend solely on the revenues that will accrue to the issuing authority. Among these issuers are water and sewer authorities; highway, port, and airport authorities; college dormitory authorities; sports authorities; industrial development authorities; and pollution control authorities. In this area, "caveat emptor" is often good advice.

Regular broker-dealers play major roles in both the primary distribution and the secondary markets for municipals, but commercial banks are also quite active in these fields. The latter often join regular broker-dealers in underwriting new issues of municipals, and some new issues are underwritten solely by commercial banks. Many banks also serve as dealers in the secondary market. In most cases banks probably assume these roles voluntarily for reasons of profit; in some cases, however, local pressures to "cooperate" provide an additional stimulus.

Continuity of trading in this market, as in the market for corporate bonds, depends heavily on dealers, including some banks, acting as market makers. Bonds of most states and of the larger municipalities in good financial standing enjoy broad and continuous markets. However, markets for issues by smaller governmental units and by governmental units and authorities of questionable standing tend to be narrower and less continuous.[1]

MONEY MARKETS

We shall now explore what is popularly known as the "money market." More specifically, we shall deal with markets for the following types of

---

[1] The secondary market for debts of the federal government and its agencies will be considered later.

financial claims: short-term debts of the federal government and its agencies; short-term obligations of state and local governments; federal funds; bankers' acceptances; large-denomination negotiable certificates of deposit; loans to securities dealers; commercial and finance paper; and Eurodollar claims. Though these various types of claims differ in some respects, they have important characteristics in common: they are of short maturities; they are highly safe; and they can be bought and sold quickly and at low transactions costs. In short, they are so safe and so liquid that they are often called "near-moneys."

These financial claims serve several closely related purposes in the economy:

1. They are close substitutes for money itself as a form of holding liquid purchasing power. Though less liquid then money, they are almost as safe and have the advantage of yielding explicit income. In the absence of such claims, households, business firms, and others would undoubtedly elect to hold more money relative to their total wealth and also relative to their rates of expenditure.
2. They are a major means of adjusting liquidity positions by banks, other financial institutions, nonfinancial business firms, and others.
3. They serve as instruments or vehicles for increasing the mobility of funds among geographic regions and the various sectors of the economy.
4. They are important channels through which the effects of Federal Reserve policy actions are disseminated through the financial system.

We shall now look at the various types of money market instruments and the market facilities that enhance their liquidity.

MARKETABLE SECURITIES OF THE U.S. TREASURY

At the end of 1975, the marketable debt of the U.S. Treasury stood at $363.2 billion.[2] (See Table 10 − 3.) Of this total, about $107 billion was held by government agencies and trust funds and by the Federal Reserve, leaving $255.9 billion in the hands of private investors. Of the latter amount, $150.1 billion, or 59 percent, had maturities within a year, and

---

[2] We concentrate on marketable debts because these are the ones that are bought and sold in the money market. On that date the Treasury also had over $200 billion of nonmarketable debt which was held by government agencies and trust funds, foreign official institutions, and individuals.

Table 10−3   **Marketable Securities of the**
U.S. Treasury, December 31, 1975
(in billions of dollars)

		Maturities				
	Total— All Ma- turities	Within 1 Year	1−5 Years	5−10 Years	10−20 Years	Over 20 Years
Total outstanding	$363.2	$199.7	$112.3	$26.4	$14.3	$10.5
Holders						
U.S. government						
agencies and trust funds	19.3	2.8	7.1	3.3	4.2	2.1
Federal Reserve	87.9	46.8	30.5	6.5	1.5	2.6
Private investors—total	255.9	150.1	74.7	16.7	8.5	5.9
Commercial banks	64.4	29.9	29.6	4.1	0.6	0.3
Mutual savings banks	3.3	1.0	1.5	0.4	0.2	0.1
Insurance companies	7.6	2.0	2.4	1.6	1.2	0.4
Savings and loan associations	2.8	0.9	1.6	0.2	1.0	—
Nonfinancial corporations	9.4	7.1	2.0	0.2	0.1	—
State and local governments	9.3	5.3	1.8	0.8	0.9	0.6
All others	159.2	103.9	35.9	9.4	5.5	4.4

Source: *Federal Reserve Bulletin*, November 1976, p. A35.

$224.8 billion, or 88 percent, had maturities within five years. All of these securities are virtually devoid of default risk, and the market risk on the shorter maturities is very low. These securities are held by almost every type of institution in the economy (see Table 10−4). Individual holdings of these securities, which were at least $25 billion, are included in the

Table 10−4   **Outstanding Debt Issues of Federally**
Sponsored Credit Agencies, December 31, 1975
(in millions of dollars)

Issuing Agency	
Federal Home Loan Banks	$18,863
Federal National Mortgage Association	29,963
Banks for Cooperatives	3,643
Federal Intermediate Credit Banks	9,211
Federal Land Banks	14,773
Total	$66,453

Source: *Federal Reserve Bulletin*, November 1976, p. A37.

residual category "all others," which also includes some holdings by foreign central banks and international institutions.

The Treasury securities discussed above are of three principal types:

1. Treasury bills. Most of these have initial maturities of between 30 days and a year, though some run for as long as 18 months. These are sold at discounts below their face values, so that holders receive a return in the form of an excess of the redemption price over the issue price. Large amounts of these are sold in weekly auctions.
2. Treasury notes. Most of these have initial maturities of between one and five years, though some run longer. They are usually, but not always, issued at par, and interest is paid periodically on their par values. They are sometimes called "coupon issues."
3. Treasury bonds. These have initial maturities of five years or more, and are also coupon issues.

The data above refer only to marketable securities that are direct debt obligations of the Treasury. Also outstanding on that date were more than $66 billion of so-called "federal agency issues," of which many had maturities within a year. (See Table 10–4.) These are issued by institutions that have received varying degrees of sponsorship by the federal government and that operate in the fields of agricultural credit and home mortgages. Though they are not obligations of the federal government and are not formally guaranteed by the government, they are generally considered to be almost as safe as the Treasury's own obligations of comparable maturities, and most of the dealers that make markets for direct Treasury issues also do so for federal agency issues.

At the heart of the market for Treasury obligations and federal agency issues are some 24 dealers that serve as market makers. Ten of these are specialized departments of commercial banks; the others are nonbank dealers, most of whom also deal in other securities. Though most of them are domiciled in New York City, they have branches in leading cities and a network of correspondent dealers throughout the country. Each of these market-making dealers is connected with the others and with the Federal Reserve Bank of New York by private wire. Many buyers and sellers deal directly with the specialized dealers; others place orders through local dealers, banks, and brokers.

The volume of transactions in this market is huge—far larger than in any other securities market in the world. For example, in September 1975 the daily volume of transactions averaged $5566 million.

Table 10 — 5   **Daily Average Dealer Transactions in U.S. Government Securities and in Federal Agency Issues, September 1975** *(amounts in millions of dollars)*

	Amounts	Percent of Total
U.S. government securities	$5,566	100.0
Maturities		
within 1 year	4,032	72.4
1– 5 years	1,315	23.6
5– 10 years	128	2.3
10 or more years	91	1.7
U.S. government agency issues	787	

Source: *Federal Reserve Bulletin,* November 1976, p. A36.
Note: These figures do not include transactions in new or maturing issues.

(See Table 10– 5.) More than 72 percent of these transactions were in maturities of less than a year, partly because of the large volume of outstanding securities in this maturity range, but also because these securities are bought and sold more frequently as a means of adjusting liquidity positions. Daily transactions in federal-agency issues averaged $787 million.

Several characteristics of the market for Treasury securities merit emphasis:

1. It is international in scope. Participants include not only every type of buyer and seller located throughout the United States but also foreign official institutions, foreign banks, and other foreigners.
2. It is a major channel through which commercial banks, other financial institutions, nonfinancial business firms, and others adjust their liquidity positions. However, other branches of the money market also perform this function, as we shall see later.
3. The structure of this market and the volume of transactions facilitate Federal Reserve open-market operations in government securities, and especially in the shorter maturities. The Federal Reserve can quickly buy or sell large amounts of these securities with only minimum direct effects on their prices and yields, and the expansionary or restrictive effects are widely disseminated. For example, though the Federal Reserve buys securities from New York dealers, the money thus created flows to sellers who may be located anywhere.

SHORT-TERM DEBTS OF STATE AND LOCAL GOVERNMENTS

Of the $231 billion of state and local government debt outstanding at the end of 1975, at least 10 percent had maturities within a year. Some of these claims initially had longer maturities, but many were initially short-term and were issued in anticipation of tax receipts or of proceeds from planned sales of longer-term bonds.

Several hundred brokers and dealers, including many commercial banks acting in these roles, serve as middlemen in this market. Some serve as market makers and maintain significant inventories; others act more as brokers. The breadth and continuity of the markets for these claims vary considerably. Markets for short-term claims against state governments and their larger political subdivisions are generally very broad, and even large transactions can be consummated quickly and with little effect on prices and yields. This is less true of the issues of some of the smaller political units.

LOANS TO DEALERS AND BROKERS IN SECURITIES

Not only government security dealers, but also other dealers and brokers in securities, issue claims against themselves that are liquid assets for banks, other financial institutions, nonfinancial business firms, and others. Dealers require funds to finance their inventories of securities, and brokers require funds to finance their customers' purchases of securities on margin. Since their equity funds are typically far too small to cover their requirements, dealers and brokers acquire most of their funds in other ways, the most important of which are the following:

1. Call or demand loans. These are one-day loans that are automatically extended day by day unless the lender calls for repayment or the borrower repays voluntarily. During the 1920s call loans were a major source of liquidity for financial institutions and large nonfinancial corporations. Though still used, they are now less important than many other sources of liquidity.
2. Loans with specified maturities, usually not more than 90 days.
3. Sales of securities under repurchase agreements. A security—often a government security—is sold at one time but the seller agrees to repurchase it at a stipulated time in the future. The time between sale and repurchase may be only one day, or it may be longer. For example, a government security dealer may sell a security for $1 million, agreeing to repurchase it two days later for $1 million

plus interest for two days at the going rate. Thus, the buyer acquires a highly liquid asset for two days and the seller acquires funds for that period and retains the right to reclaim the security for sale to others.

Though commercial banks and other financial institutions are the largest suppliers of funds to dealers and brokers, large amounts are also provided by nonfinancial corporations, mostly through repurchase agreements.

THE FEDERAL FUNDS MARKET

The term "Federal funds" is simply a short name for immediately available deposit claims against a Federal Reserve bank. They are often given an even shorter name—Fed funds. The term "immediately available" means that the funds are available for use on the day that the loan is made, as contrasted with funds that will be collected and available for use only one or more days later. In the parlance of the market, lenders sell Fed funds and borrowers purchase them.

In most, though not all, Fed funds transactions, deposits at Federal Reserve banks, which are legal reserves for banks that are members of the Federal Reserve, are transferred from the seller to the buyer. Such transfers are effected in two principal ways:

1. Through one-day loans. For example, on Day 1, Bank A orders the Federal Reserve to transfer $1 million of its reserve balance to Bank B, which the Federal Reserve does immediately through its electronic transfer system. On Day 2, Bank B repays the loan with interest for one day at the prevailing rate on Fed funds, so that reserves are transferred back to Bank A. Most transfers of Fed funds are effected in this way. Though the initial maturity of most of these loans is only one day, the loans may be extended from day to day if sellers and purchasers agree.
2. Through purchases and sales of securities of the U.S. government and federal agencies under repurchase agreements. In this case, Bank A may purchase $1 million of these securities from Bank B on Day 1 under an agreement that requires Bank B to repurchase them the next day for $1 million plus interest. Bank A transfers reserves to Bank B on Day 1 and receives them back the next day.

Commercial banks are by far the largest borrowers, or purchasers, of Fed funds. Some other types of institutions also purchase Fed funds. For example, brokers and dealers in securities obtain significant amounts of immediately available funds by selling government securities under repurchase agreements, and other financial institutions and even some nonfinancial corporations acquire such funds through sales of securities under repurchase agreements or by direct borrowing.

Commercial banks are also by far the largest lenders, or sellers, of Fed funds. Some other types of institutions also lend Fed funds. For example, under prevailing regulations commercial banks may purchase Fed funds directly not only from other commercial banks but also from savings and loan associations, mutual savings banks, the Federal Home Loan Banks and the Federal Home Loan Bank Board, other agencies of the federal government, securities dealers, and some others. A bank may also acquire Fed funds by purchasing government securities under repurchase agreements not only from the types of institutions listed above but also from business corporations, state and local governments, foreign banks and foreign official institutions, and some others.

In the example cited earlier, the Fed funds transaction involved a direct transfer of a deposit at the Federal Reserve between two member banks. Today, however, a significant share of Federal funds borrowing never goes through a Federal Reserve account or results in a shift of funds to or from a bank. An example will clarify the process involved. Suppose that a customer has a $20 million demand deposit at a bank. Under existing laws and regulations the bank may not pay interest on demand deposits, and it must hold reserves against the deposit. Moreover, the bank fears that the customer may withdraw the deposit to purchase earning assets, which would drain reserves from the bank. The demand deposit can be exchanged for Fed funds at the bank in either of two ways:

1. The customer relinquishes the $20 million demand deposit to buy and lend to the bank a like amount of Fed funds. On the books of the bank this will appear as a $20 million decrease of demand deposits and an equal increase of its own liability in the form of "Federal funds borrowed."

2. The customer relinquishes his $20 million demand deposit to purchase from the bank a like amount of government securities under a repurchase agreement. On the books of the bank this will appear as a decrease of demand deposits and an equal increase of its liabilities in the form of "securities sold under agreements to repurchase."

Such transactions can be advantageous to both the bank and its customer. The bank gains because it thereby avoids the loss of reserves that would result from withdrawal of the deposits, and it experiences a decrease of its required reserves, thereby enhancing its lending power, because no reserves are required against its liabilities in the forms of Fed funds borrowed and securities sold with agreement to repurchase. The customer gains by exchanging sterile demand deposits for interest-yielding Fed funds. These are only two of the many ways that customers have found to earn interest on their liquid funds despite the prohibition of interest on demand deposits.

The Fed funds market grew to considerable importance during the 1920s, though participation in it at that time was largely confined to big banks, and there was only one middleman—a bond dealer who assembled information and put potential lenders and borrowers in touch with each other. The Fed funds market then dwindled during the period from the mid-1930s to 1951, when most banks were highly liquid, demands for bank loans were small relative to the banks' lending power, and interest rates were generally low. As these conditions came to be reversed after 1951, the market grew markedly, and its growth accelerated during the 1960s and early 1970s. The number of participating banks and other institutions rose sharply, the market came to be organized more efficiently, and the volume of transactions in Fed funds rose to record levels. For example, in mid-1976, the total liabilities of commercial banks in the forms of Federal funds purchased and securities sold under agreements to repurchase amounted to $60.7 billion. Of this total, $35.2 billion was owed to commercial banks, $8.1 billion to securities brokers and dealers, and $17.4 billion to others.[3]

There are two principal types of middlemen in this market—two nonbank brokers, and large commercial banks. The two nonbank brokers put potential lenders and borrowers in touch with each other. Large commercial banks also perform this function sometimes. However, the middleman function is now performed predominantly by large banks acting as dealers in Fed funds. Such a bank in a financial center buys Fed funds from its correspondent banks and others, retains such amounts as it wants for its own purposes, and sells the remainder to others. Though banks of almost all sizes sometimes appear in the market as buyers and sometimes as sellers of Fed funds, smaller banks are typically net lenders and larger banks net borrowers of these funds. In some cases, banks lend Fed funds only temporarily. However, when rates on Fed funds are quite high relative to other rates, some banks lend these funds almost continuously for protracted periods. On the other side, some banks borrow Fed funds only to meet temporary reserve deficien-

[3] *Federal Reserve Bulletin,* March 1977, p. A19.

cies, but some, and especially some very large banks, borrow large amounts almost continuously.

The interest rate on Fed funds is one of the most volatile of the short-term rates. It sometimes changes several times a day, especially toward the end of a reserve period, when banks are making final adjustments of their reserve positions. When the supply of excess reserves is large relative to the demand for them, the rate can fall to very low levels, sometimes to only a fraction of 1 percent. Under the reverse conditions it can rise to high levels, sometimes several percentage points above the current Federal Reserve discount rate. For example, at times during the first half of 1974 it rose above 13 percent while the Federal Reserve discount rate was 8 percent. The fact that this rate can rise so far above the discount rate is eloquent evidence that the Federal Reserve does not stand ready to lend freely and without limit at its posted rate.

The Fed funds rate is, however, closely related to other short-term rates, and especially to yields on other highly liquid assets. This is primarily because selling Fed funds is by no means the only way that a bank can dispose of excess reserves, and purchasing Fed funds is not the only way that a bank can repair a reserve deficiency. For example, a bank may also use its excess reserves to repay borrowings at the Federal Reserve, if it has any, to buy Treasury bills or other liquid assets, or to acquire less liquid assets. And a bank may also repair a reserve deficiency by borrowing from the Federal Reserve, if it has not worn out its welcome there, by selling Treasury bills or other liquid assets, or by disposing of less liquid loans and investments. For such reasons, yields on these various types of assets tend to move in the same direction, though not necessarily to the same extent or with the same timing.

In short, the Fed funds market has become a major medium, though not the only one, through which banks make temporary adjustments of their reserve positions, and it is an important medium for transferring lending power among banks for longer periods. It also serves various other types of institutions, both as a source of short-term loans and as a supplier of highly liquid, income-yielding assets. We shall later discuss in some detail the role of this market in transmitting the effects of Federal Reserve policy actions. Suppose, for example, that the Federal Reserve creates additional reserve funds by purchasing government securities or acceptances. The initial effect will be to increase the excess reserves of some banks and to decrease the reserve deficiencies of some others. This will appear in the Fed funds market as an excess of supply over demand, the rate on Fed funds will decline quickly, and the decline will be transmitted to yields on close substitutes and also, though perhaps less quickly, to yields on assets that are less close substitutes.

BANKERS' ACCEPTANCES

Bankers' acceptances are short-term, liquid financial claims against commercial banks, mostly against large banks. Some of these originate in financing imports and exports, but some are used to finance the shipment, exchange, or storage of goods within this country. A simple example will illustrate the nature and functions of these instruments. Suppose that you wish to use a bankers' acceptance to finance an international trade transaction. You might be an exporter seeking to arrange credit for the foreign purchaser of your goods. However, we shall assume that you are an importer, that you buy $10 million worth of goods from Mr. Exporter abroad, that Mr. Exporter wants payment immediately, but that you want to defer payment for 90 days. You could, of course, finance the transactions by borrowing directly from a bank or some other source, but you may find it less expensive to use a bankers' acceptance. In this case, the following steps are involved: You approach a bank, perhaps Chase Manhattan, and ask, "Will you accept a 90-day draft drawn on you for $10 million?" The banker will reply, "Yes, if you provide assurance that you will have $10 million in our hands before the draft matures." If you provide this assurance, Chase will issue to you a *letter of credit,* containing the bank's commitment to accept such a draft. You will send the letter of credit to Mr. Exporter, who will draw a draft stating in effect: "To Chase Manhattan Bank: Pay to me or order the sum of $10 million 90 days after date." The draft will be presented to Chase, one of whose officers will write on its face, "accepted," and sign his name. This is a shorthand way of stating, "We accept this order and will pay to the holder $10 million 90 days hence." Thus the time draft or bill of exchange is transformed into a bankers' acceptance, which is an unconditional, binding obligation on Chase Manhattan to pay as ordered.

The accepting bank has not advanced loan funds to you or to Mr. Exporter, but it has, in effect, guaranteed payment. For this it charges a fee. Mr. Exporter now has a highly safe and liquid asset that he can sell in the money market at the prevailing rate of discount on assets of such high quality. Funds to finance your transaction are provided by the holder of the acceptance.

The volume of bankers' acceptances outstanding has risen markedly in recent years (see Table 10−6). The principal middlemen in this market are six dealers, all located in New York City, who maintain a

Table 10-6   **Dollar Bankers' Acceptances Outstanding in the United States**
(in billions of dollars)

End of Period	Amounts
1965	$ 3.4
1966	3.6
1967	4.3
1968	4.4
1969	5.5
1970	7.1
1971	7.9
1972	6.9
1973	8.9
1974	18.5
1975	18.7
1976	22.5

Source: *Federal Reserve Bulletin*, November 1976, p. A25, and July 1977, p. A25.

continuous market. The principal holders of acceptances are of several types:

1. The Federal Reserve. From the beginning, bankers' acceptances drawn to finance trade in real goods and services have been eligible for Federal Reserve purchases in the open market and as collateral for loans by the Federal Reserve. Traditionally, the Federal Reserve has given considerable support to this market, but in recent years it has held for its own account only a very small fraction of outstanding acceptances.
2. Foreign central banks. These banks hold a significant fraction of their claims against dollars in the form of dollar acceptances but much more in other short-term claims, such as Treasury obligations and time deposits.
3. Foreign private banks and business firms.
4. Large American commercial banks. Many banks purchase and hold acceptance claims against themselves for earnings purposes and also because these can be sold in the market if a bank wishes to acquire funds. Banks also hold acceptance claims against other banks.
5. Large domestic and international nonfinancial corporations. On some occasions these institutions have held more than half of all outstanding acceptances.

OPEN-MARKET COMMERCIAL AND FINANCE COMPANY PAPER

These instruments are unsecured short-term promissory notes issued by various types of business concerns with high credit ratings. Until a decade or so ago, they were usually called "commercial paper" because most of them were issued by large commercial establishments to finance such things as shipments of goods, holdings of inventories, and accounts receivable from customers. Traditionally, this paper had original maturities of 30 days to 6 months and was held largely by commercial banks.

This market has changed markedly in recent years, in the following ways:

1. Many more types of firms have come to issue such paper. Huge amounts have been issued by various types of finance companies. For example, consumer finance companies, and especially the larger ones, sell their notes, which are usually in large denominations, and retail the proceeds to consumers. Large sales finance companies, such as the General Motors Acceptance Corporation (GMAC), issue notes and use the proceeds to finance loans to their dealers to enable the latter to carry inventories and accounts receivable from their customers. In recent years there have been large issues of "bank-related paper." Most of this is issued by bank holding companies or their affiliates. The proceeds are used to finance a wide variety of activities of these holding-company systems, but a considerable part of them is put at the disposal of subsidiary banks through loans to them, deposits with them, or purchases of earning assets from them. Such notes are also issued by public utility companies and many other types of corporations with high credit ratings. In fact, issuers are now so diverse that the term "commercial paper" is almost obsolete; some term like "short-term corporate notes" would be more appropriate.
2. The maturities of this paper have become much more varied. Many notes still have initial maturities in the traditional 30-day to 6-month range and few run beyond a year, but maturities of less than 30 days have become much more common. In fact, some issuers tailor maturities to conform precisely to the wishes of buyers, even if this means maturities of only a few days.
3. Holders of this paper have become more numerous and varied. These now include not only commercial banks but also many other types of institutions, including large nonfinancial corporations. The latter, denied explicit interest on their demand deposits, find

especially attractive the very short maturities that are tailored to meet their maturity preferences.

4. The volume of outstanding commercial and finance company paper has increased tremendously. It rose from $13.5 billion at the end of 1966 to $52.7 billion at the end of 1976. (See Table 10 − 7.)

New issues of commercial and finance company paper are distributed in two ways — through commercial paper houses and by direct placement. A commercial paper house is simply a broker-dealer that, among its other functions, acts as a primary distributor of such paper. Six dealers account for most of this business. A commercial paper house usually buys the paper outright from the issuer and retails it to others, but it sometimes sells the paper as broker-agent for the issuer. Also, it commonly stands ready to make a secondary market for the issues that it distributed initially.

Many big finance companies, many bank holding companies and their affiliates, and some other big corporations place their new issues directly with corporations and other institutional buyers. The financial officers of these issuers are in daily communication with corporate treasurers and others with command over large amounts of funds. For most of this privately placed paper, there is not a secondary market. However, this is not as great a disadvantage as it might appear. For one

Table 10 − 7   **Commercial and Finance Company Paper Outstanding, End of Years 1966 − 1975**
(in millions of dollars)

End of Years	Total	Financial Companies[a]	Nonfinancial Companies
1966	$13,465	$12,888	$ 757
1967	17,085	14,974	2,111
1968	21,173	18,399	2,774
1969	32,600	27,244	5,356
1970	33,071	25,938	7,133
1971	32,126	25,879	6,247
1972	34,721	27,753	6,968
1973	41,073	32,691	8,382
1974	49,144	36,000	12,694
1975	47,690	37,515	10,175
1976	52,673	39,636	12,987

Source: *Federal Reserve Bulletin,* November 1976, p. A25, and July 1977, p. A25.
[a] Includes bank-related paper.

thing, the maturities of many of these issues were originally tailored to the desires of the buyers. Also, some issuers stand ready to redeem their notes before maturity at the request of the buyer.

LARGE-DENOMINATION NEGOTIABLE
CERTIFICATES OF DEPOSIT (NCDs)

These are time deposit claims against commercial banks evidenced by certificates. The certificates are in denominations of at least $100,000, and many are in denominations of $1 million or more. These denominations indicate that they are designed to appeal to large investors, and their principal holders are, in fact, business corporations, foreign central banks and other foreign investors, and state and local governments, though some are held by other institutions. Their initial maturities range from 30 days to several months. However, they are "negotiable"; that is, they can be transferred from holder to holder by endorsement. Thus, the issuing bank need not redeem a certificate before its maturity, but a holder can regain his money earlier by selling the certificate in the money market.

Though banks have long issued certificates of deposit, large-denomination NCDs were of little importance before 1961.[4] However, they became an immediate success after their introduction in that year by the First National City Bank of New York. The number of issuing banks has increased markedly, though most of the issues are still by big banks. Their appeal to institutional investors is evidenced by the rapid growth in the amount outstanding; by the end of 1975 this had risen to nearly $83 billion. (See Table 10–8.)

Most new NCDs are issued directly by banks to the initial holders. However, in some cases—especially when banks are making unusually strong efforts to raise funds from this source—they are distributed through dealers or brokers. A secondary market for NCDs is maintained by nonbank broker-dealers. About five major dealers serve as market makers in these issues, and a number of other firms also facilitate transactions, acting as brokers, as dealers, or both.

In short, NCDs have become a major source of funds for many large commercial banks and an important bearer of liquidity for other institutional investors.

---

[4] All savings and time deposit claims are, of course, sources of funds for their issuers and liquid assets for their holders. We concentrate here on NCDs because they are money market instruments.

Table 10–8   **Outstanding Negotiable Certificates of Deposit in Denominations of $100,000 or More** *(in billions of dollars)*

End of Period	Amount
1969	$11.1
1970	25.8
1971	33.8
1972	44.3
1973	64.1
1974	89.8
1975	82.9

Source: *Federal Reserve Bulletin,* September 1973, p. A16, and November 1976, p. A12.

Two types of Federal Reserve policies have at times inhibited the growth of NCDs. On several occasions in the late 1960s and early 1970s the Federal Reserve refused to raise ceiling rates on NCDs while yields on closely competing assets were rising. Also, in late 1973 it imposed an 8 percent marginal reserve requirement on increases in outstanding NCDs to decrease the ability of banks to bid for funds. Whether similar policies will inhibit NCD growth in the future remains to be seen.

EURODOLLAR LOANS

Borrowing of Eurodollars is one of the newer and more sophisticated means of shifting reserves and lending power among American banks.[5] Eurodollar deposits are dollar-denominated deposit claims against banks located in foreign countries, including foreign branches of American banks. Some of these deposits are payable on demand, but most are time deposits, with maturities ranging from a few days to several months. These deposits are owed to both Americans and foreigners. As a sort of fractional reserve against these liabilities, foreign banks hold deposit claims, mostly demand deposit claims, against American banks. On the basis of their Eurodollar deposits, foreign banks make dollar-denominated loans to borrowers of all types, among which are American banks.

[5] We shall deal here in a simplified way with only this one aspect of the complex subject of Eurodollar financial claims. For a somewhat more comprehensive treatment see pp. 291–294 below.

An example will illustrate how Eurodollar borrowings can be used to reallocate reserves among banks in this country. An American bank borrows $10 million from a foreign bank and receives the proceeds in the form of a check or an electronic order on deposits at another bank in the United States. It clears the check through the Federal Reserve collection system and gets an addition to its reserves at the expense of the bank on which the check was drawn.[6] Since such payments are usually made through an electronic transfer system, the entire transaction can be consummated quickly.

Eurodollar borrowings were used only infrequently before the 1960s as a method of transferring reserves among American banks. However, they rose to very high levels on various occasions in the late 1960s and early 1970s when the Federal Reserve was following restrictive policies, domestic interest rates were high, and many banks found it difficult to acquire funds in other ways. For example, they rose above $14 billion by mid-1969 and remained above $10 billion for many months. They thereafter declined somewhat but were above $4 billion in mid-1974. There is reason to believe that this method will continue to be employed even when monetary and credit conditions here are less stringent.

SUMMARY OF MONEY MARKET INSTRUMENTS

The preceding sections have dealt with only those types of short-term liquid assets that are actively traded in the money markets. A complete inventory of liquid assets available in the economy would also include, at a minimum, money itself and various types of savings and time deposits other than NCDs at the various depository types of financial intermediaries. However, both the variety and the amounts of money market instruments are impressive. (See Table 10 − 9.) The total volume of transactions in these instruments, if we had this information, would be far more impressive, for the annual transfers of funds from buyers to sellers of these instruments is many times as large as the amount outstanding at any time.

We shall later have many occasions to refer back to the principal functions of money market instruments: As substitutes for money itself;

[6] In some cases the borrowing bank will receive the loan proceeds in the form of a check drawn on itself. In this case, the bank will simply cancel its deposit liability to the foreign bank and will receive no addition to its reserves. However, its reserve position will be improved because its deposit liabilities, and therefore its required reserves, will be decreased.

Table 10 – 9   **Principal Money Market Instruments in the United States**

	Approximate Amounts Outstanding Circa the End of 1975 (in billions of dollars)
U.S. Treasury obligations with maturities within one year held outside the government and the Federal Reserve	$150
Federal agency issues with maturities within one year	19
Short-term state and local government debt	40
Loans to dealers and brokers in securities	7
Federal funds	15
Bankers' acceptances	19
Commercial and finance company paper	48
Large denomination negotiable certificates of deposit	83
Eurodollars loans to American banks	4
Total of above	$385

Note: The data in this table are far from precise and indicate only general orders of
      magnitude. Some are only approximate estimates, and there is no clear dividing
      line between instruments that should be considered money market instruments
      and those that are not so actively traded but are very close substitutes.

as a means of holding liquid purchasing power; as a source of liquidity for almost every type of entity in the economy; as a means of increasing the mobility of funds among geographic areas and among sectors of the economy; and as a medium for transmitting the effects of Federal Reserve policy actions.

CONCLUSION

This chapter, and the two preceding, have described the interrelated markets for various types of financial claims. There remain, of course, many types of financial claims for which there is no broad and well-organized market. These include, for example, equity claims against individual proprietorships and partnerships, whose unlimited liability makes them unsuitable for broad trading; equity claims against small corporations that are only rarely offered for sale; and many debt claims against households, small business firms, and small governmental units. The high cost of collecting, analyzing, and disseminating economic and financial information about the millions of these small units is a major obstacle to the development of broad markets for the financial claims that they can issue. Fortunately for many of them, they have access to funds from local financial intermediaries on terms almost as favorable as those available in national markets. However, some are not so fortunate.

A very large fraction of all financial claims in the United States does enjoy broad markets. Included in this category are both equity and debt claims against business corporations that hold the bulk of all business assets; debt claims against the federal government and its agencies; debt claims against state and local governmental units of at least moderate size; and both equity and debt claims against many types of financial intermediaries. Primary markets contribute to economic efficiency in ways that are almost obvious. They enable each issuer to sell its financial claims over broad national and even international areas to those buyers offering the highest prices. In this process, they so increase the interregional and intersectoral flows of securities and funds as to reduce markedly, and even to eliminate, regional and sectoral differentials in yields on a given class of security. Thus they serve to allocate the scarce supply of financial resources to those who can use them most productively.

Secondary markets contribute to economic efficiency in ways that are less obvious but no less important. In the first place, as noted earlier, enhanced marketability of a security is one way of reconciling differing maturity preferences of issuers and holders and of increasing the liquidity of the security. In the absence of a continuous and orderly secondary market for proposed new issues, sellers may be able to sell them only at considerably higher yields. In the second place, the prevailing prices and yields in secondary markets for the various classes of securities are an important determinant of the terms on which comparable new issues can be sold. And in the third place, the secondary market enhances the interregional and intersectoral mobility of funds. Huge amounts of funds are transferred among regions and sectors through purchases and sales of outstanding securities. For example, a financial intermediary may sell some of its holdings of money market instruments or less liquid securities to buyers located in one region and use the proceeds to purchase new issues originating in another region or regions.

SELECTED READINGS

I. Primary markets

Carosso, V. P. *Investment Banking in America: A History.* Cambridge, Mass.: Harvard University Press, 1970.

Friend, I., et al. *Investment Banking and the New Issues Market.* Cleveland and New York: World Publishing Co., 1967.

Robinson, R. I., and Wrightsman, D. *Financial Markets: The Accumulation and Allocation of Wealth.* New York: McGraw-Hill, 1974. Chaps. 13 – 18.

II. Money markets

Lindow, W. *Inside the Money Market.* New York: Random House, 1972.

Robinson, R. I., and Wrightsman, D. *Financial Markets: The Accumulation and Allocation of Wealth.* New York: McGraw-Hill, 1974. Chaps. 7 – 11.

Woodworth, G. W. *The Money Market and Monetary Management.* 2d ed. New York: Harper & Row, 1972.

INTERNATIONAL MONETARY AND FINANCIAL RELATIONSHIPS

Up to this point we have concentrated largely on the domestic functions of money and finance. However, our monetary-financial system also plays important roles in transactions across national boundary lines, our monetary and financial policies have profound effects on other countries, and the policies of other nations affect monetary and financial developments in this country. This chapter will explore some of the most important of these international relationships.

BASIC FUNCTIONS OF MONEY AND FINANCE IN INTERNATIONAL TRANSACTIONS

These functions are essentially the same as those in domestic transactions: to decrease the real costs of trade and to enable traders to exploit to the maximum extent the potential gains from both spot exchanges and exchanges involving time. And the potential gains from exchanges across national boundary lines are of essentially the same types as those from domestic exchanges. Because of differences in preferences and in initial endowments of specific goods, persons in different countries can be made to feel better off through pure spot exchanges, in which the total amount of goods is given. Even greater are the potential gains from international exchanges that are an integral part of a system of specialized production, which increases the total real output available for sharing by traders. There are great differences in both the total amounts and the specific types and proportions of productive factors available in the various nations. There are differences in the specific types of natural resources and in the ratios of these to capital and labor; differences in stocks of capital; differences in the supply of labor relative to other factors, and in the types and degrees of skill of the labor force; and differences in states of technology. Such differences in factor endowments result in great differences in relative efficiencies in producing specific types of goods and services. World real output and income can be maximized only if each nation specializes in producing those things in which it has a comparative advantage, which means those things in which it is most efficient or least inefficient in comparison with other countries. The extent to which such potential gains can be realized depends heavily on the efficiency and smooth functioning of international exchange processes.

There are also large potential gains from international exchanges involving time. Some of these are comparable to domestic exchanges involving time on consumption account. For example, members of a nation may borrow from foreigners at one point in time in order to meet unusual current needs, promising to repay later with interest, and both borrower and lender may feel better off. Even greater are the potential gains from international exchanges involving time to finance capital formation. Stocks of capital vary greatly from nation to nation, as do rates of current real saving. One would therefore expect that in the absence of international transfers of investing power there would be wide differences in the marginal efficiency of investment. For example, the marginal efficiency rate may be 12 percent in the United States and 25 percent in some other country. A transfer of investing power from the United States to the other country will increase the total real income of the two countries, and both will benefit if the interest rate is somewhere between 12 and 25 percent.

All of the above types of exchanges might, of course, be effected under a system of pure barter, but such a system would be operationally expensive and many of the potential gains from trade would remain unrealized. Efficiency in international transactions has been greatly enhanced through the development and use of money and various types of financial instruments and institutions. We shall discuss these further after surveying the principal types of transactions across national boundary lines.

TYPES OF INTERNATIONAL TRANSACTIONS

Essentially, these are similar to the types of transactions within a nation—purchases and sales of goods and services, purchases and sales of financial claims of various types, and gifts or grants.

TRADE IN GOODS AND SERVICES

American exports of goods and services to the rest of the world (ROW) include not only many types of commodities but also a wide variety of services, the latter including services supplied to foreigners visiting this country, shipping and other transportation services, financial services, and services rendered by American property located abroad. Foreign purchasers of American exports must pay for them, doing so by surrendering dollars or foreign moneys.

On the other hand, Americans purchase from the rest of the world large amounts of imports of goods and services. These include not only many types of commodities but also a wide range of services, such as services supplied to American travelers abroad, transportation services, and services rendered by foreign properties in the United States. American purchasers of imports must pay for them, doing so by surrendering dollars or foreign moneys.

TRADE IN FINANCIAL CLAIMS

Americans also buy from and sell to the rest of the world many types of financial claims. These are of two broad types:

1. Direct financial claims against nonfinancial entities, such as business firms and governmental units. Some of these are claims against American entities; others are claims against foreign entities. Some are equity claims, principally equity claims against corporations; others are debt claims with maturities ranging from very short to very long. Some are new issues; others are part of the outstanding stock.
2. Indirect financial claims against banks and other financial intermediaries. Thus foreigners may purchase claims against American financial intermediaries or repurchase claims against foreign intermediaries formerly held by Americans. And Americans may purchase claims against foreign intermediaries or repurchase claims against American intermediaries formerly held by foreigners.

Table 11−1   **U.S. Exports and Imports of Goods and Services, 1972−1975**
(amounts in billions of dollars)

Year	U.S. GNP	Exports of Goods and Services		Imports of Goods and Services	
		Amount	Percent of GNP	Amount	Percent of GNP
1972	$1171.1	$ 72.7	6.2	$ 75.9	6.5
1973	1306.3	101.5	7.8	94.2	7.2
1974	1406.9	144.2	10.2	136.5	9.7
1975	1498.9	147.8	9.9	126.5	8.4

Source: *Federal Reserve Bulletin,* May 1976, p. A54.

When foreign entities buy financial claims from Americans, they must pay for them, doing so by surrendering dollars or foreign moneys. And American purchases of financial claims from foreign entities must be paid for by surrendering dollars or foreign moneys.

Two aspects of such international purchases and sales of financial claims deserve emphasis:

1. They transfer purchasing power from the purchaser to the seller. The seller of a financial claim receives money that he can use as he sees fit—to purchase imports of goods and services, to transfer to others, or for other purposes.
2. They alter the portfolios of both the buyer and the seller. We shall later emphasize that a major motive in many transactions is to adjust the income-safety-liquidity characteristics of portfolios.

INTERNATIONAL GIFTS AND GRANTS

These are essentially similar to domestic transfer payments, for the donor surrenders goods or purchasing power without receiving anything of value in return. Thus foreign individuals and governments may make gifts or grants to American entities in the form of money or goods, and American individuals or governmental units frequently make gifts or grants to foreigners in the form of money or goods.

SUMMARY

We have now identified the three broad categories of international transactions that give rise to payments between American entities and entities in the rest of the world. During any period, American entities receive payments in these types of transactions: (1) exports of goods and services; (2) exports of financial claims; and (3) receipts of gifts and grants.

Also, during any period, American entities make payments to the rest of the world in three broad types of transactions: (1) imports of goods and services; (2) imports of financial claims; and (3) gifts and grants to the rest of the world.

THE INTERNATIONAL PAYMENTS MECHANISM

Most payments across national boundary lines are effected by transferring deposit claims against banks. Some transfers are effected with written orders, similar to ordinary checks, but large payments are usually effected through orders by cable, telegraph, or other electronic means. Thus distance need not mean delay. Huge amounts of payments are made throughout the world by transfers of deposit claims against large American banks. This is one reason, though not the only one, why foreigners hold large amounts of deposits in American banks.

We shall now survey the principal institutional arrangements that facilitate international payments. Though it is common to speak of "the international monetary system," there is no "international system" in the sense of some institution or set of institutions that are operated by a supranational or international authority and that provide the money used in ordinary international transactions. The one truly international monetary institution, the International Monetary Fund (IMF), does not itself provide a medium used for international payments. Instead, it operates through the various national monetary authorities, serving as a source of liquidity for them and as a channel for consultation and cooperation. The so-called "international monetary system" is composed of more than 150 national monetary systems. Each nation claims, as a right of national sovereignty, the right to define its own monetary unit, to establish and govern its own monetary authority, and to determine its own monetary policy. The principal components of each national monetary system are its central bank and institutions performing commercial banking functions. These are monetary intermediaries; they supply national money primarily by purchasing various types of financial claims, and they reduce the nation's money supply primarily by selling financial claims of various kinds. These national monetary systems are interconnected in various ways, as we shall see later.

CENTRAL BANKS

Just as the United States has its Federal Reserve System, almost every other nation has its central bank. Thus, there is the Bank of England, the Bank of France, the Bank of Canada, the Bank of Japan, the Reserve Bank of India, and so on. The major domestic purpose of each central bank is to manage its nation's monetary policy, but it also performs other domestic functions, such as clearing and collecting checks, serving as the government's banker, and supervising commercial banks. In the usual case, a central bank also manages its nation's international liquidity position, buys and sells foreign moneys and other international reserve assets, and regulates the exchange rate between its own national money and foreign moneys.

A nation's international liquidity position refers to its ability to meet its payments to the rest of the world fully and promptly. For this purpose it needs access to some sort of asset that will be acceptable to foreign payees. It uses such access for two principal, related purposes:

1. to meet at least temporary excesses of its payments to the rest of the world over its receipts from the rest of the world
2. to prevent undesired declines of the exchange rates on its own national money in terms of foreign moneys

In effect, it sells these assets and uses the proceeds to purchase any excess supply of its money in exchange markets.

The sources of international liquidity to each national central bank are of two broad types: its holdings of international reserve assets; and its facilities for borrowing foreign money or assets easily convertible into foreign money.

INTERNATIONAL RESERVE ASSETS

The components of international reserve assets are of three broad classes:

1. Gold. Some years ago, this was a major source of international liquidity. When virtually all central banks stood ready to buy gold in unlimited amounts and at fixed prices in terms of their national moneys, any holder of gold could acquire any foreign money that it wanted by selling gold to the central bank of the foreign country. However, the importance of gold as an international reserve asset has declined markedly during recent decades and is likely to

decline still further. Though central banks still hold large amounts of gold, their gold purchases and sales with each other have become much more limited and may be discontinued entirely. In short, gold may become "demonetized."

2. Special Drawing Rights, commonly called SDRs. These are financial claims against the International Monetary Fund, which the latter creates and issues to national central banks, and which are transferable among central banks. Thus a central bank can acquire a desired foreign money by selling some of its SDRs to the central bank of that country. SDRs, whose outstanding volume can be controlled by the IMF, are likely to become an increasingly important component of international reserves.[1]

3. Claims against foreign national moneys.

The composition of official international reserves varies considerably from country to country. Almost all countries hold some of their international reserves in the form of gold and SDRs, and most of the official international reserves of the United States are in those forms. However, most foreign central banks and governments hold a much larger fraction of their international reserves in the form of claims against foreign national moneys. These include a number of other national moneys—such as British pound sterling, German marks, and French francs—but by far the largest part consists of claims against U.S. dollars. The size and composition of these claims at the end of 1975 are shown in Table 11−2. The total, at more than $80 billion, is indeed impressive. Only a small fraction is in the form of demand deposit claims, which yield no income; the remainder is in the form of a wide variety of dollar-denominated earning assets. These include time deposit claims against American banks; large amounts of Treasury bills and other short-term Treasury debt, and some longer-term Treasury obligations; commercial paper; and bankers' acceptances. Thus foreign official institutions are major participants in most branches of the American money market.

We find, then, that one international role of the dollar is to serve as a major source of international reserves and liquidity for other countries. Foreign central banks transfer these claims to others to cover deficits in their balances of international payments and also use them to influence the behavior of exchange rates. For example, a nation can

---

[1] Some writers also include as a component of official international reserves an item called "Reserve Position in the IMF." This is simply the amount that the nation can borrow from the IMF without question. I prefer to consider this as a part of a nation's official borrowing facilities.

Table 11–2	**U.S. Liabilities to Official Institutions of Foreign Countries, December 31, 1975** *(in millions of dollars)*	
Total		$80,150
Types of claims		
	Demand deposits	2,644
	Time deposits[a]	3,438
	U.S. Treasury bills and certificates	34,175
	Other short-term liabilities[b]	8,913
	Marketable U.S. Treasury bonds and notes	6,575
	Nonmarketable U.S. Treasury bonds and notes	19,976
	Other readily marketable liabilities	4,429

Source: *Federal Reserve Bulletin,* May 1976, pp. A63 –A65.

[a] Does not include large-denomination certificates of deposit, which are included in "other short-term liabilities."

[b] These consist largely of negotiable certificates of deposit, commercial paper, and bankers' acceptances.

present an unwanted decline of the exchange rate on its money by using dollar claims to purchase the excess supply of its money in exchange markets. And it can prevent an unwanted increase of the exchange rate on its money by supplying more of its money to purchase dollar claims.

OFFICIAL INTERNATIONAL BORROWING FACILITIES

The other major source of international liquidity for a central bank consists of its facilities for borrowing foreign moneys or assets readily convertible into foreign money. These facilities are of three principal types:

1. Borrowings from the International Monetary Fund. Under the IMF agreement, each nation is entitled to borrow a stated amount "without question" and further amounts if approved by IMF officials. In effect, a central bank buys from the IMF the desired foreign money, paying for it by delivering an equivalent amount of its own national money.
2. Borrowings from other national central banks. These occur frequently and sometimes in very large amounts. Some occur under formal, continuing arrangements. An outstanding example is provided by the Federal Reserve reciprocal currency, or swap, arrangements with 14 foreign central banks and the Bank for

International Settlements in Basel. (See Table 11 – 3.) Under these arrangements, the Federal Reserve and each of the foreign institutions agrees to supply to the other its own money up to some stipulated maximum in exchange for the money of the other. For example, the Bank of England can draw up to $3 billion from the Federal Reserve, giving in return an equivalent value in sterling, and the Federal Reserve can draw from the Bank of England up to $3 billion worth of sterling, giving in return an equivalent value in dollars. In addition to their borrowing and lending under formal arrangements, central banks borrow from and lend to each other under *ad hoc* arrangements, especially in times of actual or threatened crisis.

3. Other borrowings. Central banks, and especially those of less developed countries, sometimes borrow from foreign private sources. For example, they borrow on short or intermediate term from a consortium of foreign commercial banks, or they float intermediate- or longer-term securities on the international market.

Table 11 – 3   **Federal Reserve Reciprocal Currency Arrangements, January 31, 1976**

Institution	Amount of Facility (in millions of dollars)
Austrian National Bank	$ 250
National Bank of Belgium	1,000
Bank of Canada	2,000
National Bank of Denmark	250
Bank of England	3,000
Bank of France	2,000
German Federal Bank	2,000
Bank of Italy	3,000
Bank of Japan	2,000
Bank of Mexico	360
Netherlands Bank	500
Bank of Norway	250
Bank of Sweden	300
Swiss National Bank	1,400
Bank for Internal Settlements	
Swiss francs/dollars	600
Other European currencies/dollars	1,250
Total	$20,160

Source: *Federal Reserve Bulletin,* May 1976, p. 208.

SUMMARY

Each national central bank has access to international liquidity in the form of several types of international reserve assets and several types of international borrowing facilities. These enable a country to cover temporary excesses of its international payments over its international receipts. However, they do not free a country from the need to bring its international payments and receipts into balance over a longer period. A country with large and persistent deficits would exhaust its holdings of international reserves and also its international borrowing facilities. And a country with large and persistent surpluses would court price inflation because its central bank would have to purchase large amounts of international reserve assets, thereby creating reserves for its commercial banks.

To describe fully the various methods of equilibrating balances of international payments is beyond the scope of this book. However, it may be useful to mention briefly some of the actions that can be taken for this purpose by a deficit country, a surplus country, or both:

1. Adjustment of exchange rates among national moneys. A decrease of the exchange rate on the money of a deficit country will make its exports cheaper to foreigners and its imports more expensive to its own people, thereby tending to raise its exports relative to its imports. On the other hand, a rise of the exchange rate on the currency of a surplus country will tend to decrease its exports relative to its imports.
2. An increase of interest rates in the deficit country relative to those in the surplus country. This may be achieved through a more restrictive monetary policy in the deficit country, a more expansionary monetary policy in the surplus country, or both. This should at least serve to reduce the outflow of loan funds from a deficit country and may induce a flow of loan funds from surplus to deficit countries.
3. More restrictive monetary and fiscal policies in the deficit country to reduce, or restrict the rise of, its levels of national money income and prices; more expansionary monetary and fiscal policies in surplus countries to enhance the rise of its national money income and prices; or both. Such actions should serve to decrease the excess of imports over exports of deficit countries and to raise imports relative to exports of the surplus countries.

How, and to what extent, each of these various methods of equilibrating balances of international payments should be employed remain difficult and controversial questions. We shall later have more to say about this.

COMMERCIAL BANKS

We have already noted that most payments across national boundary lines are effected by transferring deposit claims against banks. These payments are facilitated by the commercial banking systems of the various countries and by a network of interconnections among these systems. In some of the least developed countries commercial banks do not extend much beyond the larger cities, but in more developed countries banking facilities are to be found in all areas. The banking systems of most countries consist of a limited number of nationwide branch banking systems. Thus virtually all branch offices have direct access to the nation's principal financial centers. However, as noted earlier, the United States does not permit nationwide branching; no bank is permitted to operate a domestic branch outside the state in which it is domiciled. Nevertheless, banks throughout the country have direct or indirect access to the principal financial centers through a nationwide network of correspondent relationships with New York City as their center.

The banking systems of the various nations are interconnected in many ways. One is through international correspondent relationships, similar to those among domestic banks within the United States. Under such arrangements, banks in different countries hold deposits with each other, usually with banks in lesser centers holding deposits with banks in the major centers; they lend to each other; they draw drafts on each other and accept such drafts, thereby creating bankers' acceptances; they join in making loans; they supply to each other reports on the creditworthiness of potential borrowers; and they act as agents for each other in buying and selling financial claims, clearing and collecting checks, enforcing contracts, and so on.

National banking systems are also interconnected through international branches. Big banks in most of the industrialized nations operate branches in other countries. For example, in mid-1976 there were in the United States nearly 200 offices of foreign banks, and their total assets were about $62 billion. Most of these offices were located in New York, Illinois, Texas, and California. A majority of the parent banks were domiciled in Canada, the United Kingdom, Continental Europe, and Japan, but some were in the Middle East and other countries.[2] Though

[2] *Federal Reserve Bulletin,* October 1976, pp. 815–823.

some of these offices concentrate largely on financing international trade, most of them compete actively for both American and foreign deposits and lend in both the United States and abroad.

Big American banks operate branches throughout the world. In mid-1976, foreign branches of American banks held total assets in excess of $194 billion. These branches receive deposits from their parent banks and other Americans but many more from foreign banks, governments, and business firms. They also make loans to their parent banks and to other Americans but many more to foreign banks, governments, and business firms. These branches facilitate international transfers of loan funds in many ways. For example, a London branch of an American bank lends to and borrows from its parent bank; it does the same with branches of the parent located in other countries; it accepts deposits from a business firm located in one country and lends in other countries; and so on.

National banking systems are also interconnected through joint ownership of banks by banks domiciled in two or more countries. For example, an American bank joins with an Iranian bank in establishing and operating a bank in Teheran. Or British and German banks join in establishing a bank in Colombia or Brazil. Banks from two or more countries often form consortiums to lend in other countries. For example, banks in Britain, the United States, Australia, and Japan may jointly make a large loan to the Philippine government or its central bank.

THE ROLE OF THE DOLLAR AS AN
INTERNATIONAL MEDIUM OF PAYMENTS

International payments may be made by transferring deposit claims against a bank in the payor's country, deposit claims against a bank in the payee's country, or deposit claims against a bank in a third country. Americans usually pay foreigners with claims against American banks, and most of their receipts from foreigners are in this form. Deposit claims against American banks are also widely used as the medium of payments among other countries in transactions that do not involve Americans as either payors or payees. For example, a Frenchman may pay for Brazilian coffee with claims on an American bank, and the Brazilian recipient can use the dollars as it sees fit. It is partly because dollars are so widely used as a medium of international payments that foreigners hold large amounts of deposit claims against American banks. For example, at the end of 1975, foreign private banks held more than $7.5 billion of demand deposit claims against American

Table 11−4   **U.S. Liabilities to Foreign Official Institutions and
Short-term Liabilities to Other Foreigners, December 31, 1975**
(in millions of dollars)

	Amounts by Component	Total
I. Liabilities to foreign official institutions		$ 80,150
II. Short-term liabilities to foreign banks other than official institutions		28,988
Demand deposits	$ 7,549	
Time deposits	2,140	
U.S. Treasury bills and certificates	335	
Other short-term liabilities	18,964	
III. Short-term liabilities to other foreigners		10,036
Demand deposits	3,248	
Time deposits	4,901	
U.S. Treasury bills and certificates	349	
Other short-term liabilities	1,538	
IV. Grand total		$119,174

Source: *Federal Reserve Bulletin,* May 1976, pp. A61− A63.

banks, and other foreigners held $3.2 billion of these claims. (See Table
11 − 4.)

The foreign private sectors also hold very large amounts of short-
term, dollar-denominated debt claims as liquid stores of value. Among
these are negotiable certificates of deposit and other time deposits; U.S.
Treasury obligations, and especially the shorter maturities; bankers' acceptances; and commercial paper. We shall later have occasion to emphasize that the American monetary-financial system serves as a sort of
financial intermediary for the rest of the world. It tends to buy from the
rest of the world corporate equities and longer-term, less liquid debt
obligations and to issue to the rest of the world financial claims that are
shorter-term and more liquid.

SUMMARY

We have identified three international roles of the U.S. dollar: as a
major component of the official international reserves of other countries; as a major medium of international payments; and as an impor-

tant store of value for foreign private holders. It is largely because of these roles of the dollar that foreign holdings of dollar claims, most of them short-term, have reached the huge total of more than $119 billion shown in Table 11−4.

EXCHANGE MARKETS

International transactions typically involve one market that is not necessary in purely domestic transactions—an exchange market or, as it is sometimes called, a foreign-exchange market. This is because international payments usually, but not always, involve the exchange of one national money for another. For example, if an Englishman is to make a payment to a Frenchman, they must agree on the national money in which payment is to be made. If it is to be in francs, the Englishman will exchange British sterling for francs unless he already has francs. If it is in sterling, the Frenchman receiving payment will exchange the sterling for francs unless he wants to hold sterling. If the payment is to be made in U.S. dollars, the Englishman will exchange sterling for dollars and remit dollars to the Frenchman, and the latter may exchange the dollars for francs.

The things bought and sold in exchange markets are national moneys and short-term claims stated in national moneys. There are, of course, some transactions in coins and paper money, but the great bulk of the trade is in claims against bank deposits denominated in national moneys. Short-term claims are also traded in exchange markets. For example, if you had a high-quality note promising to pay £100 in 30 days, you could sell it in the exchange market at the prevailing price for sterling claims payable on demand less a discount at the prevailing rate of interest for 30 days. The buyer could then sell the promissory note in the London discount market, thus acquiring sterling, probably in the form of a demand deposit claim against a British bank.

By far the most important middlemen in exchange markets are the foreign departments of commercial banks. These usually function as dealers in exchange, buying and selling for their own accounts. There are also exchange brokers. These put into contact with each other ultimate buyers and sellers of exchange. Banks also use them sometimes to find potential buyers and sellers of the various national moneys. There are also independent dealers in exchange, some large and some smaller. The little independent exchange dealers that one sees along streets in tourist areas are the modern counterparts of the old moneychangers.

When things of value are exchanged for each other, there must, of course, be some ratio of exchange. In markets for national moneys this is called an *exchange rate*. For example, suppose that at some time one U.S. dollar exchanges for five French francs. The exchange rate can be expressed in terms of either monetary unit—either as $1 = 5 francs, or as 1 franc = $\frac{1}{5}$ = 20 cents, U.S. If the ratio changes to 1 franc = $\frac{1}{4}$ = 25 cents U.S., or $1 = 4 francs, this can be expressed as either a rise of the franc in terms of the dollar or as a fall of the dollar in terms of the franc. There are, of course, exchange rates among all the national moneys.

If trading in exchange markets is unrestricted, the exchange rate between any two national currencies will tend to be the same in all exchange markets at any given time. This is because arbitragers, hungry for profits, will quickly spot any difference in rates and will simultaneously buy in the cheaper market and sell in the dearer one. For example, suppose that you, with command over millions of dollars, spot the following situation at some time: in Paris, $1 = 5 francs; in New York, $1 = 4 francs. What would you do, and what would be the effects of your action and of similar actions by others? Unfortunately for you, someone else will almost certainly prevent the emergence of such a large difference.

In the following discussion we shall use as an example the exchange rate between the U.S. dollar and the British pound sterling, but the principles are generally applicable.

SPOT EXCHANGE AND FORWARD EXCHANGE

It is useful to distinguish two major types of transactions in exchange markets—*spot exchange* and *forward exchange*. In spot exchange, an agreement is reached at some time and the transaction is fully consummated, and deliveries are made immediately, or "on the spot." However, in forward-exchange transactions a contract and a price are agreed upon at some time but delivery is postponed until a stated time in the future. For example, you may agree today to buy £1 million at an exchange rate of £1 = $2.39, with delivery to occur three months hence. Of course, you and the seller of sterling must provide assurances that you will deliver dollars and that she will deliver sterling at the appointed time. Transactions in forward-exchange markets are essentially similar to futures transactions in commodity markets.

Participants in forward-exchange markets have several different purposes. One is to speculate. One can, of course, speculate by buying or selling in the spot market. For example, suppose that the spot rate is

£1 = $2.40. You may buy spot sterling now if you expect a higher spot rate in the future, or you may sell sterling now, expecting to be able to replace it later at a lower price in dollars. You can also speculate, with a smaller initial investment, by buying or selling foreign moneys in forward markets. Suppose, for example, that today's exchange rate on sterling for delivery four months hence is £1 = $2.39. You may contract to buy forward sterling at this price if you think the spot rate at the end of four months will be higher, or you may sell sterling forward if you think that you can cover the contract by purchasing sterling at a lower spot price before the contract expires. Though the motive of exchange speculators is to reap a profit, their activities may or may not be socially useful. For one thing, informed speculation can promote a more orderly behavior of exchange rates through time. Also, by assuming exchange risks the speculator can reduce the exchange risks of others. This point requires amplification.

A major function of forward-exchange markets is to reduce exchange risks in international commercial and financial transactions. Nationals who acquire assets denominated in a foreign money face the risk that the exchange rate on the foreign money will decline, thereby reducing the value of the asset in terms of their own money. On the other hand, nationals who incur a liability stated in terms of a foreign money incur the risk that a rise of the exchange rate on that money will increase their liability as measured in their own money. Such risks can be reduced, and even eliminated, through appropriate transactions in forward exchange.

A commercial example will clarify the principles involved. Suppose that you, an American exporter, have sold manufactured goods to a British importer in exchange for his promise to pay £1 million four months hence. Your costs were incurred in dollars and you reckon your profits in dollars. Your profit could be reduced, and even turned into losses, if the dollar price of sterling fell below the expected level. You can eliminate this risk by selling now, at a fixed price, £1 million for delivery four months hence. Smith, an American importer, is in the reverse position. She owes a British exporter £1 million, to be paid four months hence. Her risk is that the dollar price of sterling may rise, thus increasing her liability in terms of dollars. She can eliminate this risk by purchasing now, at a fixed price, £1 million for forward delivery. Since your risks are of opposite types, you and Smith should make a deal, in which you sell and Smith buys £1 million for forward delivery. You may do this with the aid of an exchange broker, or you may do it indirectly through sales to and purchases from dealers in forward exchange. This illustrates the general principle that exchange risk can be eliminated by combining, or "marrying," opposite risks.[3] In some cases a speculator will bear the exchange risk by buying forward from you or selling forward to Smith. Of course, he will not be speculating at all if he *both* buys from you and sells to Smith. At least for opposite risks, marriage is a wonderful institution.

Transactions in forward-exchange markets also occur on a broad scale as a means of reducing exchange risks in international borrowing and lending, thereby enhancing international flows of loan funds, and especially of short-term funds. Suppose that you, a potential lender, observe at some time that interest rates on one-year maturities for financial claims of equal quality are 6 percent in New York and 7 percent in London.[4] Though the interest yield is clearly more attractive in London, you can earn it only if you buy sterling and lend it, and at the end of the year your principal and interest will be in terms of sterling. If the dollar price of sterling should fall by more than 1 percent, your *net* return will be less than it would have been if you had lent in New York. You can avoid this risk if, at the time that you buy sterling in the spot market, you also sell forward sterling for delivery a year hence. The entire transaction will be profitable if the interest differential is greater than the excess of the spot rate at which you buy sterling over the forward rate at which you sell sterling.

The same principles apply to borrowing in terms of a foreign money. For example, to a British borrower the 6 percent rate in New York is clearly more attractive than the 7 percent rate in London. However, to take advantage of the lower rate he must borrow dollars and sell them in the spot market for sterling. If at the time of repayment the sterling price of the dollar has risen by more than 1 percent, the net cost of borrowing in New York will be higher than that in London. He can easily avoid this risk by purchasing dollars forward at the same time that he sells dollars in the spot market.

The practice of borrowing in lower-interest markets and lending in higher-interest markets with forward market protection against exchange risk is known as "covered interest arbitrage" and is widely employed. The availability of forward cover enhances markedly flows of short-term and medium-term funds among the world's major financial

---

[3] Employing this principle, some transactors try to match the amounts of their assets and their liabilities stated in a national money. What they lose on one they will gain on the other.

[4] We use a one-year maturity to simplify calculation of interest. The same principle applies to shorter and longer maturities.

centers, but the facilities of this market are less adequate for some of the lesser national moneys and for long-term contracts.

INTERNATIONAL FINANCIAL RELATIONS

Most of the remainder of this chapter will deal with the principal types of financial flows between the United States and the rest of the world and some of the instruments and institutions involved in these flows. However, it will be convenient to preface this with a survey of the stock of outstanding financial claims by residents of the United States against the rest of the world, and the stock of outstanding financial claims by the rest of the world against the United States. (See Table 11 − 5.)

THE STOCK OF OUTSTANDING CLAIMS

At the end of 1975, American financial claims against the rest of the world amounted to $271 billion while foreign claims against the United States amounted to $200.7 so that net claims by the United States against foreigners were about $70 billion. However, the composition of American claims against foreigners differed markedly from the composition of foreign claims against the United States. At least 65 percent of the American-held claims were nonliquid, and most of them were longer-term. By far the largest component was "direct investment abroad." This represents claims by American residents, mostly American business firms, against properties that are located abroad and that are controlled at least partially by the American claimants. In some cases Americans hold all the claims against these properties; in others, some funds have been raised abroad through foreign issues of equity or debt claims. The $123.2 billion figure shown in Table 11 − 5 includes only claims by Americans against such properties. Outstanding examples are claims against foreign-located properties in such forms as petroleum producing, refining, and distribution facilities; mines; factories of various kinds; and warehouses and other distribution facilities abroad. Americans also held $25.6 billion of foreign bonds and $21.8 billion of bank loans to the rest of the world.

Less than 10 percent of American claims against the rest of the world are identifiable as liquid, but some of the miscellaneous financial claims would probably fall into this category.

The pattern of foreign claims against the United States was quite different. Only 28 percent of the total was in the form of nonliquid

Table 11–5   **U.S. Financial Claims Against Rest of World and
Rest of World Financial Claims Against U.S., End of 1975**
(*in billions of dollars*)

Type of Claim	Amount of Claim, by Component	Total
I. U.S. financial claims against rest of world		
A. Nonliquid claims		
Direct investment abroad	$123.2	
Foreign bonds	25.6	
Bank loans to foreigners	21.8	
Total		170.6
B. Identifiable liquid claims		
Official holdings of claims against foreign moneys	2.3	
Private holdings of foreign currency	20.4	
Total		22.7
C. Miscellaneous financial claims		77.7
D. Grand Total		$271.0
II. Rest of world financial claims against U.S.		
A. Nonliquid claims		
Foreign direct investment in U.S.	26.7	
U.S. Corporate equities	26.7	
U.S. Corporate bonds	2.6	
Total		56.0
B. Identifiable liquid claims		
Demand deposits	14.0	
Time deposits	20.9	
U.S. government securities	66.5	
Acceptances	8.4	
Total		109.9
C. Miscellaneous financial claims		34.8
D. Grand Total		$200.7

Source: Board of Governors of the Federal Reserve System, *Flow-of-funds accounts.*
Note: Rest of world claims against the United States do not include $47 billion of gold and
SDRs held by the official institutions of those countries. Though some of this
amount might conceivably be used to buy resources in the United States, this is
not a specific claim against the United States.

claims. These consisted largely of foreign direct investment in the United
States and foreign holdings of stock in American corporations and
American corporate bonds. Most of the other 72 percent of total foreign
claims against the United States consisted of claims by official foreign
institutions and liquid claims by private foreigners. As noted earlier,

these are largely in the form of deposit claims against American banks, obligations of the U.S. Treasury, commercial paper, and bankers' acceptances.

In summary, American nonliquid claims against foreigners far exceed foreign holdings of nonliquid claims against the United States. On the other hand, foreign holdings of liquid claims against the United States far exceed American holdings of liquid claims against foreigners. These data support our earlier statement that the American monetary-financial system serves as a sort of financial intermediary for the rest of the world, issuing indirect claims that are more liquid than the securities that it acquires. Many of the funds that these American institutions use to purchase securities from foreigners are of American origin, but considerable amounts come from foreign sources.

We turn now to international flows of funds and financial claims.

INTERNATIONAL FLOWS OF FUNDS

Funds are transferred across national boundary lines through two broad types of transactions: through purchases and sales of direct financial claims, and through purchases and sales of claims against financial intermediaries.

INTERNATIONAL PURCHASES AND SALES OF DIRECT FINANCIAL CLAIMS

American individuals, private institutions, or governmental units can transfer funds to foreigners by purchasing from them direct financial claims of any type. These may be claims against households, business firms, governmental units, or any other entity except a financial institution, and the issuer may be either an American entity or a foreign entity. They may be equity claims or debt claims of any maturity, and they may be denominated in dollars or in a foreign money. Similarly, foreigners can transfer funds to Americans by purchasing from them an equally broad variety of direct financial claims.

In practice, very few funds are transferred internationally through purchases and sales of direct financial claims against households, unincorporated business firms, small corporations, and small political units whose securities are not guaranteed by some higher authority. This is because most of these issues are not widely known and do not enjoy broad, continuous, and efficient markets. However, very large amounts of funds are transferred internationally through purchases and sales of direct financial claims against national governments and their major political subdivisions and against large nonfinancial corporations. Among the latter are large national corporations that do most of their business domestically; large national corporations that also operate some facilities in other countries; and corporations that do business in so many countries and on such a large scale that they are truly international or multinational corporations. Among the best known are large petroleum companies, with producing facilities, refining capacity, and distribution systems throughout the world; large automobile companies that produce parts, operate assembly plants, and distribute in many countries; copper mining companies; and chemical companies. The total resources of these and other international companies are huge.

National governments and their major political subdivisions and large nonfinancial corporations affect international financial flows in many ways:

1. Their new issues of equity and long-term debt claims are sold in many national financial centers.
2. Outstanding issues of such equity and debt claims are traded internationally in secondary markets. This is true even if they are listed on only one exchange, and some are listed on the exchanges in two or more countries.
3. Such concerns have access to bank credit and other sources of short-term and intermediate-term credit in all the major national financial centers, and they shift their borrowing from center to center to get the best available terms.
4. Many of these concerns command large amounts of liquid funds that they can shift among the various financial centers and among the various types of financial claims. The outstanding example is, of course, the huge amount of funds commanded by the Middle East oil countries and the petroleum companies that they control. In all these ways, large nonfinancial concerns facilitate international flows of funds and tend to reduce interest differentials among the major national financial centers.

American investment bankers play important roles in the international distribution of new security issues. For example, some part of a new American issue may be sold abroad through foreign offices or correspondents of American investment banks that are members of the underwriting syndicate. Moreover, American investment banks play major roles as distributors of new foreign issues. This is true not only where a major part of a new foreign issue is expected to be sold in American markets but also where all, or virtually all, of the issue is to be distributed through foreign markets. For example, suppose that a multinational corporation wishes to issue a large volume of bonds to be sold through financial centers in most of the financially important countries. An American investment bank may assume a leading role in organizing an underwriting and selling syndicate including a hundred or more investment banks domiciled throughout Western Europe and in Canada and Japan.

In the case of international issues, this question arises: In what national currency or currencies shall the security be denominated? The security is unlikely to enjoy a good market if it is denominated in a national currency that potential buyers consider to be "weak" and to entail large exchange risks. One solution is to issue "optional currency loans," in which the holder may choose between two or more national currencies. For example, a holder may be permitted to receive payment in U.S. dollars or German marks. However, the solution that is used more commonly is to issue Eurobonds denominated in a single national currency that is generally considered to be "strong." Though some of these are denominated in other national currencies, such as German marks or Swiss francs, dollar-denominated Eurobonds are by far the most common. Even if all of a new issue of dollar-denominated Eurobonds is initially sold in foreign markets, Americans may later purchase at least some of it in secondary markets if its yield becomes attractive relative to yields on domestic bonds.

Large amounts of funds are transferred internationally through purchases and sales of outstanding securities in secondary markets. Thus Americans export funds by purchasing from foreigners outstanding issues of foreign or American securities, and such transactions occur in both foreign and American secondary markets. Foreigners are active buyers and sellers in American markets for longer-term claims. It is estimated that during 1976 foreign purchases of corporate stocks and bonds in American markets exceeded $30 billion and that their sales of such securities exceeded $35 billion. Foreigners were large net sellers of these claims against foreign issuers and large net purchasers of long-term claims against U.S. corporations. They also made $5.4 billion of net purchases of longer-term claims against the U.S. Treasury. (See Table 11–6.)

The sections above concentrated on transfers of longer-term direct securities. Large amounts of funds are also transferred internationally through purchases and sales of short-term, liquid, direct-debt

Table 11–6   **Foreign Transactions in Securities
in U.S. Markets During 1976**
(*in billions of dollars*)

Type of Security	Foreign Purchases	Foreign Sales	Net Purchases or Sales (−)
I. American securities			
Corporate stock	$18.2	$15.5	$ 2.7
Bonds	5.5	4.3	1.2
II. Foreign securities			
Stocks	1.9	2.3	−0.4
Bonds	4.9	13.6	−8.7
III. Total	$30.5	$35.7	$−5.2

Source: *Federal Reserve Bulletin*, June 1977, p. A65.
Note: Data above do not include transactions in the securities of the U.S. government.

claims. We have already mentioned the large foreign purchases of short-term claims against American entities. In a similar way, but usually to a lesser extent, Americans purchase comparable claims in London and other major financial centers.

INTERNATIONAL FLOWS
THROUGH FINANCIAL INTERMEDIARIES

Huge amounts of funds flow internationally through purchases and sales of financial claims against financial intermediaries. For instance, an American entity—an individual, business firm, or financial intermediary—supplies funds to a foreign intermediary by purchasing deposit or other indirect financial claims against it. And similar foreign entities supply funds to American intermediaries by purchasing deposit or other indirect financial claims against them. In such transactions, the holder of the indirect financial claims is the ultimate supplier of funds, but the recipient financial intermediary performs the functions of investigating and evaluating the creditworthiness of potential borrowers, of making and servicing loans, and of bearing risks of default. Through such channels, foreign funds can be made available even to borrowers whose direct financial obligations cannot command an international market.

The intermediaries involved in such international transfers can be divided into three broad classes:

1. Official international and regional financial intermediaries. The most important of these is the International Bank for Reconstruction and Development, commonly called the World Bank. This institution sells its highly regarded debt obligations through the major financial centers and lends the proceeds in many countries, mostly in less developed countries. There are also some regional intermediaries that perform similar functions for their respective regions.
2. Financial intermediaries sponsored by national governments. Many governments sponsor financial intermediaries, and some guarantee the obligations issued by these intermediaries. For instance, almost every less developed country has some sort of economic development bank, and many governments in both developed and less developed countries sponsor intermediaries to provide finance for agriculture, housing, backward areas, and industries in which the government has an interest. Many of these institutions have access to foreign funds.
3. Commercial banks and other private financial intermediaries. Though some other types of private intermediaries also have access to foreign funds, commercial banks play the major role. We have already noted some of the institutional arrangements that facilitate international flows through commercial banks: the presence in every important financial center of large banks with reputations for safety and reliability; the network of correspondent relationships among such banks; the large number of foreign branches of banks; and the frequent formation of international consortiums of banks to make large loans.

Now we shall explore another type of international relationship among commercial banks—the so-called Eurodollar market.

THE EURODOLLAR MARKET

The international mobility of short-term and intermediate-term funds has been enhanced markedly by the development of what is popularly, and misleadingly, known as the "Eurodollar market." As noted earlier, this refers to an arrangement under which a bank located in one country issues deposit claims against itself that are denominated not in terms of its national money but in terms of a foreign money. Though some of these are demand deposits, most of them are interest-bearing time deposits with maturities ranging from a few days to more than a year. This system was originally called "Eurodollar" because most of the banks issuing such deposits were located in Britain and Continental Europe, and most of these deposits were denominated in American dollars. Later developments have made this terminology obsolete. For one thing, dollar-denominated deposits are now issued not only by European banks but also by banks domiciled in other areas, such as the Bahamas, the Caymans, Canada, and Southeast Asia. Moreover, banks located in some countries are now issuing deposits denominated in other foreign moneys, such as British sterling, Dutch guilders, German marks, and Swiss francs. We shall continue to use the term "Eurodollar" because it is customary and because we shall use as an example dollar-denominated deposits and the associated dollar-denominated loans to illustrate the principles involved.

In our example, a Eurodollar deposit originates as someone surrenders a demand deposit claim against an American bank in exchange for a dollar-denominated time deposit claim against a bank in London, which may be either a British bank or a London branch of an American bank. The depositor may be anyone who formerly held deposits at an American bank—American business firms or wealthy households, international corporations, foreign private banks, Middle Eastern oil countries, or foreign central banks. Their primary reason for preferring dollar deposits in London over dollar deposits in the United States is usually their higher yield.[5] There can be no doubt that the American policies of prohibiting interest on demand deposits and of limiting interest paid by domestic banks on time and savings deposits have spurred the development of the Eurodollar market. However, the latter would survive, and probably prosper, even in the absence of such artificial stimulants.

At this stage the London bank has issued interest-bearing, dollar-denominated time deposit claims against itself and has acquired as an asset an equal value of demand deposit claims against American banks. It may now lend this amount, and in order to balance its assets and liabilities in terms of dollars, its loans will probably be denominated in dollars. The borrowers are of many types—American banks and business firms, business firms and banks in other countries, governments, central banks, and so on. The borrowers, whoever they may be, receive the proceeds in the form of demand deposit claims against American

[5] In some cases, secrecy is another reason. For example, the Soviet Union has usually avoided holding deposits in the United States in order to avoid surveillance by the American government. Also, it is rumored that some individuals and business firms hold Eurodollar deposits to avoid surveillance by American tax authorities.

banks, which they can use as they see fit. They can use the dollars directly to make payments to Americans or to anyone else who will accept dollars, or they can sell the dollars in exchange markets for other national moneys, which they can use as they see fit.

Though interest-bearing Eurodollars are not ordinarily used as a medium of payments, they serve other very important functions. First, they serve as a means of transferring loan funds and of intermediating between the preferences of ultimate suppliers of funds and ultimate users of funds. Suppliers of funds acquire deposit claims against prestigious banks, maturities adjusted to their preferences, and higher yields than those available on deposits in the United States. These claims are likely to be most attractive to those who, in order to avoid exchange risk or for other reasons, prefer assets denominated in dollars rather than in other moneys. For most borrowers, the principal attraction of loans denominated in dollars is that their interest cost is often lower than that on loans from their own banks denominated in other moneys. However, some with large amounts of assets and income denominated in dollars prefer to incur dollar-denominated liabilities as a means of reducing or eliminating their exchange risks. Other borrowers in terms of dollars can eliminate their exchange risk by purchasing dollars for forward delivery.

Second, Eurodollar deposits serve to increase total lending power in the countries to which they flow. In our example, the attraction of Eurodollar deposits to London enabled banks there to make more loans than they could have made on the basis of their sterling deposits alone. Third, international flows of Eurodollars serve to reduce interest differentials among the principal financial centers. Eurodollar deposits grow fastest when interest rates abroad are high relative to those in the United States, and they tend to flow to those countries where interest rates are highest.

A simple example was sufficient to clarify the nature and functions of the Eurodollar market, but it should be noted that this market is indeed extensive and complex. For example, the London bank initially receiving the Eurodollar deposit may not itself make loans to ultimate borrowers but may redeposit the funds, taking Eurodollar deposit claims in exchange, in banks in such places as Paris, Amsterdam, Rome, or Singapore, thereby enabling the recipient banks to increase their loans. And the borrowers of dollars, or those to whom they pay dollars, may redeposit them with banks in various countries.

In short, the Eurodollar market is by no means the only way of transferring short-term and intermediate-term funds across national boundary lines, but it has greatly increased the international mobility of such funds. The latter is generally desirable on grounds of allocative efficiency, but it sometimes reduces the autonomy of national monetary policies.

INTERNATIONAL ECONOMIC AND FINANCIAL INTERDEPENDENCE

The preceding sections have focused on various institutional arrangements that facilitate payments in international transactions of all kinds and that promote international movements of investible funds. Though its functioning has been far from perfect, this system has contributed greatly to the efficiency of the world economy. In these same processes, it has increased international economic and financial interdependence. For instance, economic and financial developments in the United States have profound effects on other countries, and we have found that our economic and financial system is by no means immune from the effects of economic and financial developments abroad.

We shall only mention here a few of the ways in which developments abroad can affect the ability of the United States to achieve its domestic macroeconomic objectives of "maintaining continuously high levels of employment and low levels of unemployment, the highest sustainable rate of economic growth, and reasonable stability in the purchasing power of the dollar." Foreign economic and financial developments can be transmitted to the American economy through trade in goods and services, or trade in financial claims, or both. For instance, a sharp drop in foreign demands for American exports will directly decrease the total demand for American output and lower incomes of those in our export industries, and the latter are likely to respond by decreasing their own demands for output. The result is likely to be at least a temporary decline of employment and real output. On the other hand, an increase in foreign demands for American exports increases directly total demands for American output and the incomes of those in export industries, and the latter are likely to increase their own demands for domestic output. Such a development may be welcome if total demands for our output are not excessive, but not if the American economy is already under inflationary pressures.

With a high degree of international mobility of capital funds, financial developments abroad can have significant effects on financial conditions in the United States. For instance, a large rise of interest rates in foreign financial centers can induce a large flow of funds from the United States to those centers, thereby tending to raise interest rates in this country. Under some circumstances this can discourage American investment spendings for output enough to produce at least temporary unemployment. Induced international flows of funds may also militate against the success of American efforts to restore full employment through expansionary monetary policies, especially if interest rates abroad remain at higher levels. Decreases of American interest rates may be inhibited by large outflows of funds.

EXCHANGE RATE SYSTEMS AND RELATED MATTERS

In our earlier brief discussion of exchange rate systems and methods of equilibrating international payments, we concluded that these remain difficult and controversial questions. This was certainly true in the mid-1970s; the set of arrangements that had prevailed from 1946 to 1971 had broken down, the system remained in a state of flux, and the nature of future arrangements had not yet been determined. A brief survey of developments during the period since World War II will clarify the principal issues.

The arrangements that prevailed from 1946 to 1971 are usually referred to as the Bretton Woods System because they were based on plans formulated by a group of experts from 44 nations meeting at Bretton Woods, New Hampshire, in July 1944. This has been described as "a system of stable but not rigid exchange rates." Each nation agreed to establish with the International Monetary Fund a par value for its money, this being stated in terms of gold or the United States dollar, and to maintain the exchange rate on its money within a band ranging from 1 percent below to 1 percent above its declared parity. But there was one important exception: each nation was not only permitted but also expected to adjust the level of its exchange rate to "correct a fundamental disequilibrium." As so often happens in international negotiations, the key terms were not defined. The general meaning and intent of this provision were clear: exchange rates should be adjusted to correct surpluses or deficits in balances of payments so large and so persistent that to correct them by adjusting relative national levels of interest rates, incomes, and prices would be too costly in terms of their effects on domestic economies. But the agreement did not specify how large and persistent payment imbalances had to be to constitute a "fundamental disequilibrium" and to justify changes of exchange rates. In the event, most countries were excessively reluctant to alter the exchange rates on their moneys. Only rarely did countries with surpluses raise their exchange rates to eliminate their surpluses, and most countries with deficits either failed to lower their exchange rates or did so only belatedly.

If actual exchange rates were to be held within a narrow band, the logic of the system required that balances of payments be equilibrated through adjustments of relative national levels of interest rates, incomes, and prices. This, in turn, required that each country allow its domestic monetary policy to be dominated, or at least strongly influenced, by its balance-of-payments position. For instance, when the exchange rate on the money of a surplus country rose to the top of its band, the central bank of that country would supply enough of its money to meet the excess demand for it in exchange markets, doing so by purchasing international reserve assets, primarily gold or American dollars. The domestic effect of such purchases, if no counteractions were taken, would be to increase the reserves of the nation's banking system, which would tend to increase the nation's money supply, to lower interest rates at least temporarily, to stimulate investment spending, and to raise the nation's level of money income. On the other hand, when the exchange rate on the money of a deficit country fell to the lower limit of its band, the central bank of the country would purchase the excess supply of its money in exchange markets, doing so by selling international reserve assets, primarily gold or American dollars. If no countermeasures were taken, the domestic effect of such central bank sales would be to decrease the reserves of the nation's banking system, which would tend to decrease the nation's money supply, to raise interest rates at least temporarily, to retard investment spending, and to lower the nation's national money income. In short, both the induced monetary expansion in surplus countries and the induced monetary restriction in deficit countries would serve to equilibrate international payments.

It turned out, however, that most countries were unwilling to allow their domestic monetary policies to be dominated by their balance-of-payments positions. Many surplus countries resisted monetary expansion because of their fear of price inflation. Central banks of those countries therefore took domestic actions to offset at least in part the expansionary effects of their balance-of-payments surpluses—such actions as selling domestic securities in their open markets and raising legal reserve requirements of their banks. Most deficit countries were even more unwilling to allow domestic monetary restriction in response to deficits in their balance of payments. Almost immediately after World War II, the United States adopted the Employment Act of 1946, which asserted for the first time the responsibility of the federal government "to promote maximum employment, production and purchasing power." Most other Western industrialized countries proclaimed similar policies. These countries were not about to permit monetary restraint at the cost of domestic employment and production. They therefore took various kinds of domestic expansionary actions to offset the restrictive effects of the deficits in their balances of payments. In the United States, these were mostly in the form of large Federal Reserve purchases of government securities.

With nations unwilling to adjust their exchange rates promptly and adequately and also unwilling to allow their domestic monetary policies to be dominated by their balance-of-payments positions, it was virtually inevitable that the Bretton Woods system would break down sooner or later. Some countries, such as West Germany and Japan, ran large and persistent surpluses and amassed huge stocks of international reserves. Many others incurred large and persistent deficits and suffered serious deterioration in their international liquidity positions. The United States was a member of this group. Its total deficit during the years 1950 – 1970 exceeded $30 billion. During most of these years, its exports of goods and services exceeded its imports, but these surpluses were more than offset by its net purchases of financial claims from the rest of the world and by its net gifts and grants to foreigners. However, by 1970 American imports were exceeding its exports. By that time it was evident that the exchange rate on the dollar was too high. In 1971 it became increasingly clear that the international position of the dollar was precarious. The nation's stock of international reserves had fallen to only $15.5 billion; its liabilities to foreign central banks had risen to $20 billion; its short-term liabilities to other foreigners were nearly $22 billion; and the deficit in its balance of payments was increasing.

After several international financial crises and near crises, the Bretton Woods system came to an end in August 1971. At that time President Nixon ended the convertibility of the dollar in terms of gold and stated that this country would thereafter take no official action to stabilize the exchange rate on the dollar. Since that time the dollar has been floating in exchange markets.

After the termination of the Bretton Woods system of stable exchange rates, the principal nations might have agreed to establish an exchange rate system of the opposite type—a pure system of flexible exchange rates. Under such a system, central banks and other official institutions would not intervene at all to influence the behavior of exchange rates; the latter would be determined solely by other supply and demand forces in exchange markets. It turned out, however, that most countries were unwilling to adopt such a pure system and to forgo official intervention. They have indeed allowed large adjustments of exchange rates, not only between the dollar and other moneys, but also among other moneys. But they have also intervened frequently and sometimes on a large scale. American official intervention in exchange markets has generally been on only a modest scale, but intervention by foreign official institutions has at times been massive. These foreign institutions have sometimes sold dollars to lower the exchange rate on the dollar or to cushion its rise; but on a much larger scale they have purchased dollars to raise the exchange rate on the dollar or to reduce the extent of its decline. In this process they have added large amounts to their already large holdings of dollar claims. Many countries appear determined to protect their export industries and their import-competing industries from the consequences of a sharp decline of the exchange rate on the dollar.

In 1978, more than seven years after the end of the Bretton Woods system of stable exchange rates, international monetary arrangements were still in a state of flux. Though the system of floating exchange rates, tempered by extensive official intervention, had functioned better than many had expected, there was general agreement that further reforms were desirable. However, there was not yet agreement on the nature of these reforms.

Though it is still too early to foresee the shape of future international monetary arrangements, we can indicate briefly some of the major unresolved issues:

1. The exchange rate system. After their experience with the Bretton Woods system, nations are unlikely to accept a system of fixed rates that are adjusted only very infrequently. On the other hand, recent experience suggests that they will also reject a system of "pure" flexible rates without official intervention. The future system is likely to afford more flexibility of rates than did the Bretton Woods system, but exactly how much and how this will be achieved remain to be seen.
2. The international liquidity system. Choices in this category should depend somewhat on the nature of the exchange rate system that is adopted. It is unlikely that any national currency will be allowed to play the dominant role as an international reserve asset that

the dollar played under the Bretton Woods system. The role of gold, though still controversial, will probably decline. This leaves a greater role for SDRs or some other asset whose quantity can be controlled through the IMF or some other international agency.

3. Equilibration of balances of international payments. There is no reason to believe that national monetary authorities will in the future be any more willing than they have been in the past to sacrifice domestic objectives in order to equilibrate their balances of payments through adjustments of relative national levels of interest rates, output, and prices. This suggests a greater future reliance on adjustments of exchange rates.

CONCLUSION

It is difficult to foretell the implications of future reforms for the international roles of the American monetary-financial system. The dollar is likely to lose relative importance as an international reserve asset, giving ground to some asset whose volume can be controlled by an international authority. Other national moneys, or money issued by the European Economic Community, may gain in importance relative to the dollar, and other financial centers may offer a greater challenge to New York. Yet it seems probable that the dollar will continue to be the most widely used medium of international payments, and that the American financial system will continue to be the most powerful center in the world financial system. However, a caveat is in order. All bets are off if international monetary and financial relations come to be dominated by political considerations or if American authorities follow such inflationary monetary and fiscal policies as to bring the dollar into disrepute.

SELECTED READINGS

Cooper, R. N. (ed.). *International Finance.* Baltimore: Penguin Books, 1969.

Fellner, W., et al. *Maintaining and Restoring Balance in International Payments.* Princeton, N.J.: Princeton University Press, 1966.

Holmes, A. R., and Schott, F. H. *The New York Foreign Exchange Market.* New York: Federal Reserve Bank of New York, 1965.

Little, J. S. *Euro-dollars: The Money Market Gypsies.* New York: Harper & Row, 1975.

Prochnow, H. V. (ed.). *The Eurodollar.* Skokie, Ill.: Rand McNally, 1970.

Scott, I. O., Jr. *European Capital Markets.* Washington, D.C.: Comptroller of the Currency, 1968.

_____ . *The Euro-Dollar Market and Its Public Policy Implications.* Joint Economic Committee, 91st Congress, 2d Session. Washington, D.C.: U.S. Government Printing Office, 1970.

Solomon, R. *The International Monetary System, 1945 — 1976.* New York: Harper & Row, 1977.

Yeager, L. B. *International Monetary Relations.* New York: Harper & Row, 1966.

THE MONETARY-
FINANCIAL SYSTEM
AS A WHOLE

The preceding chapters have discussed separately the principal elements of our monetary-financial system and the functions that they serve, with some attention to interrelations among the various parts. The major purpose of this chapter is to explore further these interrelationships and to suggest how the various components, interacting in both competitive and complementary ways, function collectively as an organic whole. However, the interrelationships are so numerous and complex that to try to describe all of them would defeat our purpose of achieving a broad perspective. Our treatment will therefore be illustrative and suggestive rather than exhaustive. We shall try to achieve our objective by considering, in order, two broad topics:

1. the roles of the various components of the system in translating positive saving into spending for output in the forms of investment and of household and government dissaving
2. the roles played by the various components in promoting the interregional mobility of funds and, by analogy, the mobility of funds among the various sectors of the economy

This approach leaves to each reader a major part of the task of developing his own perspective on, and understanding of, the functioning of the system as a whole. To this end, it is suggested that you pay special attention to Table 12−1, which lists the principal components. You will find it useful to study this list, to recall the functions of the various components, and to think about interrelationships among the parts.

Table 12−1   **Principal Elements of the
American Monetary-Financial System**

I. Stock of outstanding financial claims at any time
   A. Direct securities
      1. By legal type of claim: equity claims and debt claims of all maturities
      2. By types of principal issuers: households, nonfinancial business firms, governmental units, foreigners
   B. Indirect securities—equity and debt claims against various types of financial intermediaries
II. Sources and uses of saving
   A. Sources of saving: households, business firms, governmental units, and foreign
   B. Uses of savings: gross private investment, household dissaving, and government dissaving
III. Markets to facilitate purchases and sales of financial claims
   A. Principal middlemen: securities brokers and dealers
   B. "Places" through which trading occurs
      1. Organized securities exchanges
      2. Over-the-counter markets
   C. "Branches" of the market, on various bases of classification
      1. Primary markets and secondary markets
      2. Markets for corporate equities
      3. Markets for long-term debts of households, business, government, and foreign
      4. "Money markets": markets for short-term, liquid debt claims
IV. Financial intermediaries
   A. Monetary intermediaries
      1. The Federal Reserve and the "monetary section" of the U.S. Treasury
      2. The commercial banks
   B. Private nonbank financial intermediaries
      1. Mutual savings banks
      2. Savings and loan associations
      3. Credit unions
      4. Life insurance companies
      5. Other insurance companies
      6. Private pension funds
      7. State and local government employee retirement funds
      8. Finance companies
      9. Open-end and closed-end investment companies
      10. Real estate investment trusts
      11. Securities brokers and dealers
   C. Principal federally sponsored financial intermediaries
      1. Federal Land Banks
      2. Federal Intermediate Credit Banks
      3. Banks for cooperatives
      4. Federal Home Loan Banks

Table 12 – 1   *(continued)*

      5. Federal National Mortgage Association
      6. Federal Home Loan Mortgage Corporation
      7. Government National Mortgage Association
 V. Some providers of services to the financial system
   A. Government and private producers and disseminators of economic and financial intelligence
   B. Insurers of direct financial claims
      1. Insurers of mortgages
         a. Federal Housing Administration
         b. Veterans Administration
         c. Private insurers
      2. Private insurers of some other credit risks and against hazards that affect the ability of debtors to meet their obligations
   C. Insurers of claims against financial intermediaries
      1. Federal Deposit Insurance Corporation
      2. Federal Savings and Loan Insurance Corporation
      3. National Credit Union Share Insurance Fund

SAVING, DISSAVING, AND INVESTMENT

We shall first survey the roles played by the various components of the monetary-financial system in translating positive saving into spending in the form of investment and of household and government dissaving. To make our discussion more concrete we shall cite some data relating to GNP, saving, dissaving, and investment, and to simplify exposition we shall deal with only one year—1975. Though data for other years would differ somewhat, both in absolute amounts and in the proportions of the components, those for 1975 are sufficient for our present purpose, which is only to indicate general principles and approximate orders of magnitude.

SAVING SUPPLY

During 1975, gross national product or income at current prices amounted to $1529 billion. Gross saving, including both private and government saving, was $195.1 billion, or 12.8 percent of GNP. (See Table 12 – 2.) Gross private saving alone was $259.4 billion, or 17 percent of GNP. As usual, gross business saving accounted for a major fraction of total private saving. Of the latter, depreciation and other capital consumption allowances accounted for 62.7 percent, undistributed corporate profits for 6.4 percent, and personal saving for 30.9 percent. As a group, governmental units were negative savers, with total dissaving of $64.3 billion. This reflected $70.2 billion of negative saving by the federal government and $5.9 billion of positive saving by state and local governments as a group.

It will be recalled that the amount of saving by each sector is equal to the total amount of positive saving by entities in that sector minus the amount of negative saving or dissaving by entities in that sector. And total gross saving, at $195.1 billion, is equal to the total amount of positive saving in all sectors minus the total amount of dissaving in all sectors. This net figure for gross saving is the appropriate one to use in analyzing the translation of gross saving into gross private investment. However, it

Table 12 — 2   **Gross Saving and Gross Private Investment in 1975**
(in billions of dollars)

	Subtotals	Totals
I. Gross Saving		
Personal saving		$ 84.0
Gross business saving		
Capital consumption allowances	$161.3	
Undistributed corporate profits	10.3	
Total		171.6
Government saving		
Saving by federal government	−71.2	
Saving by state and local governments	6.9	
Total		−64.4
Statistical discrepancy		4.0
Grand total		$205.3
II. Gross Private Investment		
Net foreign investment		$ 11.9
Gross private domestic investment		183.7
Fixed investment		
Residential structures	51.2	
Nonresidential structures	52.0	
Producers durable equipment	95.1	
Change in business inventories	−14.6	
Grand total		$205.3

Source: Various tables in *Survey of Current Business,* November 1976. Because of rounding, items may not add to totals shown.

should be remembered that during any period very large numbers of households are dissavers, and that even when governmental units as a group are positive savers, many of them may be dissavers. In a typical period, very large amounts of positive saving by some entities are translated into spending for output in the form of household and government dissaving.

GROSS PRIVATE INVESTMENT

Part II of Table 12−2 shows the types and amounts of gross private investment during 1975. As your knowledge of national income accounting would lead you to expect, gross private investment was equal to gross saving. One component, net foreign investment, was only a small fraction of the total, as is usually true; in 1975 it was $11.8 billion.[1] The major component, gross private domestic investment, was $189.1 billion, or 13.1 percent of GNP. Business inventories actually declined by $11.5 billion. Private fixed investment amounted to $200.6 billion. Though 1975 was not a good year for housing, expenditures for new residential construction, including both single-family and multifamily units, were $51.5 billion, equal to 27.2 percent of gross private domestic investment and 3.4 percent of GNP. In many years these percentages are significantly higher. New construction for nonresidential purposes was $52.8 billion, equal to 27.9 percent of gross private domestic investment. The largest component was producers' durable equipment, at $96.3 billion, which was equal to 50.9 percent of gross private investment and 6.3 percent of GNP.

TRANSLATION OF POSITIVE SAVING INTO DISSAVING AND INVESTMENT

We now turn to this question: Through what processes and channels is positive saving translated into spending for output in the forms of investment and of household and government dissaving? Table 12−3

---

[1] You will remember that net foreign investment (NFI) for any period is equal to our exports of goods and services minus our imports of goods and services and minus also our net gifts and grants to ROW. When it is positive, it reflects the net value of our output or income that is used to increase our net claims against ROW. When it is negative, it reflects the decrease of our net claims against ROW resulting from the excess of our imports and gifts and grants to ROW over our exports to ROW.

Table 12–3   Methods of Disposing of Saving by Positive Savers and of Acquiring Funds by Dissavers and Spenders for Investment

Methods of Disposing of Positive Saving	Methods of Acquiring Funds by Dissavers and Spenders for Investment

I. Methods that do not directly involve transactions in financial markets
  A. Finance of own current investment
  B. Purchase of "old" physical goods
  C. Increase in holdings of money
II. Purchases of financial claims of some sort
  A. Outstanding financial claims against others
    1. Direct securities
    2. Claims against financial intermediaries
  B. Newly created financial claims against others
    1. Direct securities
    2. Claims against financial intermediaries
  C. Purchase and retirement of outstanding financial claims against self formerly held by
    1. Financial intermediaries
    2. Other holders
	I. Methods that do not directly involve transactions in financial markets
	  A. Own positive saving (for spenders for investment)
	  B. Sales of "old" physical goods
	  C. Decrease in holdings of money
	II. Sales of financial claims of some sort
	  A. Outstanding financial claims against others
	    1. Direct securities
	    2. Claims against financial intermediaries
	  B. Newly created financial claims against self

FINANCIAL MARKETS

Brokers & Dealers	Other Security Holders
Financial Intermediaries	

provides information that is essential for answering this question. As mentioned earlier, every positive saver, be it a household, a business firm, or a governmental unit, faces this question: How shall I dispose of the money representing my current saving? The available methods are listed on the left-hand side of Table 12 — 3. On the other hand, every dissaver or spender for investment, be it a household, business firm, or governmental unit, faces this question: How do I acquire funds to finance my expenditures? The available methods are listed on the right-hand side of Table 12 — 3.

SELF-FINANCE

In the first chapter we presented a simple model in which every entity relied exclusively on self-finance. In that model, no household or other entity could spend for consumption in any period more than its current disposable income, and no entity could spend for investment more than its own current saving. The bonds of self-finance have long since been broken. Now, in a typical year, millions of households and some governmental units spend more than their current disposable incomes, and many entities spend for investment more than their own current saving. On the other hand, many entities save more than they spend for investment. Even today, however, self-finance remains an important means of translating positive saving into investment spending. This is especially true of business saving and investment. In a typical year, many business firms finance some or all of their investment out of their own current gross saving in the form of capital consumption allowances and undistributed profits. Obviously, this method involves no transfer of funds from savers to others for their use and no transaction in financial claims. However, most business firms are by no means confined to self-finance.

TRANSFERS WITHOUT FINANCIAL TRANSACTIONS

We also noted earlier that funds can be transferred from savers to others in ways that do not involve transactions in financial claims. For example, a dissaver or spender for investment acquires funds by selling some of its stock of "old" physical assets or by decreasing its holdings of money. And a positive saver uses some of its current saving to acquire "old" physical assets or to increase its stock of money. Though some transfers are effected in these ways, this method is now of only minor importance.

Most transfers of funds from savers to others are now effected through purchases and sales of financial claims of many kinds. Savers supply funds by purchasing financial claims of some sort, and dissavers and spenders for investment acquire funds by selling financial claims of some sort.

FINANCING THROUGH THE CREATION
AND SALE OF DIRECT FINANCIAL CLAIMS

By far the most important single method of financing investment and dissaving is through the creation and sale of new direct financial claims. Households and governments issue new direct debt claims against themselves, and business firms issue both direct equity and debt claims.

We can arrive at a very approximate estimate of the fraction of total investment and dissaving expenditures that was financed through the creation and sale of new direct financial claims by comparing total investment and dissaving during 1975 with the amount of funds raised in financial markets by the nonfinancial sectors during that year. We know that gross private investment was $200.9 billion and that the federal government's deficit on income and product account was $70.2 billion. Unfortunately, we do not know the total amount of dissaving by households and by state and local governmental units that were dissavers during the year. However, we do know that outstanding consumer credit increased by $8.5 billion. If we use this as a very rough approximation of the amount of household dissaving, we can say that total expenditures in the form of gross private investment, federal government dissaving, and household dissaving were *at least* $280 billion.

Table 12—4 shows the amount of funds raised in U.S. financial markets during 1975 by the various nonfinancial sectors—governmental units, households, nonfinancial business firms, and foreign. This is the net increase during the year in the amount of outstanding direct financial claims against these entities. It is therefore equal to total new issues of these securities during the year minus the amounts retired. In 1975 this was $210.4 billion. This was equal to 75.1 percent of the estimated total of gross private investment and dissaving by the federal government and households. However, we must not assume that this figure measures with any precision the percentage of investment and dissaving on income and product account that was financed through the creation and sale of new direct financial claims. For two reasons, the figure may be too high. First, we have not included in expenditures any allowance for

Table 12—4	**Funds Raised in U.S. Financial Markets During 1975 by the Nonfinancial Sectors** *(in billions of dollars)*	

I. Total funds raised in financial markets by the nonfinancial sectors		
Direct equity issues	$ 10.1	
Direct debt issues	200.3	
Total		$210.4
II. Funds raised, by sector		
U.S. government		85.2
State and local government		14.9
Foreign sector		13.0
Households		49.7
Farm		9.4
Nonfarm noncorporate		1.2
Corporate		37.1
III. Funds raised, by type of security issues		
U.S. government debt		85.2
Corporate bonds		17.3
State and local government debt		14.9
Corporate equities		10.1
Residential mortgages		40.7
Commercial mortgages		10.9
Farm mortgages		5.2
Consumer credit		8.5
Open-market paper		6.6
Bank loans n.e.c.[a]		−14.2
Other		−2.2
Foreign (mostly debt)		13.0

Source: *Federal Reserve Bulletin,* November 1976, p. A56.
[a] n.e.c. = not elsewhere classified.

dissaving by state and local governments, and our figure for total household dissaving is too low. Second, some funds raised in financial markets were not used to finance investment and dissaving on income and product account but were used to purchase types of assets not included in those accounts—such things as land, "old" houses and other "old" physical assets, and liquid financial assets. On the other hand, total new issues of direct securities far exceeded the net amount of funds raised in financial markets by the nonfinancial sector; this is because retirements of these securities during the year were undoubtedly very large. We noted earlier that one method of disposing of positive saving is to reduce outstanding financial claims against the saver, that this is the only method of disposing of positive saving that serves to reduce the outstanding stock of direct financial claims, and that it is widely used. (See item II — C in the left-hand column of Table 12 — 3.) For example, many of the state and local governmental units that were positive savers used a large part of their surpluses to reduce their debts. Many business firms with positive gross saving did the same. And many households dispose of their positive saving primarily by reducing their mortgage and other debt. For example, the outstanding volume of home mortgages at the beginning of 1975 was $450 billion. If only 5 percent of this was retired during the year, the amount retired would be $22.5 billion. Many positive savers also reduce their consumer debt. For instance, though new extensions of consumer installment credit during 1975 amounted to $163 billion, repayments were $156.2 billion, so that the net increase in the amount outstanding was only $6.8 billion.

Despite such uncertainties, we can safely conclude that the creation and sale of new direct securities is by far the most important method of financing investment and dissaving, and that in a typical year considerably more than 50 percent of these expenditures are financed in this way.

All the major nonfinancial sectors made net issues of direct financial claims against themselves. The federal government increased its debt by $85.2 billion, considerably more than its deficit of $70.2 billion. State and local governments, which as a group were positive savers, increased their debts by $14.9 billion. Households increased their debts by $49.7 billion, mostly in the form of increases of home mortgages and consumer credit. Foreigners raised considerable amounts of funds in our financial markets, but we shall see later that they also supplied funds to these markets. Nonfinancial corporations raised $37.1 billion.

Only a small part of the total funds raised, $10.1 billion, was through issues of corporate equities. Issues of direct debt claims accounted for the rest. These were issued by every major type of nonfinancial entity, and their maturities ranged from those of long-term mortgages and bonds to those of short-term commercial paper. (See Part III of Table 12 — 4.)

SOURCES OF THE FUNDS RAISED IN
FINANCIAL MARKETS BY THE NONFINANCIAL SECTORS

Who advanced the funds raised by the nonfinancial sectors? It would, of course, have been possible for the ultimate savers, mostly nonfinancial business firms and households, to provide all the funds by purchasing and holding the new issues of direct securities. But, as indicated by Table 12–5, this is not what happened. Of the $210.4 billion of total funds advanced, $40.8 billion was advanced by the federal government and its agencies and by foreign sources, and $169.6 billion was advanced by the private domestic sectors. The volume of funds advanced by private financial intermediaries was $116 billion. This was equal to 68.4 percent of the total amount advanced from all private domestic sectors, and to 55.1 percent of all funds advanced. Of the funds advanced by private financial intermediaries, commercial banks accounted for 24 percent, other depository institutions for 44 percent, and insurance companies and pension funds for 33.9 percent. Other private intermediaries actually withdrew funds in that period.

Thus, we find, as we did earlier, that the flow of funds from

Table 12–5 **Funds Advanced in U.S. Financial Markets to the Nonfinancial Sectors During 1975** *(in billions of dollars)*

I. Total funds advanced		
In purchase of direct equities	$ 10.1	
In purchase of direct debts	200.3	
Total		$210.4
II. Sources of funds advanced to purchase direct debt		
1. By U.S. government and its agencies	29.6	
By foreign	11.2	
Total		40.8
2. Private domestic funds advanced—total		169.6
3. Funds advanced by private financial intermediaries		116.0
III. Funds advanced by private financial intermediaries as percentage of total private funds advanced	68.4	
IV. Funds advanced by the various types of private financial intermediaries		
Commercial banks		27.6
Other depository institutions		51.0
Insurance and pension funds		39.3
Other finance		−1.8
Total		$116.0

Source: *Federal Reserve Bulletin*, November 1976, p. A57.

Table 12 — 6   **Net Issues of Indirect Financial Claims During 1975**
(amounts in billions of dollars)

Institution	Principal Issues	Amount of Net Issues	Principal Assets Acquired
Federally sponsored credit agencies	Agency debt	$ 12.1	Mortgages
Monetary authority	High-Powered Money	11.1	U.S. government securities
Commercial banks	Demand deposits	5.5	Wide variety of debts
"	Time and savings deposits	30.1	"
Mutual savings banks	"	11.2	Bonds and mortgages
Savings and loan associations	"	43.1	Mortgages
Credit unions	"	5.5	Consumer credit
Life insurance companies	Insurance and annuity rights	19.4	Bonds and mortgages
Other insurance companies	Insurance policies	4.5	Long-term debt
Private pension funds	Pension rights	12.7	Stocks and long-term debts
State and local government employee pension funds	Pension rights	11.6	Bonds and mortgages
Finance companies	Equities and debts	3.9	Consumer credit
REITs	Equities and debts	−1.6	Mortgages and real estate
Open-end investment companies	Equity shares	1.6	Corporate equities
Security brokers and dealers	Debts	2.2	
Total		$170.7	

Source: Board of Governors of the Federal Reserve System, *Flow-of-funds accounts.*

ultimate savers to dissavers and spenders for investment is primarily through financial intermediaries. Savers buy various types of indirect financial claims against financial intermediaries, and the latter use the funds to acquire earning assets, mostly direct securities. Table 12 − 6 shows the net increases during 1975 of the principal types of indirect financial claims. The table includes net issues by the monetary authority and by the principal federally sponsored credit agencies as well as those by the private financial intermediaries. These indirect financial claims differ significantly from the direct securities acquired by the inter-mediaries in terms of their denominations, maturities, safety, and liq-uidity. For example, $85.2 billion, or 40 percent, of all net issues of direct debt and equities during 1975 were in the form of real estate mortgages, long-term corporate bonds, and corporate equities of varying degrees of risk and illiquidity. On the other hand, most of the net issues of indirect financial claims were of shorter maturity and greater safety and liquidity. For instance, the federally sponsored credit agencies acquired long-term, relatively illiquid farm and residential mortgages by issuing federal agency debt, which is considered almost as safe and liquid as the government's own debt obligations of the same maturities. The Federal Reserve increased the stock of High-Powered Money by $11.1 billion through purchases of government securities, and the commercial banks increased the stock of demand deposits by $5.5 billion in the process of purchasing a wide range of financial claims against others. Thus the monetary intermediaries "monetized" $16.6 billion of debt. Commercial banks and the other types of depository intermediaries also made net issues of $89.9 billion of time and savings deposits and acquired an approximately equal amount of mortgages, bonds, and a variety of other debt claims. These deposits are predominantly short-term and are considered to be as safe as demand deposits, though not quite as liquid.

In general, the indirect financial claims issued by the nondepository types of intermediaries are not as liquid as those discussed above, but their characteristics differ from those of the financial assets acquired by these institutions, and these characteristics are valued by holders. For example, the insurance, annuity, and pension rights issued by life insurance companies and pension funds provide protection against some of the financial hazards of death and old age.

In short, financial intermediaries, both private and government-sponsored, play vital roles in intermediating between the preferences of issuers of direct securities and the preferences of asset holders, in enhancing safety and liquidity, and in serving as major conduits for transferring funds from savers to issuers of direct securities.

PRIMARY DISTRIBUTION OF NEW SECURITIES

We have already seen that a major part of investment and dissaving is financed through the creation and sale of new direct securities and that most of the latter are purchased and held by financial intermediaries, though some are purchased by others. Now we ask this question: How are the newly created direct financial claims distributed from their issuers to their buyers and holders? Many are placed directly with buyers without the use of any middleman. For instance, a household or business firm borrows directly from its bank. A new mortgage is sold directly to a savings and loan association or other financial intermediary. Some commercial paper is issued directly to its buyers. And some corporate bonds and stocks are placed directly with financial intermediaries.

However, very large amounts of new issues are distributed through middlemen of various types. The federal government usually distributes its new issues through the Federal Reserve banks and their branches, commercial banks, and dealers in government securities. Issues by federally sponsored agencies are marketed through dealers acting as primary distributors. Most state and local government issues with initial maturities of more than a year are distributed through regular broker-dealers and commercial banks acting as investment banks. Investment banking syndicates play a major role in distributing new corporate issues of equities and longer-term debt obligations. For example, new corporate issues of stocks and bonds amounted to $52.5 billion during 1975. Only about 20 percent of these were privately placed; most of the remainder were sold through investment banks. Much new commercial paper is also distributed through commercial paper houses.

Though many new mortgages are placed directly with institutional buyers, a large volume is distributed by various types of middlemen. Mortgage brokers serve to bring sellers and buyers together. Mortgage banks originate mortgages, assemble blocks attractive to institutional buyers, sell them, and continue to service them. The middleman function is also served by some federally sponsored agencies, including the Government National Mortgage Association, the Federal National Mortgage Association, and the Federal Home Loan Mortgage Corporation. These buy mortgages and resell them. In some cases they also pool mortgages and sell guaranteed bonds and participations in the pool, thereby serving as a financial intermediary.

Through the various facilities of the primary markets, a huge volume of new issues of direct securities is enabled to achieve nationwide and even international markets.

Middlemen also play important roles in distributing new issues of indirect financial claims against financial intermediaries. In general, new deposit liabilities are placed directly with holders without the use of a middleman, but there are exceptions. For instance, a broker solicits funds from savers in the East and deposits them with savings and loan associations on the West Coast. Less frequently, a bank uses a broker to distribute its issues of large-denomination NCDs. Middlemen play larger roles in distributing new issues of indirect equity claims and longer-term debt claims against financial intermediaries. For instance, investment companies sell their shares through their own sales organizations and through regular broker-dealers. Investment banks distribute new issues of common stock, preferred stock, and long-term and intermediate-term debts for commercial banks and their affiliates, for finance companies, for REITs, and for others.

In summary, the various sectors of the primary markets for financial claims, both direct and indirect, facilitate the sales of new securities and increase the mobility of funds among geographic areas and the various sectors of the economy, thereby promoting allocational efficiency.

SECONDARY MARKETS FOR FINANCIAL CLAIMS

Since secondary markets are, by definition, markets for securities that are already outstanding, it is not immediately evident that they contribute in any way to the initial distribution of new securities. Yet their contributions are real and of several related types:

1. The terms on which a new issue can be sold depend heavily on the quality of the secondary market for it.
2. The prices and yields on comparable securities in the secondary markets are major determinants of the prices and yields at which new issues can be sold.
3. Though a large part of the purchases and sales of securities in secondary markets are merely for the purpose of rearranging portfolios, some are directly related to transfers of current saving for use by others. For example, households and business firms use some of their current saving to purchase "seasoned" securities in secondary markets. Financial intermediaries often sell securities from their portfolios and use the proceeds to buy new issues. Households frequently sell securities from their portfolios to finance at least part of the cost of an expensive consumer durable good or to make a down payment on a house. Business firms often save over a considerable period and accumulate securities that they later sell to cover at least part of the cost of expensive investment projects.

Though we do not know how much current saving is used to purchase securities in secondary markets or how much dissaving and investment is financed through sales of securities in secondary markets, we have reason to believe that the amounts are quite large.

OTHER FINANCIAL SERVICES

We shall merely mention here some other functions and institutions that promote economy, or allocational efficiency, or both in the transfer of funds from savers to others:

1. The collection, analysis, and dissemination of economic and financial intelligence to serve as bases for rational decision making.
2. Reduction of risk through insurance of claims against financial intermediaries.
3. Reduction of risk through insurance of direct financial claims, such as mortgages.
4. Reduction of risk to both issuers and holders of securities through insurance against hazards affecting the future income and wealth of the issuer. Among these are insurance on the life and health of a debtor and insurance against defective titles to property, damage to property, embezzlement, and liability to third parties.
5. Reduction of risk through a legal system that defines, protects, and enforces property rights.

SUMMARY

We have now completed our brief survey of the processes through which the various components of the monetary-financial system, interacting in both competitive and complementary ways, promote the translation of saving into spending for output in the form of investment and dissaving. Instead of attempting a summary, we invite the reader to refer back to Table 12−1 and to review at least briefly the roles played by the various components. If you have a flair for graphics, you might enjoy replacing the box in the middle of Table 12−3 with a Rube Goldberg model of complex pipes representing the channels through which funds can flow to dissavers and spenders for investment as positive savers employ the various available methods of disposing of the funds representing their saving.

INTERREGIONAL MOBILITY OF FUNDS

For another way of viewing the functioning of the monetary-financial system as a whole, we shall now look at the principal ways in which this system contributes to the mobility of funds among the various geographic regions and sectors of the economy. We shall deal primarily with interregional mobility, but the same principles apply to intersectoral mobility. We start by asking why a high degree of interregional mobility is economically desirable.

INTERREGIONAL MOBILITY AND ALLOCATIONAL EFFICIENCY

Ideally, the interregional mobility of funds, the latter representing command over real resources, would be so great that interest rates in the various regions would differ by no more than enough to compensate for differences in risks and transactions costs, with both risks and transactions costs reduced to their economic minimums. Only under such conditions is it possible to achieve maximum efficiency in the allocation of scarce financial and real resources and a maximum total amount of real output or income. To clarify this point, consider the opposite situation, one in which there is no interregional mobility of funds; each region is a completely isolated market for funds. Suppose that in Region A the supply of funds is so large relative to demands for them that supply and demand are equated only at a very low rate of interest, such as 4 percent on a security with a given degree of safety and liquidity. In contrast, the supply of funds in Region B is so small relative to demands for them that supply and demand are equated only at a very high rate of interest, such as 9 percent on a security with the same degree of safety and liquidity as that in Region A. Suppose further that in each region potential spenders for investment exploit all investment opportunities whose mean expected rates of return are at least equal to the interest rate in that region.[2] Thus enterprisers in Region A exploit all investment opportunities with expected rates of return of at least 4 percent, but enterprisers in Region B exploit only those investment opportunities with expected rates of return of at least 9 percent. This is clearly an inefficient allocation of scarce financial and real resources, for some resources are being used in Region A for investments whose rates of return are only 4 or 5 percent while in Region B investment opportunities with higher rates of return, such as 6, 7, and 8 percent, remain unexploited. Total output and income can be increased by a transfer of investment resources from Region A to Region B, and this can be ef-

---

[2] In an uncertain world, spenders for investment are likely to require a rate of return somewhat in excess of the interest rate to compensate them for risk bearing. However, this does not invalidate our conclusions because the same principle applies to all regions and there is no *a priori* reason to expect that the required compensation for risk bearing will differ by region.

Table 12 — 7   **Regional Demands for Funds
and Supplies of Funds to a Region**

I. Demands for funds in a "typical" region
   A. By state and local governmental units
   B. By business firms of all types and sizes
   C. By households
      1. Funds for mortgages
      2. Consumer credit
II. Sources of funds for use in a region
   A. Savings originating within the region ("Regional supply of funds" = saving within the region minus exports of funds to other regions)
   B. Imports of funds
      1. Sales of direct securities to buyers outside the region
      2. Flows of outside funds to financial intermediaries operating within the region

---

fected through an interregional flow of funds. Suppose that funds become perfectly mobile among regions so that interest rates in all regions are the same at some intermediate level, such as 6 percent. In this case, all potential spenders for investment, regardless of their location, face the same structure of interest rates, and the scarce supply of funds can be allocated to those investment opportunities, regardless of location, that promise the highest rates of return.

Having established the economic desirability of a high interregional mobility of funds, we now survey the principal ways that the monetary-financial system promotes this end. We start by considering the principal demands for funds in a region and the principal sources of funds to a region. (See Table 12 — 7.)

REGIONAL DEMANDS FOR FUNDS

The total demand for funds within a region, whether the term "region" is narrowly or broadly defined, is typically composed of several parts, the relative importance of which can differ greatly from region to region:

1. Demands by a state government and its political subdivisions. Most of this demand is to finance durable public improvements, such as highways, streets, schools, other public buildings, sewers, and so on. Such demands may be quite small in regions with stable or declining populations but very large in rapidly growing regions.

2. Demands by business firms in the region to finance purchases of durable capital goods, inventories, and accounts receivable. These include demands by regional agriculture, manufacturing, and all other lines of private economic activity in the region. In size, the business firms are likely to range from small to large, and the size distribution is likely to differ markedly from region to region. Business demands may be relatively small in a static region whose industries are stable and not capital-intensive, but very large in a region that is industrializing rapidly and shifting to more capital-intensive technologies.
3. Household demands for mortgage money to finance purchases of homes and for consumer credit to finance purchases of durable goods and for other purposes. These demands, too, may be small in regions with static or declining populations but very large in a region with a rapidly expanding population.

The types of financial claims that the demanders of funds within a region are prepared to offer are likely to differ in their income-safety-liquidity characteristics and also in the extent to which they are known outside the region. Some of these claims will be highly safe and liquid while others are less so; and some will be known only within the region, or only in a locality within the region, while others are so widely and favorably known that they can command nationwide and even international markets.

REGIONAL SUPPLY OF FUNDS

The potential sources of funds to meet total demands for funds in a region can be divided into two broad classes: saving originating in the region and saving originating outside the region. The amount of household, business, and government saving typically varies considerably from region to region, but regional saving, whatever its amount, can be made available to demanders within a region in two principal ways. Savers can buy direct financial claims issued by the regional demanders of funds, or they can entrust their saving to regional financial intermediaries, which in turn make funds available to the demanders. In most cases some part of the saving originating within a region will be exported to other regions. One reason for this is that regional savers and intermediaries often seek geographic diversification of their portfolios. Another is that the income-safety-liquidity characteristics of the direct securities generated within a region may not conform to the portfolio preferences of regional savers and intermediaries. We shall use the term "regional supply of funds" to denote total saving within a region minus the amounts exported to other regions.

It would indeed be an unlikely coincidence if, in each and every region, the regional supply of funds were exactly equal to the regional demand for funds at a structure of interest rates and yields that was uniform for all regions. In some areas regional supply will exceed regional demand. These are often called "capital surplus areas." In others, regional demands will exceed regional supply. These are often called "capital deficit areas." We shall concentrate on the latter and explore the principal ways in which such deficit areas can import funds from outside. There are two principal ways:

1. by selling direct securities to buyers outside the region
2. through flows of outside funds into regional financial intermediaries

SALES OF DIRECT FINANCIAL CLAIMS
TO BUYERS OUTSIDE THE REGION

The ability of any issuer to import funds by selling its direct securities outside its region depends, of course, on how widely and favorably the issuer is known. In most cases, the regional issuers who can sell their securities most widely and on the most favorable terms are state governments and their larger political subdivisions and large business corporations.

The securities of state governments and at least their major political subdivisions are typically so widely known that they can be sold in the national market at yields generally prevailing on comparable securities. These issuers can, if they wish, finance all their needs for durable public improvements without drawing on the scarce regional supply of funds. The ability of smaller political units to tap outside markets varies widely. The securities of such units may enjoy no more than a regional market if each issue must be sold on its own merits. However, some states have solved this problem ingeniously by establishing state-administered "bond funds." These are, in effect, a type of financial intermediary that stands ready to buy claims issued by political subdivisions within the state, pools these claims, and sells in the securities markets financial claims against itself. These financial claims against itself are generally considered safer and enjoy greater marketability and liquidity than the individual issues held by the bond funds.

Very large interregional flows of funds and of real capital occur through big corporations that carry on economic activities within a region but also operate in other regions and even on a nationwide or international scale. Some examples are: auto companies that provide and operate parts manufacturing and assembly plants in many regions; chemical companies that establish and operate plants in many regions, including the South and West; national trucking companies that supply transportation facilities in many regions; petroleum and gas companies that produce oil and gas and operate refineries and wholesale and retail distribution facilities throughout the nation; and various types of chain stores that provide trading facilities and inventories over wide areas. These examples could be multiplied. Such national corporations can perform for a region the various types of functions that an international corporation can perform for a less developed country. They can import funds from outside, provide real fixed capital and inventories, introduce more advanced technologies, and supply entrepreneurship and management. Such national corporations need not draw upon a scarce regional supply of funds. They can sell equities and long-term debts in the national markets, either through investment banks or by direct placement; they can issue open-market commercial paper through commercial paper houses or by direct placement; and they have access to banks in many financial centers. Most regions also contain other corporations which, though not nationwide in the scope of their operations, are nevertheless big enough and widely enough known to be able to sell their direct claims on favorable terms to outside buyers.

Some other types of direct claims originating in a region can also be sold to outside buyers. For example, insurance companies have traditionally purchased farm mortgages originating in many regions, though their activities in this field have recently been small. Farmers in a region can sell their mortgages to the Federal Land Banks, which acquire funds by selling their highly regarded debt issues in the national securities markets. Farmers can get short-term and intermediate-term loans from regional Production Credit Associations, which acquire funds from the Federal Intermediate Credit Banks, which in turn acquire funds by issuing their highly regarded debt claims in the national market. Agricultural cooperatives in a region can finance both their long-term and their short-term needs by borrowing from the federally sponsored Banks for Cooperatives, which also acquire funds by selling their highly regarded securities in the national market.

Residential mortgages originating within a region can be sold to outside buyers in several ways. Insurance of mortgages by the FHA and the VA facilitates such interregional sales, but a major fraction of new mortgages continues to be uninsured, or "conventional." The extent to which private insurance of conventional mortgages will develop and enhance the marketability of mortgages over wide areas remains to be seen. We noted earlier that mortgage brokers facilitate sales of mortgages, and that mortgage bankers help originate mortgages, pool them in amounts attractive to institutional buyers, sell them over wide areas, and continue to service them. Similar functions are sometimes served by regional financial intermediaries, such as savings and loan associations and commercial banks. Mortgages originating within a region can also be sold to the Federal National Mortgage Association or the Federal Home Loan Mortgage Corporation, which will either resell them to others or hold them with funds acquired by selling their own issues in the national market. Though large interregional movements of mortgages do occur, it remains generally true that their interregional mobility is less than that of issues by large and widely known governmental units and business firms.

In summary, the financial system does achieve very large interregional flows of funds through sales of direct securities originating within a region to buyers in other regions. In many cases, sales of direct securities outside a region finance such a large part of the total regional demand that the remaining regional demands can be fully satisfied by the regional supply of funds. This is most likely to occur when the capital deficit of a region is small or when the region includes types of issuers that are able to sell large amounts of direct securities to outside buyers. Under the reverse conditions this method alone may not suffice to eradicate a regional scarcity. However, there is another major method of importing funds to a region, which we shall now consider.

FLOWS OF OUTSIDE FUNDS TO FINANCIAL
INTERMEDIARIES OPERATING IN A REGION

The term "financial intermediaries operating in a region" includes not only intermediaries that provide funds almost solely in the region but also those that operate in other regions as well. Among the latter are intermediaries that are legally domiciled in other regions.

A financial intermediary can acquire outside funds to supply in a region in two principal ways: by selling some of its earning assets to buyers outside the region; and by issuing financial claims against itself to outside buyers. As noted earlier, financial intermediaries typically hold some liquid assets that they can sell when they need funds for other purposes. Such sales are useful to meet seasonal or other temporary needs but are likely to be insufficient to meet chronic excess demands in a region. A financial intermediary may also sell to outside buyers some of its other earning assets, especially if these are claims against large and widely known debtors. However, many earning assets, and especially claims against small debtors, do not enjoy good secondary markets.

The extent to which the financial intermediaries operating in a region can provide funds in that region by issuing claims against themselves to outside buyers depends heavily on the size and geographic coverage of those intermediaries. Conditions are most favorable when the intermediaries can attract funds from all parts of the country. For example, a number of other countries have nationwide branch banking systems. Each bank operates branches throughout the country, each branch acquires funds by issuing deposit claims, these funds are pooled through the head office, and they are redistributed, partly through the branches, to areas with the largest demands. Thus a high degree of interregional mobility is achieved within the branch banking systems. As noted earlier, the United States prohibits nationwide branch banking; no bank may operate a domestic branch outside the state in which it is domiciled. Nevertheless, some of the big branch banks and also some big banks with only one banking office contribute very substantially to interregional flows of funds.

Outstanding examples are big banks domiciled in such places as Boston, New York, Philadelphia, Cleveland, Chicago, Denver, San Francisco, Dallas, New Orleans, and Atlanta. Such banks can acquire huge amounts of funds in various ways: from deposits by business firms, governmental units, and banks located in very broad areas and even nationwide; from issues of large-denomination NCDs to buyers in all parts of the country; and from issues of commercial paper and debentures in the national markets. The funds thus acquired are made available in many regions and in many ways: through loans to banks and other financial intermediaries, or through participation in loans made by those intermediaries; through purchases in the open market of both long-term and short-term direct financial claims; and through loans to governmental units and large business firms throughout the country. Some of these loans are made directly by the bank or its branches; others are made through *loan production offices* located in many regions. Though these are not legally considered to be branches, they certainly facilitate interregional bank lending, and they are unlikely to forgo opportunities to solicit deposits for the parent bank.

In some areas the banking structure is less favorable to promoting interregional flows of funds. Consider, for instance, a state that prohibits branching or restricts branching to local areas, and whose banking system consists largely of small and medium-sized banks. Such banks must rely largely on locally generated funds. They are not in a favorable position to solicit funds from distant depositors, to sell large-denomination NCDs in distant markets, or to sell commercial paper and debentures in the national market. Nevertheless, they can draw some funds from outside their respective areas. They can borrow from the Federal Reserve if they are members, but in some areas most banks are not members. They can borrow from the Federal Intermediate Credit Banks to make agricultural loans. They can buy Federal funds. They can borrow from their city correspondents, or sell loan participations to them. They can sell some of their earning assets to distant buyers and use the proceeds to make new loans. Despite these alternatives, a banking system composed largely of small banks is not conducive to interregional flows of funds.

In most regions there are also other types of financial intermediaries, or outlets of such intermediaries, that can acquire funds from outside the region. Thus a large savings and loan association may sell shares to distant buyers, either directly or through a broker. It may borrow from its Federal Home Loan Bank. It may originate mortgages and sell them to distant buyers through a mortgage broker, a mortgage banker, or a federally sponsored credit agency. A branch of a large finance company may lend in a region funds acquired by the company's head office by selling equities, long-term bonds, or commercial paper, or by borrowing from banks located in other regions. An insurance company domiciled in the region or operating a loan production office there may buy mortgages or bonds originating in the region with funds acquired from distant policy holders.

THE DEGREE OF INTERREGIONAL MOBILITY OF FUNDS

Having surveyed the various channels through which funds move among regions, we now ask this question: How closely do actual conditions approach the ideal, in which the interregional mobility of funds would be so great that interest rates in the various regions would differ by no more than enough to compensate for differences in risks and transactions costs, with both risks and transactions costs reduced to their economic minimums? It would have been easy to answer this question in the period before World War I. At that time the interregional mobility of funds was still so limited that interest rates in the West and South remained systematically higher than those in the North and East.

The situation has improved greatly since that time. Through the principal channels described above, and through others to a lesser extent, the financial system now achieves huge interregional flows of funds. Governmental units and large business firms whose financial positions and prospects are widely known suffer from no regional scarcity of funds, no matter where they may be located; they have full access to the national financial markets where yield differentials depend not on the location of the issuers but on other characteristics of the issuers and on the qualities of their issues.

If regional scarcities of funds persist, those who suffer from them are entities that do not have ready access to outside funds—households, small governmental units, and small business firms. Even for these users of funds, the situation has improved markedly, and for several reasons:

1. The ability of governmental units and large business firms to finance their needs from outside sources leaves a larger part of the regional supply of funds for these users.
2. Changes in the banking structure. Before World War I the banking system was composed of a very large number of banks, most of them small and operating only a single banking office. Since then the trend has been toward a smaller number of larger banks, many of them operating branches, or related through bank holding companies, or both. Such banks can acquire funds from wider areas and disperse them more widely.
3. Provision of agricultural credit through federally sponsored agencies. At the end of 1975, the Federal Land Banks held $16.6 billion of farm mortgages, or 31 percent of the total outstanding, and the Banks for Cooperatives and the Federal Intermediate Credit Banks had provided an additional $12.9 billion for various agricultural uses.
4. Improved facilities for financing residential mortgages. These are of several types: the authorization of federal charters for savings and loan associations, and the subsequent establishment of thousands of these institutions across the country; insurance of financial claims against these and other large lenders on residential real estate; and the establishment of several federally sponsored agencies that acquire mortgages, make secondary markets for them, and lend to institutional holders of mortgages.

Because of such developments, and perhaps for other reasons as well, regional differences in the rates paid by households and by small business firms and governmental units have narrowed markedly. In fact, it would be difficult to prove statistically that there remain significant differences among most of the regions. However, there is still room for improvement. For instance, in areas with the most rapid population growth, interest rates and other terms on home mortgages are sometimes more onerous than those prevailing in other regions. Also, it appears that in some states that prohibit branch banking or limit branching to local areas, small borrowers pay higher rates than those prevailing elsewhere on similar loans. Where borrowers find it difficult to acquire funds from distant sources, greater efficiency can often be achieved by bringing competing outlets closer to the borrower. Small borrowers are usually the major beneficiaries of increased competition in local credit markets. Even if the additional competition does not result in lower interest rates, it often makes lenders more sympathetic to the needs of small local borrowers, more willing to work out financial plans appropriate for the borrowers, and more willing to assume risks.

CONCLUSION

Though our treatment of the functioning monetary-financial system has of necessity been illustrative rather than complete, it should have established at least one major point: that the sum of the various interrelated elements do indeed constitute a "system" that achieves a high degree of efficiency in allocating scarce financial resources among their many alternative uses and users. This is not to say, however, that the system achieves complete allocational efficiency or that further improvements are not feasible. The final chapter will consider a number of proposed reforms.

MACROECONOMIC ASPECTS OF MONEY AND FINANCE

Up to this point we have concentrated largely on the roles of money and finance in promoting efficiency in exchange processes and in the allocation of scarce financial and real resources. We turn now to some of the relationships between money and finance and such macroeconomic variables as aggregate money demands for output, as represented by GNP at current prices; the rate of real output, as measured by GNP at constant prices; the average price level, or its reciprocal, the purchasing power of the dollar; the state of employment and unemployment of labor and other productive resources; and the level of interest rates.

Money and finance are interrelated with the behavior of such variables in numerous and complex ways. For example, some economic disturbances are caused, or at least exacerbated, by inappropriate monetary and financial policies, including government fiscal policies. On the other hand, monetary and fiscal policies are often employed affirmatively to promote a more satisfactory behavior of the macroeconomic variables, and monetary policies achieve their results largely through their effects on conditions in financial markets. Moreover, misbehavior of aggregate demands for output for whatever reasons can have devastating effects on the financial system. For example, the great depression of the 1930s was accompanied by widespread failures of financial intermediaries, and many that survived became largely inoperative. Rapid price inflation may not cause bankruptcies of financial institutions, but it brings its own types of distortions and strains, as Americans were reminded in the 1970s.

The high importance that Americans attach to the behavior of the macroeconomic variables is suggested by the Employment Act of 1946, in which the federal government for the first time assumed for itself and its agencies a responsibility to promote the achievement and maintenance of "maximum employment, production and purchasing power." More recently, it has been customary to state such objectives in terms of "achieving and maintaining the highest sustainable rate of economic growth, continuously high levels of employment and low levels of unemployment, and reasonable stability in the purchasing power of the dollar."

We have enjoyed an impressive rate of long-term, real economic growth. This is borne out by the data in Column 1 of Table 13 − 1, showing indexes of real GNP, or of GNP in the various years valued at the average prices prevailing during 1972. The increase in real GNP was 300 percent between 1929 and 1976, and 170 percent between 1947 and 1976. Much of the increase was accounted for by the expansion of the labor force accompanying the large growth of population; the latter grew 78 percent between 1929 and 1976 and 49 percent between 1947 and 1976. However, total real output rose so much faster than population that real output per capita increased 123 percent between 1929 and 1976 and 81 percent between 1947 and 1976. Many factors have combined to produce the increases in real output per capita. Among the most important are the huge increase in the stock of real capital, both in absolute amount and in amount per worker; improvements in the quality of labor; and a wide range of technological innovations. Some of the credit should go to the monetary-financial system for promoting efficiency in production and exchange processes and for facilitating capital accumulation.

The secular growth of real output has not, however, been accompanied by economic stability. On various occasions the growth of output has lagged behind its potential and at times output has actually declined, unemployment has risen, and the price level has been far from stable. The greatest departure from stability occurred during the Great Depression, which began in 1929 and ended only after America's entry into World War II. During the downward phase of the cycle, which lasted from 1929 to 1933, nearly 25 percent of the labor force became wholly unemployed and many others could find only part-time jobs; real output fell 30 percent; the price level of output declined 25 percent; and the money value of national output and income fell by about 50 percent. Prices of most types of assets, both physical and financial, also fell sharply. The fall of output did not reflect any decrease in the productive capacity of the economy. It occurred because the decrease in aggregate

Table 13—1   Behavior of Selected Macroeconomic Variables, 1929—1976

Year	Col. 1 Index of GNP at Constant (1972) Prices 1972 = 100	Col. 2 Index of Price Level of GNP 1972 = 100	Col. 3 GNP at Current Prices 1972 = 100	Col. 4 Index of Size of Popu- lation 1972 = 100	Col. 5 Real Output per Capita 1972 = 100	Col. 6 Unemployment as a Percentage of the Civilian Labor Force
1929	27	33	9	58	47	3.2
1933	19	25	5	60	32	24.9
1939	27	28	8	62	44	17.2
1940	29	29	8	63	46	14.6
1941	34	31	11	64	53	9.9
1942	39	35	14	65	60	4.7
1943	45	36	16	65	69	1.9
1944	48	37	18	66	73	1.2
1945	48	38	18	67	72	1.9
1946	41	44	18	68	60	3.9
1947	40	50	18	69	58	3.9
1948	42	53	22	70	60	3.8
1949	42	53	22	71	59	5.9
1950	46	54	25	73	63	5.3
1951	49	57	28	74	66	3.3
1952	52	58	30	75	69	3.0
1953	53	59	31	76	70	2.9
1954	52	60	31	78	67	5.5
1955	56	61	34	80	70	4.4
1956	57	63	36	81	70	4.1
1957	58	65	38	82	71	4.3
1958	58	66	38	83	70	6.8
1959	62	68	42	85	73	5.5
1960	63	69	43	87	72	5.5
1961	64	69	44	88	72	6.7
1962	68	71	48	89	76	5.5
1963	71	72	51	91	78	5.7
1964	75	73	55	92	82	5.2
1965	79	74	58	93	85	4.5
1966	84	77	65	94	89	3.8
1967	86	79	68	95	91	3.8
1968	90	83	75	96	94	3.6
1969	92	87	80	97	95	3.5
1970	92	91	84	98	94	4.9
1971	95	96	91	99	96	5.9
1972	100	100	100	100	100	5.6
1973	105	106	111	101	104	4.9
1974	104	116	121	101	103	5.6
1975	102	127	130	102	100	8.5
1976	108	134	145	103	105	7.7

Source: Various tables in *The President's Economic Report*, February 1977.

demands for output made it unprofitable for producers to employ all the available labor and other productive facilities. For the severity of the decline of aggregate demand for output, both monetary and fiscal policies must bear a large part of the blame. The money supply was allowed to decline nearly 30 percent, and the government's tax and expenditure policies were on the whole depressive rather than expansionary. Under the stress of the declining values of output, income, and assets, the financial systems virtually collapsed. Thousands of debtors defaulted on their obligations and most others suffered a decline of their creditworthiness; the flow of saving dwindled; financial intermediaries lost their ability to command funds and therefore lacked funds to lend; and thousands of banks and other financial institutions failed. Though the economy began to improve in 1933, the recovery was slow and erratic, and full recovery was not achieved before 1942.

The American economy has been less unstable since World War II, but its record for stability has been far from perfect. Though we have thus far avoided a depression of the depth and duration of that during the 1930s, we have experienced six recessions—in 1949, 1954, 1958, 1961, 1970, and 1974 – 1975. In some of these recessions, real output did not actually decline; it merely failed to rise as fast as the productive capacity of the economy. In others, output actually declined. The most serious of the recessions was in 1974 – 1975, when real output fell more than 3 percent and unemployment reached a peak of 9 percent of the labor force. In general, the postwar period has been one of price inflation. Between 1947 and 1976 the most comprehensive price index, that of total GNP, has risen 168 percent. The consumer price index and the wholesale price index rose by similar amounts. In retrospect, the rate of price inflation before 1965 seems rather modest; during the 18 years between 1947 and 1965 the price level rose 48 percent. However, price inflation has since accelerated. During the eleven years between 1965 and 1976, the price level rose 81 percent, and in the six years following 1970 it rose 34 percent. In some years the inflation rate exceeded 10 percent. In the face of these prolonged and apparently accelerating increases of the price level, people generally became "inflation-minded"; they came to expect that inflation would continue but were uncertain as to its future rate or duration.

The period since 1970, and especially that since 1973, has been described as one of "stagflation"—price inflation in the face of stagnant output and excessive unemployment. Under these conditions, the financial system came under serious stress. Interest rates rose to historically high levels. Prices of bonds and other debt securities fell sharply. Stock prices also fell. Many financial intermediaries that were unable to raise the rates that they offered for funds, either because they lacked earning power or because of government restrictions, suffered disintermediation or at best a sharp decline of their inflows of funds. We shall later have more to say about this episode.

SOME MACROECONOMIC THEORY

We shall now explore some of the interrelationships between money and finance and the behavior of such macroeconomic variables as real output, employment, and price levels. To present a complete and rigorous theory of the determination of the behavior of such macroeconomic variables is beyond the scope of this volume. For example, we shall not discuss at all the aggregate supply functions of labor and output, whose behavior has all too often made it difficult, if not impossible, for the stabilization authorities to achieve simultaneously their multiple objectives of full employment and a stable price level. We shall concentrate on the behavior of aggregate demands for output, with special emphasis on the roles of the monetary-financial system.

AGGREGATE DEMANDS FOR OUTPUT

In an earlier section, we noted that the aggregate demand for output, or the annual rate of total expenditures for output, which we designated by Y, is equal to $C + I + G$, where the symbols represent, respectively, consumption, investment, and government demands for output.[1] This is, of course, only a definitional identity, asserting that during any period the total value of output must be equal to the sum of its components. However, it does make it clear that any increase of the rate of aggregate expenditures for output must be accompanied by an equal increase in real output, the average price per unit of real output, or some combination of the two. On the other hand, a decrease in the rate of total expenditures for output must be reflected in an equal decrease in real output, the average price per unit of output, or some combination of the two.

To explain the equilibrium level of Y at any time, and changes in its level, we must analyze the determinants of the behavior of its components, $C + I + G$. It will be convenient to state our analysis in terms of

[1] See pp. 82–86 above.

the saving supply function (S) and the investment demand function (I). As we shall see later, this analysis takes fully into account the consumption function (C) and the government demand function (G). We shall argue that Y can be in equilibrium only at that level at which investment demand and saving supply are equal.

SAVING AND INVESTMENT

We noted earlier some definitions and relationships that are essential to our analysis:

1. We defined I as the sum of gross private domestic investment and net foreign investment. Since gross private domestic investment is by far the larger component, we shall concentrate on it. Thus investment demand during any period is that value of current output demanded for the purpose of maintaining and increasing the private stock of capital goods.
2. We defined gross saving (S) in two ways, which amount to the same thing. (a) S is the sum of personal saving (S_p), gross business saving (S_b), and government saving (S_g). This definition looks at S in terms of income disposal and notes that it is that part of the nation's disposable income, which must be equal to the value of output, that is not used for consumer spending (C) or government spending (G) for output. (b) $S = Y - C - G$. In other words, S is that value of current output that is not demanded for consumption and government purposes. We shall stress this definition because it emphasizes that any value of output represented by saving must remain unsold, thereby depressing the value of total output, if investment demand is insufficient to take it off the market. On the other hand, an excess of investment demand over the value of output represented by saving supply would tend to increase the total value of output.

We shall now analyze both the investment demand and the saving supply functions.

THE INVESTMENT DEMAND FUNCTION

We assume that the private demand for output for capital formation purposes is a positive function of the marginal efficiency of investment and a negative function of the level of interest rates. The marginal efficiency rate is the reward for investment. The interest rate is an explicit cost if the spender for investment acquires funds from others; it is an opportunity cost if he uses for investment his own funds that he could have lent to others.

This is, of course, simply an extension of our earlier discussion of rational decision making by spenders for investment. We noted first that in a riskless world of perfect certainty the rational objective would be to maximize net income, and that to achieve this a spender should rank all investment opportunities according to their marginal efficiency rates and undertake all whose marginal efficiency rates were at least equal to the market rate of interest. However, in a world of uncertainty and risk this rule is not appropriate for a risk averter. Such a spender will undertake only those investments on which the mean expected rate of return exceeds the prevailing interest rate by at least enough to compensate him for risk bearing. Even in this case it remains true that his investment demand will vary inversely with interest rates. We arrive at the same conclusion if we assume that he demands only those new investment goods whose present discounted values are at least equal to their costs of acquisition.[2] Suppose that he has a given set of expectations concerning the amounts and timing of the future cash flows that will be generated by an investment. A rise of the interest rate at which he discounts the future cash flows will reduce the present value of the investment good, thus reducing his demand function for it. And a decrease of the interest rate at which he discounts the future cash flows will increase the present value of the investment good, thus increasing his demand function for it.

It is, of course, an oversimplification to assume that at any time there is only a single interest rate in the market. We have already seen that there are many interest rates, applying to financial claims with differing degrees of safety and liquidity and differing maturities. Moreover, some investment is financed by the issue of ownership shares, in which cases the cost of equity funds is most relevant. Despite these facts we shall, to facilitate exposition, assume that "the" interest rate will serve as a satisfactory proxy for the cost of funds available to finance investment.

The investment demand function represented in Figure 13–1, showing investment as a negative function of interest rates (i), assumes a given state of expectations concerning the marginal efficiency rates that will be yielded on various levels of investment. If such expectations increase, the II curve will be increased—shifted to the right—at each level

---

[2] See pp. 67–69 above.

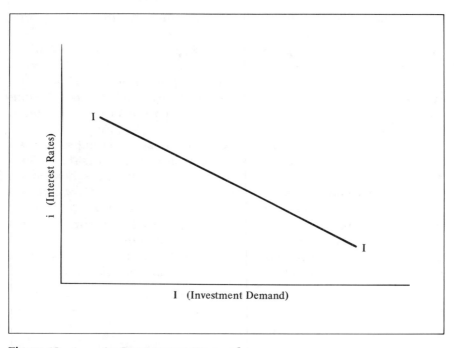

Figure 13 — 1   **An Investment Demand
Function with Given Expectations
Relating to the Marginal Efficiency of Investment**

of interest rates, and the reverse will occur if such expectations deteriorate.

THE SAVING SUPPLY FUNCTION

The supply of saving at any given level of national income or
output depends on many things, such as the distribution of income
among high-income and low-income households; attitudes of households toward current consumption versus saving for the future; business practices relating to capital consumption allowances and to the
division of net earnings after taxes between dividend distributions and
retained earnings; and the relationship between the government's net
revenues and its expenditures for output. Economists are not agreed on
the effect of the level of interest rates on the supply of saving at a given
level of national income. An older view was that a higher interest rate

would entice people to save a larger share of their incomes. On the other hand, it has been pointed out that the objective of some savers is to achieve some level of total interest income, and that the higher the interest rate the less they need to save for this purpose. For the sake of simplicity, we shall assume that saving supply is not significantly responsive to interest rates, but neither our analysis nor our conclusions would be invalidated if the supply of saving were in fact moderately responsive to interest rates.

With the above conditions given and constant, saving supply is a positive function of the level of national income or output. This is illustrated in Figure 13−2. As the value of national income rises, households consume more but also save more; business firms enjoy larger profits after taxes and save more in the form of retained earnings; government revenues rise and government saving will increase if government spending for output does not rise by an equivalent amount.

Since saving supply is equal to $Y - C - G$, it is evident that the supply function of saving can be shifted upward or downward at each

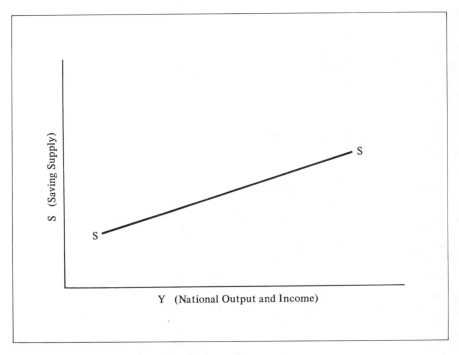

Figure 13−2   **A Saving Supply Function**

level of national income by a decrease or increase of $C + G$ at that level of Y. A decrease of $C + G$ at each level of Y will shift the saving supply function upward, and an increase of $C + G$ at each level of Y will shift the supply function of saving downward.

EQUILIBRATION OF SAVING
SUPPLY AND INVESTMENT DEMAND

As already noted, the level of national income or output can be in equilibrium only if saving supply and investment demand are equal. In other words, the total amount of output demanded can be equal to the value of the output produced only if investment demand is just sufficient to take off the market that part of output not demanded for $C + G$ purposes. Any tendency for investment demand to exceed saving supply at any level of Y would be reflected in an excess total demand for output, which would serve to raise the level of Y. On the other hand, any tendency for saving supply to exceed investment demand at any level of Y would be reflected in an excess supply of total output, which would serve to lower the level of Y.

With the supply of saving any given positive function of the level of national income, and investment demand any given negative function of interest rates, saving and investment can be equated at various combinations of the levels of national income and interest rates. This is illustrated in Table 13−2. For example, saving and investment can be equated at the relatively low level of $150 billion a year with national income at the relatively low level of $1000 billion and interest rates at the relatively high level of 9 percent. And saving and investment can be equated at progressively higher levels of national income, which increase saving supply, and progressively lower levels of interest rates, which increase investment demand. This is summarized by the $I = S$ line in Figure 13 −3. This line includes all the combinations of the levels of national income and interest rates which, with given saving supply and investment demand functions, would equate I and S. At any combination lying above the $I = S$ line, such as that represented by Point A, saving supply would exceed investment demand. And at any combination lying below the $I = S$ line, such as that represented by Point B, investment demand would exceed saving supply.

Though given saving supply and investment demand functions determine the $I = S$ line, on which the equilibrium level of national output and income must lie, they cannot by themselves determine a unique equilibrium level of national income because they cannot by

Table 13–2   **Hypothetical Investment Demand
and Saving Supply Functions**
(amounts are annual flows in billions of dollars)

Y	S	i	I
$1000	$150	9%	$150
1200	180	8	180
1400	210	7	210
1600	240	6	240
1800	270	5	270
2000	300	4	300
2200	330	3	330

themselves determine a unique equilibrium level of interest rates. To achieve the latter they need the assistance of yet another function, which economists call, perhaps for lack of a better term, the supply function of loanable funds. Though the term "investable funds" might be more appropriate, we shall bow to common usage and use the term "loanable funds."

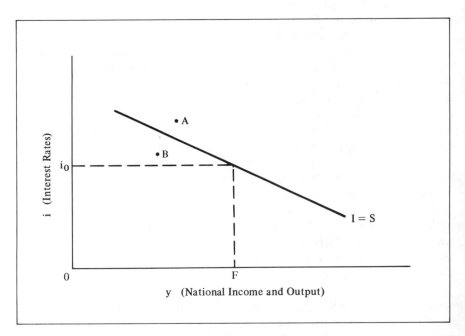

Figure 13–3   An $I = S$ Line with Given
Saving Supply and Demand Functions

THE SUPPLY FUNCTION OF LOANABLE FUNDS

This refers to the supply of funds made available to finance investment. The term "loanable funds" is not accurately descriptive. For one thing, the supply of funds for investment includes the amount of its own funds that a spender for investment uses to finance its investment expenditures as well as the amounts acquired from others. Also, it includes funds acquired through the sale of equity claims as well as those acquired through the sale of debt claims.

The supply of loanable funds and the supply of saving are not the same thing and they need not be equal to each other. It is true that the flow of current saving is normally by far the largest source and component of the supply of loanable funds. But the supply of loanable funds can be less than the supply of saving because of "leakages," and it can exceed the supply of saving because of "infusions" from other sources. Leakages can occur in two principal ways:

1. Some part of current saving is offset or absorbed by a decrease of the money supply.
2. Some part of current saving is absorbed as some members of the community increase their money balances instead of making the funds available for investment. This is often referred to as "hoarding."

On the other hand, "infusions" of two types can contribute to the supply of loanable funds:

1. An increase in the money supply can augment the supply of loanable funds without any prior act of saving by any entity in the economy.
2. Some members of the community provide loanable funds directly or indirectly by making net reductions in their holdings of money balances. This is often called "dishoarding" or "negative hoarding."

In an earlier chapter we discovered why increases and decreases in the money supply are normally associated with additions to or subtractions from the supply of loanable funds. We found that the monetary institutions, primarily the Federal Reserve and the commercial banks, create money in the forms of currency and checking deposits predominantly by making net purchases of nonmonetary types of financial claims, and that they reduce the money supply predominantly by making net sales of nonmonetary types of financial claims. Suppose that these institutions create $2 billion of new money in the form of currency and checking deposits to pay for their net purchase of an equal amount of direct debt securities, which may be either newly created or a part of the outstanding stock. The sellers of the securities are supplied with an additional $2 billion of funds that they can use, if they wish, to finance investment. On the other hand, the monetary institutions can reduce the supply of loanable funds by reducing the money supply. Suppose that they reduce the money supply $1 billion by making net sales of direct debt obligations; these may represent a reduction of bank loans to customers or net sales of securities from the banks' portfolios. In either case, those who repay bank loans or purchase securities from the monetary institutions must surrender $1 billion of funds that might otherwise have been available to finance investment. These funds are absorbed or extinguished by the decrease of the money supply. This is clearly a "leakage" in the flow of funds.

As already indicated, the flow of loanable funds can be augmented by "dishoarding," as some members of the community make net reductions in their money balances. This can occur in various ways. For example, individuals or institutions may reduce their holdings of money in order to purchase and hold more securities, thus increasing the volume of loanable funds available to the sellers of securities. Or spenders for investment may finance a part of their investment expenditures by making net reductions in their own holdings of money balances. If the money supply remains constant, the community as a whole cannot dishoard in the sense of reducing its total holdings of money balances. The smaller money holdings of dishoarders must be balanced by larger money holdings by others. In the statistics, the process of dishoarding will appear as an increase in the velocity of money—an increase in the average number of times each dollar of the money supply is spent for output each year. But the most important point here is that the process of dishoarding can augment the supply of loanable funds.

Several types of developments can lead members of the community to decrease the quantity of money balances that they demand:

1. A decrease in the level of national income and an accompanying decline in the volume of transactions. With a smaller volume of transactions, the community will demand only smaller money balances for transactions purposes.
2. A rise in the level of yields on nonmonetary financial assets. With a rise in the reward for holding nonmonetary assets, the community is likely to prefer to hold a larger part of its portfolio in the form of securities and only a smaller part in the form of money balances.

3. The development of more optimistic expectations concerning the future prices, safety, and liquidity of securities. In these circumstances the community will prefer to hold a larger part of its portfolio in the form of securities and a smaller part in money balances.

On the other hand, as already noted, the supply of loanable funds can be reduced by "hoarding," as some members of the community make net additions to their money balances. For example, positive savers may use some of their current saving to increase their own money balances rather than spending the funds for investment or making them available to others. Individuals or institutions may sell securities and use the proceeds to increase their money balances. Business firms or others may borrow more and add some of the proceeds to their money balances instead of spending them. If the total money supply remains constant, the larger money balances of the hoarders must, of course, mean smaller money balances for the rest of the community. In the statistics, the process of hoarding will be reflected in a decrease in the velocity of money. The salient point here is that hoarding can reduce the supply of loanable funds.

The types of developments that can lead members of the community to increase their demand for money balances are just the reverse of those that induce decreases of demands for money balances: an increase in the level of national income and the accompanying rise in the value of transactions, which tends to increase the volume of money balances demanded for transactions purposes; a decline of the level of yields on nonmonetary assets, which lowers the reward for holding earning assets rather than money balances and decreases the opportunity cost of holding money; and the development of less optimistic or more pessimistic expectations concerning the future prices, safety, and liquidity of securities.

The relationship between the supply of loanable funds and the supply of saving is summarized in the following equation:

$$L_S = S + (\Delta M - \Delta H)$$

where

L_S = the supply of loanable funds, stated as dollar flows at annual rates

S = the supply of saving, stated as dollar flows at annual rates

ΔM = change in the money supply, stated at an annual rate in dollars

ΔH = change in the community's demand for money balances, stated at an annual rate in dollars

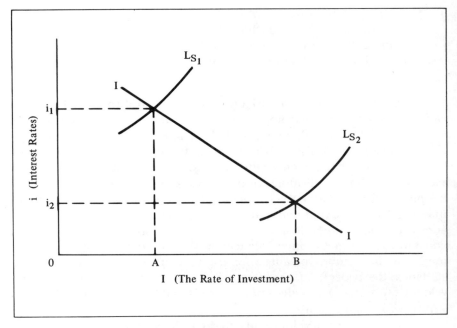

Figure 13 — 4   **A Supply Function of Loanable Funds and an Investment Demand Function**

ΔM may be either positive or negative; it is an infusion of funds if it is positive and a leakage if it is negative. ΔH may also be either positive or negative; it is a leakage of funds if it is positive and an infusion if it is negative. The algebraic sum of $(\Delta M - \Delta H)$ measures the amount of net infusion or net leakage; it is a net infusion if it is positive and a net leakage if it is negative.

DETERMINATION OF THE EQUILIBRIUM LEVEL OF INTEREST RATES

The supply function of loanable funds together with the investment demand function determine both the equilibrium level of interest rates and the equilibrium level of investment. Suppose that the investment demand function is that represented in Figure 13 — 4. If the supply function of loanable funds is that represented by the L_{S_1} curve, the equilibrium level of interest rates will be i_1 and the equilibrium rate of investment will be the horizontal distance OA. However, if the saving supply function is larger, as represented by the L_{S_2} curve, interest rates will be in equilibrium at the lower level i_2 and investment will be at the higher level *OB*. Note that this analysis does not ignore the role of the saving supply function as a determinant of interest rates; saving supply is included as a major component, but not the only one, of the supply of loanable funds.

EQUILIBRIUM LEVELS OF INTEREST RATES AND NATIONAL OUTPUT OR INCOME

Having introduced the supply function of loanable funds, we can now complete the task of explaining the determination of equilibrium levels of income and output. As noted earlier, given saving supply and investment demand functions will be reflected in an $I = S$ line, such as that in Figure 13−5. The equilibrium level of income and interest rates must lie somewhere on that line. But the point at which equilibrium will occur depends on the supply function of loanable funds. The level of output or income *OF* in Figure 13−5 has special significance, for we assume it represents the full-employment level of output with a stable

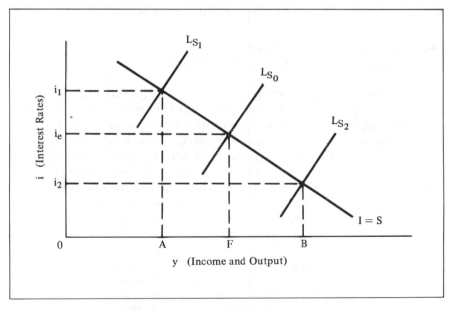

Figure 13−5   **Determination of Equilibrium Levels of Income and Interest Rates**

price level. This level of aggregate demand for output can be achieved and maintained only if the supply function of loanable funds is such as to intersect the $I = S$ line at the level of interest rates i_e, which is the only level of interest rates that will generate a full-employment level of aggregate demand.

Suppose that the supply function of loanable funds is smaller, such as that represented by the L_{S_1} curve. Interest rates will be at the higher level, i_1, and national income at the lower level OA. At such a higher level of interest rates, investment demand for output will be smaller, the lower level of investment expenditures will decrease the amount of income received by the community, and the latter will in response reduce its expenditures for consumption purposes. The lower value of output must reflect lower real output, lower prices per unit of output, or some combination of the two.

Now suppose that the supply function of loanable funds is much larger, such as that represented by the L_{S_2} curve. Interest rates will be at the lower level, i_2, which will generate a higher level of aggregate demand, OB. Since OB is much larger than the full-employment supply of output at stable prices, OF, the result must be a rise of prices. We shall later have more to say about attempts to depress interest rates below the level consistent with full employment and price stability.

SHIFTS OF THE INVESTMENT
DEMAND AND SAVING SUPPLY FUNCTIONS

Having noted that the equilibrium levels of interest rates and income can be changed by shifts of the supply function of loanable funds, we must emphasize that the equilibrium levels of interest rates and income also depend on, and can be changed by, the investment demand and saving supply functions. We start with saving supply and investment demand functions that are reflected in the $(I - S)_0$ line in Figure 13—6. Under these conditions the level of interest rates i_0 is the only one consistent with the generation of the full-employment level of aggregate demand, OF. Now the $I = S$ line shifts upward and rightward to $(I = S)_1$. This could reflect either or both of two events:

1. An increase of investment demand at each level of interest rates. This could result from anything that increases expectations concerning the marginal efficiency rates of investment.
2. A decrease of saving supply at each level of Y. This would reflect an increase of $(C + G)$ at each level of Y. Such shifts increase the level

of interest rates, in this case to the higher level i_1, that will result in the level of aggregate demand OF. At any lower level of interest rates, aggregate demand would exceed OF, which would obviously be inflationary.

Suppose now that the $I = S$ line shifts downward and leftward to $(I = S)_2$. This could reflect either or both of two events:

1. A decrease of investment demand at each level of interest rates, reflecting less optimistic expectations concerning marginal efficiency rates of investment.
2. An increase of saving supply at each level of Y, reflecting a decrease of $(C + G)$ at each level of Y.

Such shifts lower the level of interest rates, in this case to the lower level i_2, that will result in the level of aggregate demand, OF. At any higher level of interest rates, aggregate demand would be below OF, which would mean a lower rate of real output, a lower price level, or both.

As we discuss later the role of monetary policy in regulating the behavior of interest rates, we should bear constantly in mind that the saving supply and investment demand functions are also important de-

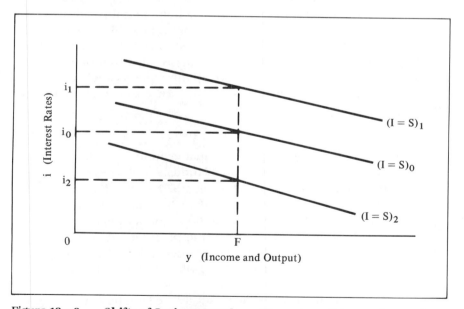

Figure 13 − 6   **Shifts of Savings Supply and Investment Demand Functions**

terminants of the behavior of interest rates and income levels, and that they are of predominant importance in determining the "appropriate" level of interest rates.

THE ROLE OF MONETARY POLICY IN ECONOMIC STABILIZATION

We shall now consider briefly the role of Federal Reserve monetary policy in economic stabilization. Suppose that its dominant objective is to maintain total output continuously at full-employment levels with a stable price level. For this purpose it must rely on its control over the money supply and the latter's direction and rate of change (ΔM), for it has no direct control over the other variables affecting the behavior of income and interest rates. The Federal Reserve has no direct control over the supply functions of labor and output, which may behave adversely. It has no direct control over the investment demand function, which reflects decisions of spenders for investment. It has no direct control of the saving supply function, which is determined by savers. And it has no direct control over the public's demand function for money balances or over the direction and rate of change of ΔH.

In short, the Federal Reserve can only hope that through its control of the behavior of M it can make the supply of loanable funds behave in such a way as to achieve the level of interest rates that will generate a level of aggregate demand for output that will produce continuously full employment with price stability. To develop these points it will be useful to recall the earlier equation $L_S = S + (\Delta M - \Delta H)$, and to restate it as follows:

$$\Delta M = L_S{}^* - (S - \Delta H)$$

In this version, $L_S{}^*$ is the supply of loanable funds that the Federal Reserve wants to achieve. The amount of funds supplied by $(S - \Delta H)$—the two components over which the Federal Reserve has no direct control—may be either less or greater than $L_S{}^*$, the desired level. In principle at least, the Federal Reserve can offset, or compensate for, any deficiency or excess of $(S - \Delta H)$ through appropriate changes in ΔM. Thus it can increase ΔM to compensate for a deficiency of $(S - \Delta H)$, and it can decrease ΔM, or even make it negative, to compensate for an excess of $(S - \Delta H)$.

In trying to implement such a policy, the Federal Reserve encounters serious difficulties, only a few of which will be mentioned here. First is the difficulty of identifying the appropriate target level of interest rates—the level that will generate a full-employment level of aggregate demand. As emphasized earlier, the appropriate level of interest rates is determined by the saving supply and investment demand functions, and it is changed by shifts of these functions. If the Federal Reserve tries to achieve and maintain inappropriate levels of interest rates, its policy actions will have destabilizing rather than stabilizing effects on the economy. Further difficulties are posed by lags in the operation of money policy and errors in economic and financial forecasting. When the Federal Reserve takes expansionary or restrictive actions, the full effects are not achieved immediately; instead, the full effects on conditions in financial markets are spread over several months, and full effects on aggregate demands for output may be spread over an even longer period. Moreover, the Federal Reserve and others cannot forecast with perfection either the time distribution of the effects of monetary-policy actions or the behavior of other relevant variables, such as the saving supply and investment demand functions and the public's demand function for money balances. For these and other reasons, monetary policy may be unable to reach its objectives even if Federal Reserve officials are highly able and completely dedicated to the goal of economic stabilization.

In the following chapter we shall have more to say about monetary policy.

FINANCIAL INSTITUTIONS AND THE MACROECONOMIC BEHAVIOR OF THE ECONOMY

The sections immediately preceding gave almost no attention to sectors of the monetary-financial system other than the monetary intermediaries. However, it should not be inferred from this that the other financial sectors do not have significant effects on the macroeconomic behavior of the economy. Earlier chapters discussed in some detail various ways in which the financial sectors encourage saving and investment and promote secular economic growth. Among these are: making available to savers financial claims with more attractive combinations of income, safety, and liquidity, thereby encouraging both saving and transfers of saving for use by others; enabling spenders for investment to issue types of financial claims that are more favorable to the issuers in terms of the cost of funds and effects on the issuers' solvency and liquidity positions; reducing risk, and transferring the function of risk bearing to those who will perform it for the lowest price; reducing the transactions costs of transferring funds and real resources; and increasing efficiency in the allocation of scarce investable resources to their most productive uses. There can be little doubt that in such ways the various sectors of the financial system have promoted the secular growth of both the stock of capital and the rate of real output.

THE FINANCIAL SYSTEM AND
AGGREGATE DEMANDS FOR OUTPUT

Many sectors of the monetary-financial system other than the monetary intermediaries also influence the behavior of aggregate demands for output. It is true, of course, that the supply or stock of money is a major determinant of the rate of expenditures for output. However, the latter also depends on the income velocity of money. Or, to put the same thing another way, the rate of expenditures also depends on the community's demand for money balances relative to its rate of expenditures. The smaller the amounts of money balances demanded at each level of expenditures, the higher the level of expenditures that can be supported by each dollar of the money supply. The nonmonetary sectors of the financial system affect the level of aggregate demands for output primarily by making available types of financial claims that serve as substitutes for money itself in the portfolios of the public, thereby tending to reduce the public's demand for money balances. And the degree to which these other financial claims serve as substitutes for money depends on their income-safety-liquidity characteristics relative to such characteristics of money. Suppose, for example, that the financial system is still so primitive that the only assets available for holding are physical goods, money, and very long-term bonds, and that the bond market is inefficient and involves high transactions costs. Under such conditions, the community would elect to hold large money balances relative to its total wealth and also relative to its income and expenditures. In sharp contrast, we have seen that the present financial system provides a wide variety of alternative assets; that a great volume of these are almost as safe and liquid as money itself and yield an income; and that many securities enjoy efficient markets. Among these are various types of time and savings deposit claims against all depository types of financial intermediaries, and also a large volume of highly safe and liquid short-term direct claims, such as government securities, acceptances, and commercial paper.

The easy availability of these income-yielding, close substitutes for money has clearly reduced the public's demand for money balances at each level of national income, thereby enabling any given money supply to support a higher level of expenditures for output.

CONCLUSION

This chapter has not attempted to present a fully developed theory of the behavior of such macroeconomic variables as aggregate demands for output, the price level of output, and the levels of employment and real output. Instead, its purpose has been the much more limited one of highlighting some important interrelationships between money and finance, on the one hand, and macroeconomic variables on the other hand. The lines of causation run both ways. After noting briefly that misbehavior of macroeconomic variables can have profound effects on the monetary-financial system, attention was shifted to the effects of money and finance on selected macroeconomic variables, with special emphasis on interest rates and aggregate demands for output.

Some of the principal findings were that both the equilibrium level of interest rates and the equilibrium level of national income, or output, depends on three functions:

1. The saving supply function $(Y - C - G)$. Other conditions given, this is a positive function of the level of national income.
2. The investment demand function. This is a positive function of expectations concerning marginal efficiency rates on investment, and a negative function of interest rates.
3. The supply function of loanable funds $[L_S = S + (\Delta M - \Delta H)]$.

Equilibrium levels of aggregate demand and of interest rates are determined simultaneously by all three functions, and shifts of one or more of the three functions can shift equilibrium levels of aggregate demand and interest rates.

The monetary-financial system affects the level of aggregate demand, and thereby the behavior of the levels of real output and prices, primarily through its influence on the supply function of loanable funds. For example, a monetary policy that increases the supply function of loanable funds tends to lower interest rates, thereby stimulating investment spending, and the resulting increase in national income elicits an increase of consumption expenditures. On the other hand, a monetary policy that decreases the supply function of loanable funds tends to have the opposite effects. These facts are basic for monetary policy. However, it should not be forgotten that the saving supply function and the investment demand function play crucial roles in determining the "appropriate" level of interest rates and the actual behavior of both interest rates and aggregate demands for output.

These subjects will be discussed further in the next chapter.

SELECTED READINGS

Branson, W. H. *Macroeconomic Theory and Policy.* New York: Harper & Row, 1972. Chaps. 5, 13, 14.

Brunner, K. (ed.). *Targets and Indicators of Monetary Policy.* San Francisco: Chandler Publishing Company, 1969.

Chandler, L. V., and Goldfeld, S. M. *The Economics of Money and Banking.* 7th ed. New York: Harper & Row, 1977. Chap. 11.

Friedman, M. "A Theoretical Framework for Monetary Analysis." *Journal of Political Economy,* March/April 1970.

Maisel, S. J. *Managing the Dollar: An Inside View by a Recent Governor of the Federal Reserve Board.* New York: W. W. Norton & Co., 1973.

MONETARY POLICIES AND THE FINANCIAL SYSTEM

This chapter consists of two main parts. The first deals with the channels through which Federal Reserve monetary policies achieve, or fail to achieve, their objectives; the second considers further relationships between monetary policies and interest rates.

THE MODUS OPERANDI OF MONETARY POLICY

Our brief discussion, in the preceding chapter, of the role of monetary policy in economic stabilization was inadequate in at least two respects: First, it dealt too briefly with the channels through which monetary policy actions affect the behavior of aggregate demands for output. Second, it virtually ignored the roles played by the nonmonetary sectors of the financial system. This chapter attempts to remedy both deficiencies.

As a first step, it will be useful to recall some of our earlier findings concerning the characteristics of our contemporary monetary system. We found that in this system increases of M occur as the monetary intermediaries—the Federal Reserve and the commercial banks—issue currency and demand deposits to purchase financial claims, which may be either newly created or a part of the outstanding stock. And decreases of M are effected predominantly through net sales of financial claims by the monetary intermediaries. Such exchanges of money for financial claims and vice versa do not directly change either the net income or the net wealth of the public; they merely change the composition of the portfolios of the public. For example, those who borrow more from the banks to get more money increase their liabilities as much as they increase their assets, and those who exchange outstanding earning assets for money merely change the composition of their portfolios without increasing their total value. Since there is no clear reason to expect that changes of M effected in these ways will directly affect the rate of consumption expenditures, monetary-policy actions must achieve their results through other channels. We shall find that these effects are achieved primarily through altering the supply of funds and the levels of security prices and yields in financial markets.

The Federal Reserve does not control directly and precisely the size of the public's money supply. It is true that the Federal Reserve can increase directly the public's money supply by purchasing securities from entities other than commercial banks, and that it can directly reduce the public's money supply by making net sales of securities to such entities. However, it exercises its control primarily through regulating the reserve position of the commercial banking system. It does this both by regulating the dollar volume of reserves available to the banks and by setting and changing the levels of reserve requirements. (See Table 14 − 1.)

If it wishes, the Federal Reserve can indeed force the banks to

Table 14 − 1   **Federal Reserve Instruments of General Monetary Management**

Instruments	Restrictive Actions	Expansionary Actions
I. Instruments for regulating the dollar volume of bank reserves		
A. Discount (loan) policy actions	Raise discount rates, tighten nonprice rationing	Lower discount rates, relax nonprice rationing
B. Open-market operations in acceptances and government securities	Sell	Purchase
II. Legal reserve requirements against demand and time deposits	Raise	Lower

reduce the money supply. By decreasing the volume of bank reserves, by raising reserve requirements, or both, it can put the banks in such deficient reserve positions that they are compelled to make net sales of earning assets. The Federal Reserve can also enable and encourage the banks to expand by providing them with excess reserves, doing so by increasing the dollar volume of bank reserves, by reducing reserve requirements, or both. But the banks are not compelled to expand; they could, if they wished, simply hold the excess reserves even though the latter yield no income. However, for reasons of profit banks usually expand their earning assets to, or near to, the maximum permitted by their reserve positions.

Neither the Federal Reserve nor the commercial banks can compel the nonbank sectors to borrow more or to make net sales of earning assets to the monetary intermediaries; they can only induce the nonbank sectors to do so by bidding up the prices and lowering the yields on earning assets. As this process continues, the portfolios of the nonbank sectors, with more money and fewer earning assets, become safer and more liquid but earn less. If their portfolio preferences have not changed, the nonbank sectors will seek to restore their desired portfolio balances by increasing their own demands for earning assets. Through such processes, interest rates will tend to be lowered throughout financial markets. And in response to these changes of conditions in financial markets, spenders for investment, and perhaps others as well, will be induced to increase their expenditures for output.

We shall have more to say about such processes as we consider restrictive and expansionary types of monetary policy.

RESTRICTIVE MONETARY POLICIES

We shall deal first with Federal Reserve policies aimed at restricting the level, or the rate of growth, of aggregate money demands for output. We assume that the economy is in a strong boom. Unemployment has already been reduced to a low level, spending is rising faster than real output, and prices are already rising. The banking system has at most only a small amount of excess reserves, but loan demands by bank customers, including large business firms, are insistent and rising. Federal Reserve officials decide that a more restrictive policy is in order.

We noted earlier the principal policy actions that the Federal Reserve can take for restrictive purposes:

1. Increase legal reserve requirements against commercial bank demand deposits, or time and savings deposits, or both. This does

not, of course, change the dollar volume of reserves available to banks, but by increasing required reserves it decreases excess bank reserves and can even put banks in a deficient reserve position.
2. Restrict the dollar volume of reserves available to the banks by limiting the stock of High-Powered Money, H. The Federal Reserve can limit its loans by raising its discount rate and by resorting to various types of nonprice rationing. It can also sell in the open-market acceptances and government securities, or at least limit its purchases of such assets.

The Federal Reserve can use its policy instruments to achieve various degrees of restrictiveness, which for convenience we shall measure in terms of the behavior of M:

1. It may seek to force an absolute decrease of M. Though this may be done if "the situation has gotten out of hand," Federal Reserve officials recognize that such drastic action could precipitate a financial crisis and recession.
2. It may seek to hold M constant until inflationary pressures have subsided. Even with M constant, the rate of expenditures for output may continue to rise for some time as the community, in response to rising interest rates and to expectations of rising prices, elects to hold smaller money balances relative to its income and expenditures. However, with the passage of time, the rise of money income and expenditures will raise the quantity of money balances demanded for transactions purposes, bring the quantity of demanded money balances into equality with the constant money supply, and thus bring the rise of expenditures to a halt. Even this may be accompanied by stringencies in financial markets and may precipitate a recession.
3. It may allow M to continue to increase but at such a slow rate that it will bring the rate of increase of expenditures for output down to the desired level. The hope is that such a gradualist policy will squeeze out inflationary pressures with less danger of precipitating either a financial crisis or a recession.

The various degrees of restrictive policies have at least this in common: they so restrict the reserve position of the banking system that the latter is unable to meet all current demands for loans at the prevailing levels of interest rates. The banks could adjust solely by reducing their loans to customers, doing this by raising interest rates or through various types of nonprice rationing. However, they rarely do this in the early stages of restriction. This is primarily because a bank's lending to customers is so closely related to its ability to attract and retain deposits, which for an individual bank are the major source of its lending power. A bank that failed to give preference to customer loans in times of credit restriction would lose deposits to other banks and alienate borrowers whose business would be welcome later when credit supplies became more plentiful relative to demands. Moreover, the ability of a bank to refuse loans to business customers is sometimes limited by large outstanding lines of credit, under which the bank has agreed to lend to customers on demand up to some limit. Some of these are formal contracts that are legally binding on a bank because the customer has paid a commitment fee. Others may not be legally binding, but a bank that failed to honor an informal understanding would probably lose the customer. For such reasons, loans to bank customers, and especially to "valuable" customers, are usually curtailed significantly only after the restrictive policy has been in effect for some time.

In the meantime, banks struggle competitively to repair their reserve positions and to maintain their lending power, doing so by curtailing their holdings of open-market assets and through various types of borrowing, thus tending to raise market rates of interest. Some increase their borrowings from the Federal Reserve, but the latter responds by raising its discount rate, reminding banks that borrowing is a privilege and not a right, admonishing banks to reduce their borrowings, and in some cases refusing to make new loans. Banks turn to the Federal funds market, where the rising demand for funds and a shrinking supply of excess reserves push the Federal funds rate to high levels. At times during the early 1970s the Federal funds rate rose above 13 percent. They make special efforts to induce the public to hold more time and savings deposits, not only through advertising campaigns but also by raising interest rates to the extent permitted by Federal Reserve ceilings. Large banks intensify their attempts to sell large-denomination negotiable CDs. They also turn to various other types of borrowing. Bank holding companies and their affiliates issue open-market commercial paper and longer-term debt obligations. Banks themselves issue promissory notes of various maturities. They borrow in the Eurodollar market. Loans from the Federal Reserve are the only type of bank borrowing that serves to increase the total supply of bank reserves. All the others are methods of competing for a larger share of the limited supply of reserves.

While banks are striving to borrow more, thus tending to increase market rates of interest, they also limit their holdings of open-market types of earning assets, such as government securities, commercial paper, bankers' acceptances, and loans to brokers and dealers in securities. At the very least they decrease their purchases of such assets, and many make net sales. At first the major impact may be on short-term liquid assets, but as market rates of interest and discount on these assets rise sharply, at least some banks sell some of their longer-term assets, such as bonds of state and local governments or of the federal government. Some of these earning assets of banks are sold outright, others under agreements to repurchase them later. The decrease of bank demands for open-market assets and bank net sales of such assets tend to raise both short-term and long-term rates of interest.

To the extent that commercial banks fail to meet the credit demands of their customers, at least some of the latter compete for alternative sources of funds. Households increase their accounts payable at retail stores and seek to borrow more from finance companies. Small business firms increase their debts to their suppliers and borrow more from sales finance companies on the basis of their accounts receivable. Large and well-known business firms have more alternative sources of both short-term and long-term funds. They sell more commercial paper or other short-term or intermediate-term debts in the open-market. Large corporations may also seek to acquire more long-term funds by issuing equities or bonds. This is especially likely to occur when short-term interest rates become very high and current yields on bonds are not yet high relative to those expected to prevail in the future.

In short, Federal Reserve restrictive actions lead to a rise of interest rates throughout financial markets. The upward movement may begin as the Federal Reserve sells a significant amount of government securities, thus both decreasing the money supply directly and increasing the supply of securities to be held by others. Greater upward pressures on rates result as commercial banks both increase their own demand for funds and curtail their supply of funds to others.

NONBANK FINANCIAL INTERMEDIARIES

During the 1950s many expressed fears that the rapidly growing nonbank financial intermediaries would seriously reduce the effectiveness of monetary policies, and especially of restrictive monetary policies. The principal fear was that as commercial banks were forced to reduce supplies of credit, the nonbank financial intermediaries would expand their loans enough to prevent a reduction of the total supply of funds. Events since the mid-1960s have shown that such fears were largely groundless. In fact, a common complaint now is that restrictive monetary policies have excessively severe impacts on at least some types of nonbank financial intermediaries and on the sectors of the economy that they serve.

Savings and loan associations provide the best case in point. As noted earlier, these are outstanding examples of institutions that lend long and borrow short. Their earning assets consist largely of long-term residential mortgages with fixed interest rates, so that their average rate of return at any time is the weighted average of the rates prevailing when the mortgage loans were made. On the other hand, the associations acquire funds predominantly by issuing various classes of time and savings deposit claims that are most directly competitive with similar claims against commercial and mutual savings banks and with such open-market assets as Treasury bills and other short-term obligations of the federal government, open-market commercial paper, and acceptances. Savings and loan associations are placed in a difficult position when, in response to a restrictive monetary policy, market yields on competing short-term assets rise above the average yields on the mortgage portfolios of the associations. If they raise interest rates on their liabilities to the extent required to maintain "normal" inflows of funds, their interest costs will exceed their earnings. On the other hand, if they refuse to raise yields on their liabilities to the required level, they will suffer at least a dwindling net inflow of funds and perhaps large net withdrawals. In fact, most of the associations have followed the latter type of policy during periods of restriction, at least partly because of ceilings on their deposit rates, with the expected results. Residential construction, heavily dependent on funds from the savings and loan associations, fell sharply; in some periods the decline of home construction was as much as 50 percent.

Nor are other types of nonbank financial intermediaries immune from the effects of restrictive monetary policies. Mutual savings banks also experience a decrease of net inflows of funds, and sometimes net outflows, when they fail to increase interest rates on their time and savings deposits in line with the rising yields on competing assets. Thus they are forced to curtail their purchases, and even to make net sales, of their principal types of earning assets—long-term bonds and real estate mortgages. The impact on inflows to credit unions is usually less severe, partly because of the loyalty of members of credit unions and partly because individual deposit accounts at these institutions are typically smaller and less sensitive to interest differentials. Finance companies—including both consumer finance and sales finance companies—acquire most of their funds by issuing both short-term and longer-term debts in the open market and by borrowing from banks. They experience at least an increase in their costs of funds, and some are likely to find bank credit less available in periods of restriction. They are therefore impelled to raise interest rates on their loans. Life insurance companies usually do not experience a reduction of their gross inflows of premium receipts during periods of monetary restriction, but they have less to invest in their major types of earning assets—long-term bonds, mortgages, and common stocks. This is because at least the major companies are legally required to lend to their policy holders at fixed rates of interest, in most cases at 5 or 6 percent, and policy holders increase their borrowings markedly when market rates of interest rise much above these levels.

At this stage, we have shown how the effects of Federal Reserve restrictive actions are transmitted through the commercial banks and other financial institutions to all branches of the financial markets. However, we have not yet explored the channels through which such developments in the financial sectors can affect the behavior of aggregate money demands for output. It is to this subject that we now turn.

EFFECTS ON AGGREGATE MONEY DEMANDS FOR OUTPUT

Restrictive developments in financial markets are translated into effects on aggregate money demands for output through three principal channels: cost-of-funds effects; nonprice rationing effects; and wealth effects.

COST-OF-FUNDS EFFECTS

These include both the interest cost of financing through debt issues and the cost of financing through new equity issues. When long-term interest rates rise, new shares of stock can be sold only at lower prices relative to expected earnings per share. Most corporations are reluctant to issue new shares at prices so low as to "dilute," or decrease, earnings per share on their outstanding shares. This can be clarified by an example. Suppose that a corporation has outstanding a certain number of shares, and that annual earnings per share are $2. If yields on long-term bonds are relatively low, the market price per share may be $24. But if long-term interest rates are higher, the price per share may be only $16. Suppose that the corporation has available to it further internal investment opportunities that would yield 10 percent annually, or 10 cents for each $1 addition to its assets. If it can issue new shares at a price of $24, each new share issued will add that amount to the corporation's assets and $2.40 to its annual earnings, thereby raising average earnings per share. But if each new share can be sold for only $16, the addition to earnings will be only $1.60, which will reduce earnings on outstanding shares.

We noted earlier that with a given state of expectations concerning the marginal efficiency of investment, a rise in the costs of funds tends to reduce private investment in such forms as residential construction, business expenditures for plant and equipment, and increases in business inventories. However, it should not be assumed that every increase in the cost of funds will reduce actual spending for investment. A major reason for adopting a restrictive monetary policy is often to counteract a rising investment demand function, the latter reflecting expectations of increased rates of return on investment. Thus to prevent an actual increase of investment spending, the cost of funds must rise at least enough to offset expected increases in rates of return. In some cases, and especially in periods when inflationary expectations predominate, this may require large increases in the cost of funds.

An increase in the cost of funds is likely to have quite uneven impacts on the various specific types of private investment. Restrictive effects are likely to be largest on the types of investment on which expected rates of return have risen least, financing costs are a large fraction of the total operating costs of the project, and costs of delaying the investment are least. In this category are typically residential construction and investments in business plant and equipment whose major purpose is to lower production costs rather than to expand total capacity to meet rising demands for output. Restrictive effects are likely to be least under the reverse conditions.

Though the largest impact of an increase in interest rates is on private investment, there is also some downward impact on expenditures by state and local governments, primarily on large capital expenditures by local governments. In many cases the annual service charges on debt issued to finance such lumpy projects are large enough to have a significant effect on local property tax rates. The higher the interest rates on these debts, the more likely local government officials and their constituents are to disapprove long-term bond issues to finance large public improvements. In some cases they postpone the projects, hoping for lower interest rates in the future. In others, they undertake some part of the projects but finance at least part of them temporarily with issues of short-term debt.

An increase of interest rates may also decrease household borrowings to purchase consumer durable goods. However, it seems unlikely that this effect is very large, partly because interest rates on consumer installment loans usually rise only sluggishly, and partly because consumer purchases of durable goods seem rather insensitive to interest rates. The effect of increased interest rates on household consumption and saving functions remains a controversial subject. As noted earlier, a classical view was that a rise of interest rates would increase saving and decrease consumption at each level of household disposable income. Most economists now assume that this effect is at best small. The subject merits further investigation.

NONPRICE RATIONING EFFECTS

There would be no place for nonprice methods of rationing credit during periods of restriction if all branches of credit markets were perfectly competitive with no obstructions to changes in interest rates, and if interest rates in fact adjusted quickly to equilibrium levels. Nonprice methods of rationing appear to play no more than a small role in the highly competitive open markets for financial assets, where interest rates are highly mobile, but they are significant where "customer relationships" between lenders and borrowers are involved. Home mortgages and bank loans to customers will serve as examples.

We noted earlier that in periods of restriction flows of funds to savings and loan associations and other principal holders of mortgages decline sharply, so that these lenders are forced to decrease the amount of mortgage funds that they supply. They could, of course, respond by raising interest rates on mortgages to the level required to bring effective demand into equality with the reduced supply of funds. In fact, this usually does not happen, at least not quickly. Even when they are legally free to rise, mortgage rates typically rise more slowly than other long-term yields, such as those on corporate bonds. Moreover, many states impose legal ceilings on mortgage rates, and in several periods these ceilings have been below the rising yields on other types of long-term debt. Under such conditions, mortgage lenders resort to various types of nonprice rationing. They simply decline to make mortgage loans, saying, in effect, "Sorry, we just don't have the money." They shun higher-risk loans, lending only to the safest borrowers. They require larger down payments, which some borrowers cannot make. They lend for only shorter periods, thus increasing the burden of monthly carrying charges. Because of such practices, a restrictive monetary policy can reduce mortgage lending and construction activity considerably more than might be expected solely from the increase of mortgage rates.

Though banks do increase the interest rates they charge on loans to customers during periods of restriction, the increases are in many cases insufficient to reduce customers' demands to the level of the banks' ability to supply funds. Among the reasons for such bank policies are the oligopolistic nature of local markets for bank loans to customers, a fear of alienating customers by charging "all the traffic will bear," and an unwillingness of each bank to acquire a reputation of raising rates faster and further than other banks. Banks employ various types of nonprice rationing, of which the following are examples: A bank refuses to take on new loan customers, explaining that, "We must take care of our old and loyal customers first." It raises its credit standards and rejects some loan applications as too risky. It requires more collateral, which some applicants cannot supply. It lends for only shorter periods and requires more rapid repayments. It tries to convince applicants that it is not in their own interest "to borrow so much in uncertain times like these." And in some cases it simply denies loan applications, in whole or in part. Nonprice rationing is likely to impinge most heavily on loan applicants who are not considered to be among a bank's most valuable customers.

Though we have no reliable quantitative estimates of the effects of nonprice rationing, there is reason to believe that these methods do have significant effects on both the total amount of credit extended and on the rate of spending for output.

WEALTH EFFECTS

As already noted, increases of interest rates, and especially of long-term rates, tend to lower the prices of income-yielding assets of all kinds. Prices of long-term bonds and of other assets yielding fixed dollar amounts of return always fall under such conditions. Prices of common stock also decline if expected earnings per share fail to rise enough to offset the rise of long-term interest rates. A major reason for the sharp decline of stock prices during the early 1970s was the extraordinarily large increase of interest rates. Such declines of their wealth lead at least some households to reduce their consumption and to increase their saving at each level of disposable income.

Though we are unable to estimate the quantitative impact of the wealth effect on spending, it is believed to be significant, especially in periods when interest rates rise markedly.

RESPONSES OF OUTPUT, EMPLOYMENT, AND PRICES

When the Federal Reserve takes actions to restrain the rate of growth of expenditures for output, it hopes, of course, that the impact will be almost solely on the price level with little or no depressive effect on the growth of real output and employment. Too often, however, events do not turn out so favorably; fighting inflation with restrictive monetary policies can be costly in real terms.

EXPANSIONARY MONETARY POLICIES

We shall now explore the use of monetary policy actions to increase the rate of growth of aggregate money demands for output. Our discussion of this can be relatively brief because both Federal Reserve actions and the processes through which these achieve, or fail to achieve, their purposes are largely symmetrical with those discussed above.

The principal actions that the Federal Reserve can take to promote monetary expansion have already been noted: decreases of legal reserve requirements against demand deposits, or time and savings deposits, or both; reduction of discount rates and relaxation of other restrictions on bank borrowings from the Federal Reserve; and purchases of acceptances and government securities in the open market. Which of these instruments will be employed and how vigorously they will be used will depend on the economic outlook as viewed by Federal Reserve officials. For example, at some time they may see no danger of an economic recession but conclude that expenditures for output may rise a little too slowly. In such cases they may merely increase slightly their rate of purchase of government securities. In other circumstances much more vigorous action will be appropriate. Suppose, for example, that the economy has for some time been in a period of high prosperity with inflationary pressures, but it is becoming increasingly apparent that unemployment may be developing. Fearing false signals, the Federal Reserve may at first act cautiously, perhaps relaxing only slightly its degree of restriction. However, when it becomes convinced that the threat of recession is real, it may use all its instruments aggressively to encourage expansion. We shall deal with this case because it facilitates exposition.

The Federal Reserve may well lead off with a large purchase of government securities, thereby increasing bank reserves. This directly increases the amount of money and decreases the amount of securities available for holding by others, thereby tending to lower interest rates. The Federal Reserve may quickly reduce discount rates and legal reserve requirements, or it may postpone such actions for some time. The immediate responses of short-term and long-term interest rates to such actions will depend to some extent on how these actions affect investors' expectations concerning the future course of interest rates. If the Federal Reserve makes it clear, through the vigor of its actions and official statements, that it has abandoned its restrictive policies and has embarked on a policy of expansion, bond prices may rise dramatically as investors seek capital gains. If, however, Federal Reserve actions appear tentative and experimental, investors may fear an early return to restriction. In such cases the initial downward impact on interest rates may be largely confined to short maturities, and bond yields may fall only later.

The Federal Reserve should expect that some part of the additional bank reserves that it creates by purchasing securities, and some part of the excess reserves that it creates by lowering reserve requirements, will be used to reduce bank borrowings at the Federal Reserve, especially if the latter had become large during the preceding period of prosperity. Some banks may also elect to hold more excess reserves as interest rates fall. However, the Federal Reserve can offset these effects and exert net pressures for expansion by supplying still more reserves. On the basis of their excess reserves, banks proceed to increase their earning assets and to reduce at least some types of their outstanding debts. They increase their net purchases of open-market assets, such as government securities, commercial paper, acceptances, and claims against brokers and dealers. At first the downward impact on yields may be confined largely to short maturities, but as these yields fall and it becomes clear that the decline of rates is not merely temporary, banks step up their purchases of longer maturities. At some stage they also liberalize their lending to customers, reducing rates and relaxing nonprice rationing. In the meantime, banks also reduce their own demands for funds. They decrease their demands for Federal funds, and this, together with an increase in the supply of excess reserves, brings a sharp decrease of the interest rate on these funds. In some cases this rate falls to only a fraction of 1 percent. Bank holding companies and their affiliates reduce the interest rates that they offer on their issues of open-market commercial paper. Banks reduce the rates they offer on their issues of large-denomination NCDs and also, though sometimes only after a delay, rates on their other types of time and savings deposits.

As the Federal Reserve and the commercial banks make net purchases of earning assets, issuing additional money in exchange, they alter the portfolio composition of the nonbank sectors. These portfolios become safer and more liquid but earn less. If these holders have not altered their portfolio preferences, they will seek to restore the balance in their portfolios by increasing their demands for earning assets.

NONBANK FINANCIAL INTERMEDIARIES

As market yields on competing assets fall, savings and loan associations, mutual savings banks, and credit unions receive larger inflows of funds. Policy holders demand fewer loans from life insurance companies, so that the latter have more funds to purchase corporate bonds, mortgages, and other long-term assets. Finance companies and real estate investment trusts are enabled to sell their issues of long-term and short-term debt on more favorable terms, and to borrow more cheaply from banks.

In short, all the principal types of nonbank financial intermediaries are enabled to acquire funds on more favorable terms and to lend more to others.

EFFECTS ON AGGREGATE MONEY DEMANDS FOR OUTPUT

Expansionary monetary-policy actions and the resulting developments in financial markets are translated into effects on aggregate money demands for output through the three principal channels mentioned earlier:

1. Costs-of-funds effects—in this case a decrease in the cost of borrowing.
2. Nonprice rationing effects. As financial institutions experience an increase in their lending capacity relative to customers' demands for loans, they relax some of their nonprice rationing methods that had prevailed in the preceding period of restriction. They court new borrowers instead of turning them away; they no longer confine their loans to the safest types of borrowers; they lend for longer periods and require less collateral; and so on.
3. Wealth effects. As long-term interest rates fall, the prices of bonds and other assets with fixed dollar returns are increased, and prices of common stocks will also be increased if expected earnings per share do not decrease enough to offset the effects of the decline of long-term interest rates. In response to the increase of their

wealth, at least some households are likely to increase their consumption at each level of disposable income.

When the Federal Reserve adopts an expansionary policy to halt a decline of total expenditures for output or to increase the rate of growth of such expenditures, it usually hopes that the effects will be reflected almost solely in increases of real output and employment, rather than increases in prices. Its hopes are likely to be realized in large part so long as there are large amounts of unemployment and unused capacity. However, the responses have too often become considerably less favorable before full employment was reached.

FEDERAL RESERVE
POLICIES AND INTEREST RATES

Almost from the time that the Federal Reserve began operations more than 60 years ago, it has been obvious that this system has some power to influence the behavior of market rates of interest, and it has used these powers frequently and in some periods almost continuously, sometimes because of its concern for interest rates per se, and sometimes as a means of promoting other objectives. Yet there still remain controversies over the extent of these powers and their appropriate use. We shall discuss these by considering two broad questions:

1. What are the limits, if any, to the power of the Federal Reserve to control the level of interest rates?
2. To what ends should these powers be used?

To understand the nature and sharpness of these controversies it will be helpful to survey some attitudes of the public and some members of the government toward interest rates.

ATTITUDES TOWARD INTEREST RATES

Outside the financial community, and even among some members of that community, there is strong opposition to high interest rates, even in periods of high prosperity. A monetary policy that causes or condones high interest rates is likely to bring loud protests; one that is accompanied by low interest rates is likely to receive general approbation. Some even demand that the dominant objective of the Federal Reserve should be to maintain interest rates at continuously low levels.

The reasons for these attitudes are numerous and confusing:

1. A continuing feeling that interest is a form of exploitation of debtors by creditors rather than a legitimate form of income received for services rendered. Those sharing this attitude, which has persisted since the Middle Ages, concentrate on the effects of interest rates on income distribution and tend to ignore the roles of interest rates as incentives to save and to make savings available for use by others, as rationers of scarce financial resources, and as a determinant of aggregate demand.

2. Interests of debtors in low interest rates. Debtors include some of the most vocal and influential groups in our society—farmers, homeowners, nonfinancial business firms, and on some occasions the government itself. Even some who are not themselves debtors or creditors, or who are in a balanced creditor-debtor position, tend to sympathize with debtors because they believe that higher interest rates transfer income from poor debtors to wealthy creditors. This view is far too simplistic. For example, a rise of interest rates on the bonds of a business corporation can transfer income from wealthy stockholders to less-wealthy creditors. Or higher interest rates on government bonds financed by a highly progressive personal income tax can transfer income from the wealthiest taxpayers to less-wealthy creditors.

3. Antipathy to the depressing effects of high interest rates on the capital values of assets.

4. Belief that under all conditions low interest rates promote real economic growth. Though valid when growth is inhibited by a deficiency of investment demand, this belief becomes invalid if the limiting factor is a shortage in the supply of real saving.

5. Belief that the Federal Reserve can in fact maintain interest rates at any level that it chooses, and can do so without adverse economic effects. Many of those holding this belief implicitly assume that interest is a purely monetary phenomenon, that the level of interest rates is determined solely by the nominal money supply and the demand for nominal money balances, and that the "real functions"—the investment demand and saving supply functions—are irrelevant to the outcome. In the following sections we shall investigate some of these contentions.

LIMITS ON FEDERAL RESERVE
CONTROL OF THE LEVEL OF INTEREST RATES

Beliefs that interest is a purely monetary phenomenon, that the level of interest rates is determined solely by the supply of nominal money relative to the demand for nominal money balances, and that the Federal Reserve can fix interest rates at any level that it chooses by manipulating the nominal money supply are clearly erroneous. It would be closer to the truth to say that "the equilibrium level" of interest rates is determined basically by the investment demand and saving supply functions, but that under some circumstances the Federal Reserve can produce or correct deviations from this level by manipulating the nominal money supply.

To aid in developing this point, it will be useful to recall our earlier discussion of the determinants of the "full-employment, equilibrium level of interest rates," which means that level of interest rates that would equate investment demand and saving supply at a full-employment level of output.[1] The conclusion was that this level of interest rates depends solely on the investment demand and saving supply functions, and that this equilibrium level can be shifted upward by an increase of the investment demand function or a decrease of the saving supply function, and the equilibrium level of interest rates can be shifted downward by a decrease of the investment demand function or an increase of the saving supply function. In our example we shall assume that the investment demand and saving supply functions are such as to produce the $I = S$ line shown in Figure 14−1. The horizontal distance OF represents the full-employment level of output with stable prices.

Interest rates can be at the full-employment equilibrium level only if the supply function of loanable funds is such as to intersect the $I = S$ line at the level of interest rates i_0, the only level of interest rates consistent with a full-employment level of aggregate demand, OF. The Federal Reserve can establish the appropriate supply function of loanable funds, L_{S_0}, by regulating the direction and rate of change of the money supply, ΔM.

By decreasing the money supply the Federal Reserve could, if it wished, decrease the supply function of loanable funds and raise the level of interest rates. This is represented by the L_{S_1} curve, which intersects the $I = S$ line at the higher level of interest rates i_1. At this higher level of interest rates, aggregate demands for output would be only OA, which is significantly below the full-employment level. The lower value of output must be reflected in lower real output, lower prices, or both. If prices and wage rates are less than fully flexible downward, so that the decrease of aggregate demand is not fully reflected in a decrease of

[1] See pp. 346−348 above.

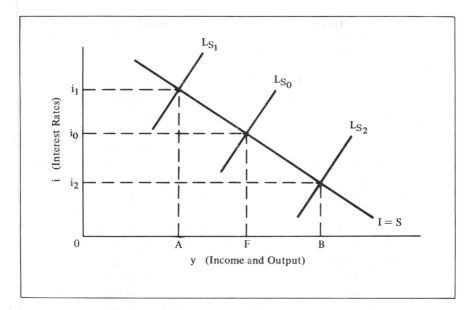

Figure 14–1   **Interest Rates and Income Levels**

prices, the result must be some loss of potential real output and employment. However, the Federal Reserve can, by increasing the money supply, increase the supply function of loanable funds to L_{S_0} and lower interest rates to the full-employment level, i_0.

We can now reach some limited conclusions concerning the power of the Federal Reserve to regulate the level of interest rates by controlling the behavior of the nominal money supply. It can indeed establish and maintain a level of market rates of interest above the level consistent with a full-employment level of aggregate demand, but if prices are not fully flexible downward, interest rates can be maintained at such a higher level only at a cost in terms of lost output and employment.

Consider now Federal Reserve attempts to hold market rates of interest below their full-employment equilibrium level, doing so by increasing the nominal money supply. In Figure 14–1, it is assumed that an increase of the money supply initially reduces interest rates to the lower level i_2. But this is only the beginning of a longer story. To analyze subsequent developments and outcomes it will be useful to distinguish two cases.

Case 1. The increase in the nominal money supply is a "once only" increase effected in such a way that it does not create general expectations of future price increases. We can envision the following sequence of events:

1. The increase of the nominal money supply initially lowers interest rates to i_2.
2. The decline of interest rates increases investment expenditures. This, together with an increase of consumption induced by the rise of national income, increases aggregate demand to the level OB.
3. This level of aggregate demand is considerably in excess of the full-employment supply of output at constant prices, so that the excess demand must be reflected in a proportional increase in the price level. The rise of the price level will be reflected in increased money values of national income and output. In particular, investment expenditures at each level of interest rates will increase proportionally with the prices of investment goods if the investment demand function in real terms remains unchanged. This increase in investment expenditures will be reflected in an upward and rightward shift of the $I = S$ line. This serves to raise interest rates, for the new equilibrium level of interest rates must lie somewhere on the higher $I = S$ line.
4. The higher money values of national income and output will be accompanied by a higher value of total transactions, which will increase the community's demand for money balances for transactions purposes. In effect, the rise of prices, by increasing the community's demand for money balances, will eradicate the initial excess of the money supply over the demand for money balances.
5. The above developments will raise the level of interest rates. If the saving supply and investment demand functions have not shifted in real terms, interest rates will return to the original equilibrium level, i_0.
6. The only permanent effect of the "once only" increase of the nominal money supply is to raise the price level.

Case 2: The Federal Reserve is adamantly determined to hold interest rates at the selected low level and attempts to increase the nominal money supply to the extent necessary to prevent market rates of interest from rising above this level. Such a continuous increase in the nominal money supply will support a continuous, and perhaps accelerating, rise of prices. At some stage members of the community will come to expect prices to continue to rise in the future. In popular terms, "inflationary expectations" or an "inflationary psychology" will emerge. This usually does not occur at an early stage; people continue to think for some time that even though prices are rising currently they may stabilize or even decline in the future. However, after prices have risen almost continuously for a considerable period, and especially if the rate of inflation appears to be accelerating, both borrowers and lenders come to have inflationary expectations, and these can have profound effects on both the demand for and supply of funds in financial markets and on the behavior of market rates of interest. Paradoxically, it often turns out that the faster the monetary authority increases the nominal money supply in order to hold down interest rates, the faster the rate of increase in market rates of interest becomes.

To explain this, we must now make a distinction that has been avoided up to this point— a distinction between *nominal rates of interest* and *real rates of interest*. Nominal rates of interest are simply the rates observed in financial markets—the rates received by lenders and paid by borrowers. Real rates of interest are the nominal rates adjusted for changes in the price level, or more specifically, for changes in the purchasing power of the monetary unit. The relationship between nominal and real rates of interest can be expressed as follows:

$$R = \frac{1+i}{1+g} - 1$$

where

R = the real rate of interest, stated in percent per annum
i = the nominal interest rate, expressed in percent per annum
g = the rate of change of the price level, stated in percent per annum.

Thus, $1/(1+g) - 1$ reflects the annual rate of change in the purchasing power of each dollar. The real rate of interest and the nominal rate are equal if the price level does not change. The real rate exceeds the nominal rate if the price level declines, and the real rate is less than the nominal rate if the price level rises. The real rate is zero when the rate of price inflation and the nominal interest rate are equal, and it is negative when the rate of price inflation exceeds the nominal rate of interest. (See Table 14−2.)

Table 14 — 2   **Relationships Between Nominal and Real Rates of Interest**

i Nominal Rate of Interest	g Annual Rate of Increase of Price Level	R Real Rate of Interest
6	−5	+11.6
6	0	+6
6	+6	0
6	+12	−5.4
20	+30	−7.7

Expectations of price inflation tend to raise nominal rates of interest by increasing demand functions for funds at each nominal rate of interest and also by reducing supply functions of funds at each nominal interest rate. Spenders for investment offer higher interest rates because they expect price inflation to increase the nominal rates of return on investments. For example, a specific investment project may be expected to yield a 10 percent annual rate of return over its current cost if the price level and the nominal value of the flow of services rendered by the project remain constant. But suppose the price level is expected to rise by 15 percent a year, with an equal increase in the nominal values of the services rendered by the project. The expected nominal rate of return may be 25 percent, leading spenders for investment to increase sharply their demand functions for funds. Dissavers may also increase markedly their demands for funds, expecting to pay interest and principal with depreciated dollars. Their motto may be, "Borrow and buy now; avoid higher prices later." Supply functions of funds in financial markets decrease as owners of funds save less or use their funds for their own purposes.

If the rate of price inflation were perfectly foreseen by market participants and interest rates were perfectly free to respond, expected inflation rates would be reflected in nominal market rates of interest so that the real rate of interest could remain unchanged. In many cases, however, nominal rates of interest fail to rise enough to offset the rate of inflation, so that real rates of interest are reduced and even become negative. For this there can be many reasons, such as imperfections in forecasting the rate of inflation, government attempts to place ceilings on nominal rates, and various institutional rigidities that delay adjustments of the terms of financial contracts. A failure of nominal interest rates to rise enough to compensate for increases in the price level can have profound effects on saving, the portfolio choices of asset holders, and the flow of funds. Savers are likely to save less and consume more. And in disposing of their current saving and in managing their portfolios, people tend to shun assets that are fixed in terms of monetary units and to seek types of assets whose prices are free to rise—such things as equities, land, claims on foreign moneys, gold, jewelry, and art objects. Flows of funds through financial intermediaries, and especially through those issuing claims fixed in terms of money, dwindle, and large net withdrawals may occur. Since real rates of interest are too low to allocate the scarce supply of funds to those who can use them most productively, these must be rationed by nonprice methods, which are usually based more on some sort of favoritism than on considerations relating to efficiency.

On the other hand, inflationary expectations can raise nominal interest rates more than enough to compensate for the rate of inflation that will actually be realized. For example, suppose that a nation has experienced an inflation so prolonged and rapid that the community generally expects that prices will continue to rise at least 20 percent a year. Many households and business firms are likely to buy land, houses, and other physical assets at high prices that would be justified only if the 20 percent inflation rate actually continued, and to commit themselves to paying high nominal rates of interest on large debts. Now suppose that because of monetary and fiscal reforms or for other reasons the inflation is stopped, or at least reduced to an annual rate of only 2 or 3 percent. Many of those who made earlier commitments based on inflationary expectations will find it difficult, if not impossible, to meet their obligations.

We shall have more to say about inflation in the following chapter.

CONCLUSION

The preceding discussion suggests the answer to a question raised earlier: To what ends should the Federal Reserve use its power to influence the behavior of market rates of interest? Ideally, the Federal Reserve would use its powers to maintain rates at that level which, with prevailing investment demand and saving supply functions, would produce a level of aggregate demand just sufficient to maintain a full-employment level of output without price inflation. It would resist higher rates because of their cost in terms of lost output and employment, and it would resist lower rates because of their cost in terms of price inflation and its accompanying inequities and inefficiencies. However, as noted earlier, it is much easier to propound this rule than to implement it successfully. A basic reason for this is the imperfection of our knowledge concerning investment demand and saving supply functions, and therefore our difficulty in identifying the level, and changes in the level, of interest rates that would produce the desired results.

SELECTED READINGS

See list at end of Chapter 13.

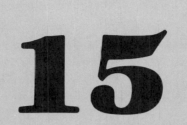

THE MONETARY-
FINANCIAL SYSTEM
OF THE FUTURE

The preceding chapters have described the structure and functioning of the American monetary-financial system as it had developed by the mid-1970s. That complex system was by no means static; it had changed dramatically during the preceding century and even during the preceding fifty years, and there was no reason to believe that the process of change was at an end. In fact, some changes were already under way and others were in prospect with widely differing probabilities of happening. The purpose of this chapter is to suggest the nature of some future changes. As a first step, it will be useful to survey briefly some of the principal sources of change.

SOURCES OF CHANGE

The various components of the monetary-financial system are shaped by a complex of interacting forces, some operating through the market and some through government, and changes in the complex of forces tend to change the functioning of the system, or its structure, or both. Some forces for change originate within the system itself, as participants "learn by doing" and introduce technological innovations. However, the most powerful forces for change originate outside the monetary-financial system in the various sectors of the economy and in the society at large.

For example, a full explanation of the transformation of the relatively simple monetary-financial system of a century ago into the vastly different and more complex system of today would have to take into account all the forces that have transformed American society from one that was relatively small, largely agrarian, and characterized by relatively small firms into the much more populous, highly industrialized, and highly urbanized society of today. This would require attention to many forces, including the following:

1. Widespread and continuing innovations in methods of agricultural production. Substitution of capital for labor and almost innumerable technological innovations have freed most of the labor force from farms and made it available for other types of production.
2. A series of innovations in transportation that have increased the speed and reduced the costs of transporting goods, thereby broadening markets.
3. Many innovations in communications. These include not only faster and more economic transportation of paper messages but also such things as telegraph, telephone, telex, wireless, and sophisticated computer-based electronic communications systems. The contributions of these innovations to the broadening of financial markets have already been noted; these innovations have also served to broaden and integrate markets for commodities and other services.
4. Many other innovations that have increased the average size of business firms and made the large business corporation dominant in many lines.
5. The many forces that have expanded the role of government as a demander of resources, as an issuer of securities, as administrator of social security programs, as regulator of the private sector, and so on.

There can be little doubt that the monetary-financial system of the future will continue to be changed by continuing changes of the types noted above and by other forces that cannot yet be foreseen.

The government affects the structure and functioning of the monetary-financial system most directly through its regulatory policies. These are of several types:

1. Chartering policies. These relate to the types of institutions to receive charters and the number of charters granted.
2. Branching policies. These relate to limitations on the number of physical facilities that an institution may operate, their locations, and their geographic coverage.

3. Portfolio policies. These relate to the permitted types and mixes of the assets and liabilities of an institution.
4. Limitations on the range of services that each type of institution may supply.

At any given time, these types of government restrictions do indeed affect the structure and functioning of at least some parts of the system. It is, however, more difficult to assess the long-run effects of government restrictions and regulations on the structure and functioning of the system. Some have argued that in the longer run basic social and economic forces will prevail; government restrictions will be relaxed if they prevent entrepreneurs from exploiting profitable opportunities to establish new institutions or undertake new functions. There is some truth in this contention. In fact, we shall later argue that some existing government restrictions are likely to be relaxed because they have become obsolete and uneconomic. However, lags in the adaptation of government policies can be long indeed, sometimes extending over decades.

The objectives of government regulatory policies relating to financial institutions are numerous, conflicting, and confused. Part of the confusion results from the division of regulatory responsibilities among numerous agencies at the federal level and among agencies in the fifty states, but another part derives from the multiplicity of objectives. The latter are often stated as "promotion of competition, efficiency, soundness, and integrity of the system." But the relative weights attached to the objectives, and the interpretations of the objectives, change from time to time. For example, in the 1930s, following widespread failures of financial institutions, the emphasis was on promoting "soundness." Allegedly to promote this objective, a number of highly anticompetitive measures were adopted. Among these were the prohibition of interest on demand deposits, imposition of legal ceilings on rates on time and savings deposits, and limitations on the establishment of new banks and bank branches. In recent decades, statements of the regulators have placed more emphasis on promoting competition and efficiency, yet these agencies continue restrictions that contribute little, if any, to the promotion of soundness and are clearly anticompetitive and damaging to efficiency. The confusion and inconsistencies of regulatory policies also result to a significant extent from political pressures by the regulated institutions. As so often happens, those that are regulated bring strong political pressures on the regulators to grant favorable treatment to themselves and to repress competition from others. Thus, the Congress, state legislatures, and the regulatory agencies become focal points in the controversies of big banks vs. small banks, banks vs. thrift institutions, banks vs. investment banks and brokers, and so on. And regulatory policies shift as the relative political powers of the institutions change. The structure and permitted functions of the commercial banking system provide a case in point.

COMMERCIAL BANKS

The branching power of each commercial bank is determined by the state in which it is domiciled. Some states permit no branches at all, some others permit branching within a locality or region within a state, and some permit statewide branching, but no state permits branches of banks domiciled in other states. Yet many banks, and especially the larger ones, want to branch outside their own states and even nationwide. And in many situations interstate branching into at least adjoining trade areas would clearly promote competition and efficiency. The present branching restrictions are largely the result of political pressures from banks. Little banks resist competition from bigger banks, and both little and big banks within a state resist competition from out-of-state banks.

There is reason to believe that restrictions on branching will be relaxed somewhat. In many states restrictions on intrastate branching have already been liberalized as the advantages of larger-scale banking have become increasingly apparent, and, perhaps more important, as political power in the state legislatures has shifted from rural areas and small towns, where small banks predominate, to larger urban areas. Also, more of the larger banks that would like to branch into other states would now condone interstate branching on a reciprocal basis. That is, they would accept entrance of branches of out-of-state banks if they received in return the right to operate branches in other states. Moreover, it is possible, though perhaps not very probable, that the federal government will assert its right to determine the branching powers of the national banks that it charters, rather than leaving these to be determined by the states. As we shall see later, the development of the Electronic Funds Transfer System (EFTS) is likely to exert further pressures for relaxation of restrictions on branching.

Relaxation of branching restrictions could well be followed by dramatic changes in the structure of the commercial banking system. For example, the number of commercial banks could decrease from the present level of about 14,500 to 1,000, or even less. And some of these may be nationwide systems. Nor should one rule out the possibility that at least some nonbank depository institutions will be permitted to branch more widely. At present, branching by almost all of them is confined to their own states or to even smaller areas. Yet some would find it advantageous to branch interstate. For example, a large savings and loan association might operate some offices in areas where it accumulated funds in excess of the local demand for mortgage money and other offices in areas where the demand for mortgage funds exceeded the local supply of funds for this purpose, thereby facilitating interregional flows of funds.

It is also possible that commercial banks will receive broadened powers in the fields of investment banking and as broker-dealers in securities. In many other countries, institutions performing commercial banking functions also play major roles as investment bankers and as broker-dealers. However, in 1933 the federal government decreed that commercial banks should divest themselves of their security affiliates, and that they should act as brokers only on specific requests from their customers. Since that time, commercial banks have performed investment banking functions only with respect to government securities. It is not at all clear that the mandatory separation of investment banking from commercial banking was wise policy in 1933 or that it is appropriate today. It is true, of course, that in the period before 1933, when there was virtually no federal regulation of the securities industry, some of the securities affiliates of commercial banks were guilty of bad judgment, or worse. However, their conduct appears to have been no worse than that of independent investment banks. It might have been wiser to permit commercial banks and their affiliates to continue to act as investment banks, subject to appropriate regulations and safeguards.

Such a policy might be socially useful. There appears to be no shortage of investment banking services at reasonable prices for large corporations, but the situation seems to be different for some small and medium-sized corporations. The position of the latter could be improved if they had access to investment banking services at a commercial bank that is familiar with their financial conditions and prospects and with regional sources of longer-term funds.

Commercial banks may also acquire greater powers to serve as brokers and dealers in securities. For at least some customers, it would be more convenient to place orders with their banks and to use bank officials as investment advisers. Brokers generally oppose such "intrusions," but at least some of them are likely to find that it is more efficient to use banks as sources of orders than to maintain a large number of expensive retail offices.

We shall later have more to say about the future of depository institutions. Before doing so, however, it will be useful to survey some conditions in the mid-1970s that were so stressful that further changes seemed almost inevitable.

THE OUTLOOK FOR ECONOMIC STABILITY

Price inflation, and uncertainty concerning its future rate and duration, were matters of major concern in the mid-1970s. Inflation during the preceding dozen years, in a few of those years at a double-digit rate, had already exerted highly disturbing effects on financial markets. Nominal interest rates rose to historically high levels, bond prices sagged and behaved erratically, and stock prices were depressed. Depository institutions, especially savings and loans associations, were subjected to severe cycles of disintermediation and reintermediation, with highly destabilizing effects on the construction industry. Many observers became convinced that reforms were needed for the asset and liability policies of these institutions and for methods of housing finance. Though the rate of inflation had decreased to about 6 percent by 1977, its future course was highly uncertain, as noted earlier.

After a dozen years of continuous inflation, a prolongation of inflation at an annual rate of 6 percent or more, and especially an acceleration in the rate of inflation, could have serious consequences for the financial system. For one thing, it could lead to marked changes in the characteristics of direct securities. As noted in earlier chapters, a major part of all outstanding direct securities is in the form of debt contracts in which both principal and annual interest are stated in fixed numbers of dollars, and many of these are in the form of mortgages and bonds with initial maturities of 25 years or more. Such contracts have real advantages for issuers and holders when the purchasing power of the dollar remains relatively constant, but they become less acceptable in the face of prolonged price inflation.

Under conditions of prolonged and widespread inflationary expectations, conventional, direct debt contracts are likely to be modified in one or more of the following ways:

1. Long-term debt contracts may virtually disappear, leaving only maturities of a year or so. This may not protect creditors against loss of purchasing power, but it does permit frequent renegotiation of the level of interest rates in line with current expectations concerning future inflation rates.

2. Long-term debt contracts may continue to be written, but their rate
   of interest may be adjusted periodically. For example, a mortgage
   or bond may be payable only at the end of 25 years, but the rate of
   interest would be adjusted annually in line with prevailing rates
   on comparable one-year obligations. This could protect holders
   against a decline in the dollar values of these obligations, but it
   would protect them against loss of real purchasing power only if
   nominal rates of interest were high enough to compensate for the
   rate of inflation actually realized.
3. Long-term debts, and perhaps shorter-term debts as well, may come
   to be "indexed." In such contracts, the "basic amounts" are
   stated in dollars, but the amounts actually payable are arrived at
   by applying a price index. For example, a contract may provide
   for "basic amounts" of $1000 at maturity and $70 a year in interest, but stipulate that the amounts actually payable will be the
   "basic amounts" multiplied by some broad price index, such as
   the consumer price index or the GNP price deflator.

Though indexation would protect both debtors and creditors
against the direct effects of inflation as measured by the selected price
index, it would also present difficulties. One is the difficulty of achieving
indexation of all outstanding contracts as well as new ones. Another
arises from the dispersion of prices during inflation. General price inflation is usually accompanied by widely differing rates of increase of the
prices of individual goods and services. One result is that the wealth and
income of some debtors, measured in terms of money, rise more than
the general price level while the nominal wealth and income of other
debtors rise less. Many in the latter group of debtors would find it difficult to meet their indexed debt obligations, and some would be forced
into bankruptcy. For example, the revenue system of the federal government is such that a rise of the price level tends to increase its money
revenues more than proportionally, thus increasing its real revenues,
but many state and local governments are in the reverse position.

Inflationary developments of the types described above could also
have serious consequences for financial intermediaries, and especially
for those whose liabilities are fixed in terms of dollars. We have already
mentioned the cycles of disintermediation and reintermediation engen-
dered by wide fluctuations of the nominal yields on competing assets,
the latter reflecting at least in part inflationary expectations. Insolvency
for at least some of these institutions could also result. Suppose, for
example, that the assets of a depository institution are largely in the

form of conventional long-term debts whose principal and interest are stated in fixed numbers of dollars and that nominal long-term interest rates rise sharply because of inflationary expectations. The market values of the institution's long-term assets will fall so much that the institution is likely to become insolvent. Bankruptcy is likely to follow in the absence of massive financial assistance from the government.

In short, the present common practice by depository intermediaries of borrowing short and lending long is unlikely to survive a prolonged period of high but unstable and imperfectly predictable rates of inflation. The institutions may seek to adjust in various ways:

1. They may come to make only short-term loans. This would frustrate home buyers and others who wish to be assured of the continued use of funds over long periods. Also, during a transition period the institutions would face the problem of disposing of their existing long-term assets at nonruinous prices.
2. They may continue to acquire long-term bonds and mortgages, but only those on which interest rates are adjusted frequently. Proposals to authorize such securities under the name "variable rate mortgages" (VRM) have met considerable resistance from borrowers, presumably because the latter dislike uncertainty concerning the future amounts to be paid. However, attitudes may change as borrowers come to realize that the alternative of borrowing on conventional mortgages may be even more objectionable because the interest rate paid throughout the life of these mortgages may contain an "inflation hedge" greater than that justified by the rate of inflation actually realized.
3. They may avoid all long-term debts that are not indexed. If indexation of direct debts becomes widespread, financial intermediaries will be put under strong pressure to index their own issues of deposits and other indirect financial claims.

Such prolonged inflationary developments are also likely to impinge heavily on other parts of the financial system. For example, life insurance and annuity companies may find it increasingly difficult to sell policies that are fixed in terms of dollars and that involve large amounts of current saving; the public may shift its demands away from ordinary life policies and other types involving even more saving in their early stages and toward term policies that involve little current saving. Effects on stock prices and on holders of stock are difficult to predict. It used to be believed that common stocks were an excellent hedge against inflation. In fact, it was believed that earnings per share would rise faster than the price level because important business costs would lag behind—such costs as wages, rentals and leases, and interest. After inflationary expectations have become widespread, such cost lags become less likely and may not occur at all; in fact, at some times costs may outrun prices. When such developments are accompanied by high nominal long-term interest rates, the result is inevitably bad news for the stock market. If you doubt this, ask anyone who held stocks in the first half of the 1970s.

The preceding paragraphs have dealt only with some direct effects of prolonged inflation on the monetary-financial system. Indirect effects may be even more important. In extreme cases, prolonged inflation may create conflicts and frustrations so intense and widespread as to jeopardize the ability of a society to maintain social and political order.

While stressing the distorting effects of prolonged inflation, we should not forget that severe and prolonged unemployment can be at least as damaging.

DEPOSITORY FINANCIAL INTERMEDIARIES

Some of the most important changes in the monetary-financial system that can now be foreseen relate to the depository types of financial intermediaries—commercial banks, mutual savings banks, savings and loan associations, and credit unions. A number of proposals for change have already been introduced in Congress, and it seems likely that most of them will be adopted sooner or later. Adoption of these measures could lead to marked changes in the numbers of the various types of institutions, in the types and amounts of financial assets that they can accumulate, and in the functions that they perform.

As noted earlier, all types of depository institutions have at least one common function: they all issue various types of time and savings deposit liabilities that are quite similar and competitive with each other. However, there have also been important differences among these types of institutions and in public policies relating to them:

1. Traditionally, only commercial banks were permitted to create and issue liabilities transferable to third parties in payment. Now it is proposed that all the other depository types of intermediaries—often referred to collectively as "thrift institutions"—be given this power. In fact, a number of thrift institutions, most of them located in the New

England area, are already exercising this power. What is transferred to third parties in payment is a special type of interest-bearing savings deposit, called a NOW account. The orders used to transfer payments are called by various names, the most common of which is *negotiable order of withdrawal,* or NOW. In effect, they are checks, and there is no sensible reason for calling them anything else.

Bills introduced in Congress in 1977 would authorize the issue of interest-bearing NOW accounts throughout the country by all types of thrift institutions and also all types of commercial banks. But the bills do not provide final answers to some important questions. (a) To what types of holders will NOW accounts be issued? The bills introduced in 1977 would confine them to individuals, thus ruling out partnerships, corporations, and governmental units. It seems likely, however, that thrift institutions, and especially the larger ones, will press for powers to issue NOW accounts to a wider range of holders. And if thrift institutions achieve these powers, commercial banks will seek them too. (b) What will happen to the prohibition of interest on demand deposits? Logic suggests that if it is "sound" to permit interest on NOW accounts, which are demand deposits in fact if not in name, it is equally "sound" to permit interest on things called demand deposits. However, Congress is inclined to retain the prohibition. The outcome for demand deposits if Congress sticks to this position is not difficult to predict.

2. The types and proportions of financial assets acquired by the various types of depository intermediaries have differed widely. Commercial banks have been permitted to acquire and hold almost every type of debt obligation, though their holdings of mortgages have been restricted. In contrast, savings and loan associations have been largely confined to mortgages, primarily to home mortgages. Mutual savings banks have been confined largely to mortgages and long-term bonds, while credit unions have made mostly consumer loans. Now it is proposed that the asset powers of all these institutions be liberalized. Restrictions on commercial bank holdings of mortgages would be relaxed, and all thrift institutions would be permitted to acquire mortgages, consumer loans, and also limited amounts of other earning assets. Many thrift institutions aspire to become one-stop, family financial centers, advertising that "we can supply all the financial services that your household may need—checking accounts, time and savings accounts, mortgages, consumer credit, credit cards, travelers' checks, and credit life insurance."

3. Federal as well as state charters have been available to com-

mercial banks, savings and loan associations, and credit unions, but only state charters have been available to mutual savings banks, and only 18 states have authorized the establishment of these institutions. Now it is proposed that federal charters be made available to them. Thus, mutual savings banks may appear throughout the country and become even more important elements in the financial system.

Adoption of these proposed changes would blur the historic distinctions among these types of institutions, make them somewhat more similar to each other, and alter their competitive relationships. A major result should be enhanced competition for the financial business of households. Some other implications will be discussed later.

It is difficult to explain fully why the thrift institutions have become so aggressive in seeking expanded powers and why they are likely to get them. However, the following forces are clearly relevant:

1. Dissatisfaction with the past performance of the thrift institutions as sources of mortgage funds. It is hoped that permitting these institutions to issue monetary liabilities will enable them to command more funds and that permitting them to acquire consumer credit and some other short-term financial assets will enable them to increase their earning power more quickly and to a greater extent in periods of credit stringency, thereby reducing disintermediation.

2. More aggressive commercial bank competition for savings. During the period from the 1930s into the 1950s, commercial banks did not compete aggressively for savings. However, their competition became increasingly intense as market rates of interest rose, demands for bank loans increased, and demand deposits grew only sluggishly. Their advertising stressed the advantages of saving at "one-stop, full-service institutions." The thrift institutions now seek to outdo the commercial banks on this score.

3. The electronic funds transfer system (EFTS), already in the process of introduction, is a major reason why the thrift institutions are likely to be granted expanded powers, and especially power to provide means of payment to third parties. Members of the thrift industry, and some congressmen as well, fear that thrift institutions will be placed in a highly adverse competitive position relative to commercial banks if they are not permitted to participate fully in the EFTS. This is indeed a serious danger, as will become evident later.

THE ELECTRONIC FUNDS TRANSFER SYSTEM (EFTS)

The EFTS is a sophisticated, computer-based communications network whose principal function is to transmit payments electronically. This is no longer just a technologist's dream; all the necessary technology and hardware are already available, and some parts of the system are already in operation. The full development of the system may be delayed by government restrictions or slow acceptance by consumers, but its ultimate triumph is virtually assured by its great superiority over paper checks as a means of transferring payments.

TRANSFERS OF PAYMENTS BY CHECKS AND OTHER WRITTEN ORDERS

We noted earlier that checks written against bank deposits became the principal means of transferring payments because this proved to be cheaper than the use of coins and paper money and had other advantages as well.[1] Now paper checks are in the process of losing their primacy to an EFTS because the latter is more economical and also has other advantages. A simple example will suggest some of the reasons why the use of checks is expensive. (See Figure 15−1.) The payor must write a separate check for each payment and make a record of it, thus incurring some cost, and transport it to the payee, at some additional cost. The payee will record its receipt and transport it to his bank, at some cost. The payee's bank will do the accounting necessary to credit the payee's account and transport the check to a clearing-and-collection agency, again at some cost, and the latter will sort the checks it receives and transport each check to the payor's bank. The latter will deduct the amount of the check from the payor's account and transport the check to the payor. Thus a paper check must be handled and transported several times, and numerous accounting entries must be made to complete the payments process.

To make such a payment through an EFTS is simpler, faster, and cheaper. In effect, the payor orders his bank electronically to transfer a payment to the payee, the payor's bank transmits the order electronically to the payee's bank, which credits the payee's account, and payments among banks are cleared through entries in computers. The

[1] See pp. 135–138 above.

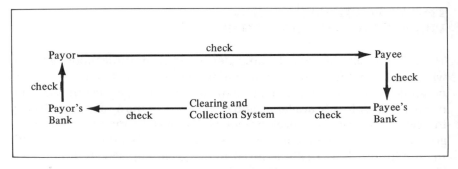

Figure 15—1 **Mechanics of Payment by Check**

entire process is completed without the use of a check or any other paper order. A brief survey of the structure of the EFTS will clarify the process. Because many details of the system remain to be determined, we shall describe it only in general terms.

GENERAL STRUCTURE OF THE EFTS

The center of the EFTS is likely to be the Federal Reserve Communications System (FRCS), which is a much more powerful successor to the old Federal Reserve wire transfer system.[2] The FRCS consists of high-capacity computers linked electronically to form a nationwide network. At the center of the FRCS is the central switching system, located in Culpeper, Virginia. This is connected with the Board of Governors in Washington and to 12 district switching systems, one at each of the Federal Reserve banks. These, in turn, are connected with what will eventually be about 32 Automated Clearing Houses (ACHs) located in as many regions. Computers at each regional ACH are linked into the computers of the participating commercial banks and other financial intermediaries in the region. Finally, the computer facilities of many business firms will be linked with those of their banks. This will be a truly nationwide electronic network.

[2] However, it is possible that this will be replaced by a similar system owned and operated by some other entity, such as a cooperative formed by the financial institutions using the system, a private firm, or a government corporation. Also, it is not necessary for all parts of the system to be controlled by a single entity.

DIRECT INCOME CREDITING

Orders to make payment can be entered into the electronic system in various ways. We shall deal first with "direct income crediting." This can be used not only for payrolls but also for other types of payments that occur at regular intervals, such as interest, welfare, pension, and social security payments. Under this arrangement, employees and other recipients of payments authorize their employers or other payors to pay them by direct crediting to their accounts at designated financial institutions. By 1977 a large number of private employers were already making payments in this way, the federal government was already paying many military personnel and millions of recipients of social security benefits by direct credits to their accounts, and the practice was growing rapidly. This suggests one reason why mutual savings banks, savings and loan associations, and credit unions insist so strongly that they be permitted to participate in the EFTS on a full parity with commercial banks; they would be placed at a serious competitive disadvantage if payrolls and other similar payments could be credited directly only to accounts at commercial banks.

The following steps are involved in payments by income crediting through an EFTS:[3]

1. The employer delivers to his bank a magnetic tape including the data necessary for payments; the payroll may cover only a few employees or thousands. The data include for each employee the amount to be credited to his account, a number indicating the institution he has designated to receive the payment, and the number of his account there.

2. A computer at the payor's bank automatically deducts the amount of

---

[3] The system described here might well be called "an electronic giro system," for it is an electronic modification of a giro system that has long been employed in various parts of Europe but which used written orders to effect transfers. Payments are in some cases made through banks and in others through postoffices. In explaining the system, we shall assume that payment is through a postoffice system. Under the giro system, each person or firm has an account number, which identifies his postoffice as well as his own account. When a payor wishes to make a payment, he delivers a set of instructions to pay, which may include only one payment or many. The instructions include the account number of each payee and the amount to be paid into it. The payor pays the local postoffice with cash or by check. The instructions are then sent to the central office of the system, which sorts them out and sees that the various accounts are credited as ordered. Both parties are notified by return post that payment has been completed. Note that in this system orders flow from the payor through the payment institutions to the payee and that there is no return flow of checks or other paper.

the payment from the payor's account and credits the accounts of those who have designated that bank to receive payments for their accounts. The remaining data are transmitted to a computer at the regional ACH.

3. Computers at the ACH order the banks and other intermediaries that are members of the clearinghouse to credit the accounts of those payees who have designated those institutions to receive funds for their accounts. The remaining data, relating to payments to accounts in banks that are not members of the ACH, are electronically relayed to the FRCS, which distributes the orders to the other designated recipient insitutions.

4. All claims of banks against each other are automatically cleared through the electronic system, and payments among banks are made by debiting and crediting their reserve accounts at the Federal Reserve.

Note that this payment system utilized no checks and no other paper unless payees were given written notices that their accounts had been credited. Though the initial investment in an EFTS is very large, costs of electronic transfers made in large volume are far below those of a check system, and lower costs are enjoyed by all participants in the process—by payors, who do not have to prepare checks, by banks, and by payees. The system of direct deposits also provides other advantages to payees:

1. reduced possibility of loss, destruction, or theft of checks
2. elimination of the inconvenience of getting checks cashed
3. assurance of uninterrupted deposits during periods of temporary absence from their places of residence

Such advantages virtually assure that very large numbers of payees will authorize income crediting, and the economies accruing to employers and other payors will attract them to the system.[4]

PREAUTHORIZED PAYMENTS

Orders may also enter an EFTS through preauthorized payment arrangements. These are used mostly for repetitive payments, such as insurance premiums, utility bills, rentals, and mortgage and consumer

---

[4] However, at least one employee complained that the system enabled his wife to find out how much he really made. His wife's attitude is not recorded.

credit installments. Under this arrangement, a payor authorizes the payee to send bills to his bank or other financial institution and authorizes his financial institution to pay them on stated dates. On these dates the financial institution deducts from the payor's account and forwards payment to the payees through the system. A variant of this is a system called "bill-check." When a customer gets a bill he signs it, indicates the date on which it is to be paid, and sends it to his bank. On the indicated date his account will be charged and the payment transferred.

POINT-OF-SALE TERMINALS (POS)

A highly important method of entering orders into the system is through point-of-sale terminals, or POS. These are located in grocery stores and other establishments where large numbers of people make purchases, and are connected through a local Switching and Processing Center (SPC) to all or most of the banks and other financial institutions in the area where customers have accounts. A customer seeking services through a POS terminal presents to the attendant a plastic card that includes his picture, his signature, the name and identification number of his financial institution, and the number of his account. Several types of services are available through a terminal:

1. Credit authorization. In this case, an issuer of a credit card authorizes the extension of credit to the customer and agrees to pay the charge.
2. Check verification. A financial institution verifies that the customer has the required amount in his account at that time but does not guarantee that the check will be honored upon presentation.
3. Check guaranty. A financial institution guarantees that a check for the indicated amount will be paid.
4. Interaccount transfers. This service permits a consumer to debit one of his accounts at a depository institution and to credit another of his accounts.
5. Cash withdrawals. The consumer receives cash, his account at a depository institution is debited, and the account of the store is credited.
6. Payments for purchases or for debt retirement. An account of the consumer at a depository institution is debited and an account of the payee is credited.
7. Acceptance for deposit of cash and other items.

AUTOMATED TELLER MACHINES (ATMs)
AND CASH DISPENSING MACHINES (CDMs)

These machines perform various functions for customers of depository institutions, including acceptance of deposits, withdrawals of cash, transfer of funds between accounts, and accepting instructions to pay third parties. Some are linked to computers, but others are not. Though some are located on bank premises, others are located outside in such places as large retail stores, airports, and railway stations. Many of these machines operate 24 hours a day and 7 days a week. Several thousand were already in operation by the mid-1970s.

ACCESS BY TELEPHONE

In the future, households and business firms will also have access to the electronic system through their telephones. They will gain access to a computer by inserting their identifying plastic cards into an attachment to their telephones, and then transmit orders by punching the telephone buttons or by dialing.

CAPABILITIES OF EFTS

A summary of the principal capabilities of the EFTS, defined broadly to include the computers involved as well as the communications components, will help to explain the effects that are likely to accompany the development of the system:

1. Rapid transfers of payments over long distances. Funds transferred in payment will become available for respending by payees almost simultaneously with their deduction from the accounts of payors. This will tend to increase the velocity of money—the volume of payments that can be made with a given stock of money. Payees will, of course, welcome the earlier availability of money to them, but payors will not welcome their earlier loss of funds and may resist the change from a paper system. The likely outcome is that payees will insist on receiving payment in immediately available funds.
2. Reduction of the costs of providing financial services. The EFTS will change markedly the cost functions of producing and distributing

financial services. Cost functions under the present paper system are characterized by relative large variable costs, including labor costs. In contrast, the EFTS involves very large initial investment and very low marginal costs. The EFTS can achieve much lower cost per unit of service, but only if volume is high, and high volume can be achieved only if consumers can be induced to shift away from the paper system. The present system of pricing payment services does not reflect the high real costs under the paper system and therefore does not promote shifts to the EFTS. For example, customers typically receive large amounts of "free" services in lieu of interest on their deposits, and the Federal Reserve makes no charge for clearing and collecting checks. The transition to EFTS will be more rapid, and the system more efficient, if all parties receive interest on their deposits and if payment services are priced on the basis of their costs.

3. Ability to accumulate, store, analyze, and retrieve very large amounts of information at low cost. In the course of receiving and making payments each financial institution will accumulate and store much information about the financial history and position of each customer—his income, his expenditure patterns, his debts, and perhaps also his net worth. As many have pointed out, this could lead to invasion of the customer's privacy. However, it also provides virtually all the information needed for extending lines of credit. The development of the EFTS is expected to be accompanied by the extension of lines of credit to most households and business firms.

4. Ability to transfer funds from one type of account to another almost instantaneously and at very low marginal cost. Many depositors are already permitted to use the telephone to shift funds between demand and savings accounts. The EFTS will extend the practice and make it faster and cheaper. For example, a financial institution's computer may be instructed as follows: "When you receive a payment order in excess of the customer's demand deposit balance, shift the required amount of funds from his savings account to his demand account. If the amount in his savings account is insufficient, make a loan to him under his line of credit, not to exceed $X million. If that is not sufficient, buzz your attendant." Though transfers among accounts at the same financial institution are fastest and cheapest, such transfers involving two or more institutions will also be fast and economical.

SOME IMPLICATIONS OF THE EFTS AND OTHER INNOVATIONS RELATING TO DEPOSITORY INSTITUTIONS

Though all the implications are not yet foreseeable, the following appear to be among the most important:

DEFINITIONS OF MONETARY INTERMEDIARIES AND THE MONEY SUPPLY

As thrift institutions issue liabilities that are used as a medium of payments, they should be included in the category of monetary intermediaries, along with the Federal Reserve and commercial banks. It is at least possible that the legal power to participate in the payments process will be extended to still other types of financial intermediaries, such as consumer finance companies.

As new types of liabilities come to be transferred in making payments, we shall have to expand the definition of the money supply to include these as well as currency and demand deposit claims against commercial banks, even if we define the money supply narrowly to include only those things that are actually used as means of payments. However, it is not yet possible to forecast precisely the nature of the new types of monetary liabilities or how large they will become. Much will depend on government policy regarding interest on demand deposits. If the government repeals the prohibition of interest on demand deposits, and permits all monetary intermediaries to issue these deposits and to pay interest on them at competitive rates, all or most of the monetary liabilities of these institutions may remain demand deposits in name as well as in fact. However, deposits under this name will virtually disappear if the prohibition of interest on demand deposits is retained. Those eligible to hold interest-bearing NOW accounts will certainly shun sterile demand deposits, and others will easily find ways of earning interest on their liquid funds. On receiving payments, they will shift the funds almost immediately into some interest-bearing asset and convert them back to demand deposits only moments before making payments to others.

For similar reasons, the EFTS will exacerbate cycles of disintermediation and reintermediation if authorities attempt to hold ceiling rates on time and savings deposits below the level of yields on liquid open-market assets. In the end, the EFTS may force the elimination of such ceilings.

IMPLICATIONS FOR COMPETITION AND PHYSICAL
FACILITIES OF BANKS AND OTHER PAYMENT INSTITUTIONS

Under the EFTS, the location of banking offices will become a less important determinant of customers' choices among financial institutions, for customers will have less need to visit the institutions. With direct income crediting to their accounts, they will not need to visit a banking office to make deposits. With access to currency at numerous conveniently located ATMs, CDMs, and POS terminals, they will not need to visit a bank to get cash. Borrowing almost automatically under a line of credit, they will not need to go to a banking office to arrange normal consumer loans. And they can pay their bills through preauthorization arrangements or through orders transmitted by telephone. In short, they will need to visit a banking office only infrequently for extraordinary transactions, such as arranging a line of credit for the next year or so, or to arrange an unusually large loan, and even some of these transactions can be effected by telephone.

Such developments will enhance competition, for customers will have more convenient and more economical access to financial institutions located over wider geographic areas. These developments will also decrease a financial institution's need for branch offices, and especially for the familiar type of branch office with a large building, tellers' cages, a conspicuous safe, drive-in facilities, and so on. Many of these may be rendered obsolete. In physical appearance, the "branch" of the future may resemble a well-appointed office of a lawyer or a real estate agent, where consultations can occur under pleasant circumstances.

Developments accompanying the EFTS will have important implications for geographic restrictions on branching by commercial banks and other financial intermediaries. A major purpose of these restrictions is obvious, as was noted earlier: bankers within a restricted area hope to escape effective competition from banks outside the area. Such attempts are already largely ineffective for large business firms and large banks. The EFTS will make such restrictions relatively ineffective for more customers and more banks.

The EFTS is bringing further confusion to an already confused issue—the legal definition of a bank branch. Legal restrictions apply to the physical facilities of a bank that are legally defined as branches, but not all physical facilities of a bank are so defined. For example, as mentioned earlier, some big banks maintain loan production offices in many regions. Such an office usually solicits deposits for its parent, though it does not accept deposits at that location, and it accepts loan applications but does not finally consummate loans. Officials have ruled that these are not branches within the meaning of the law. Now this question has arisen: Are POS terminals branch offices within the meaning of the law? For example, some New York City banks established POS terminals in stores located in nearby New Jersey. The Comptroller of the Currency ruled that these were not branches and were therefore permissible. However, the New Jersey legislature decreed that they were branches and therefore illegal. Perhaps the next step will be a ruling that a telephone capable of communicating with the computer of a bank located outside the state·is a branch and therefore illegal. Such restrictive decisions may retard the growth of the EFTS, but the long-run outcome is more likely to be some relaxation of geographic restrictions on branching.

IMPLICATIONS FOR MONETARY MANAGEMENT

Neither the introduction of the EFTS nor the extension of monetary powers to the thrift institutions should alter substantially either the methods or the effectiveness of monetary management by the Federal Reserve. However, the Federal Reserve should expect that during the period of transition to the new system, which is likely to be several years, there will be new uncertainties, changes in the public's demand for money balances relative to its rate of expenditures, and changes in the reliability of its traditional intermediate policy guides.

The introduction of EFTS and related developments will almost certainly reduce the public's demand for currency relative to its retail types of expenditures because of the easy availability of ATMs, CDMs, and POS terminals. For one thing, the public will pay for more of its retail purchases by transfers of deposit claims through POS terminals. Also, because currency can be acquired so conveniently, people may withdraw only smaller amounts more frequently. For example, instead of withdrawing $100 of currency each time, thereby incurring greater risks of loss and robbery, you may withdraw more frequently, but only $20 each time.

More uncertain is the net effect of EFTS on the public's demand for transferable deposit claims relative to its rate of expenditures for output. As already noted, this demand will tend to be increased, or not to decline so much, if the prohibition of interest on demand deposits is repealed and if the depository institutions come to pay a significant rate of interest on their monetary liabilities. However, at least two other developments will tend to decrease the public's demand for such balances. One is the much greater speed of monetary transfers under the EFTS, which will enable each dollar of deposits to effect a greater volume of payments during any period of time. Another probable development under EFTS is a greater use of lines of credit. In making loans in the "ordinary" way, banks lend to customers for a stated period, thereby creating deposits, and the deposits remain outstanding until the loans are repaid at maturity. Under a line of credit, however, the lending institutions create deposits only to the extent that the borrowers actually draw on the line of credit, and any funds deposited by borrowers are used directly to reduce their borrowings, thus tending to reduce outstanding deposits. The borrowers' accounts at the lending institutions show at any time only their net deposit there or their net borrowing. Thus a given volume of payments can be effected with a smaller average volume of outstanding deposits. In effect, unused portions of lines of credit serve as "potential deposits," thereby reducing the demand for "actual deposits."

Both the EFTS and the extension of monetary powers to thrift institutions will bring new uncertainties and questions for Federal Reserve policy making. For example, the Federal Reserve will have to consider such questions as these: What monetary magnitude is the most appropriate intermediate guide to monetary policy? Is it some narrowly defined money supply, such as M_1 adjusted to include other liabilities actually used as means of payments? Is it some broader measure of M, such as M_5, that includes all depository claims? Or is it some still broader magnitude, including additionally some highly liquid direct securities? There are some *a priori* reasons to believe that broader magnitudes should be accorded more weight as policy guides as the EFTS reduces sharply both the time and marginal costs involved in shifting funds between M_1 and other highly liquid financial claims. It is to be hoped that the Federal Reserve will be able to develop more precise answers to such questions as it gains experience with the evolving EFTS.

CONCLUSION

We do not pretend to have discussed all the developments that will have important effects on the future structure and functioning of the American monetary-financial system. Some of the possible changes that were discussed may not happen at all, or only in modified forms. Also, there are likely to be highly influential changes that have not even been mentioned. Yet this chapter should have established one point—that there is no reason to expect that future changes in the system will be any slower, less numerous, or less sweeping than those of the past.

SELECTED READINGS

I. Proposed reforms relating to depository intermediaries

> Federal Reserve Bank of Boston Conference. *Policies for a More Competitive Financial System: A Review of the Report of the President's Commission on Financial Structure and Regulation.* Boston: Federal Reserve Bank of Boston, 1972.
>
> President's Commission on Financial Structure and Regulation. Report [popularly called the Hunt Commission Report]. Washington, D.C.: U.S. Government Printing Office, 1971.

II. An electronic monetary, or funds, transfer system

> Flannery, M. J., and Jaffee, D. M. *The Economic Implications of an Electronic Monetary Transfer System.* Lexington, Mass.: Lexington Books, 1973.
>
> Arthur D. Little, Inc. *The Consequences of Electronic Funds Transfer: A Technology Assessment of Movement Toward a Less Cash Less Check Society.* Cambridge, Mass.: Arthur D. Little, 1975.
>
> National Commission on Electronic Funds Transfers. *EFT and the Public Interest.* Washington, D.C.: 1977.

INDEX